NATIONAL BESTSELLER

1453 THE CONQUEST

THE OTTOMAN EMPIRE TRILOGY

BEYAZIT AKMAN

kopernik

First published by Kopernik Inc.

Editor-in-Chief: Abdülkadir Özkan
Advisor: Prof. Halil Berktay
Series Editor: Dr. Yaşar Çolak
Director: Dr. Cengiz Şişman
Translated by: Peter Klempner
Design: Ali Kaya
Application: Sinopsis

Kopernik Publishing House
Kopernik Inc.
108 Olde Towne Avenue Unit: 308 Gaithersburg Maryland 20877 - USA
www.kopernikpublishing.com

Certification no: 35175
ISBN: 978-625-7852-07-4
First Edition: October 2020

Printed in ISTANBUL
Elma Basım ve Yayın İletişim Hizmemetleri
San. Tic. Ltd. Şti. Küçükçekmece/İSTANBUL
ISTANBUL - LONDON - NEW YORK – WASHINGTON DC

NATIONAL BESTSELLER

1453 THE CONQUEST

THE OTTOMAN EMPIRE TRILOGY

BEYAZIT AKMAN

kopernik

BEYAZIT AKMAN: (1981) is a Turkish author of historical fiction, short stories, essays, scholar, book critic and professor of English literature. He earned his B.A. from Middle East Technical University of Ankara in 2003. He received his M.A. in English literature at Illinois State University, as a Fulbright Scholar in 2006, and completed his Ph.D. at the same university in 2012. For his doctoral degree, he focused on the image of Turks and Islam in Western discourse. He taught many courses at Illinois State on East-West discourse in the Department of English. In 2010, he was awarded the Smithsonian Baird Society Fellowship and conducted research at archives and libraries in Washington DC. He also taught courses on world and comparative literature as a visiting professor at State University of New York, Geneseo from 2012 to 2014. Akman has also been published many times in national and international peer-reviewed journals. He started writing historical fiction after years of archival research at university libraries in the United States. His first novel, *1453: The Conquest,* was an instant success when first published and became one of the bestselling novels for a first-time author in his native Turkey. It quickly became a contemporary classic and has been used as inspiration for many historical TV series, movies and novels, launching a new era of historical fiction in Turkey. Proving himself to be a top-notch historical fiction writer, he later wrote *1492: The Gates of Heaven,* which he describes as an ode to the lost Andalusian civilization. Recently, he published *1302: Othman Khan: The Birth of an Empire* in two volumes about the origins of the Ottoman Empire based on the most up-to-date research and scholarship about the Ottomans. Akman was awarded *The International Prize for Historical Fiction* and History in Fiction by the Writers' Association of Turkey. He has been invited to speak at international book fairs in Frankfurt, London and Istanbul. His latest work of nonfiction, *In Search of Lost History: East-West from Mehmed the Conqueror to Shakespeare,* dedicated to Edward Said, was published in 2017 by Kopernik Publishing. Akman became an associate professor in 2019 and works at Social Sciences University of Ankara. He is married with one daughter.

PROLOGUE
The Archer's Secret

1
CONSTANTINOPLE

A needle-like arrow pierced the blue sky in a wide arc and fell back to earth among clouds of dust and the smoke of black powder. It hissed through the air so quickly and with such a sound that the people below swore it was a flying serpent.

The hiss of the ivory arrow tip made itself felt amid the din of cannon fire, clashing swords, cries and screams. The expert archers were using these ivory-tipped arrows as if taking revenge on Timur's majestic elephants that once in times past had so terrified their horses. The arrow was bearing down on its target, its shaft fashioned from young pine from the forests of Ilgaz, three hundred miles away. Isfendiyar Bey's loyal men carefully selected each and every one of these trees—the younger the pine sapling, the higher quality the arrow shaft. It seemed this arrow wanted to prove itself to the lush mountains of the Black Sea that it was quickly leaving behind as it flew through the sky this day.

It had waited seventy-seven years for today, to be an arrow and to change the fate of the siege. It was well-fashioned, the only example of its kind—first baked in an oven and then set to season for no less than fifty years. The waistcoat of its fletching was from the wing of an eagle, itself able to pick out a small rabbit through a forest canopy from thousands of feet up. It had sprung from the bow like an eagle on the hunt, attaining its freedom.

Yet it didn't seem it would be so easy for it to reach its target. It would have to overcome three sets of fortified walls that had been set in the earth for more than a millennium.

It flew over twenty yards of the moat—now red with blood—surmounted the three-foot supporting wall and licked passed the six-foot-thick outer wall that rose twenty-five feet above the ground. It continued over the piles of corpses that stretched for miles, reminiscent of the mountains along the Mediterranean, and wended between the siege towers and cannons. It then struck a crenel in one of the towers on the forty-five-foot inner wall with such force that it sent shattered stone flying, more like one of Timur's elephants than an arrow. Stone fragments hurtled out and blinded one of the two Constantinopolitan soldiers who were bringing pitch to a furious boil to pour over the Ottomans trying to scale the next wall to reach the breaches.

This hadn't been the archer's target.

He was exhausted and worn, and the pain in his back was only getting worse.

He again reached back over his right shoulder to his quiver, his thumb and index finger curled in a crescent. He plucked another eagle feather-fletched arrow and quickly fitted it to the string of the bow he was holding firmly in his left hand. There was a slight bump on the middle finger of the hand he held the arrow with, but this callus wasn't from shooting arrows, it was from writing with a reed pen. As every janissary in the corps, he also had to be skilled in a form of art, and he'd been studying calligraphy ever since he was brought to the corps when he was seven years old.

He saw the thousands of letters he'd written—*vav, kaf, mim, nun*—pass before his eyes. He saw an *elif* woven into the marbled paper of the pitch mixed with blood flowing toward him and a *mim* to his side. It was like a *vav* was sailing as a ship on a crimson sea. He hadn't progressed in calligraphy as fast as he had in archery, though, and had only been able to receive his certificate when he was twenty.

One of his compatriots in the chaos behind him bumped into his back as he knelt on the ground, knocking his arrow from the bowstring and out of his hand. He remembered dipping his reed pen into the inkpot as he picked up the arrow from a pool of blood.

His hand again wrapped firmly around the bow's grip—first his little finger, then ring finger and middle finger all in fine alignment. This top recruit from the Devshirme had labored for many years to master this movement, which he now did unconsciously within a second. After all, he was the one who ensured he would become a janissary through a strange twist of fate.

His left hand holding the bow had blistered and he would secretly cry at night back at the guild. His drills started with drawing the bowstring thirty-three times a day, then sixty-six, and then ninety-nine not much later. Within a year at the guild he could draw the bowstring a thousand times a day as if it were nothing. In one quick motion, he drew the bull sinew string that no one else would venture to touch and then look around as if to show it was child's play.

This is not what he should be thinking about at this moment, though, as his mind should have been on the days of carrying firewood. He'd struck his target many times since the war began and he was maybe a little boastful.

The secret of archery his master had whispered only to him out of the most dexterous archers seven years earlier passed through his mind again. He drew the arrow, its tip dripping with blood, back to his ear and tried to pick out the renowned Genoese knight he'd heard so much of since the beginning of the war. He aimed through the battlements that had given way in parts, and without blinking from both sides of the bow as only so many men on earth could.

"*Ya Haqq!*" he cried as he let fly the arrow into the sky. It sailed behind the ramparts five hundred yards away and sped between the city's soldiers who were fighting with heart-wrenching bitterness, striking his target in between two battlements.

It pierced the Genoese knight's armor and emerged out his back.

Iskender the janissary felt he couldn't stand the pain from the spear lodged in his back any longer.

2
Rome

Aluvixe Diedo dismounted in such haste when he got to the Castel Sant'Angelo where the city walls stretched out that he nearly fell when he reached the ground. He would've been very proud and delighted to be in Rome if it had been any other day. This day, however, he was very tired. He'd been around the Mediterranean on a journey of more than a month that had started in Constantinople.

It wasn't captaining this difficult sea voyage or sometimes only getting two hours of sleep a night over the past fifty-four days that so disturbed him, but the weight of the news he had to give. The pain he felt as his feet left his stirrups for the streets of Rome was well beyond the deep gash in his leg from a sword that for weeks he hadn't known how to heal and that had now become completely infested with maggots. If asked, Diedo would've much preferred to cut off his leg altogether rather than give the news he had.

The people who saw him thought him a thief as he limped along the crowded street. His sea blue uniform, expensive boots and flapped hat of high order looked much above the station of this man's appearance of a looter. If they hadn't suspected him of being afflicted with plague, two thieves who had taken to watching him could've easily stripped him of his shirt. He could also have been a pirate wearing the shirt of some Venetian captain he'd held prisoner for months. Or was it that his quick pace was a sign that he had been up to some nefarious business and was running away from somewhere?

Diedo, however, kept on his way regardless of those around him. He wasn't attracting the notice of more than a few people staring at him, as the street was already bustling enough for his presence to not make much of a difference.

"Forgive us, Jesus!" a group of monks wearing brown felt robes blacked up from filth all cried out in unison. The group of monks believed the scourge of the plague that had befallen the land for the past few years had arisen from their own sins. They called the people to torture them with the belief that this was the only way to purify themselves.

Papal States guards in groups of two, easily recognizable by their uniforms, went from door to door and painting large, red crosses on houses stricken with plague. The haphazard and unsightly crosses, some on walls, some on doors, forbade anyone from entering or leaving those houses.

The guards were painting a red cross on a house Diedo was passing. A man came running out protesting that neither he nor his family had been afflicted with plague. He was more than aware that this cross on his door meant death. From this hour on he'd no longer be able to go out for bread or bring water home. His neighbors would become his sworn enemies and would stop coming to visit. But the man needed food, most of all for the little baby inside who was crying with no respite. One of the guards had grown accustomed to such protests and clenched his hand around his sword as soon as he saw the man at the door.

"Don't take one more step!" he ordered.

"But, honorable guards, you're mistaken! I beg of you, I haven't fallen with plague and neither has my family. We're healthy—look, look—there's no sign of it on me," the man said, lifting up his shirt to try to show that he had no mark of plague.

"Don't take another step and go back inside!" the guard warned again. The other guard with the paintbrush was trying to get away from the man so he wouldn't fall to the pestilence.

The guard was at a loss for what to do as the man came straight toward him, and so lifted his sword and ran the man through the stomach. A woman was in tears as she stared out from the doorway, holding a baby and with two small children at her side. The guards moved on to mark another house without a care.

Diedo was trying not to step in all the human filth as he moved to get to the middle of the street so he could walk faster. The middle of the road was empty other than for being full of excrement, as the people did their business in tin pans and tossed it out into the streets from their doors and windows. It was always safer to walk along the walls, although those in a hurry, like Diedo was now, would chose the middle of the street so they could pick up their pace.

The captain's wounded leg didn't help him go as fast as he'd like to as he stepped through the filth, and now he was at danger of falling into excrement at any moment. He might have thought going to the middle of the street hadn't been so wise, but his haste made him forget it.

He saw Saint Peter's Basilica from where he stood at the end of the long street, which appeared like the base of a *Tau* cross from overhead, and felt as though he had reached its heart. Papal guards surrounded him as he entered the magnificent building Constantine the Great, the first Christian emperor of Rome, had built it in the fourth century over the tomb of the Apostle Peter.

"I'm here to see Cardinal Pietro Barbo," he said as he pulled out a sealed letter from Constantinople.

He'd been told he would have to find the cardinal who was the archpriest of the basilica before he could reach the pope. The cardinal came up the dark corridor behind the guards and looked at Diedo anxiously. He said he was the cardinal he was looking for and motioned for Diedo to follow him.

There were pairs of guards from the priesthood waiting at each of the hauntingly large doors at the head of every labyrinthine corridor. They opened the doors with a nod from the cardinal and then immediately shut them again. The flickering torches on the walls penetrated the darkness. The smell of mildew and damp grew stronger the further they descended down the floors. Diedo had expected to go up, and he was growing more distressed as they wound down the stifling, stuffy stairways. He started to hear screams as they neared the crypt and an unpleasant smell was burning his nose.

They came to a long corridor lined left and right with barred cells when they reached the seventh floor below where the musty smell of mold mixed with cries and screams. Diedo realized he was among the cells of the Church's Holy Inquisition that he, like everyone else, had always heard of but had never had the opportunity to see.

There was a naked, young woman tied to a stone slab in a narrow cell to the right. The two priests next to her were searing her vagina with a pair of tongs they had heated in the nearby fire. The one holding the tongs was irate.

"You filthy witch. You'll pay the price for betraying our Lord and Savior Jesus Christ. You'll suffer the punishment for giving birth to the Devil!"

The priest on the other side of the stone was reading Bible verses in Latin in a firm, loud voice.

There was an old man in a cell on the left a little further ahead with his hands bound behind him and his neck in a ring with two iron bars, one attached to a plate under his chin and the other down to the iron over his shoulders and chest. A torturer standing over him turned the screw in the middle, pushing the prongs out and creating great stress on the man's chin and chest. Diedo had heard of this device that could be placed around the neck for days and expanded every day until it broke the chin and jaw before snapping the neck. A victim could live for many days after having their neck broken, as the process didn't snap any veins or spill one drop of blood, but with the spinal cord broken, the head was effectively detached from the body. Diedo was himself of the Latin Rite, but he was disgusted seeing these scenes in Rome. He could never accept the barbarities done in the name of religion—this was not Christianity.

They came to a larger cell at the far end where one of the many people inside opened the gate for the cardinal and his guest. There was an elderly man speaking with his back turned. He was short and grey haired, wearing a black cassock with a white belt and a tall, conical hat and looking at the wretched man before him whose wrists and ankles were bound in chains.

"We promise you, Jacobo, that we will kill you swiftly if you tell us where your family and the other Jews have escaped to," the old man said.

Jacobo repeated the same thing for the hundredth time from where he was kneeling, struggling to speak from the wounds and bruising on his face from two weeks of torture.

"I don't know."

"Your brother immediately cut out his own tongue and still couldn't save himself from torture."

The man with his back turned looked over at the half-conscious young man next to Jacobo. The young man's head was in a device called a skull crusher. An iron headpiece over his skull could be tightened with the thick screw on top and the iron bar that firmly fastened the screw from the right and left was attached to his feet on the ground.

Jacobo looked hopelessly at his brother.

"Your Grace," said Cardinal Barbo, "I don't mean to interrupt, but news has come from Constantinople."

Diedo bowed as soon as the short man turned around, but couldn't bow so low due to his wounded leg. The pope carefully but worriedly looked Diedo up and down.

"How long have you been traveling?"

"Thirty-two days all together."

"What's your name?"

"Aluvixe Diedo."

"The Aluvixe Diedo who's the famous captain of the Venetian fleet?"

Diedo nodded.

"There are rumors that the siege has dragged on. What news do you bring?"

"Mehmed—" Diedo said with a trembling voice. "Sultan Mehmed—"

He realized he wouldn't be able to speak and so took out the papers from his pocket to hand to Cardinal Barbo. The pope angrily snatched them from his outstretched hand. His eyes went red when he read the two-line note from Cardinal Isidore in Constantinople.

"Did they take it? Have the Turks taken the city," they heard Jacobo say from behind them, his voice hoarse but hopeful.

It was very important for him to know since one of his brothers had been taken as a slave to Roman Constantinople.

The pope's face had already gone red with rage. He drew the knife from his servant's belt and plunged it into Jacobo's brother's heart. He twisted the blade and pulled it out as blood splattered across Jacobo's cheeks.

"We'll see to you later," he said.

3
CHICAGO

The bright armor caught the eye of a young man with blond hair and blue eyes. The knight's armor on display at the Art Institute of Chicago's exhibit of medieval armor and arms were foreboding. The masses of metal were so imposing it seemed they could fit two people at once. The pointed shoulders on one set of armor that resembled rhinoceros horns and the hundreds of beastly shields had a chilling effect on the museumgoers. Some of the swords were even the length of a person's entire body.

Some of the suits of armor opposite Beyazit were even more formidable than the two, open-mouthed lion statues to both sides of the museum's entrance. The Art Institute of Chicago on Michigan Avenue—the most famous street of one of the United States' most populous metropolises—is one of those exceptional, shrine-like buildings that had managed to collect artifacts from all the world's civilizations in one place. The tall stairs at the grandiose entrance with columns in imitation of Rome, and the cut stone of its towering walls, like those of the mosques built under patronage of the Ottoman sultans, all made the building look like a shrine—much more than what the concept of a museum evokes.

Beyazit walked into the Ottoman exhibit in the neighboring Islamic arts collection. He was growing anxious to find the man he was looking for. A guide in the hall with a group was explaining the painting of a sultan that was going to be presented at the auction further down the exhibit.

"As you've all probably noticed, this large gallery is exclusively dedicated to Mehmed II, also known as the Conqueror, who captured Constantinople from the Eastern Roman Empire in 1453, after a two-month siege—"

It seemed everything in the hall had been presented meticulously and with great care in white. The high ceilings with simple spotlights, the color of the walls, the edges of the panels and the frames of the paintings shined in places and were matte in others, but all white, and they together gave a feeling of expansiveness. The pieces on display were already eye catching enough, giving the sense there was no need for any other color.

It was as if the paintings of the palace, the flower-filled gardens of Edirne and Constantinople, all kinds of Ottoman women's clothing, the blindingly intricate works of calligraphy in *Naskh* script, the caftans embroidered with tulips, the oil marbling adorned with crescents and the thousands of various items bedecked with the greens and reds of emeralds and rubies along with countless other gems and gilding all seemed to say that they wouldn't accept any other color. There was a simplicity to the portrait of a ruler between the rubies and emeralds. The stillness of the sultan's face, his serene look and the ordinariness of his turban and caftan was surprising.

The group passed by the display case. Only the few people in the group who knew Arabic could truly express their admiration when they looked at the meticulous replica of the inscription from Topkapi Palace's *Bab-i Hümayun*—the Imperial Gate—which had been created to complete the exhibition. The people in the group couldn't help but look over at the simple man in the portrait while the guide read the translation of the inscription.

—Sultan Mehmed Khan, Sultan of the Lands and Emperor of the Seas, the Shadow of God over Men and Spirits, Deputy of God in the East and the West, Champion of Water and Land, Conqueror of Constantinople—

Beyazit saw that he'd come just in time when he entered the Auction Hall. The portrait was just about to go on the block. Two employees wearing white gloves slowly lifted the painting and carefully placed it on a platform.

A hum started amid those in the Auction Hall. The bidders and everyone else were all excited to be so close to the original work whose replicas they'd all seen so many of up until now.

The auctioneer began the explanation. "This is a portrait of Mehmed II by Venetian artist Gentille Bellini. Some scholars interpret it as proof that Islam doesn't actually prohibit the use of images of the human form in art given that this sultan was a devout Muslim—"

The first bid came after the auctioneer finished.

"Five hundred thousand dollars!"

The painting was still going to be on display at the National Gallery of London, but had been brought over specifically for the auction.

"One million dollars!"

Everyone in the hall was listening in suspense to the suddenly increasing bids and many bidders lowered their numbers. The people at the back with Beyazit were waiting excitedly for the result for this portrait of the renowned sultan they'd heard so much about.

"Three million dollars!"

A group of people was also surprised looking on the portrait for the first time, as this couldn't be the bloodthirsty, barbaric and ruthless Mehmed of their imaginations. They wondered if this could be the man who put an end to the grand Roman Empire and spilt rivers of blood for three days and three nights in Constantinople, if this pale-faced man was Bathomet or the antichrist who the Church had for centuries said would put an end to Christendom.

"Five million dollars!"

The man in their imaginations was always nastier of feature with a fiery face, scowling like the descriptions of Satan from the Middle Ages as a horned goat. There were also many paintings that imagined him as such, but the painting they saw now was of a pale man with a strange turban and fur-lined clothing.

"Ten million dollars! And the winner is number forty-seven," the auctioneer said as he pounded his gavel.

Beyazit had found the man he was looking for.

An old man with white hair and a white mustache and Beyazit sat across from each other in the well-lit cafe of the Art Gallery.

"Oh, I wish they had Turkish coffee," the old man said as he added sugar to his coffee. "And the cool breeze off the Bosporus. This is a big day for me. I've worked years to be able to buy that painting."

"Why's this painting so important to you?"

"I'd be revealing my identity if we get into that. And don't forget, we agreed in our correspondence that we're meeting on the condition that you don't divulge my identity to anyone. I can say this much, though—I've always been a great follower of all the works the sultan had made."

"Where'd you get this interest?"

"The late Süheyl Ünver had a saying. Everyone has a job and a pastime, and it's that pastime that is our entire history."

"So where are all these pieces?"

"They're far away from where they should be. Take his medallions, for example. It's thought three survive from the sultan to the present day. I think there's more, but of these there's three on display. There's one in Oxford, another in the Bibliothèque nationale in Paris, and another at the Smithsonian in Washington DC. Interesting, isn't it? Three countries and three medallions."

"It's like the world's three superpowers all snatched them up."

"Even more interesting, the medallions witness the movement

of civilization. For instance, the oldest medallion of the sultan is in Paris, then the second oldest is in England, and the latest is in the US—the world's newest superpower. And this portrait was painted six months before the sultan died. It show his state in his final months."

"Is that why he's so pale?"

"It is. They say he had begun to be poisoned around the time the painting was done."

"They also said it was the end of civilization when he conquered the Byzantines, didn't they?"

"You're right, but it wasn't the Byzantines. You can call them many names, but don't call them Byzantines."

"Why?"

"Byzantium was the name of a kingdom established long before Rome. The Eastern Romans never called themselves Byzantines. They called it New Rome or Eastern Rome, New Jerusalem even, but they never used the name Byzantine. According to Constantine and the Greeks who founded the city, this empire was the heir of the Rome of Julius Caesar, and it was accepted as such for centuries. European historians who couldn't accept the fall of Rome started calling them Byzantine much later."

"I've read most of all of those historians' travelogues. All of them except for one."

The old man smiled. "The travelogue of Alberti Balbi. The very one who brought the first medallion to the sultan."

"It's the actual reason we're meeting."

"I found his notes in a second-hand bookshop in Venice years ago. If the bookseller would've taken them to the Vatican archives straight away if he'd known their value. He could've made a small fortune. Not many people have read it since it's in Latin, there's quite a few pages missing and there're inconsistencies. It's the personality in the notes that really sets it apart form typical travelogues."

"It's objective, right?"

"It is, but it's from a time in his journeys when he was experiencing mental turmoil. He was mourning his beloved wife when the sultan invited him to Edirne, so the actual reason why he went was to try to save himself from his depression."

"Did he know Turkish?"

"As much as any other Venetian envoy going abroad in those days. His speaking improved when he was in Edirne for a while. Of course, he also had a talent for language that came from his family. His brother Bernardo had already tutored the sultan in Venetian years earlier."

"Was Alberti sent to the sultan as an envoy?"

"You could say that, but you'll see when you read it that he acted independently from his retinue of diplomats. It'd be more accurate to call him a traveler."

"So why was the sultan so interested in the Venetians?"

"It might seem right for you to ask that question now, but back then it would've been quite ridiculous. Venice was the West in the fifteenth century. It was the most powerful after Eastern Rome. But the best part of his travelogue is that it's a bit distant from all that and it's personal. His notes of his experiences are quite personal."

"Like what?"

"I wouldn't want to detract from your pleasure of reading it. You'll understand what I'm getting at when you do."

With this, the old man handed a folder over to Beyazit. His hands shook with the excitement of finding the missing piece to a great puzzle as he took the folder.

4
The Travelogue of Alberti Balbi

The calm canals of Venice come to mind, the smooth water in front of the Doge's Palace and the port filled with peaceful sailors from around the Mediterranean who come to bypass storms. The ships sailing into the tranquil port come to me along with the evening's setting sun. And my house at the head of the harbor, the moonlight reflecting off the water as Cristina and I made love until morning, our panting breath as if we were dying, and then born again. Was the sweat pouring from my brow when she was on top of me any different than the holy water used the baptize a newborn?

But I'm full of torment now. The burning ships outside, the fires on the ramparts and the janissaries' torches are all lighting up my tent at this uncertain hour of night. The flashes of jumping flames against the cloth of my tent and the silhouettes of soldiers passing on one side and the dark shadows of smoke on the other remind me of Nilüfer's magic letters on a piece of paper. I write with one hand while the other holds firmly onto a cosmetic case she uses to line her eyes. The figure of a swan in ink next to me and these letters bring me maybe a little closer to her.

I don't remember how many nights have been like this. I really can't remember at all.

I wonder if it's true that people are really created in pairs. Can a woman carry with her the spirit of someone else who's died? Can a man love two women at the same time? Isn't every different land a traveler goes to a different world? Is so, doesn't a traveler have a right to a new life, a new home and a new, second love in these new worlds? Maybe that's why the Mohamatans justify polygamous marriage.

Nilüfer doesn't think like this. She's never thought like this, and I couldn't convince her.

I don't think I can take much more. This Mohamatan girl isn't willing to run off to Venice with a Christian no matter how hard I try to convince her. I could even have welcomed her into one of the most beautiful houses in Venice. I could've transformed that house on the harbor with the rising sun, one door opening to the street and another to the canal into a charmed world that can scarcely be found outside of tales of the Arabian *One Thousand and One Nights.*

I can't sleep again tonight. The sounds of cannons and wounded and dying soldiers don't allow for any sound sleep, but the difficulties inside me drown out all the sounds from outside. The silence in my heart smothers all the howling and clatter outside my tent and the torches flashing against its cloth around me aren't nearly enough to bring light to the darkness of my spirit.

I wish I weren't in this state and could run out into the claws of death without batting an eye. I wish I was under the burning pitch the Constantinopolan soldiers pour from the ramparts so I wouldn't now have to suffer this pain inside me.

I see Nilüfer's big, black eyes, what the Turks would call almonds, in the shadows hitting my tent. The Turks liken the features of a woman's face to food and her body to beautiful animals. Lips are cherries, cheeks apples, and a woman's suitors would say that she is like a gazelle or a mare.

Her eyes put their stamp on my heart with the black rub she put around them, like the archers always at the sultan's side, like the blank ink of a unique seal. This case is all I could get from her after pleading with her over and over. A metal stem comes out from the mouth of the little, tulip-shaped case plated in gold. The place to hold the stem is perforated with fine workmanship like the parts of the handholds for the faucets on the Turks' fountains. How interesting that, like a traveler who's gone through the desert for days without water and kneels at the mouth of a fountain, I quench my thirst amid the drought around me with this case of black rub in my hand. Like how the faucets turn, which I've filled pages explaining, I rotate the case from the stem in my fingers and bring it to my nose to smell. The brass case and the stem both smell of Nilüfer.

I start with this complete blathering in my most desperate moments. If I can find a dusky woman with black eyebrows and eyes when I get back to Venice, and if I apply this rub to her eyes, maybe I'll think of her as Nilüfer and be able to quite this agony.

I don't know why I keep these notes anymore. It must be a habit from traveling and it's a natural consequence of an envoy's obligation to report everything. Now, though, writing is perhaps the only thing that connects me to Nilüfer. This is definitely the reason. This air I breathe envelops the entire world, and as Mullah Lütfi explained for hours that one night, if it goes about the earth and wraps around the miniscule grains, then the words and letters of Nilüfer's elegant writing maintain these lines, the words I write and letters I scratch out. They're all products of the same source, and it, that spring, unites us. It's as if this moment of writing that's a part of her life seats me across from her. These handsome Latin letters look rough and characterless next to Arabic letters that go from one shape to another and wrap in changing colors. They're cold, formless and brutish. Doesn't this graceful swan she made out of letters for me look as if it could jump from the paper flapping its wings? How long I pleaded for her to make me this swan, and I couldn't make her listen. She made it before my eyes the next time we met to reconcile my heart. Those hours that I didn't want to end passed as if it had been a couple of minutes. She looked at me and said that knowing Arabic isn't enough to know Ottoman, that it needs much more and that I should be able to read the writing of the sawn. I strived for days and weeks to read it, but I couldn't. Then I showed it to Mullah Lütfi. He looked at it for a moment, moved his lips vaguely in the way the Turks do when they express gratitude and then easily read it out to me. I was taken aback when Nilüfer wanted me to point out all the letters and words when I told her I could read her swan. She knew straight off that I'd cheated. No cheating, she told me, angry at what I'd done. I should read it for real, and more than read it, I should feel it. Now I can only look with a heavy and dark disposition at the words this that form this swan, its thin neck and spread wings yelling out to me.

I've already ordered my servant boy to prepare the horses and we'll set out for the port at Gallipoli at first light of morning. I won't wait anymore for the siege to end. No one believes the city can be taken any longer. There are even pashas who evaluate the situation and say Constantinople will be bound to pay a higher tribute than before and Mehmed will withdraw in success. The envoys who come after me will note whether or not this sultan, who's nearly emptied the treasury by amassing tens of thousands of soldiers, will have influence over his janissaries after this.

What will happen when I return? I wish I could wrap my arms around Cristina. And what about Nilüfer? Would she wait in hope for me like Penelope waited for Odysseus? Who am I kidding?

I read a few hundred verses from Homer's epic that night again as I tried to ease my mind and focus on my decision. I identify with Odysseus more and more these days. Mehmed sniffed at this notion the first time I said it. He said I'm like Odysseus and Constantinople is like Troy. If only I had been able to give Mehmed's mind-boggling plan a few weeks before, as Odysseus had done to Achilles. I have no power to persuade a sultan toward war or peace as Odysseus convinced Agamemnon and Achilles to go to war. We envoys only watch, listen and convey. Decisions are for sultans, emperors and kings.

I am similar to Odysseus in one way, though.

I have to give it to Mehmed the more I think about how the port I'll set off for tomorrow morning sits right off the fabled Troy. The only thing I hope to find on my return journey is the lotus that made Odysseus' men forget the way home and completely lose their memories. The Turks call this flower *nilüfer.*

After having read the first pages of the notes in the institute's library, Beyazit could tell they weren't in historical order and they'd have to be rearranged. It would take quite some time to get them to line up with the historical events.

He would have to go back much further to understand how they unfolded.

BOOK ONE

Alexandros

5

Mullah Gürani could tell right away that the young man riding a swift horse five hundred yards from him on the vast plains of Manisa was a prince. Seeing the child for the first time, he recognized by instinct that it couldn't be anybody other than a prince wearing a red shirt with golden embroidery and a specially made caftan. He couldn't reckon how a boy of nine years old could already be such a good horseman. He wanted to see just how talented this young prince was.

He straightened out the sides of his green robe that had been fluttering for the past hour as he rode. He fixed his scholar's turban around his head again, stroked his increasingly white-speckled yet not fully grey beard as he always did before embarking on an important task, and then set back off on his horse holding his cane together with the reins in his left hand.

"Mehmed!" he called out from behind as he quickly caught up to the fast-moving prince.

The prince turned and looked over his left shoulder as he cut the wind and saw a man of middle age with a speckled beard quickly approaching him.

He was cross—no one would call him by his name, he was accustomed to being addressed as Sir or Your Royal Highness the Prince. He glared back at this insolent man.

He spurred his horse on faster.

Mullah Gürani smiled to himself as the prince started to pull away from him. It was what he'd expected. There was the fire of a rebel in this child, but it was a fire he used to serve himself instead of to smelt ore into steel and then fashion a sword. The mullah also brought his horse to a faster gallop.

"Mehmed!" he shouted as he again neared the boy.

The prince looked back at the man again—he'd never come across a man who could catch up to him this easily. He spurred his horse on even faster, pulled the reins left and started to cross away.

Mullah Gürani quickly followed in his tracks. The boy was a skilled horseman, he thought, but no master.

The plain on which the prince was riding would give way to a craggy rock drop in half a mile and the mullah was paying particular attention to this. They sky stretched out from behind a slight hill, but the drop on the other side wasn't visible. Mullah Gürani got the answer to what he was looking for when he saw a bird drop down after cresting the hill.

He was going to stop the boy this time, come what may.

He neared the prince for a third time, but now from the other side with less than three hundred yards left before the crest of the hill. He waited for the horses to be side by side. The prince sped up even more, excited and angry, but the man was more agile with his horse than him.

Mullah Gürani waited until his horse's nose was just in front of the prince's. He reached out his staff with his left hand and pushed the boy off his horse. Then he veered his horse off to the other side. The prince hit the ground and rolled for a while with his momentum as his horse came to an abrupt stop at the rocks.

Gürani circled back around to the prince and was surprised when he saw that he didn't even have the slightest scratch on his face.

"It's clear you're used to falling off your horse, Mehmed," he said half teasing.

"You could've killed me!" the prince yelled back, his face glowing with anger.

"But you were already going to your death. There's a rocky cliff just over the hill."

"How would you know?!"

"I saw the birds gliding down below the crest."

Mehmed looked at the slope, dazed and thinking if the other side could really be a cliff and if the man was telling the truth. He'd never been in this area outside the city before and had been looking to ride over more diverse terrain.

The prince would escape his daily palace life and the wash of sycophantic servants to ride his horse over the green plains around Manisa, speeding forth as if leading a gigantic army. He didn't like being disturbed, and he'd run out again after the ways of the palace got to him. He didn't know, however, who this man was who called him by his name or where he'd come from.

"So you're saying you saved my life, are you?"

"No one can save anyone's life. I was just in your fortune."

Mehmed was angry at the man's insolence, but couldn't find any words.

"You're lost inside yourself with every passing day," Mullah Gürani said from atop his horse. "There's something you're looking for, but you don't know what it is. You have a fire inside you, but it's a slave to the wind out in these plains and it's the winds that will extinguish it."

"Who're you and what right do you have to speak to me that way?!" Mehmed was getting angrier, but what the man said touched a nerve and he felt an odd jolt inside.

"You look at the stars at night—sometimes until morning—and you search for the meaning of your life on these hillsides in the day. You're trying to find your station on earth."

"I'm going to tell my father the sultan about you and then you'll be sorry. Who the hell are you?!"

"I've come to teach you."

"What'll you teach me?!"

Mullah Gürani looked up at the wide, arching sky. "I'm going to teach you of you."

Mehmed tried to understand what that meant for a while before returning to his anger. "You'll explain that to my father, too!"

"As you wish, Prince, Your Highness. Let's go together. Your father's already waiting for you."

Now the prince was thoroughly confused as he approached the man to mount behind him. He wondered whether his father had come from Edirne to Manisa, and if so, if he had he also assigned this man. None of it made any sense.

Mehmed realized his father really had come when he saw a small army of the sultan's janissaries around the palace. His father had made surprise visits before, but never to Manisa at this time of year.

He hadn't said a word on the way back with Mullah Gürani. His attendants surrounded him as soon as he jumped from the horse.

"Oh, Your Highness, where were you? You gave us quite the fright!"

"Your father, His Excellency the Sultan has come. He wishes to see you—"

Some were trying to clean off the boy's arms and hands while others wanted to say which of the shirts they were holding out like dishes of food the prince would wear. Mullah Gürani frowned seeing Mehmed's attendants' flattery and was convinced that his first order of business was to clear them out of the palace.

6

A teenage boy and girl held hands as they quietly walked through the trees. The sunlight filtered through the branches and leaves and dappled their anxious but smiling faces. The boy bent down and strayed from side to side from time to time to make sure there was no one around and then motioned for the girl following behind to do the same.

"Please, Alexis, let's go back. I'm scared. What if they catch us?" she said softly.

Alexandros lifted his finger to his lips, "Shush. Don't worry, Mariam. Nothing's going to happen. I've done this before a whole bunch of times. I've been watching for days to show you. All of the regimental guards are with the officers."

Her blonde hair was shining in the sun when he glanced up at her. He looked again at her hair gathered in curls to each side of her head and her small, sea-blue eyes that would make anybody jealous. Her dress was tattered and her feet bare—no different than his own clothes and feet—but he saw Mariam as one of the palace women in their gleaming dresses he would see from afar in the city square. If he could, he would buy her the world's most beautiful dress and jewelry with the most precious gems. He was disappointed that he was going to give her something much less valuable this day, although he reckoned Mariam would like his gift if he girded himself with enough courage while he presented it.

He quickly hid himself behind a tree with his back pressed against its trunk. He pushed Mariam behind the tree next to him to make sure she was hidden.

"Be quiet," he said slowly as he looked her in the eyes.

Two Greek soldiers, both holding lances and shields, their chests covered with breastplates and helmets on their heads, were making their routine rounds a hundred yards away. Mariam was frightened and was unconsciously squeezing Alexandros' hand.

"Don't be afraid," he said. "They're going away."

Mariam looked at him with fearful eyes. "They look like the ones who beat my father the other day."

"No, Mariam, they're different. These are palace guards. It's just their uniforms that look alike. Don't think about them now. I have a surprise for you."

Mariam was terrified of Constantine's nobles and soldiers. Her elderly father had fainted from the heat in a field just the other day. Soldiers thought he was lazing around when they came upon him as they passed through the field. She had been running with a pail of water for him, but he'd been soundly battered by the time she finally got to him.

"Let this be a lesson for you," one of the soldiers had said as they left. "It'll be much worse if you can't produce enough by the end of the season."

An empty clearing paved with stone extended toward them and into the trees after a slightly rough slope where they could see the battlements of the ramparts. The blue waters of the Bosporus over the ramparts and the sunlit hill meeting the horizon looked like a dreamscape.

Alexandros still loved Mariam's dimples when she smiled more than the scenery. He wanted to tell her so, too, but couldn't find the courage.

"Come on, come on," he said as he pulled on her hand.

They were right next to the ramparts. They went behind the overhang that was nearly as tall as them and Alexandros tried to keep Mariam from the cliff in front of them.

"Don't be scared, there's no one from the palace coming here to-day."

"How do you know?"

"They're all at the western ramparts today. I heard the guards talking—they're waiting to receive the emperor. Didn't you see the crowds in the square? They started gathering at the Gate of Saint Romanus in the early morning. And anyway, they all stay at the Blachernae Palace when they come here on one of their random visits. I've been watching it for weeks."

"Where'd the emperor go?"

"He went for talks in some far-off land. They're off making agreements to fight against the Turks."

"But how do you know all that, Alexis?"

"I heard the guards talking—"

"What if they come and catch us here?"

"Trust me. What? Would I ever want anything bad to happen to you?" Alexandros wanted to reach out and caress Mariam's hair when he spoke, but he couldn't bring himself to do it. "Don't wor-ry and just enjoy the view."

She looked down the sheer, stone walls ascending high above the sea and shivered, but the view was amazing.

"Hold me, Alexis. I'm afraid I'll fall."

Alexandros went behind her and held her waist as they looked down together. He felt like his heart would burst through his chest, not from looking down the cliff, but from finally being this close to Mariam.

"Do you see the lions?" He pointed to the gigantic statues Em-peror Theophilos had erected six hundred years before.

The two lions on either side of a spectacular gate with columns and arches looked as if they had walked in from the sea and that they let all passing ships know that they were entering Constantine's city. The aquamarine walls extended with triangular-arched windows, holes for the passing wind and echelons of columns in a terrifyingly magnificent show on the southern face of the city.

"Is this my surprise?" Mariam said as she smiled and looked over at Alexandros.

"A part of it. You have to wait and watch me a bit for the real present. Run into the woods right away and hide behind a tree if you hear anybody coming, but don't be scared."

"Oh, and what're you going to do?"

"Just watch," Alexandros said as he pulled her back toward the walls.

He put his back against the stone wall and went off some twenty yards as Mariam watched curiously. Then he looked back down at the sea and put one bare foot in front of the other as if he were going to take off running, he stopped and looked back at Mariam.

Mariam put her hand up to her mouth. "What're you doing?! No, Alexis, please don't! It's so dangerous, are you crazy?!"

"Don't worry," Alexandros said right before he ran toward the battlements and jumped headfirst off the walls with all his strength as he came to the drop.

Mariam ran to where Alexandros had just jumped and looked down, her heart thumping, as he hurtled to the water.

Alexandros sped toward the water with the form and grace of someone who'd been diving in these waters his entire life, passed the columns, loopholes and finally the lions. He paid attention to ensure he hit the water at a steep angle with his arms outstretched to lessen the impact. He'd chosen this part of the sea walls to hide his gift because the rocks here were well below the surface. He'd decided he could dive here after combing over the shore for days.

"Alexis!" Mariam cried, her head bent down as he plunged into the water.

The rings spreading out from Alexandros' dive splashed against the sea walls as he disappeared under the surface.

Mariam looked around as Alexandros vanished under the water and started to plead as if in prayer.

"Please, Lord Jesus, please let Alexis come up out of the water. Don't let him die. Please, Lord Jesus, don't let anything happen, don't let anything happen to Alexis. Let him came back to me!"

She felt the passing seconds as hours and grew more worried seeing no movement in the water below. There were stories of the many Romans who'd been lost to the strong currents where the Bosporus emptied to the sea and she was losing her mind thinking that Alexandros would join them. Her blue eyes were open wide looking at the blue water as if she were looking at a reflection in a mirror as memories of the countless times they'd spent together since they were children came rushing to her mind. She thought about the castles they used to make out of mud, playing hide and seek in the fields, how Alexandros had worked throughout the night in her father's field after working in his own during the day when the man had fallen ill so the patrician's men wouldn't notice he was gone. All the confidence he had in his tiny world passed before her eyes one by one, like how just the past week, he had climbed the Column of Constantine in the city square and gave her the daisies he had put there earlier.

She saw a head emerge from the water just below the lions as her little eyes were welling with tears.

"Oh, Jesus Christ, thank you. Thank you, Jesus!" she cried, then jumping up and down and waving her arms, "Alexis, Alexis!"

She saw something in the boy's mouth but couldn't make out what it was from where she was.

He took hold of the feet of the lion statue and pulled himself out of the water, latching onto its back and then head with his strong arms. He stepped up onto the backs of the statues and quickly scrambled up the wall like a spider, using the holes as hand and footholds. He climbed over the overhang of the arched gate, the stone around the crenels and the capitals of the marble columns with the ease of climbing a staircase.

Mariam ran over to where he was climbing and saw his hand appear over the battlements as he hauled himself over the wall.

She slapped his face as soon as she got to him. "I was so scared something would happen to you! You awful boy, what if you died, what if you drowned, what if you hit your head on the walls?!"

Alexandros wasn't surprised by her reaction in the slightest and gave a tricky smile. "Don't be afraid, nothing was going to happen to me, Mariam. I'm used to it."

"I'm not scared. I'm never going to forgive you for this!"

He held out what he was holding. "Maybe this will help you forgive me. I did it for you."

Mariam's eyes sparkled as she looked at the necklace of coral intertwined with thick, hemp string in his hand.

"I collected all the coral from the different coasts around the city. I only chose the finest ones. It's kind of simple, though."

"It's the most beautiful thing I've ever seen. It's so pretty."

Alexandros saw Mariam's eyes shining and reckoned he'd made her quite happy.

She turned around for him to fasten the necklace around her neck. The boy's hands were shaking so much that for a moment he thought he wouldn't be able to tie the knot. Mariam looked out at the Maiden's Tower as Alexandros tied the string.

"Would you like to go there?" he said when he saw her looking out.

"Have you lost your mind again? How would we get there? There's no way."

"If you want to, I'll find a way."

"No, Alexis, I don't want to go there at all."

She lied, knowing the boy would do what he said. She looked down at the necklace and then back up at Alexandros. She gave him a kiss on the cheek in a flash and then, embarrassed, ran back toward the trees.

Then Alexandros heard a voice, "Don't move!"

He looked over and saw two palace guards running toward him. It was much too late to run. If he ran into the trees, Mariam wouldn't be able to keep up, and even if he were able to escape, the guards would get her—and he'd heard around what these men would do to peasant girls.

He motioned for Mariam to run without letting the guards see. She ran in and disappeared among the trees in silent fright, but instead of running away, she hid behind a thick tree and watched, worried and anxious. Alexandros went in the other direction as if trying to escape, pulling the guards along with him.

"I said stop! Stop or I'll put this lance straight into your back!"

Alexandros did as he was told.

"Well, well, looks like a fish has jumped up from the water," one of the guards said with a smile as water dripped from the boy.

"Out with it, boy. What're you doing here?" The guard pointed the sharp, steel tip of his lance at the boy's throat.

Alexandros felt he could take the guards who didn't do anything other than wander around the palace, and swipe away the lance from his throat, but decided against it, afraid Mariam could be given away if something small went wrong.

"Uh, well, sir—I was working in the fields and the village kids wanted to play a prank on me. They don't like me very much. They've got a grudge against me because I work so hard in the fields and they don't leave me alone. Then three of the five of them took me to the shore and threw me in the water. The current took me here. I would've drowned if I couldn't hold on to the walls. And I climbed up."

The guards looked at each other, trying to make out if the boy was telling the truth or not.

"Look here, you urchin, and don't lie to us. What're you doing here?" one of them said, trying to test him.

"I'm not lying, sir. Look at me. How else could I get this wet? I was about to die."

"So, what? You're saying you climbed up the walls? That's impossible."

"You'd have done it to for dear life, sir. I was scared, but I didn't have a choice. I don't know how I did it, either. I was so scared."

One of the guards looked over the boy's strong arms and shoulders. "You'd be useful to us in the army with that spryness. It's a shame you're just a simple peasant boy."

The other was looking into the boy's eyes, mulling over whether he should believe his story.

Another guard came up behind them. "There's word Manuel Palaiologos has entered the city. He could make an inspection and we've been ordered to take our positions at once."

"There's no time to waste with this boy," the guard said as he squeezed the back of Alexandros' neck. "Fall in line in front of me," he said, and marched the boy away.

He looked back from between the two guards pulling him along out of the palace and saw Mariam in the trees. He gave her a wink as if to say not to worry and he'd find her in a little bit.

There was concern over Mariam's face as she poked her head out from the trees, but Alexandros had succeeded in building her confidence in him.

7

Sultan Murad smiled at the sight of his son as he sat in the palace's large hall. He was sitting cross-legged and waiting on a divan in front of a large window. The sunlight filtering through the latticework over the pane fell on the sultan's entire body and gave an even more divine look to his solemn command.

Mehmed noticed as he knelt in front of his father that his beard had gone quite grey, the lines in his face had deepened since the last time they'd seen each other and his face was much paler.

Mullah Gürani bowed to the sultan as soon as he entered, like everyone else, and then turned to the viziers. Halil Pasha was in the palace and Saruja Pasha and Ragip Pasha were each at the sultan's side. Next to them was a white-bearded man in a white turban and white robe who greeted him with more respect. The prince had his attention on the man who had earlier almost killed him—or saved him—as he greeted everyone and stood next to him. The man's looks were piercing his heart.

"So, it seems you've met Mullah Gürani," Sultan Murad said without taking his eyes from the boy. "His Holiness Sheikh Akshamsaddin said it would be best if he went to find you."

"Yes, I agreed to it. I would never think of not listening to Sheikh Akshamsaddin's suggestions," Mullah Gürani said.

"I hope you'll do the same," the sultan said when he saw the uncertainty on the prince's face, "as from now on Mullah Gürani will be your head tutor. I give him full authority over the goings on in this palace." He looked at the man next to Gürani. "He and Mullah Hüsrev will educate you in every field of science." After pausing for a while, he added, "They will prepare you to be sultan."

This sounded strange to Mehmed.

"I've got no designs to be sultan, Sir. It's Alaaddin's right to rule, anyway. He's older than me and more experienced."

Mehmed couldn't get it out of his mind, though, how this mullah—his tutor—could be such a skilled horseman. All the hajjis and tutors who'd come to teach him something so far were all unlikable, either always telling him he'd never be a man and leaving after a few lessons or always taking breaks. Mehmed had so far always been able to play games with the teachers sent to him after a short while and skip out on his lessons. Now, though, looking at those waiting over him, he felt things wouldn't be the same as they had been.

"But, father—" he said after a little hesitation. "He tried to kill me. There's no way he can be my tutor."

Going against his father's bidding was the last thing he wanted to do, but he felt the mullah had defeated him and he wanted revenge.

Murad stood up and waved for everyone to leave. Ragip Pasha was the last to leave, shutting the door behind him. Now with everyone having made a hasty exit, the prince was alone with his father. He already regretted what he'd said.

Seeing his rebelliousness, Murad reckoned the boy had abandoned his lessons again.

"Your brother Alaaddin, with His mercy, joined God in paradise two days ago," the sultan said as his eyes misted over.

The loss of his dear and beloved son had affected him deeply. And Mehmed was right—he'd been looked upon for years as the successor to the sultan and had been brought up that way. Mehmed was successor now with the untimely death of a second son.

The prince looked at his father, bewildered by the news, but the sultan had turned from his son and was gazing out the window.

"But when, how, father?"

"The cause isn't known yet—it could be a conspiratorial assassination. We also suspect the Karamanids and the Greeks. It could be anybody and all the information coming is murky. But I don't want to get into this now, my boy. You'll learn the details from your teacher later." He gathered himself and looked back at the prince. "Being sultan is in your destiny now, my son. You will be the ruler of the Sons of Osman and it'll be you who carries the flag of the realm." He paused for a moment and sighed. "Life is capital, and its profit is goodness. Everything that walks and breathes will one day die. Many glorious warriors and rulers have come to the world and every one of them has passed. All that remains is a name. A horse dies but the square remains and a brave, young man dies but his glory remains, my boy. My time is also getting close.

"You need to grow up already and prepare to be sultan. I have to go back to Edirne and see to my own work again. I'm leaving you with three valuable tutors here. Mullah Gürani and Mullah Hüsrev will teach you in every field of the sciences. Don't mistake them for your previous teachers—you'll be wrong."

Mehmed listened in silence as he stared straight ahead. His father's words held a different weight and had a strange effect on him. He wanted to defy them with all his ill temper and say he had no need for anyone, but it was as if he couldn't open his mouth and he couldn't go against what his father had said.

"Don't forget this, my boy. There are two types of people—one learns and the other teaches. Which one are you? There's a third, and you should avoid them and run from them as you would from a pack of jackals. They're vile cowards and leeches. Don't have anyone other than these two first types of people with you.

"Jafer Agha is one of the most experience and skilled janissary aghas under my command. He will prepare you in all the arts of war. You can't preside over a land without a sword in one hand and a pen in the other, my son. If you don't have those with the pen and those with the sword with you, neither will you frighten your enemies nor bring peace to your people. If you have the choice, always choose the peaceful way.

"People think of victory and splendor when they think of war. But war is blood and filth. Feet freeze off from the cold, foul corpses rot in the heat and there's only muddy water to stave off thirst. War is only right when it's necessary. Run from barbarity and cruelty and exalt knowledge and intelligence.

"Heed your teachers. They'll provide you a treasure trove.

"I'm leaving you with a few conscripts, as well, who you can spar with for your swordsmanship and will grow up with you and will be there at your side when you ascend to the throne. Know them like they're your brothers. Vlad is a son of a prince who must spend some time away from Edirne. He'll also spend some time with you. Remember that everything that prevents war is good. Give great importance to your language lessons. Try to understand the culture and habits of the people in your administration. I am also going to send more competent language teachers for you and word should come from the Venetian gentleman in Constantinople."

8

"This child is turning things around again, Abram," Alexandros' mother, Berenike, said to her husband as she raised her eyebrows at the boy.

The whole family had to turn over the field by evening. Alexandros, his three older brothers and older sister had all spread out over the field and were working without saying a word. As he usually did, Alexandros had woken up before the sun had risen and started working in the field hours earlier. This is what he always did when he would run off to meet Mariam. He was constantly working, taking up his pickax and working before sunrise and sometimes at night so too much of the labor wouldn't fall on his family.

Abram was well into his fifties and had spent his entire life in these fields. He looked over at Alexander without stopping his work. His hands were calloused with dirt under his fingernails and having spent nearly twenty hours a day in the fields, the many lines on his face showed that that's where he'd his life had worn on. He could've told the story of every line if asked.

Abram and Berenike were talking as turned over the field.

"That's for sure. He's going through the field like mad again. He's close to disappearing," Abram said.

"What harm is there in running after happiness?"

"That hope isn't for people like us. Don't you know these types of boys? He escaped from the old palace again just the other day. I heard him bragging to his brothers about it. But I'm scared one day he won't be able to save himself, and who knows where he'll be off to next." Abram straightened himself with his hand on his back, then leaned on his pickax and looked closely over his son.

"Let him live the way he wants. He reminds me of myself."

Abram's eyes were filling with tears. He was going to say something, but couldn't. Berenike knew what he was thinking and patted him on the back.

"I wish," Abram said, "I wish that boy could have a wonderful life somewhere else if he could just get away from here."

"What're you talking about, man? We were born peasants and we'll die peasants. You've been putting these ideas in his head. His place is here and he needs to learn how to be happy here."

"I hope he doesn't wear his life out in the fields and can use his strength and smarts instead."

Abram had vacillated for a long time about whether to open up to his wife about what he'd been thinking.

"Down, down, get to work!" Berenike said.

One of the men of the emperor's cousin and close confidant, Theophilos Palaiologos, in charge of checking over the fields was riding his horse toward where the family was working. Abram quickly bent back over and started turning over the field again. The overseer slowed his horse as he came to the field and rode around the vast land. He carefully looked over the laborers as if trying to find some shortcoming. He brought his horse over and stopped close to the girl working on her knees like the others and started watching her. He thought maybe he could sling her over his horse, bring her to the woods and have a bit of fun as he pinned her down, but he thought twice about it since there were so many young men around. Maybe he could if there were a couple other soldiers with him. He was wary, though, as he heard that an overseer had tried the same thing the other day and the girl's father planted an ax into his skull. Mind that, a small army came and raped his wife, then tied him to a horse and dragged him through the fields to his death.

None of this changed the overseer's urges, though. He figured it would be better to come back to the girl later with a large group as he pulled his horse away from her. Maybe he could also make up to Theophilos with mention of this girl.

Alexandros was running swiftly through the main stone-paved Mese road only about an hour later. Horses could reach the city center from the fields much faster, but Alexandros was running so fast he saw nothing else and didn't tire.

He quickly weaved through the crowds in the streets and kept going, flying through the Forum of Theodosius and by the Column of Marcian with bronze inscription and image of Nike, the Goddess of Victory. He sped through the Forum of Constantine and past the Column of Constantine—built by the city's founder—and the shining, gold cross at its pinnacle. With his eyes firmly fixed on the road, Alexandros didn't see the two men in front of him as he sped along. He ran straight into one's belly and fell to the ground. The man hadn't even been knocked off balance, let alone shaken up, and Alexandros thought he'd run into a stone wall.

Alexandros looked up from the ground at the man standing over him, his strange, yellow boots, red leggings and full trousers from the knee up. He saw the man's crimson sash around his waist and the handle of the dagger tucked into it as he lifted his head further. He'd never seen such a finely engraved dagger before. He carefully looked at the tulip designs on the handle and the green leaves and shining, golden lines. He didn't understand, though, why the sheath of the sword hanging from the man's side was so thin and curved. The sandy, long-sleeved coat the man wore widened from the waist down to his ankles. Alexandros wasn't surprised that he'd ended up on the ground when he saw the man's thick arms and broad shoulders. The strangest thing about this man, though, was his tall hat that folded back at the top.

Scared of the man's grandeur, Alexandros started to scoot back, worried he'd get a beating. He figured he'd just turn and run.

The janissary knelt down and tussled the boys head. "What's the matter, kiddo."

The man spoke Greek with a strange accent, but Alexandros could still understand.

He pulled the boy to his feet from the arm. "Where're you off to, running like this?"

Alexandros was still staring at the two men's clothing and hats. The man speaking had a long mustache curled up at the ends. The other was completely clean-shaven.

"Don't worry, son. Come on and talk, there's no problem here."

"No, no. I'm fine, sir." Alexandros finally said. "I'm going to meet my sweetheart. That's why I'm running." He felt he didn't have to hide anything after seeing the kindness on the janissary's face, but he didn't get why he'd just mentioned Mariam to strangers.

The janissaries looked at each other and smiled. "Watch out, though. Some people around here might not be so pleased to find a child underfoot. There're a lot of palace guards around."

Alexandros looked around and saw that there really were quite a few palace guards in and around the forum. Emperor Manuel II Palaiologos had yet to conclude the meeting with Sultan Murad's envoys in the Senate just behind the Forum of Constantine.

"You're not going to turn me in, are you?"

"Of course not, my boy. Come on, don't make your sweetie wait. If you do, you'll do her wrong."

Alexandros didn't understand the last thing the janissary said and ran off about two hundred yards in the opposite direction to the *Milion* mile marker.

Alexandros pointed out the letters and figures on the *Milion* to Mariam as he spoke. "These all show the distance from here to far-away cities and other places in the empire."

He wanted to show off to Mariam that he could read all the letters and figures. She would see him in a totally different light knowing that he could read like a child from the palace.

The monument they were looking at was splendidly built with four thick walls supported by columns and adorned with reliefs of soldiers. The end of the Mese road with the *Milion,* Hagia Sophia, Hippodrome, and old Great Palace, was the center point of the empire with the city's main roads stretching out like a web to Europe.

"How do you know that?"

"My father explained it to me. He carried stones once when it was being repaired."

Mariam was playing with the necklace that Alexandros had given her as she spoke.

"This road goes all the way to old Rome. Constantine built him himself."

"Where's old Rome? Isn't this the Roman Empire?"

Alexandros climbed over the stone monument as he explained to Mariam what he knew. "Way before it was here there was Rome. Then Constantine founded this place, old Rome was scattered and all the kings and lords came here. The Latins were jealous so they attacked and sacked the city hundreds of years ago."

"I suppose you didn't invite me here to tell me all of this," Mariam said as if she was getting bored. "My mother will already give me a good scolding again when I get back home."

Alexandros jumped down from the stones. "No, no. I was waiting for the right time." He saw Mariam look at him questioningly and went on. "We're going on a little trip today. Come on."

He went in front of Mariam and they quickly walked south along the Mese road.

"But Alex, where are we running off to?

"Don't worry. Come on and follow me."

Mariam was sweating as she tried to catch up with Alexandros ten steps ahead of her. "Go a bit slower, would you. I can't keep up."

She saw the masts of ships and the harbor when she looked up and realized they'd run to the shore. The Maiden's Tower was the only thing visible from where they were. Mariam regretted ever telling Alexandros she wanted to go there. She was scared they'd run into danger again and something could happen to Alexandros.

"I told you not to," she said as they got to the pier. "What've you prepared this time?"

"There's a fisherman I know who brings fish there every other day. The emperor's family eats there."

"But what if they catch us?!"

"Don't be afraid. I've arranged everything."

The Kontoskalion harbor was the only one of the many in Constantinople where ships of all sizes anchored. There were just as many people from other lands as there were Greeks in the crowd, Venetians and Genoese foremost among them. Mariam looked curiously at all these men in their floppy hats, not knowing where they were from.

Alexandros was weaving through the throngs of people toward the end of the pier as he looked for the fisherman.

"Master Demetrios, we're here."

An old man looked up from the middle of his boat at the teenage boy and girl on the pier. Mariam lowered her eyes as she looked at this stranger with a scruffy beard and mustache holding pieces of net.

"You're going to get me in trouble, but not so fast."

"But that's not what we agreed, Master Demetrios. I'll come tomorrow morning and the next ten days and carry the fish crates. Just like we said—"

The displeased look on the old man's face lightened a bit when he remembered the good side of the deal.

The old fisherman sat at the front of the boat as Alexandros rowed with all his strength.

"Whatever happens, don't talk," Demetrios told Mariam as they approached the islet. "I'll answer if they ask you anything."

Mariam nodded as she looked over and smiled at Alexandros.

Demetrios reached out to the pier with a long rope to tie the boat up when they got to the edge of the islet.

"Who're they?" a guard said after greeting the fisherman.

"I'm getting old already. My son and daughter are helping me."

The guard looked Alexandros and Mariam up and down. "I wouldn't reckon they'd give you permission to come to the island with this many people. We'll have to find someone else if you can't see to your work yourself."

"I've been ailing a bit these past few days. I'll be better soon, though." Demetrios said anxiously. He hadn't ever thought about the possibility of losing this work.

The guard stood for a while, thinking over the situation, before he spoke back up. "Alright, let's see about it this time around. But I want three extra crates of fish for myself."

"Yes, sir." Demetrios knew many of the palace guards took bribes and so wasn't at all surprised.

He turned around to Alexandros as the guard was walking away. "The days you're going to work for me have just doubled, young man."

Alexandros nodded.

The little island was relatively quiet and empty since there weren't any of the emperor's relatives there. There wasn't anyone else save for a few guards in the tower, where Alexandros and Mariam carried the crates as Demetrios unloaded his boat. As soon as he saw that no one was around, Alexandros slowly opened the door at the top of the tower and pulled Mariam outside to show her the view.

The skyline of the city enchanted them both. This enormous city where they lived and where they'd grown up stretched out proudly between the indigo sea and blue sky. The white gulls above the shore seemed as if they were greeting Constantinople as they passed by the great sea walls. The majestic dome of the Hagia Sophia rose from behind the Boukoleon Palace and next to the Obelisk of Theodosius as if to the envy of the vault of heaven.

They both pointed out as they tried to name all of the buildings. "Look, there's the Column of Theodosius sticking out," Alexandros said.

"And those're the chimneys of the old Great Palace," Mariam said.

They looked to the right and saw the conical cap of Galata Tower.

"Look, look. That's where the Genoese live," Alexandros said.

He looked at how Mariam's eyes sparkled and the excitement on her face. "Mariam, I have something to tell you." He turned to face her. "I—"

"Hey you!" a voice called out from below. The guard at the base of the tower had noticed them and motioned in an order for them to come down immediately.

They were both scared as they descended the stairs. The guard grabbed them both by the scruffs of their necks when they got to the bottom and dragged them over to the fisherman.

"The crates of fish you're going to give me just went up to five, Demetrios! Take your kids and get out of here. Don't bring anybody with you again, or else don't ever come back!"

9

The prince rolled up his sleeves up to his elbows in the middle of the variegated flower garden and set to pulling up brambles and tossing them aside. He knew the garden would turn into a thicket if the weeds weren't cleared in time. It had been nearly a full year since he'd started this garden in a large plot behind the palace. The first task Mullah Gürani had given him was to get his hands dirty clearing the soil and planting seeds. No one was going to help him and all the responsibilities—the stones, the soil, the mud and watering—were his own. The water from the four arms of the fountain in the center of the garden flowed and gurgled out to the flowers and trees and created a pleasant atmosphere as much as it was useful for the plants. *You won't squander anything,* his tutor always said. The design of the fountain was also made in consideration of this golden rule.

"He who can look after a garden can rule a country well enough," Mullah Gürani said, his hands clasped behind his back. "There are flowers, and they need to be watered every day. There are weeds, and they'll choke out the flowers if they're not pulled out by the roots. There are also trees, and their shade is cool and they form the boundary. And just like this, like watering flowers, a sultan should look after the rights of his subjects, punish injustice like pulling weeds and, like the powerful trees, he should place trustworthy commanders along the borders of the realm so the people may feel safe. Thusly, flowers of all kind come into bloom."

Beyond the fountain, a waist-high fence surrounded a canopy that was closed off by carpets with dominant reds and yellows, and next to it, the slightly raised platform of a hexagonal gazebo made of cedar.

The shade from the rows of cypresses, poplars, plane trees and willows provided relief from the hot summer days, and grape vines and flowers covered the high walls around the rest of the garden. What gave the garden its true color, though, was the thousands of different flowers in the large field around the canopy—pink-speckled white lilies; purple, orange and violet hyacinths; the rows of larkspur running along the fence and the hydrangeas, their balls of flowers like dyed and crumpled muslin with bent stalks, seemed to be in friendly conversation with each other. Fragrant clusters hung from the lilac trees, snapdragons roared out from their green foliage, yellow lilies swam in the waterways and snow-white peonies bloomed with orange on green in the center.

The prince had specifically asked for red carnations, white tulips and purple sweet peas from around the realm and had planted each of the seeds and bulbs himself.

There was a fresco painter depicting the flowers in fine detail in the middle of the canopy. Sultan Murad had personally sent one of Edirne's most talented artists, Baba Nakkash, to Manisa upon the prince's request. He had carefully painted Mullah Gürani in the center of the fresco with a sheet of paper on his knee.

"Have you ever thought about it, Mehmed?" Mullah Gürani said after smelling a magnolia hanging above him. "Why do we so like these beautiful scents? Why do they give us such pleasure and why do they make us so happy?"

Mehmed pulled up another weed and threw it aside. Sweat was pouring from his forehead as his hands busily moved through the garden.

"It's because there is beauty in people," Gürani continued. "There's a fondness for man's goodness and beauty in creation. Isn't it the admiration of beauty that means to be human?"

Next to Baba Nakkash was Burhan, one of the conscripts who'd been sent to be a friend to Mehmed. He was doing his calligraphy lesson, writing out an *elif* for maybe the hundredth time. He knew he wouldn't be able to go back to his teacher without having first filled five pages with *elifs*.

The palace's head doorkeeper, wearing a quilted cap with a wound turban with his curls hanging to his cheeks, slowly approached the prince.

"A Venetian has come bearing the sultan's seal. He wishes to see you."

"He must be the language teacher," Mehmed said. "Show him in."

The doorkeeper returned fifteen minutes later with the Venetian man who had a black chaperone wrapped around his head, a light beard, the tight breeches of the Europeans in red and a dark-blue jacket.

The thirty-something-year-old man looked around as he came beside the canopy, trying to figure out which one was the prince. He couldn't be the old painter. The boy pulling weeds must be one of the palace gardeners, but he couldn't reckon who the old man next to the boy was. So, the boy writing next to the painter must be the prince, he figured.

"Greetings, Your Highness," he said with a strange accent and bowed slightly. He didn't know whether he was to greet a prince as he did a sultan, but figured it was better to be safe. "Your father the sultan has sent me specially for your Venetian lessons—"

Burhan laughed. "I'm not who you're looking for." He turned his head to Mehmed, who was standing up in the garden and looking at him.

The Venetian man's face went red as he went to Mehmed.

"My apologies, Your Highness. I thought—"

"It's nothing," Mehmed said. "You're not the first to be surprised. It happens."

"The children in the Most Serene Republic don't do this work. Servants, or what you call slaves in your language, do this type of work."

"My teacher always says we're all servants of God." He looked over at Mullah Gürani.

"Whether a peasant or a king," Mullah Gürani said, "a servant who forgets his servitude strays from Truth."

Mehmed finished Gürani's saying. "A slave who worships God is freer than an emperor who strays from Truth."

The Venetian teacher was surprised to hear something so lofty from a boy.

"You take a seat," Mehmed said. "Let me go wash my hands and I'll be back."

The language teacher nearly forgot to remove his shoes as he stepped into the canopied gazebo. The first thing he'd been warned of before he set off from Constantinople was that the Turks take off their shoes in places where the sit. He felt strangely embarrassed as he removed his shoes, as is he were naked and defenseless.

He crouched down beside Baba Nakkash and started looking over the fresco. The colors were vivid. He looked at the artist's paints—he'd rarely seen so many different eye-catching pigments.

The prince carefully washed his hands and face at the fountain and then dried off at the edge of the garden with towel embroidered with tulips. He put his red, leather cap back on and wound his muslin turban back up before he entered the gazebo and took a seat on a divan.

"The colors seem even more alive than in real life," the Venetian man said.

"Very true," Baba Nakkash said with a laugh. "Life's an illusion, so art must show what's beyond it. So yes, it really is more real." He dipped his brush into the paint and continued paining the various flowers.

"Don't worry," Mehmed interjected. "I wouldn't say that I understand much of what Baba Nakkash says, either. I'm not so different from you. All I know is that the picture immortalizes the beauty of this garden. Maybe I'll get what he says later on. But anyway, what's your name?"

"Forgive me, Prince, I was amazed and got lost in the painting and forgot to introduce myself. I'm Bernardo Balbi from the branch of the prestigious Balbi family of Venice that lives in Constantinople. I was sent by His Excellency Emperor Ioannes VIII Palaiologos upon request from your father Sultan Murad in order to improve your Venetian. It is an honor to be at your service."

"You speak our language quite well." Constantinople Rome, and especially with the mediations in its relations with the sultan. The rights and laws of the Turks in Constantinople and the Greeks under your father's reign fall to us. You could say it's my father's profession. My father worked hard ever since I was a child to ensure I learned Ottoman."

"It looks like you're also interested in painting."

"I am. Artistry is all encompassing in all of Italy. Painters are sculptors and sculptors are medallion makers. They take all fields in hand."

Mehmed picked up a book from the divan and showed it to Balbi.

"Look, I draw, too."

Balbi looked in surprise at the drawings in the book that were much more than just simple figures—a horse's head, an owl's face with large eyes, the flap of a stork's wings—all wonderfully rendered.

"These don't much resemble your miniatures, though."

"I know. I draw from them, too, but it's nice to also draw from the paintings in the Europeans' books."

Baba Nakkash glared over at Mehmed.

"I must say you have a natural ability for it, Prince," Balbi said.

"Thanks. What are medallion makers, though? What's a medallion?"

Balbi removed the thin chain with a medallion the size of a coin hanging from it from around his neck and held it out to the prince.

Mehmed turned the medallion around in his hand as he looked over it closely.

"The dolphin on the front represents Venice's domination on the seas," Balbi said, "and the lighthouse on the back reminds us we mustn't fall to despair when having lost our way."

"Is Venice really as powerful on the seas as you say?"

"There's not yet been a power to rival the Venetian navy, Prince. We're born at sea and we die at sea."

Mehmed handed the medallion back to Balbi. "Do you know the story of the narcissus?" he asked. He went on before Balbi had a chance to say anything. "I'm sure you know it better since it's a tale from Greek mythology. There was a young man named Narcissus who was so beautiful everyone fell in love with him. One day he sat beside a pool and saw his own reflection. He couldn't get enough of his own beauty and stayed there for days and weeks looking at himself. He wasted away there and died and turned into the flower that we call the narcissus."

"That's why the flower goes pale from starvation like a man and is pure white."

"And it's always bent over water, looking at itself like a person would. If there's one thing I've learned from the history books I've read, it's that no power can seize eternity. Importance of self is the greatest harbinger of the end."

Balbi understood the hint was directed at him and was ashamed of his earlier remark. It was clear he shouldn't talk tactlessly with the prince or take him lightly due to his age.

"That's quite right, Prince."

"Would you tell me a bit about Constantinople. It looks like you're uncomfortable there. Here, sit here, it's better."

Balbi took a seat on the divan. "What about the city would you like to know, Prince?"

"They say the walls are impenetrable—is that true?"

"Your Highness, I spent my childhood in many different kingdoms from Europe to Anatolia and further east. I can easily say I've never seen walls like those of Constantinople in either the Italian city-states or around the grounds of the old Hindu palaces."

"Some people even say the walls have been around for a thousand years. Is that true?"

"They must be speaking of the Theodosian Walls. Yes, Prince, it's true."

"I want you to start before Constantine, though—from the Byzantines. Oh yeah, let me say while I still remember—I want you to make a medallion for me. Is that possible?"

"It is, but all my materials are in Venice. We can make one here for now and then I can send you a more beautiful one from there."

And with approval from the prince, Bernardo Balbi began to talk of Constantinople.

10

A Greek king named Byzas in the seventh century before Christ asked the Oracle of Delphi at the Temple of Apollo where he should found his new empire.

"Across from the land of the blind," the oracle said, but Byzas didn't understand a word of it.

The king set out from the temple with his fleet and armies and sailed on the Aegean for days to the north. He left Athens and Corinth behind, passed through the Dardanelles and by Troy and entered the Marmara Sea. He smiled, realizing what the oracle had meant, as he approached the shores of Chalcedon, as only the blind would settle there instead of on the peninsula jutting out into the sea on the opposite shore.

King Byzas founded the city of Byzantium there, between Europe and Anatolia and between two seas, surrounded by water to all but the northwest.

After centuries of its dominion, it became a polity closed to itself on the peninsula and was growing poorer by the day. The new successor to the city then came from the center of Europe, when one man emerged victorious in the Wars of the Tetrarchy for the throne of the Roman Empire.

As had happened in the land of Byzantium, the days of prosperity and glory in Rome also fell to quarrels and strife. The Roman

Emperor Constantine realized that the Rome of his dreams was no more and he began to search for a center to create anew from where he could reign over the world. Constantine was captivated when he saw the peninsula of Byzantium and knew he had found his capital of New Rome.

And so, Prince, Constantine decided to move the capital of the Roman Empire to the heart of the world on the edges of the Occident and the Orient a thousand years ago in the fourth century.

Constantine, the son of Saint Helena—one of the most important Christians of the empire—gave his name to the city. One of the first things he did was prohibit the pagans from killing Christians. He was the first Roman emperor to become Christian and he worked for the prosperity of all in his realm. He buried both the Christians and the saints of the pagans beneath the magnificent monument he erected in the middle of the city and tried to emphasize the importance of tolerance. They say he himself is buried in the Palladium of Troy, the ruins of Pallas Athena's monument, with the ax Noah used in building the arc, materials from Jesus' first miracle and the stone from which Moses drew water.

He brought the statue of Apollo with the world in his right hand and a crown in his left to his city.

He built a gigantic hippodrome for chariot races, games and other ceremonies whose surrounding city square and stands could hold forty thousand people. He also brought the three-headed Serpentine Column from Athens and erected it in the center of the Hippodrome.

The Hippodrome was so influential in the cultural life of the city that the colors of the chariot racing clubs—red, blue, white and green—were reflected in Constantine's power. There were the blues to the right and statesmen in green to the left. Sometimes chariot races have been held at night by torchlight under the stars. Young men die before their wedding night, experienced warriors become lame and men who want to prove their bravery lose their eyes, but the culture of the Hippodrome has always continued.

Buildings increased as the city grew and architectural achievements spread at astonishing speed in every direction. Aqueducts brought water from miles away and for weeks thousands of people came flowing in to the new sites on ships carrying cattle, slaves, monuments and statues. They came from all over the world—from Alexandria, Athens, Rome and Antioch.

The leading families of Rome, the emperor's men and patricians all moved to New Rome in time.

As if to prove that Rome had eclipsed the civilization of ancient Egypt, Theodosius I brought the Obelisk of Thutmose III, originally from the Temple of Karnak, and placed it in the Hippodrome next to the Serpentine Column after its thirty-three-day journey from Egypt. It has hieroglyphs on it that describe the pharaoh and the god Horus, and Theodosius had Roman artisans carve reliefs into a pedestal that describe the empire. One side shows the submission of barbarians bearing him gifts, another has him offering laurels of victory with wrestlers and dancing girls, another shows chariot races and the other has him and his court.

Theodosius II decided to reinforce Constantine's walls with two more layers when the empire encountered the scourge of Attila the Hun from the west. Theodosius believed the only way to stop the quickly advancing Huns was to build insurmountable walls, and that's the beginning of the famous walls that have stood for centuries.

Twenty thousand people were put to work day and night digging a very wide and deep moat in front of the first wall, which was then naturally then filled with water. The second wall is thirty feet tall and, up a tier from that, the third wall is forty feet. These walls are sixteen feet thick made from red brick and limestone with the thousand years of Roman architectural ingenuity. Every fifty-five yards there're sixty-five-foot towers. The square, hexagonal and octagonal towers were built next to, but not attached, to the walls with stairs facing the city for access.

There are also gates in the three layers of walls stretching from the Golden Horn in the city's north to the Marmara Sea in the south to maintain control over those entering and leaving. The most important aspect of these gates is that there isn't a straight line between the gates of the outer walls and those of the inner walls. This technique, named after the Greek letter *sigma*, allows defenders to easily constrict advancing enemies between the walls in any siege.

The main gate is called the Gate of Saint Romanus and is close to the Church of Saint Daniel. Mohametan centuries later called this same man the Prophet Daniel and considered him one of the Jewish prophets.

The city is protected by fortresses side by side and by the many towers each emperor built during his reign along new walls or those that have been repaired after earthquakes—which is a fate the city will never escape.

These walls are so important to the emperors that they say Justinian didn't wear his crown for forty days after they were damaged in an earthquake.

After Attila, the walls have withstood the Persians, Arabs, Bulgars, Avars, Magyars and even crusaders. No matter what armies have come or will come, they undoubtedly try to take this city.

Not many people understood what he was saying when one day Justinian said an angel had ordered him to build a magnificent church to the glory of God. The architect Anthemius of Tralles completed his drawing plans very quickly, as if he had seen what the emperor was dreaming of.

The church enigmatically faces southeast at thirty-three degrees and has a large dome in the center with a half dome to each side. There are half domes on each of its four sides that were built in order to avoid the cross shape so often seen in the west of Europe. Isidore of Miletus was the other main architect involved in its construction, which went on day and night for many years.

They brought marble from around the empire and ten thousand men worked for six years on it. Justinian also closed all the buildings of the administration, including schools, throughout the process and raised taxes as much as possible to fund the building of the church. They placed the building on a twenty-three-foot foundation and used iron and cast lead in its mortar. The bricks were made of clay from Rhodes, and each one of them has the inscription, *God is in the midst of her and she shall not be moved. God shall help her, and that right early.*

The palindromic Greek saying, *Wash the sins, not only the face,* was carved into the fountain in front of the church.

The columns for the interior were brought from the Temples of Artemis, Zeus and Apollo, and from the Sassanians in Persia, as well as from Egypt. Gold mosaics were placed on the walls that reflect the sunlight from the dozens of windows set at specific angles.

When it was finished six years later, Justinian entered and looked up in wonderment at the dome, which looks as if it is suspended from the heavens.

Constantine presenting the city from the right to the Virgin Mary and the baby Jesus is depicted in the mosaic on the main wall with Justinian on their left presenting the Hagia Sophia.

Now, Prince, Constantinople was the dearest of the entire world, its center and the queen of cities.

11

Mariam and Alexandros saw children getting up to dangerous games again on the walls of the Golden Gate when they were on their way back to their homes. One of the children was half way up one of the imposing walls. He looked like he was climbing it, but he had stopped, not going up or down. The others were watching from below and laughing.

Alexandros got closer and saw that it was Ioannes. The boy was sobbing.

"What's going on, Alex?" Mariam said.

"The kids are teasing Ioannes again. What'll happen this time?"

The children had burst into laughter and one called out, "We told you you couldn't climb it. We told you not to bother. Looks like we were right."

"How many times have I told you all to leave that kid alone," Alexandros said.

The children teased and had fun with Ioannes whenever Alexandros wasn't around.

One of the boys wasn't so happy with where things were heading and started defending it. "What're we supposed to do? The jackass fell for it again. We said climb it if you're a man and he straight on went and started climbing."

"Why doesn't he jump down?" Mariam said.

"He'd likely break something if he jumped from there."

"He'd be a goner if he fell on his noggin," another of the boys said through his laughter, although he went quite when he saw Alexandros' angry look.

"He should go up, then."

"He's afraid," Alexandros said. "He can't move."

Mariam gave Alexandros a worried look. "We should do something."

Alexandros went to the wall and started climbing up below Ioannes. He went carefully, finding hand and footholds between the stones as he went.

He put his feet in the ventilation holes when he was thirty feet up and just down and to the left of Ioannes.

He pressed his face to the wall and whispered to the boy, "How many times have I told you not to pay those boys any mind."

"I thought I could climb it, Alex," Ioannes said as he quickly drew in a breath. "It was going fine, but then I looked down and got scared. Then I got tight and stayed here."

Alexandros could see the boy's legs shaking.

Then one of the boys below yelled out, "The sentry, the guards are coming—run!"

Alexandros and Ioannes looked down and saw the boys scatter from sight. Mariam was still standing there.

"You go, too!" he yelled down to her.

"No. I'm waiting!" she shouted back.

The sentry was running along the rampart and getting closer to them.

Alexandros knew he wouldn't be able to change Mariam's mind, but there wasn't much time left.

He looked over at Ioannes. "I'm here, pal. Now keep on climbing. Don't work yourself up. If anything happens, I'll hold on to you."

"I can't, Alex. I'm really scared. What if I fall?"

"We don't have any more time, Yannis. I'm here, I'll hold on to you. Don't be scared."

Ioannes reached up for a stone above his head from where he had been clinging for the past half hour. Then he found a spot for his foot and pulled himself up. Alexandros looked over at the sentry. He was only about three hundred yards away.

Ioannes then reached up his left hand, but slipped on one of the stones he was standing on and lost his balance. He started to fall, but Alexandros grabbed him by the wrist. The boy could've died if he hadn't caught him. Ioannes was panicked and there was no way they'd be able to get up the wall that way.

Alexandros saw a set of stairs to the right running along the wall. It was their only shot.

"Listen to me, Yannis." Alexandros' forehead was dripping with sweat. "You see those stairs over to the right?"

Ioannes was scared to death and couldn't speak.

"Yannis! The sentry is almost here. My arm's already tired and we'll both die if you don't listen to me! Do you see the stairs?!"

"Yes."

"I'm going to swing you three times. On the third one I'm going to let go, and when I do, try to jump off the wall to the stairs."

"Alright."

Alexandros started counting out slowly as he swung Ioannes.

"One—"

Ioannes wasn't so sure if he could jump.

"Two—"

Alexandros swung the boy with all his strength one last time.

"Three!"

Ioannes fell face down on the stairs and clung to the steps. He took a deep breath after a dazed moment and then looked up at the sentry, who was a hundred yards away, and then immediately ran down. Nothing would ever get him close to the walls again for the rest of his life.

Alexandros pulled himself up three more times and over the rampart before he ran to and down the stairs after Ioannes.

The three of them had run through the fields to the trees by the time the sentry got to the stairs.

12

"Today I'm going to tell you the story of Alexander the Great and King Kayd of Qanuj," Mullah Gürani said. He clasped his hands behind his back and walked slowly with the prince in the palace garden in Manisa as they proceeded with the daily lessons.

They continued through the purple lilacs, white sweet peas and variegated hyacinths. The prince's literature and statecraft lessons had been set for Monday, Wednesday and Sunday mornings. Lessons on the art of war were on Tuesdays, Thursdays and Saturday, and every other day he had mathematics, physics, alchemy, engineering and astrology lesson after noon. The topic this day was politics.

The prince had quickly grown accustomed to wandering through the sweet, fresh air of the garden, checking on the roses he'd planted and tending to all the other flowers.

Mullah Gürani was pleased as he saw that the prince's rough edges from years ago had smoothed out well. He was proud the more he molded the heir to the sultanate—who had before so tormented his tutors—with the influence of his lessons, books and science. Mehmed enjoyed his lessons in the open air with his tutor as he did horse riding and archery in his spare time since he was now always closed off in the library surrounded by books.

"Is this story from Ferdowsi's *Shahnameh*? Mehmed asked.

"Ah, so you've studied your lesson, Mehmed. But let's see if you can get the rest."

The prince stopped and reached out to smell one of the countless roses in the garden. "I'm listening."

"Alexander the Great continued east after conquering the east of Europe, Anatolia and the great Persian Empire. He knew well he wouldn't be able to bring to yield the king of the long-established kingdom of Qanuj in India, as he was more powerful."

"How could he resist a force that the renowned Persian Empire's Darius III couldn't?"

"He found a remedy in consultation with his viziers when he asked them to seek a solution to Alexander. Viziers are very important, Mehmed." Gürani looked at the prince. "Very well, what are the qualities of a good vizier?"

"He must be honest above all and content with himself, right?"

"That's correct, Mehmed. A content vizier will not look to illicit activities, and such a vizier will not accept bribes. Bribes are a cancer that ruins the order of the realm. A modest, clean and kind vizier treats the people properly and doesn't tyrannize them. Viziers bear the burden and responsibilities of the ruler—they are the foundation for the ruler. A vizier's wisdom must be as immense as the sea and his intellect must be just as deep. A vizier's experience and wisdom also light the way for the ruler. You should read Yusup Khass Hajip's *Qutadghu Bilig* again so you can quote the golden rules of administration at night.

"So, Mehran—one of the viziers of Qanuj—went to the king and explained the solution they'd found. King Kayd had four marvelous things unique in the world that no one else had."

The prince was now growing more interested. "What were the four things that no other empire had?"

"The first was his daughter of wondrous beauty, the second was his philosopher whose counsel would always result in the king's greatest of victories, the third was a magic goblet that was perpetually full and the fourth was his physician who could diagnose and treat any ailment."

"And if he gave these to Alexander then he'd be able to save his kingdom, is that it?"

"That's right, Mehmed. We also have this." He continued in Arabic, "*Fight those who do not believe in God or the Last Day and who do not consider unlawful what God and His Messenger have made unlawful and who do not adopt the religion of truth even though they were given the Scripture—fight them until they pay tribute willingly and are utterly subdued.* So, in other words, if one side accepts the other's superiority and agrees to pay the tax, then the war would be forbidden."

"So, how did Alexander respond?"

"Of course, like all intelligent rulers, he formed a group of his wise men and sent them to Kayd to verify the four gifts. The wise men marveled when they saw Kayd's daughter, philosopher, ever-full goblet and physician and advised Alexander to accept the four wondrous gifts. And Alexander, as a great ruler, listened to his wise men and did as they said."

"I'm curious, though. What could the philosopher and physician do that were so important?"

"That's the main point of the story. I'll tell you of the dialogue between Alexander and the philosopher and you try to find the hidden wisdom in it."

"I'm listening," Mehmed said, full of certainty.

"When the philosopher came to Alexander's palace, the great ruler sent him a bowl of melted sheep fat. The philosopher smiled when he saw the bowl of fat and said, *What could be more simple?* He placed into it a thousand needles and then he sent it back to Alexander. Alexander pulled the needles from the fat and had a blacksmith melt them down into a black ingot and fashion a disk. Then he sent it back to the philosopher. The philosopher burnished the disk until it shined like a mirror and sent it back. When he received it this time, Alexander told his men to leave the shining disk outside."

"The iron must've gone black again when it was set in the wet outside."

"That's right, Mehmed. But there's more. This time the philosopher burnished the disk to a brilliant shine and applied an ointment to it to preserve it from damp. No matter what Alexander tried, he couldn't dull its shine. He called the philosopher to him and made him his head sage, saying he would never leave his side.

"There's more to the story, though. And the question you have to answer is why Alexander was so fascinated with this. What is the wisdom in their war of minds?"

Mehmed had started to think since the beginning of the tale that he might encounter another one of his tutor's hundreds of puzzling mind games. He would have struggled if he came across this mystifying story years ago—he would have worked at it throughout the night until he got past the objects and could see the hidden meanings behind the symbols, finally being able to find the answer after days of sleeplessness. But now he'd become better versed and learned how to use his tutor's hints and emphases. Now he was confronted with another tough tale.

"Think about Alexander and all the wars he'd fought on one side and the philosopher and his qualities, on the other. That should help you," Mullah Gürani suggested.

"The fat must symbolize the indelicate and deadness," Mehmed began. "It must mean something bad. Alexander must've sent the philosopher the pot of fat in allusion to the dozens of wars he waged and the blood he spilled and that this built up in him like a filthy bowl of fat."

"Well done, Mehmed. The fat represents Alexander's cumbersome spirit from dealing with the ruthlessness of war and world affairs. Your father Sultan Murad doesn't avoid nothing as he does war—he runs from it as he would from the devil. The ignorant sees war as brilliant victories, piles of plunder and the gaining of vast lands. But war is death. And before a soldier, death is the judgment of the ruler's spirit."

"But is a ruler to stay silent to injustice and cruelty?"

"Of course not. Quite the opposite. In such cases the ruler is the force of the powerless, the guardian of the oppressed and the sword of God on earth. No king should ever want his subjects to live in happiness and wish tyranny on his neighboring people. He should strive to be just and humane and spread Truth over the land. It's every person's holy duty to spread good just as much as it is to flee from evil. The ruler is the shadow of God on earth.

"Let's get back to the story, though. So, what do you have to say about the philosopher's answer?"

"That's easy. The philosopher putting the needles into the fat was a sign that his wisdom would penetrate Alexander's coarse spirit."

"So, the philosopher was saying that Alexander's experiences cannot surpass the wisdom he has to impart, and what he has to say will benefit Alexander, is that it?"

"Yes, Sir."

"But it didn't seem like Alexander was convinced straight away."

"In that case, a ruler must examine, as the needles were transformed into a disk, how the sage's words affect a ruler's heart blackened from battling his enemies."

"The philosopher told Alexander that the celestial wisdom from his wise soul and heart would brighten his malcontented heart."

"So, what's the hidden wisdom in the ointment the philosopher finally used?"

"There the philosopher was telling Alexander that he has such techniques that no matter what he does, he wouldn't understand, but if he heeds his counsel, his heart will be as clear as crystal. A wise ruler has no lack of wise men around him. The sword is one of the things that maintains the realm, but the other is the pen. A ruler must show a hard hand and punishment to the wicked and reverence and favor to the good. There is no punishment without the sword and there is no civilization without the pen. If your commanders aren't lion-hearted in war and your sages don't have vast experience in peace, if the treasure house is bursting its doors with gold, it will be your end, Prince."

They came to the end of the garden as the first part of the story ended and continued to walk among the gravestones in the grove where people from the earlier sultanate had been buried. Their stones were adorned with carvings of quilted and many other types of turbans.

"*Huve'l-baki,* Mehmed—*only God is eternal,*" Mullah Gürani said. "Rulers have always searched for immortality as they hold command over their lands. Even Alexander didn't say he would seize what he pleased and no one could oppose him when he established his empire within the borders of the known world. He was always among his wise men and he always strove to heed them. And so it wouldn't be wrong in the slightest to think that he could be the prophet *Dhul-Qarnayn*—He of the Two Horns—mentioned in our holy book."

Mullah Gürani noticed the prince looking at a cypress as he was thinking. "Have you ever thought about why there are so many cypresses in cemeteries?"

"I always ask myself that when I see them in the miniatures in the books I read. I keep on coming across them, but I can't seem to find the answer to it."

"The cypress is eternity, Mehmed. Its appearance represents unity and they can live for hundreds of years. The servant of God dies, but God remains. The body passes, but the soul continues on its way. That's why painters so love placing cypresses in their pieces."

"Then this place represents death, or rather, eternity."

"Absolutely."

The prince decided he'd set himself to learn more about these trees. He very much loved reading about flowers and trees and their cultivation.

"So what about the physician?" Mehmed asked, wanting to continue with the story.

"The physician told Alexander that with three things, no ailment would befall him until death—don't indulge in sleep, refrain from gluttony and rise before dawn."

"Just as our master does?"

"Precisely. That is why the sheikh always says the sun should not rise on those who haven't. He says this is how the body is best kept healthy and quick."

Mehmed remembered Sheikh Akshamsaddin, whom he'd seen years ago and whose face he would never forget. His father had told him one day that Akshamsaddin would be the teacher for his spirit, but not yet.

"From that say on, the physician used his expertise to prepare various kinds of potions, medicines and elixirs to increase Alexander's vitality."

"And what about the ever-full goblet?"

"The goblet really never emptied no matter how much Alexander drank. He gathered his wise men and ordered them to examine it and bring forth an explanation."

"Should I guess about this, too?"

"No, Mehmed. Some topics are best left to experts. It shows their ignorance when people stick their noses in things they don't understand. Never suffer the boldness of the ignorant. The wise men came to Alexander after weeks of examination and told him of what they'd found. It was all actually very simple. It was devised over many years with the input of many scholars. The material of the goblet attracts moisture like a lodestone and refills itself with the moisture and rain drops it draws to itself. The ability to devise such an instrument can only be achieved by an empire devoted to science, and Mehmed, God is the greatest scholar."

The setting sun was already glowing orange, surrounded with washed-out reds.

"But now its time for reflection," Gürani said. "Let's go see how Baba Nakkash's painting is coming along."

13

It never crossed the minds of Alexandros' family as they were scattered throughout the field that their days filled with hardship and labor would end in disaster. Alexandros had run back to the field and set back to turning over the soil after he'd finished his work with the old fisherman. Even though it was early in the morning, everyone in the family looked exhausted. They all continued breathlessly at their work, though, barefoot in the soil mixed with rocks, with streaks of dirt across their faces and sweat pouring from their brows.

When it was time to eat, the family gathered in a corner of the field and shared a loaf of dry bread. Alexandros' sister was handing a jug of water to their father when they heard horsemen approaching.

They all turned to look and Abram recognized them right away as the overseers who'd come before. This time, though, they had Theophilos Palaiologos—who owned the land—and some of his men along with them. One was so corpulent it looked like his horse was having a hard time carrying him. Alexandros' eyes were on the swords hanging from their belts.

"So then, you'd rather sit and rest than work, is it?" Theophilos said with a derisive look on his face.

"We've just sat down," my Lord, Abram said. "We were just going to have a bite and then get back to work."

"I don't know about that, but if you're not working, then I'll find other laborers to replace you all."

Abram and Berenike looked at each other, both surprised and afraid.

"I beg you, my Lord." Abram said. "Please, if you do that, we'll die!"

"We beg of you," Berenike said.

Alexandros caught the eye of the two horsemen closest to them.

Theophilos spurred his horse slowly toward the family. "Your begging's pointless. You can't change my mind once I've made a decision. However—" he looked over at the girl the overseer had told him about the other day "—maybe I can change my mind if you lend this pretty girl to me and my men for a couple hours."

The girl dropped her head as tears started down her cheeks. Abram looked at her face and tried to reckon what to do.

"But, my Lord, please, I beg you, pity us. My daughter is still very young—"

"So you defy me! Let me tell you what I'm going to do, then. I'm going to take this girl and throw you off the land!"

Alexandros slowly and gently wrapped his hand around the pickax lying next to him.

The overseer dismounted and the other horsemen drew alongside him as he started to stroke the girl's face. The rest of the family was paralyzed in place. Theophilos watched amused from atop his horse.

"There, there, don't be afraid now. If this girl pleases us, then maybe we'll think of something and can keep coming back."

The overseer was running his fingers over the girl's cheeks as she wept when Alexandros all of a sudden jumped to his feet and plunged his pickax into the man's chest. He collapsed to the ground screaming amid spurts of blood before he had the chance to reach for his sword.

Alexandros quickly wrenched the pickax from the man's chest and, as he'd planned before as he sat, ran to the oafish fat man and angrily swung it into his side. His horse seemed particularly relieved as he fell from his saddle.

Alexandros' older brothers all suddenly sprang up with their pickaxes in hand and ran to join their brother. Theophilos never thought much of peasants and had come without his armor—a decision he was now particularly starting to regret. He also didn't have enough men with him and he couldn't decide if he should put up a fight against these enraged, pickax-wielding youngsters.

"I swear to you before dark I'll be dragging this child's head through the city behind my horse!"

Abram and the rest of the family all looked with concern at Alexandros as Theophilos turned and left.

It wouldn't be long before he came back with a small army. Abram knew he had no other option and decided to use his only chance to stay alive.

Baron Christophoros Angelos held an influential place in the empire due to his friendship with Megaduke Loukas Notaras—the lord high admiral of the emperor's fleet. The respect he had gained didn't come from his relationships, but from the quiet and unassuming life he led far away from intrigue and quarrels. He lived in his small castle on a large tract of land next to the Church of Hagios Ioannes Prodromos he so loved.

His castle was beside the shore and far from the noise and bustle of the city. The only reason this man, already over sixty, retained his health was that he stayed away from the squabbles and fights in the city center, the Senate and, most importantly, Blachernae Palace farther up the Golden Horn from his own residence. His proximity to the main Golden Gate also helped him avoid going to the palace or the city whenever he received an ambassadorial duty from the emperor. He could often be found in foreign courts as an emissary, the neighboring Ottomans foremost among them, due to his mild manner and easygoing mastery of dialogue. He also without fail had an acquaintance in every land he visited.

Those higher in the aristocracy who didn't like that he was overly tolerant to the peasants also didn't speak out against him or try to raise any problems as none of them expected any malice from the aged baron.

One of his soldiers came as he was about to sit down to lunch with his wife and daughters and announced that a peasant named Abram had appealed to see him. The soldier could tell the baron would accept to see the man as soon as he said the peasant's name. He also knew that the baron sometimes lent his aid to men spouting rubbish and, albeit begrudgingly, kept the man at the gate while he went to tell his lord. He had no intention for the baron to reprimand him later.

Baron Angelos heard bells toll in his head when he heard the name. It didn't strike a chord at first as he tried to remember the name, but he thought years, decades, half a century back. Could this Abram be that Abram? Was there even a possibility? He left the table and ordered his soldier to show the man in at once. The soldier asked if he should also permit the child with the man to enter.

The baron said he should.

Abram explained all that had happened without wasting a second as Alexandros waited outside the room. The baron listened as the look on his face deepened and intensified.

"So, what would you like me to do, old friend?"

"Take the child away! Take him from here, somewhere where he can't come back." Abram looked pensively at the floor for a moment before he raised his head and continued, "As a matter of fact, I've been thinking of it for years. This child has no place here—he never fit in the fields, ever. He was going to get in trouble sooner or later. This was the last straw."

"Whisk him away? Have you lost your mind?" The baron was beside himself and didn't know what to say.

"But, Baron, don't you understand? They'll flay him alive if we don't do something in the next hour or two. You know it to be true! I have no other choice."

"But where, to whom and how?"

"To the Turks."

Baron Angelos was perplexed with this.

"I know the Turks take children from Christian lands and train them to be soldiers and palace officials."

"You're talking about the janissaries," the baron said.

"I've heard my whole life about these soldiers' successes and how they're plucked from the mires of their existence and given a bright future. I can't think of anything else. You're the only one who could make it happen."

"But how?"

"I don't know. You could take the boy right away to a nearby Christian land or deliver him to the men who take these children."

"But, Abram, what you ask of me is not as simple as you think. The Turks are very particular about this. The selection of the children, their inclusion in the records and bringing them to the palace is overseen by dozens of high officials. There are large investigations when a child is absent from the lists or something unusual happens."

Abram hadn't ever thought of this. There was no way he could've known.

"What about a bribe?" he said in dismay. "I have no money," he lowered his voice in shame, "but maybe you could help."

"You don't understand, Abram. These men aren't like the ones you and I know. They wouldn't take a bribe. You're asking me to attempt something that would put my life at stake."

Baron Angelos looked out a window of his castle and out over the city walls. He knew well that the boy by the door would experience horrific torture if something weren't done. It was as if he saw into the future as he looked out beyond the horizon toward the Ottoman lands—a lord happily gathering a small army by the walls to have a bit of fun.

"There is a way," he said a short while later as he turned from the window. "I know someone—a fiduciary of the *Devshirme* conscripts. He's in charge of this work and important. If I can find him, then maybe I can convince him. We don't have any other choice."

The baron called his men and ordered them to prepare his horse at once.

He turned back to Abram. "It's time for you to say goodbye to your son, old friend."

Alexandros' sister went running to the field where Mariam's family worked once her brother and father were gone from sight. She blamed herself for the danger her brother was in and couldn't think of anything else to do but run and explain it to his dearest friend.

The land Mariam's family worked was to the south and also quite close to the baron's castle. It didn't even cross her mind as she listened awestruck to Alexandros' sister that he and her father had actually passed by only an hour before. She was distraught and her eyes had gone bloodshot from her tears.

Mariam was dumbfounded about where Alexandros' would go as she stepped from the field to the main road when she heard a voice.

"Mariam, Mariam!"

Alexandros was behind the baron astride a horse next to a man speeding alongside them as they galloped to the Golden Gate.

He threw himself off the horse running at full speed as soon as he saw Mariam. He pulled himself together after a slight daze and started running to her.

The baron turned around and signaled his man.

The boy and girl embraced each other tenderly in the middle of the road. They were both crying.

"Where are you going, Alex, where?"

The boy couldn't say anything through his sobs.

The baron's man rode up beside them and, as an experienced knight, reached down and plucked Alexandros up by the waist.

Mariam and Alexandros' eyes were transfixed on each other as their hands slipped apart.

"I swear I'll come back one day, Mariam! Wait for me, I'll come back!"

The knight rode back to the baron with Alexandros perched behind him.

The dust flying as the horses galloped away clung to Mariam's tear-stained cheeks.

Alexandros' voice rang out more time. "I'll come back!"

14

The prince raised his stick to his head and fended off Jafer Agha as he swung his walnut rod down on him.

"Does the bull not have horns, the elephant tusks and the hedgehog spines?" Jafer Agha yelled.

The prince was at his swordsmanship lesson, as he was every Tuesday, Thursday and Saturday. They were in the field around the quarters of the soldiers responsible for protecting the prince. Jafer Agha would always wear the prince out until he could no longer lift his stick and wouldn't let him go until his arm went numb.

The mid-afternoon sun over the mountains behind them shone on Jafer Agha's head. Mehmed's thin shirt was soaked in sweat and he had to squint to see his teacher, who had taken his place with the sun behind him to make it all the more difficult for the prince.

"Do the rose's thorns not prick, do nettles not sting, does ivy not poison the cattle?"

Mehmed parried the blows with all his might as Jafer Agha continuously struck to his left and right as he talked.

"A weapon is the most natural part of a man, Mehmed," he said as he stepped back and allowed the boy a breath. "Man has created many types of weapons to defend himself just as every living thing in nature has. You do justice to the sword so long as you see it as a part of yourself. Remembering this does it justice."

He set on the prince again once he saw the boy had recovered. The sound of the clashing sticks echoed across the field.

"You will not strike a prone man, you will put no one pleading before you to the sword and you will not use your sword against an unarmed man!"

The prince felt the sting of the walnut rod when he couldn't move fast enough to evade the strike his leg.

"You will not hesitate to bring the cruel to justice. You will both punish and forgive. Could there be an emperor who didn't frighten his enemies and trust his friends, Mehmed?"

Jafer Agha came back again and again at the boy, never giving the prince a chance to rub his weltered leg. Mehmed new well enough that his teacher wouldn't feel the least bit sorry for him if he couldn't fend off the assaults coming from all sides. He blocked a strike to his chest and then started to move on his teacher. Jafer Agha knocked aside the prince's blows without much effort, but he was happy that he'd made the boy mad.

He deftly swung the rod around in his hand and struck at the boy's throat, stopping the stick just an inch away.

"Your anger has spent all your strength," he said. "Don't waste your power, Mehmed. Your survival may depend on it. You must know how to make use of your opportunities to attack, you must choose your target well and focus on one point. You know who the strongest wrestler is?" He stepped up to the boy again. "You can be struck down when you're angry. Holding rule over the world starts will ruling yourself."

The prince stepped back only to trip over a rock and fall down.

Jafer Agha smiled. "A good sultan must be aware of every danger around him. His eyes must always be open and his perception must not give way to absentmindedness. And you weren't aware of a little stone.

"This is the case both in battle and while ruling the realm. You should look over the field from the moment you enter battle, gauge your enemy and immediately identify the situations that are in and against your favor."

Mehmed took a deep breath and got back to his feet, taking his guard as if holding a sword. He stubbornly looked up at Jafer Agha. In spite of his needling, Jafer Agha knew the boy had made incredible progress, listened to everything he was told and applied it in his next exercise. It was every teacher's dream to have such a student.

Mehmed placed his feet perpendicular to each other with his front foot facing forward as his instructor had taught him. This way he could best maintain his maneuverability while also keeping good balance with his feet firmly planted to the ground.

The two started sparring again to the crack of sticks.

"You're very tense, Mehmed. Relax. Being too tense will restrict your movement. Open your legs more and widen your shoulders. You'll lose control if your feet are right next to each other."

Jafer Agha struck so hard that it sent the stick flying from the prince's hand.

"Gripping one's sword requires finesse, Prince—neither too tight nor too loose. Your arm will tense up if you grip to too tight and it'll slow you down. Your weapon will end up like this and be taken by your enemy if you grip it too lightly. Isn't that also the way to rule? Would an overly constrictive ruler bring those in his administration any peace? And would laxity ensure justice?"

Mehmed picked up his stick.

"When you best learn how to use a sword, it will mean you'll be able to manage the realm," Jafer Agha continued. "I can see from your eyes where you're going to attack me. And I'm making a plan according to that. A good warrior doesn't show in any way how and from where he'll attack. Nobody should know your target other than you. And you should weigh everything before you strike. Think twice and strike once. An attack too early can harm you."

They started to clash again.

"When are we going to start using real swords," the prince asked.

Jafer Agha liked the boy's eagerness. It was an impatience that needed to be shaved down with a sword.

"Don't you worry, Mehmed, that time will come, just as will the time you take a sword of Damascus steel in your hand and ride into battle."

As he waited for Mehmed to come back from that thought, Jafer Agha called out toward the soldier's quarters for Burhan, one of the conscripts who always practiced with the prince.

"A good leader is one who finds strength when everyone else is tired and who continues to practice as his soldiers rest," Jafer Agha said. "You must be sturdier than all the soldiers under your command. You two will keep going until dark and you can't see one another anymore."

Mehmed was happy to at least see someone his own size across from him. The muscles in his arms and shoulders and everywhere else in his body had already started to ache, but he liked sparring with Burhan.

"I almost forgot," Jafer Agha called out as he was nearly out of sight. "I have a surprise for you tomorrow. Come with your horses after morning prayers. I've already met with the mullah about it."

Mehmed liked the idea of this surprise, but he doubted he would be able to find the strength to do anything in the morning after this. He had no other choice but to resign himself to it.

He and Burhan continued to spar amid the greenery as the sun sunk behind the mountains. Their shadows grew longer—two dark giants battling each other.

15

Local boys jockeyed to get out in front of Devshirme Fiduciary Ferhad Agha, having seen his white, quilted turban. Despite not knowing the traditional protocol of the Ottomans this far from the capital, the Christians in the newly acquired lands had heard much about the importance of this turban more than those in the surrounding towns and villages.

The crowd in the city square got excited as they got closer to the man in the turban who they saw from afar, as if a bird of the empire had landed.

The town crier of the Ottoman representative in the city had a week earlier gone from neighborhood to neighborhood to announce that today, conscripts would be chosen for the janissaries of the Sublime State and that the necessary preparations should be made. The people had begun to gather in the square in front of the representative's residence since the early morning, with boys aged eight to eighteen forming a long line.

In addition to Ferhad Agha, there were also the Sanjakbey's *qadi* and priest of the city, a fief holder and those under his command from the janissaries who had been trained to perfection in the Devshirme, as many of the officials in the realm had.

"How many boys do we need to take from here," Ferhad Agha

asked his man in charge of the new tributes. His hands were clasped behind his back as he slowly walked in front of the boys.

"Twelve," the man said. The amount was calculated from the priest's baptismal record and by dividing the city's households by forty. They took one child for every forty families, as they had for a century.

Ferhad Agha began measuring up the boys opposite him who waited in trepidation and excitement. He thought to himself that the boys in the front row were very short. One was a surly little boy, another unlikable and the rest had sticks for legs. He stopped at the seventh row. The boys were taller and their cheeks were rosy. Best was their eyebrows—not too thick, though, as thick eyebrows was a sign of wickedness and malice. The agha knew Imam Shafi'i, ar-Razi, ibn Sina and ibn 'Arabi's tractates by heart, and they helped him to read the boys' characters from their appearance. One boy's earlobes were slightly too long, but that indicated a good memory. The distance between the shoulders and the center of the back was an indicator of the same thing, as well. He put his hands on the boy's shoulders and pulled him out. He was taller than the others, a fair face, and well-formed hands and feet. Two other officials immediately went to his sides. The record book in Slavonic in front of the priest of the boy's neighborhood gave the name of the child now being brought to the head of tributes along with those of his mother and father. He recorded all of this information. Next to him, another clerk carefully took down the same information in another book.

Ferhad Agha noticed how long a boy's fingers were when he got to the fifteenth row. This showed that his lungs were large, which would mean the boy could run fast and was nimble. His reddish fingernails were a sign that he was well fed. The agha learned the boy's Slavic name and then asked how many brothers he had.

Due to excitement and the weight of the man in front of him, he forgot what his mother and father had warned him not to say the whole night before, and blurted out, "I have none."

Ferhad Agha's face dropped. "Where are this boy's mother and father?" he said as he turned to the crowd.

After dozens of years of trying to perform his duty impeccably, he'd run into as many fools who squirreled away their children from the Devshirme fiduciaries as those who tried to wrangle what they could to have their only sons become janissaries. Both were unjust and unable to see the future, according to him. The first group was blind that the children taken had bright futures in front of them, and the second group had a poor understanding of the value of a single son.

He approached a man and woman in modest clothes.

"Sir, don't you know we stipulate a boy can only be taken if he has at the least one brother?"

"We know, Sir, the man said," hard-pressed and ashamed of his offence. "My wife and I are in a position to look after ourselves. "We have no need for laborers and we want the boy to be one of the Great Sultan's men. He's strong and obedient."

"There are a thousand and one wastes in the world, Sir. Wealth and youth are fleeting. Don't so quickly give up a son God has bestowed on you. God will provide him a livelihood here, as well. He'll be happy here, too, if he knows what is just."

Ferhad Agha called for the janissaries off to the side, who took the boy and his parents away before the man had a chance to say anything more.

He ruled out the boys who were too tall and those who were too short on first glance. Concerning who would become janissary conscripts, he paid particular interest to those who were neither towering beanpoles nor excessively squat. God wouldn't look on any of His servants as worthless, but Ferhad Agha believed everyone on earth had a different purpose. For him, the golden rule for the Devshirme was that future janissaries must be flawlessly handsome. He believed in his heart that those with fair faces hold fine temperament, both for himself and for conscripts.

"How old are you?" he asked a strong-looking boy in the twenty-sixth row.

"Six."

He reckoned the boy to be at least nine.

"Check this boy's age in the records," he told the head of tributes.

He and the priest flipped through the pages of the baptismal record. "The boy's correct—he's six years old."

"Too young," Ferhad Agha said with a frown.

It would be much more difficult for a child this young to grow accustomed to the conscript system than it would be for the older ones. The boys needed to at least be eight years old, although he preferred they be twelve or thirteen. He would take boys up to eighteen when forced and would allow for those up to twenty in exceptional circumstances. He believed the boys who were this old had already missed the opportunity to acquire the temperament of a janissary and would continue to live the rest of their lives as they had learned up to that point

He called for the records after checking over two well-built boys of a good height with strong arms in the fifty-fifth and sixty-third rows.

He stroked his beard as he continued on to the seventy-seventh row, where he found a boy surprising. The record said this black-browed, black-eyed boy was fourteen years old, just over five feet tall and not too light or heavy.

He noticed callouses on the boys left index finger and thumb.

"How did you get those, son?"

"From a slingshot. I'm good at hunting birds, Sir."

The boy's obedient and confident answer was exactly what he'd expected, and he like it.

"Imperial guard," he said as he turned to the head of tributes. "Put him down as imperial guard."

His attendant looked carefully over the boy brought to him. He truly had the exceptional look of an imperial guard—his arms were strong and his hands and fingers were well formed. The boy didn't know in the slightest that he'd been written down as a *solak*—a member of the sultan's elite guard.

A cry came from the crowd when Ferhad Agha chose the final boy. A woman had broken down in sobs when she saw her son selected. She pleaded as she made her way to the front of the crowd.

"Please, please, don't take my boy! Leave me my only son!"

Ferhad Agha had been pleased that the process was about to come to an end without any tragedy erupting, and this scene at the end was perturbing. There was always such an affair in every few towns without fail. All families would cry as their sons were being led away as new conscripts, but many accepted it knowing that their sons would have better futures in which they might even become the grand vizier. Some Christian Ottoman subjects often boasted that their son was a soldier for the sultan—a charmed thing that could open unexpected opportunities. The parents who were aware of this would try to do their best to help the senior Devshirme officers in their difficult tasks.

Ferhad Agha would often say that a mother's instincts were sure to show themselves every time and they would do anything, wanting to rather die than give up a son.

"Bring the woman here," he said.

The woman and her husband were in tears as they stood before him.

"Don't cry, Madam. Your son is one of the few who stands out from all these other boys. You've taken good care of him and you'll see the reward for your labor. His posture and even his look show that you've brought him up well. His broad shoulders are the sign that he'll shoot well and wield a sword beautifully. We'll get rid of this filthy tunic and replace it with a clean and new woolen shirt. We'll wash his lice-infested head at our best hamams and place on it a hat of golden brocade. We'll throw out his shredded shoes and give him boots of yellow gazelle hide made by the best cobbler in the capital. He'll have a Damascus steel sword at his side and a bull-hide quiver on his back. He will live this life, and the next, in glory. So, Madam, come now, don't cry."

Ferhad Agha's words had sprinkled water on her burning heart. She collected herself and, with her husband, kissed her son and buried her nose in his hair one last time before pulling away.

In preparation for the journey to the capital, a dozen janissaries dressed the boys in yellow, conical hats; tunics of crimson wool with red stitching; and yellow pants. The officers checked over the records one last time before the head of tributes and other officials set off with the boys chosen as janissary conscripts. The townsfolk along the hundreds-of-miles-long road to the capital likened these boys to a flock of cranes and so the head of tributes was naturally called the head crane herder, or *turnajibashi*.

The best conscripts, most gallant warriors and finest soldiers generally came from the Balkan Ottoman lands, but Ferhad Agha was vexed that he couldn't find any outstanding conscripts other than one for the imperial guard.

He silently gave thanks to God and prayed for the sultan's loyal servants to increase. His prayer would be answered in only five days as he completed the procurement of conscripts for the Devshirme.

16

The prince couldn't make sense of the stirring in front of the stables under the early morning light as the sky just began to lighten. Something black was going up and down and back and forth in front of the stables for the palace horses. It was in constant motion and surrounded by five or six people who were running to both sides.

He noticed as he got closer that it was a wild horse and the workhands around it were trying to control it with ropes. The horse was rearing back in a challenge to the men around it and whinnying as if to order them to give up their struggle. A crowd from the soldiers' quarters approached curiously, trying to reckon where this stallion had come from. They'd never seen a horse like it before.

The sleep in Mehmed's eyes melted away as he looked on the horse. He could only escape the stifling air of the palace and ride toward the endless horizon thanks to the horses he loved so well. He looked in wonder at its beauty.

Its broad forehead, large eyes, wide nostrils and arched back showed it to be a different breed. Mehmed, though, saw the main differences—its upturned tail and protruding forehead—and knew it was an Arabian.

"Jibbah," Jafer Ahga said as he came up behind the prince. "That's

what the bulge on its forehead is called. It's unique to Arabians and lets them breathe easily in hot and cold weather. The bigger the bulge, the better the horse."

"I've heard the word," Mehmed said, "but this is the first time I've seen one."

"The Arabian horse is a gift from God to the Bedouins," Jafer Agha said. "And this is a gift from your father to you."

"There's something I don't get, though. As far as I know, Arabians are either chestnut or greyish white, but this one's jet-black."

"You're right, Prince. I must've underestimated your knowledge of horses. This is an exceptional breed, and this is a rarely seen black Arabian. It only came yesterday from Arabia. Have you noticed how compact its back is and the perfect wedge of its face?"

"Yeah, it has everything an Arabian should."

"It was created to easily be able to carry a rider."

"You know what the Bedouins believe about these horses? They say God created them from the four winds—its spirit from the Northern wind, power from the Southerlies, speed from the Easterlies and intelligence from the Westerlies. Then God said, *O Arabian, I give victory in battle to your forelock and endow your belly with treasure. I choose you as one of the most majestic creatures of the world. You will fly without wings. You will rule over the land you tread with your formic color. I place good fortune on your forehead, and this the protuberance, and you will lead the other animals. People will follow wherever you go and victory will always be with you.*"

"It's a good story of their intelligence, durability and loyalty."

The horse again flailed its forelegs and strained against the ropes.

"I don't understand why it's so ornery," Jafer Agha said. "It must be tired from the journey."

"It seems like it's something else," Mehmed said. He got closer, seeing a fire in the stallion he'd not seen in any other. "He wants to go. He's not happy where he is," he said.

"He'll run off if we release him, though, Prince. There's no way we'd be able to catch him again."

"But don't you see he's in pain?" Mehmed came even closer to the horse and saw it get angrier with every pull of the ropes. "Remove the ropes," he said firmly.

The workhands first looked wide-eyed at Mehmed, then over at Jafer Agha. They didn't know what to do. Jafer Agha nodded and despairingly signaled for them to let the horse go.

The horse threw itself forward as soon as the ropes were removed and started speeding away.

Mehmed jumped on another horse in the stable and went at a full gallop after it.

They all disappeared from the view of Jafer Agha, Alberti Balbi and the crowd of soldiers.

As he followed the horse, not too close so as not to frighten it, Mehmed thought of the legend about Arabian horses attributed to the Prophet Muhammad. In order to measure the loyalty and sturdiness of the horses in his caravan, the prophet drove the thirsty animals to an oasis after a long journey through the desert, but called them back before they could drink. Only five mares returned. He considered these five horses that chose obedience to their master over water in the scorching heat to be the best. Since then, those from this line of mares have been called *al-Khamsa*—The Five.

The sun had already begun to show itself as Mehmed thought about the legend. With the black Arabian having begun to graze, Mehmed quietly prodded his horse closer. The Arabian raised its head and looked at the prince, but Mehmed didn't look it in the eye so as not to frighten it.

The prince considered the Europeans' methods of forcefully mounting a horse and bringing it to its knees to be barbarously oppressive—as far as he could reckon, this didn't so much tame a horse as enslave it.

He dismounted, walked beside the Arabian and gently stroked

its neck. It might have startled if he'd touched its forehead, so he kept below its head. Horses would become friends of man when they were domesticated on a basis of mutual trust, not subjugation. He stepped onto a stone next to the horse and slowly pulled his right leg up and over its back, careful not to move too fast and spook it. He slowly sat astride it and leaned his chest against its neck.

"Khamsa," he whispered into the Arabian's ear. "Your name will be Khamsa."

Everyone back at the palace had looks of joy when they saw the prince return riding the black Arabian with the sun shining behind him. The other horse was attached with a rope and following behind.

"Maybe Sheikh Akshamsaddin's right," Jafer Agha said to himself. "This boy will be that type of sultan."

17

Ferhad Agha was about to set off with his men for the return journey to Edirne after sending the caravan of new conscripts, who'd been taken from the towns written in the sultan's decree, off with the head of tributes. It would be three more years before more boys would be acquired for the Devshirme. The numbers of conscripts and janissaries were strictly controlled and weren't increased haphazardly. New boys could only be taken with a special decree from the sultan when he saw a need every three to five years.

He stopped at a caravanserai in Sofia on the fifth day of the return trip where he rested and performed his morning prayers. He and his men had already eaten and were preparing to set back out on the road when he heard a voice call from behind—his name was right, but it was spoken with a foreign accent.

"Ferhad Agha!"

He turned around and saw the envoy from Constantinople—an acquaintance he'd met in the days as an imperial guard in the capital.

"Sir Chistophoros, is everything alright? What're you doing here?"

"Forgive me, Ferhad Agha," the baron said in nearly flawless Turkish. "We arrived at night and I waited until morning so not to disturb you. Shall we sit? I have something to tell you. It's very important to me."

Ferhad Agha looked at Baron Angelos, the knight beside him and the boy with worried eyes waiting behind them. He was anxious to get back on the road—he never liked delays or having his plans hobbled.

"Please. We've been searching for you since we left the city two weeks ago. I thought I'd find you in Edirne, but they said you'd gone to the hinterlands. I figured I'd at least be able to catch you on your way back."

"Well, you weren't mistaken. Alright, then. Let's sit."

"What will you drink? Let me get you something."

"No, no. You're within our borders now. Don't think of playing host to us."

The Devshirme fiduciary's men and the baron's knight retired to another corner as the two men sat down. Ferhad Agha waved for the owner of the caravanserai as he was busily trying to keep the place orderly and respectable, and called for ayran for everyone.

"So, how's the emperor?"

"Not much has changed in the city, Ferhad Agha. Envy and quarrels. Ambition is spreading through the city like a plague. But I'm not here for diplomacy."

Ferhad Agha was confused with this and didn't know what the Constantinopolitan envoy could want from him.

"I've brought you a boy. Being taken for the Devshirme is the only way he can escape death."

The baron was still unable to persuade him despite having tried for half an hour. After they'd finished two cups of ayran, the owner of the caravanserai sent the two important visitors cups of complementary grape compote.

Ferhad Agha rubbed his face as he explained the situation he was in, not wanting to hurt his old friend.

"The head of tributes also has a copy of these records here and he'll be in Edirne within a few days. The janissary agha will inform the vizier if the two copies don't match and he'll immediately open an investigation. You're playing with my head, Christophoros!"

"What if you said you found the boy later in some village on your way back?"

Ferhad Agha got angry that his friend had asked him to lie and he glared at the baron. Baron Angelos knew that such a proposal wouldn't yield anything and would only serve to annoy the Ottoman officer, but he had to at least try.

"I'm sorry, Ferhad Agha, I shouldn't have said such a thing."

"And what's more, the agreements between Sultan Murad and Emperor Manuel Palaiologos are very clear—it's forbidden to take any Devshirme conscript from your empire. And this boy is a Roman Greek to the bone."

"Whatever you want from me, Ferhad Agha. I gave my word to the boy's father. The lord's men have started to pillage the whole city. Maybe they've already slaughter's his family. Dying is the best thing that could come to him other than the Devshirme."

Ferhad Agha turned his back and pulled his fur coat up over his head. He looked over at the boy sitting silently with his head down.

Baron Angelos thought about mentioning how the Ottomans constantly praised their own compassion and charity, but knowing that hearing this from a Christian would only have the opposite effect, he decided against it.

"It's these oppressed places that justify holy war, Christophoros. Let's say you saved a child, but who knows what other sundry things and suffering like this are happing right now in your city. You have to get to the root of the problem. You'll be plagued by it if you don't. God will see to a cure."

The baron stayed silent.

"I must get back on the road now, Sir Christophoros. I'm already very late," Ferhad Agha said as he stood up.

"I ask that you at least let us travel with you, if you'll permit us. They say these lands are crawling with Serb brigands."

"Gladly. *Alhamdulillah ya al-Mani*"—*Praise be to God the Protector.*

18

"You know, Mehmed, these grand mountains remind me of the gigantic walls Alexander the Great built when he confronted Gog and Magog," Mullah Gürani said.

He and the prince were riding their horses across the Manisa tablelands and talking, as they did every mid-afternoon before Mehmed's swordsmanship lessons.

They headed toward the impassable mountains rising to the west of Manisa.

"Which story is that?"

"Dust and wind came blowing into a city as never before while Alexander the Great was on campaign. There were many houses there, but nobody could see a thing. His men blew their horns from atop their elephants and the people gathered and formed a long line in front of Alexander. He asked them why the city was so quiet. The city folk responded in tears, saying their troubles were large. They said Gog and Magog lived behind the towering mountains and they had no way to defend themselves against them. Their women number in the thousands and give birth to hundreds of children at once. Their skin is harder than a dragon's and their teeth are sturdier than a wild boar's. Filthy, jet-black hair covers nearly their entire bodies. Their ears are so big they use them for pillows and sleeping mats. They attack the people and feed on their herds. They said they couldn't see to their work in the day or get a wink of sleep at night and that if the great king could help them, they'd pray for him the rest of their lives."

"So what did Alexander say?"

"Without thinking for even a moment, he said with God's permission, he would find a solution, as any merciful ruler would. He gathered his sages around him and approached the mountain. He told the people that he would provide the treasure but the men would have to come from them. Of course, the people accepted happily and Alexander told them to bring him as many blacksmiths and masons as they had. He asked for countless tons of iron and copper from the mines and block upon block of stone from the quarries. He had all the architects and engineers build enormous walls around the mountain. As thousands of workers labored day and night, he ordered for iron chutes to be built through the walls into the mountain. He had these chutes filled with coal and iron and then had oil and turpentine poured over. When the construction finished, hundreds of blacksmiths worked their bellows outside the walls, all at once raising more fantastic flames than anyone had seen before. That's how the land was saved from Gog and Magog. The people wanted to show their gratitude and offered the great ruler many gifts, but he refused them all and continued on his way."

"How did Alexander get that solution?"

"That's the important part, Mehmed. In exceptional times, exceptional people must come up with solutions that no one else could—things that no one else could imagine. It's this that's the difference between the common folk and a ruler. The simplest part of a sultan's plans would seem unbelievable to common folk. A sultan must know how to create a solution when there are none, when everything has come to an end and there's no way out." Mullah Gürani looked down at Mehmed. "One day you'll also find solutions no one else would come up with. You'll have to."

Mehmed caressed his horse's main as he thought about what Mullah Gürani had said.

"Victories don't only come from power, they come from wisdom. The mind that governs the body is the ruler seeing to his state," the mullah continued. "So, Mehmed. What is conquest?"

Mehmed answered without thinking. "Conquest is waging war, taking land, capturing cities and declaring yourself sultan wherever you go."

Mullah Gürani's face grew stern. "No, Mehmed. What you say isn't conquest, it's barbarism. Conquest is to bring serenity and spread justice. It's to spread God the Truth among the people and to speak to them of their rights.

"Do you know what we call *seyr ü sülûk*—the path of the spiritual journey?

Mehmed shook his head.

"*Seyr ü sülûk* is human dignity, it gives one the right to be human, to constantly develop, progress, to always strive for something better. It could also be to expand the holdings of the realm. Standing still neither benefits us nor the Sublime State."

The evening breeze gently swept past their faces.

"So is this related to the systems of administration?"

"The system is a form, an agent—what's important is the spirit, meaning and understanding that fills it. Aristocracy can easily turn into oligarchy, democracy into demagoguery and monarchy into tyranny."

"Like what Plato and Aristotle said so long ago, right?"

"And ibn Khaldun. But never forget, Mehmed, only a single man changes creation. This is also the monarchical order." And as such, Mullah Gürani thought that to train a sultan is to train the world. "*Seyr ü sülûk* is also innovation. The answer to deadlock is hidden in it. It's like overcoming the dragon that confronted Alexander the Great after he defeated King Darius of Persia. I told you earlier about the battle between Alexander and Darius, but I want to tell you of the meaning of the renowned Persian king's name. In his time, he was called Darab"

Mehmed would get excited when Mullah Gürani would unexpectedly test him on his foreign language lessons. He would look over all the roots, prefixes and suffixes he'd written and search for the answer.

"In Persian, *ab* means water, as in *ab-e hayat*—the water of life," the prince said. "*Dar* means trees, so water among the trees, I suppose. Darab must've come to the people as indispensable as water and he must've been much loved, so it should have the meaning of one who came from water flowing through a forest."

Mullah Gürani was always impressed with the prince's memory. He enjoyed cultivating a student who not only learned quickly, but also could remember what he learned.

"Alexander moved farther south and came to a place rife with two-horned rhinoceroses, snakes of unimaginable size and crocodiles the color of emerald. The people there had learned to live with all of this, though. But there was also a dragon that was too much for them, and they were hard put to feed and keep it full. When the people asked Alexander for help, he ordered his archers to launch thousands of arrows at it. But the arrows bounced off the dragon, and the ones that did stick had no more of an affect than a fleabite to a bull. As they were accustomed, the people once again drove their herds to the dragon for it to eat its fill. Alexander then told his men to bring him a herd of cattle. He called his physicians and told them to find plants to make a poisonous concoction. Then he had the cattle's hides flayed open and had the concoction placed underneath their skins. The next day, he drove the cattle to the dragon. A soon as the red-eyed beast ate the cattle, it bellowed so fiercely the people thought the sky would split open. It convulsed for a while and then fell lifeless to the ground.

"So you see, Mehmed. A ruler's duty is to think in a way no one else can about how to best use the resources available to him and to bring peace to the people. He must always be ten steps ahead of everyone else."

"What should a ruler's merits be, then? What are his most important characteristics?"

"Merit comes from wisdom, and wisdom from listening, Mehmed. Find tranquility before setting to any work—only hurry to prayer. There are two things that if they are found in the sultan's lands mean the sultanate has ended. One is persecution and the other is negligence. Both of these can very easily bring the system down. Peace and justice, however, happiness and living humanely—each is a part of a divine system of interconnected components. To hold the provinces, one must gather soldiers and an army, to feed the soldiers one needs treasure, the treasure comes from the people, but the people must be rich to collect this much. For the people to be rich there must be proper laws. The corruption of a single law affects all the others, and as it affects them, corruption and injustice hold reign."

Gürani looked out past the peaks of the mountains stretching out in front of them. The sun was low in the sky.

"That's enough for today. Don't forget to memorize fifty tales from the *Shahnameh* for tomorrow.

19

A hulking, Serb brigand couldn't make anything of the group of eight men he saw along the Maritsa River as he popped his shaved head over the crest of a hill he'd hidden behind. He held onto his ax tighter and looked over at his mate next to him, the man's face smeared with dirt, as if to ask what they should do. It was clear from their clothing that four of the men they were watching were janissaries and that the man with a tall, white hat with them was a high-ranking Ottoman agha. The bandits were puzzled by the knight with them, though, who they thought was most likely under their command, as well as by the older man in front of him followed by a boy. They'd never before run across a caravan whose travelers were so different from each other.

They didn't dare approach the large convoy of Devshirme conscripts that had passed along the same route two days earlier, as the sight of the many janissaries and high-ranking aghas with them was quite terrifying. It seemed now the power had been flipped—they were two dozen and the group they were watching was tiny in comparison. The brigands thought they could easily attack, wrangle the horses and take all the goods and money the company had. It's not that four janissaries weren't intimidating, but the Serbs had three times more men, which girded their daring.

First came the whistling of an ax as it split through the knight's breastplate and lodged in his chest, but by the time they realized they were under attack, the man who never left the baron's side was already lying in a pool of blood. As soon as the janissaries spotted the brigands quickly running at them from a hill two hundred yards away, they took Ferhad Agha and Baron Angelos behind them and let loose a fusillade of arrows. Each janissary targeted the horsemen immediately in front of them who were driving at them over the field, taking them down one by one.

A janissary pushed off his horse to evade a spear flying at his belly as it passed behind him and fell directly in front of Alexandros. Three of the janissaries drew their swords and charged the remaining six Serbs.

Each janissary took on two of the bandits. The first landed deadly sword blows on the two brigands coming at him. The second pulled his dagger from his waist and cut down the two men to his right and left.

One of the brigands fought off the third janissary and broke through their line unscathed with sword in hand. He came running straight at Ferhad Agha and Baron Angelos. The brigand raised his sword, taking Ferhad Agha in his white, quilted turban for an easy target. He pounced forward about to swing his sword down on the agha's head when he felt a deep, searing pain in his back and crumpled to the ground.

Ferhad Agha looked at the man's back and saw the dagger of the janissary who'd fallen in front of Alexandros as the clash broke out. The boy had quickly slid off the horse from behind the baron as the attack unfolded and quietly gone to beside the fallen janissary and sat in wait for the brigands bearing down on them. He had quickly pulled the dagger from the janissary's belt and flung it at the man's back.

Ferhad Agha looked at the boy's eyes and that moment decided what he had to do to get him into the Devshirme.

Baron Angels mourned the loss of his knight, but he'd never been this happy before to return to Constantinople alone.

20

"The great angel Jibril heard a noise rise up one day as he stood at the *Sidrat al-Muntah*a before the seventh heaven," Mullah Hüsrev said from behind his reading stand.

Two boys—Prince Mehmed and Vlad, the son of the voivode of Wallachia—were kneeling side by side in front of the mullah with their books on reading stands as they listened.

The voivode of Wallachia paid tribute to the Ottomans but was constantly in rebellion, breaking the oaths of peace he'd made to Sultan Murad. Most recently, he'd enraged Murad, who was quick to anger, with crusaders coming to the aid of the voivode's soldiers in the east of Europe. The sultan didn't want to spill any blood and avoided war as if it were the plague. Instead, he took the voivode's sons as a hostage so as to prevent the ruler of the tribute principality from breaking his word again. Expecting he was going to lose his head, the voivode was happy to have his sons raised in Ottoman palaces. His son Vlad was unlike anyone else. He got into more mischief than anybody could expect from a child and harmed everything around him with unending vigor.

"Nobody could go past the *Sidrat al-Muntah*a other than the prophet, not even the angels, right?" Mehmed asked.

That's right, Mehmed. It's the end of the seventh heaven. On the *Mir'aj*, the night of the prophet's ascension, he prayed with Jesus and Moses and rose to the seventh heaven, which he passed, and met the Creator. Jibril told him that if he himself were to take one step further, he would burn in flames.

Vlad harrumphed and pulled a face. He disliked the stories of the prophet of Islam. It wasn't because he was from a Christian family in a Christian land, though—he hated all religious tales.

The first thing that came to his mind when religion was spoken of was the stinking priests that so often visited the palaces. It was torture for him to listen to their sermons for hours so close and with their reeking breath. They would threaten to complain to his father for whatever small mistake he made, and so he was wary. He much rather preferred being forced to disrobe and stand naked for hours in front of the priest giving him his lesson than take a beating from his father for having memorized the wrong verses.

"Jibril wondered about the nature of this voice coming all the way to the ninth heaven," Mullah Hüsrev continued. "He thought a servant of God was speaking of the All Merciful, but who could it be? The only thing he could tell was that it was the voice of one who had surpassed worldly desires, strove for meaning and attained immortality. He was so curious of who's this voice was that was reaching the level of the angels that he flew to the sun, blocking its light from the world with his wings and then around the world, over mountains and plains and scoured the seas and oceans, but he couldn't find who it was. He then heard the same voice when he returned and noticed God the Merciful had accepted the prayer. He again scoured over the seas, oceans, valleys and mountains. He made an entreaty to the Creator when he again couldn't find the voice and asked the Lord of the Heavens and Earth who this servant of His was. God the Merciful told him to go to the lands of Rome, where he would find him in a Christian monastery."

"But how could God accept a prayer from a Christian?" Mehmed asked bewildered.

"So was the angel's reaction, Mehmed. Jibril went to the monastery in the blink of an eye and came across a pagan. Then he invoked God and asked the Judge of the World to lift the veil of mystery from his eyes and show how He could bestow His favor on a wailing pagan.

"God the Merciful replied that the pagan knows that he's lost his way. He knows his heart has grown dark and is searching with all his spirit for a being higher than himself. It is his ignorance that hinders him, but He has forgiven him with His mercy and opened the gates of faith. And so the All Merciful unlocked the man's tongue and intoned it with His ninety-nine names. In this way, boys, a servant of God cannot see who has true faith. Holding those in contempt who don't share one's religion or beliefs has its source in not knowing the attributes of God. Even the smallest good deeds people do can open the gates of faith to them. An evil one does to an unbeliever prevents him from understanding Islam, and his accountability is very severe.

"This story is really quite similar to the one about the former pagan who came to the prophet and asked questions."

Mullah Hüsrev remembered the hadith he'd explained to the boys a few months before, but he wanted to hear it from the prince.

"Which story is that, Mehmed?"

"The man was worried because he'd converted to Islam late in life. He came to the prophet and asked if all the good things he had done before were for nothing. The prophet said no, and that he'd found the way to true faith through those good deeds."

"Very good, Mehmed. It's just as you said. How about the tale of Abraham, you remember that?"

The prince was stumped.

Mullah Hüsrev continued so as not to further embarrass the boy. "A traveler knocked on Abraham's door one day. He showed the guest in straight away, prepared him a bowl of soup from what he had and wanted the man to feel at home. Abraham came back after preparing the soup, but when saw the man bent down in front of his fire, he said, *How dare you worship fire in my house! Get out now and my God damn you!* and chased the man from his house. Then the All Merciful told Abraham that He relieves that man's breath every second of the day and provides him air, water and all other blessings in the world for his use. He said He keeps his arms and legs healthy so the man can see to his work, his eyes open so he can see, his ears perked so he can hear and his tongue working so he can voice his troubles. He told Abraham that he had begrudged the man even a bowl of soup. After hearing this, Abraham went running after the man and begged his forgiveness. He took the traveler back home and tried to host him as best he could."

"I would've been angry with God if I were Abraham," Vlad snapped. "He's a prophet himself and God got angry with him over how he treated a fire-worshipping pagan. And in the story before, I also don't get how priests can ingratiate themselves to your God. Where's the justice in that?"

"And what is justice, Vlad?" Mullah Hüsrev had grown accustomed to the boy's contrarianism and wasn't surprised at all.

Vlad wanted to say what had come to mind, but kept his mouth shut when he remembered what the priests would do him—*justice is the powerful beating the weak and believers vanquishing unbelievers.*

"Justice is all people living happily and finding peace in this world and the next," Mullah Hüsrev said. "Justice is conferring rights on those who are right, not on the powerful." He turned to Mehmed. "It is a sultan's duty to distribute justice"

Vlad wasn't so taken with justice or peace. His hair would stand on end when he heard these words and he always wanted to scream his lungs out. He didn't know why, but he felt himself in complete opposition to them. He was happy when he felt hatred, anger and vengeance or heard them spoken of.

"Justice is mercy and tolerance, just as God the Forgiver rebuked Moses. When Moses persistently refused the oaths of mercy from Korah, who was impious and arrogant, God the Forgiver said, *Korah has implored you seventy times, but you didn't answer. If he had called on Me seventy times, I would have freed his heart from idolatry and put in him the light of faith. You, though, held him in contempt and blackened his heart. My mercy surpasses My wrath in all My creation.*"

"But Moses was a great prophet. Why would he heed a godless man? I would've done the same."

"Well, Vlad, maybe this is also the difference between us and the prophets," Mullah Hüsrev said, reckoning the boy would come out with an even more deleterious conclusion. "We are simple people whereas they are prophets with particular responsibilities. We shouldn't expect them to act like common people, just as we don't of rulers with their special duties."

Mullah Hüsrev, Mehmed and Vlad saw a bat lying on the forest floor as they walked in the small wood behind the Manisa Palace. Before they really could make sense of it, Vlad had stomped down on the creature and ground it down.

"Why'd you do that, Vlad?!" Mehmed said. "What do you get out of it?"

"I saved it from its suffering," Vlad said with a smile. "It was pretty fun, too. Way more than cutting off cats' tails."

Seeing it was too late, Mullah Hüsrev turned to the boy, angry but staid. "Pleasure is not putting an end to life, Vlad, but preserving it."

Vlad wasn't listening to a word his teacher said. He didn't see why it was so bad to kill a miserable bat—unable to look at the sunlight and condemned to live in constant darkness.

"Let me tell you boys the tale of the foolish bat who went searching for the sun," Mullah Hüsrev said as if reading the boy's thoughts.

Vlad thought this would finally be a story he'd like.

"One night, a bat grumbled to those around him, *How is it that I can't see the sun even once? I've lived my whole life in the dark. I haven't even seen it once. I've been searching for it for months, years even, and now I'm here with you all.*

"It's not because your eyes are blind to it, but for your pride, one of the other bats said. *You'd need to search for thousands of more years. How could a thing like you look at the sun? Can an ant walk on the moon?*

"Fine, the proud bat said, *I'll still continue on with my search.*

"Years passed and the bat's wings grew numb, its strength was used up and it couldn't move anymore—and it still hadn't seen the sun. *Maybe one day I flew so much that I passed it and that's why I can't see it,* it said.

"The same wise bat from before was next to him. *You're living in a dream,* it said. *You've been here flying in circles for years—you haven't even set one wing further afield. You think so much of yourself, though, that you think you've flown to the other side of the sun.*

"The bat was dumbstruck. It realized its mistake and said, *At least I'm with a bat who sees the heart. That's also enough for me."*

"If I were that bat," Vlad thought, "the first thing I'd have done is kill that other know-it-all bat."

He couldn't bring himself to tell the mullah, but he had enjoyed the fable. Years and decades later, he would feel closer to this blood-sucking animal than to anyone else around him.

21

Hasan was out of breath as he ran through the stalks of golden wheat. It was so tall that he didn't have to bend down to hide despite his large frame. He was running fast, though, and the sharp beards on the swollen ears sliced him as he sped through. The sun overhead made him sweat even more and its glare made him squint his black eyes. Having worked shirtless in the fields for years, his darkly tanned skin stood out from the golden wheat. If someone were to spy him running from afar, his dark silhouette could have given him away.

He began to whisper the prayers over and over that he'd learned from Hajji Ahmed. He had gotten over his initial fear from when Ferhad Agha had conscripted him three years before after he was sent to Hajji Ahmed's home. Like all future janissaries, he'd been placed with a Turkish-speaking family to learn the language and was made to feel at home. He didn't know why the janissary aghas had shown up now, though. He was comfortable here. Maybe the men would lose hope if he could stay lost for a while, then he'd be able to keep on with Hajji Ahmed and his wife Mürüvvet.

Kara Mustafa came flanked by two horsemen to the edge of the large wheat field. He looked out from under his black eyebrows. "You stay here," he said to his men. "And don't damage the grain."

He stepped off his horse, took off his janissary's hat and handed his sword and scabbard to his men. Then he flung off his coat and dove quickly into the field with his shirt open.

Hasan had worked out for weeks what he would do this day, where he'd run and where he could sleep for a couple nights. He figured he could fend off any jackals or wolves in the mountains—the muscle he'd built chopping wood, carrying loads and working with the scythe every day made him believe nothing could come against him.

He had been teased since he was young boy for his uncommon size, although nobody dared to say a thing again after what had happened to a couple kids who had gone too far. He hadn't been teased so much since he'd been a Devshirme conscript in a small village outside of the city of Bursa. At least he wasn't forced to have to beat anybody as he was in his own land because the children here left him alone since their parents would scold them straight off for any unkind word they said. Everything had become easier since he'd been given to Hajji Ahmed and Mürüvvet, and he spent time with the village kids as soon as he was done working in the fields. He liked being with them even though they made fun of his strange accent. Unlike at his old house, Mürüvvet didn't scold him for how much he ate and would instead constantly try to feed him more.

She would always say, "You work so much, you need to eat more than we do," and then give him more of the ayran he loved so much. Hajji Ahmed would also always ask her if she'd fed him since the boy was always so hungry.

Hasan thought that if he weren't there, there would be nobody to look after Hajji Ahmed and his wife or chop their firewood.

He ran faster as he remembered all the good from before and he had no intention of falling back into the hands of the men who had taken him from his village years ago. Like every morning, he'd made a village breakfast with a piping hot loaf of bread, butter from their own cows and wonderfully fragrant rose jam Mürüvvet had made before he'd gone out. He had been outside chopping wood when he looked up and saw Hajji Ahmed talking with the men. He knew right away who they were from their uniforms, strange hats and colorful boots.

He started to think they'd lose his trail if he crossed over the hill after the field ended. Then Kara Mustafa came from nowhere and they both tumbled to the ground and rolled out of the field.

Kara Mustafa got on top of the boy and held his shoulders down so tightly that it looked like the leather bands around his arms would snap. Hasan had walked away from a lot of fights in his life, but he'd never come across anybody who could hold him down like this. He was laboring to breath as if a boulder was on his chest and couldn't understand how a man who wasn't even that large could make his arms go dead.

"Why're you running, Hasan?" Kara Mustafa yelled. His voice was angry, but mixed with compassion.

The boy didn't answer. He had gathered his strength with his last hopes of getting out from under the man and running away.

"Does spending your days in these fields seem better than roaring on the battlefield and meting out justice? Is it that you find it easier to chop wood than to wipe out bandits?"

"You're a lion and we'll make a worthy soldier of you yet. Come on big Hasan! Answer me!"

"I—" he said, but couldn't go on. "How'll Hajji Ahmed and Mürüvvet get by without me? Who'll plant the crops, who'll harvest. I'm happy with them."

Kara Mustafa looked into the boy's eyes, astounded by his reply. He knew he should see what Ferhad had years before and trust that the agha hadn't been deceived by the boy's size, saw deep into his destiny and the light in his heart.

He pulled his knees from the boy's arms, his took his hands from his shoulders and offered Hasan a hand up.

Hasan finally took an easy breath with the weight off his chest, but then couldn't decide whether he should take the man's hand.

The man standing over him with a mustache curled up like a scimitar looked even more imposing from below—like a giant with the sun shining behind him.

Hasan reached out.

"So, is that why you don't want to leave—so nothing bad happens to these people?" Kara Mustafa said.

"I've broken bread with them for years and don't want to leave them. They look after me so well. I'm happy here. They don't have anybody else but me."

Kara Mustafa smiled. "You're mistaken, Hasan. Behind them is the Sublime State—the power of the Ottomans. We only left you here so you could learn Ottoman customs and traditions and the language. All the work you did just kept you in fine shape. Hajji Ahmed and his family get all the help they need from the state. Their lives will go on after you're gone just as they did before you came. You were just a guest—like all of us in this world."

Hajji Ahmed also always spoke like this, telling him that when the time comes, he'd leave and do what he must. Hasan only now realized that this was the day he was speaking of. He would only firmly understand much later that, like plenty of janissary conscripts before him, he'd been placed with a Turkish family for a few years, had been watched from afar and that the first stage of the process had come to an end.

"You must not have thought you'd waste away your days in the fields when we plucked you out of the mire you were in," Kara Mustafa said. "Your destiny is the bow and sword."

"Godspeed to you, son. May God give you the power of Ali," Hajji Ahmed said holding the boy's wrist with both hands as Hasan bade farewell through blurry eyes to the people he had known as parents for the past three years.

Before mounting to leave, Kara Mustafa took a purse full of gold from his waist and surreptitiously slipped it to Hajji Ahmed.

Hasan knew Kara Mustafa wasn't from the Devshirme or from the ranks of collected conscripts who had been placed with families in various villages like himself.

The only thing holding his attention now was the quiver with golden embroidery hanging from the janissary's back in front of him. Kara Mustafa was looking at a list for the next house. Next was a conscript named Iskender.

22

The Tundzha River seemed to flow with more excitement toward the Edirne Palace that day just as the boys had gathered around the barracks while dogs ran to the Justice Pavilion to see the new conscripts. The grandiose Justice Pavilion stood just after the arched bridge over the rushing river as a marker of Ottoman thought, underlying the sultanate's mission and signaling it to those coming to its center.

The new Devshirme conscripts were more anxious as they entered the city behind a procession of men on horseback while the janissary on duty held watch over it all from a pyramid-roofed tower.

"Those must be the sultan's garden guards," Dincher said excitedly as he pointed to two armed men in front of the pavilion. "The family I worked with was always talking about them. They're always on duty right here at the tower at the entrance to Edirne."

Dincher had recognized the soldiers—these *bostanji*s, the garden guards—from their high collars and open-sleeved shirts. He marveled at the size of their arms, nearly two hands around. He wondered if his arms would be that big and what kind of training it would take.

"Why do they call them garden guards?" Abdullah asked as he looked at the yellow boots of the guards his new, chatty friend he'd met in the convoy had pointed out.

"They were responsible for the gardens and fields at the beginning of the sultanate, and since the most beautiful gardens have always been at the sultans' palaces, they chose them from among the best soldiers."

"But they don't tend the gardens—they're on guard duty."

"It's not like they were looking after the gardens day and night. What's important is that the garden guards have important duties and are an impressive force."

"What do you think that stone is?" Dincher asked—his eyes on the stone in between the garden guards in front of the Justice Pavilion. The top of it was hollow and it came up to the guards' waists.

He got more annoyed the more his friend didn't join in his enthusiasm, but after thinking about the story of the garden guards, Abdullah was busy in thoughts about what his new life would bring.

"The stone of warning," Kara Mustafa said sidelong as he led the convoy. "Let it be a warning that that is where we'll put the head of anyone who betrays the sultan." He smiled as he saw the boys' faces drop. "And anyone who talks too much!"

Having collected them from the various places where they had left them after taking them from the hinterland villages and towns, top janissary officials were now taking the new conscripts to the barracks at the capital of Edirne. They had all been placed with Turkish-speaking families as laborers, tradesmen as apprentices or with wealthy men as servants for three to five years and had by now learned the language and Islamic customs of the Ottomans firsthand.

After evening prayers, the hundred boys were all in one line and trying not to fidget as they waited in front of the pavilion where the janissary agha was handing them their yellow, conical hats and dark-blue shirts along with red waist bands—but it wasn't so easy with so much around to look at.

The large field of barracks looked confusing at first glace, with soldiers piled on top of one another, but it was misleading when the boys looked closer. They started to notice that everything was according to a system. There was a company of fifty archers to the right wearing leather caps and walking in ten rows of five in archery drills in such unison that they looked like fifty reflections of the same man.

To the other side was a group of thirty men running in a line one after the other with the same order and shouting something the boys still didn't understand. Farther away was another group of janissaries around a marble, and even though the boys could see them moving their arms, they couldn't quite make out what they were doing.

A caravan of camels with woven baskets slung over both sides was entering the barracks field while dozens of cavalrymen with javelins were exercising their ambling horses in a different drill, all of which the boys couldn't make anything out of.

The walls of the barracks to the right were nearly as thick as three men. There were smoking chimneys sticking out of the little domes on the roof and the boys reckoned they must be from the kitchens. Meanwhile, they saw a man slowly descending the stairs from the agha's mansion and figured it was the renowned janissary agha known as Wolfman whose name they'd heard so much since they'd first been taken.

The agha's tall, white headpiece had two plumes rising from both sides showing that he was the most important official after the viziers. The ensemble of his ceremonial hat and long, sleeveless, fur coat in red was a sight, accompanied by yellow and red striped, buttoned shalvar and yellow boots. The inlaid handle of his dagger stuck out from his red cloth belt and his sword hung from his left.

As he was accustomed, Wolfman looked over the record books open on the table at the foot of the stairs, stepped in front of the boys and began speaking with his hands clasped behind his back.

The boys noticed from the corner of their eyes when he got closer that he was much different from how they had imagined him. He had no beard, but his mustache was ample. He was much younger than they would have thought, as well—in his thirties, tall and slender with broad shoulders. His voice was full and sharp, and his scowling brow frightened the boys more than anything else.

"I don't much like talk, boys," he said. "We're here for duty, not talk—and that duty is to serve. Let me repeat for the last time for any of you boys who are still confused—from now on you're Devshirme conscripts. If you're here today, it means you've completed the first phase. And remember—not all conscripts can complete that first stage. Today you will become true recruits and will start the second phase on the road to becoming a janissary. Years later, some of you will be janissaries, some of you will remain recruits for much longer and others will be shown the road. Those who take to their service and work hard will be rewarded and those who shirk their duties will be punished. May God open the way to you all."

A janissary clerk came to the record books next to Wolfman and signaled to the others on duty. Another clerk took the boy at the front of the line and brought him to the table.

"Give your name and where you came from, son," the clerk at the table said.

"Abdullah—Abdullah of Bosnia," the boy said as he trembled.

The janissary clerk found the boy's name, made a note next to it and turned to the agha.

Wolfman twisted the boy's ear with one hand and chopped him across the back of the neck.

"You're a recruit now, Abdullah. You will bow your head and serve when you are ordered before it goes from one ear to the other. Remember today when you're hesitant. And don't forget this slap to the neck."

He then handed him off to the janissary to his left.

The boys came before the agha one by one, gave their names and home regions as he repeated over and over the traditions of the ceremony to the smallest detail.

"Sinan. Bosnia."

"Dincher. Balikesir."

"Murat. Ainos."

"Hasan. Ulubad."

"Alparslan. Sofia."

"Abdullah. Skopje."

The boy next in line was thrilled to be closer to the girl he couldn't get out of his mind day and night for years despite everything going on around him that spoke to the adventures of the new life he was embarking on. She'd been in his mind constantly during his three years working at the Gallipoli shipyard, falling asleep to thoughts of her every night as he grew accustomed to a new language, new religion and new family. He realized a new phase had begun when Kara Mustafa came to him on the last days of his time as a deckhand on a ship off the coast between Gallipoli and Smyrna. He let out shouts of joy when he heard he'd be sent to Edirne and closer to Constantinople.

He paid great attention to the meaning of what Wolfman was saying. Hard workers would be rewarded and he'd become a janissary faster if he didn't eschew his duties. That was his way out. He should work harder than everyone else and become a janissary in the shortest time possible. He would do whatever it took.

His turn came and he approached Wolfman. He thought of the girl who he last saw so long ago, though, and as he got excited, gave the janissary clerk his old name.

"Alexandros. Gallipoli."

The clerk scowled and Wolfman twisted the boy's ear tighter than he had the others.

"It's not Alexandros, son, it's Iskender. Infidels say Alexandros—we say Iskender!"

Iskender was thankful he was able to weather his mistake after the slap across the back of the neck that felt like it came from a mallet. The Devshirme didn't look kindly on the boys using their old names that evoked their previous religions after they were given new names when they were converted. Devshirme Fiduciary Ferhad Agha had years earlier made the same connection when he saved the boy's life that Wolfman had and had given the boy the name Iskender himself. He'd personally placed the boy at one of the best places to be trained—the Gallipoli shipyard—having found him destined for good work. Ferhad Agha had gone through countless difficulties to get his name recorded in the registry, but the boy had no idea the man had stuck his neck out for him.

Iskender promised himself he'd never make such a mistake again. It was his first and last at the Devshirme.

23

Ten boys went running to the door as soon as the janissary chamberlain gave the motion. They all dashed off like lightening so as not to be the last one to finish the hundred yards and get through the door.

The competition determined the ranking of the recruits and where they would stand in lines in front of the doors of the different janissary regiments, which would then choose which conscripts they would take. The regiment's second most important soldier—the janissary chamberlain—saw over the race. The first boys were given their ranking according to their order through the door, with the first being the highest and less responsible for the daily work of the rooms than the others. The slowest ended up as the servants responsible for all the cleaning and tidying of the rooms.

Iskender had no intention of being a cleaner. He took off with such a burst of speed that he was first through the door in fifteen seconds. Hasan ran unbelievably fast despite his large size and came in second, followed by Abdullah. Dincher and Murat ran side by side and were the last two through the door. Murat was about to get a leg through the door when Dincher took off his cap and threw it inside, saving himself from being dead last. According to janissary tradition, one's clothing was considered part of the soldier.

Chief Commander Vahdeddin, the leader of the regiment, collected the boys and gave each of them two long coats, red tunics of coarse wool, undergarments, knee-length shalvar and black boots. Vahdeddin was the janissary agha's direct interlocutor as the top man in the regiment. Iskender looked at his black boots and realized that conscripts' clothing was drab and one had to be a janissary to wear the colorful yellow and red boots. This also went for the janissary hats that hung down the back of their heads. He didn't like his pointy conscript cap at all. The conical hats represented inexperience whereas the janissaries' hats, falling back over their shoulders, looked like a bowing stalk of wheat.

"Welcome to the Forty-Seventh Regiment, brothers," Vahdeddin said.

There was much more compassion in his brown eyes than fury. The black hair sticking out from the sides of his golden embroidered headpiece stood out against his fair face.

"Yes, I call you my brothers because this is a fraternity and every one of the soldiers are brothers. Our mother is the land and our father is the sultan. The fraternity is our family and the soldiers are our brothers. We have God, Muhammad is our prophet and our leader is Sultan Murad son of Mehmed forever Victorious.

"The chamberlain will show you your rooms. Go and rest well. Get good and clean in the barracks hamams. You will begin a training afforded to only a very few as of tomorrow morning. You will open your eyes with the morning call to prayer and they will stay like that until the night call to prayer. You will learn archery and swordsmanship, horsemanship, bombards and all the other aspects of warfare from the best teachers in the sultanate. You will also learn an art like elocution or calligraphy and you will push your limits of refinement and knowledge.

"We are janissaries, and as such, we are demons at wartime and angels during peace. Our friends see benevolence from us while our enemies taste the torments of hell.

"Each one of you will also be taught a craft. Some will learn cooking, some carpentry and others baking. It will be understood tomorrow morning who will work where."

Vahdeddin paused for a moment and looked over the boys' eyes. "That's enough for now. A very long day is waiting for you tomorrow. The first day is the hardest. May God give you the strength of Ali. Do not waste your strength, as we don't like either the weak or inefficient. May your holy war be blessed."

24

Master Ali was struggling to hold the interest of the boys around him.

It wasn't that the conscripts couldn't concentrate on what one of the best archers in Edirne was saying because their hands ached from a drill of slapping marble a half hour ago. What distracted them were the *solaks*—the lefties—training and racing one after another in the part of Gold Arrow Square called Coffin Square. The boys were dreaming of maybe one day becoming a *solak*—one of the most elite groups in the janissaries, and Master Ali was getting irritated.

Like the others, the large archery range outside the Edirne Janissary Barracks was arranged according to wind direction. And as they were situated parallel to the southwesterly Lodos winds and sheltered from the winds from every other direction so was it to the northerly Star winds so as not to interfere with the arrows' flight. The boys strung up their *kepaze* practice bows here every morning and continuously drew them to strengthen the muscles needed for the task.

Even after months of this exercise, when they got normal bows, they were still far from able to set string them up.

"Stringing a bow," Master Ali said, holding up a loose one, "requires coordination of all the muscles. The main load, though, is on the right leg and the arms."

He picked up the bow—its curved tips curled forward to the hand grip in a figure eight-type shape. "A common man who hasn't received months of training, slapped the marble or strengthened his grip and arms wouldn't be able to string this bow, let alone use it."

He took hold of the two ends, bent them backward and then put one end over his right knee. He looped the bowstring over the tip propped against his leg, then curled the other end farther back and attached the string with his left hand. The bow was bent the other way now, in the shape of a three with its ends bending back out.

He took hold of the handgrip in the middle and turned back to the boys. "No one other than those you've seen who are trained archers can string this bow, no one else can unstring it and no one else can shoot an arrow with it. Setting it up is a separate skill, as is using it, and those who want to pursue it first must be able to pull one hundred seventy-five to two hundred twenty pounds with one arm. It isn't something for the small or weak armed.

"An ordinary janissary, however, can easily string this bow hundreds of times a day and shoot backward from a galloping horse with perfect accuracy a hundred to two hundred times.

"But you have much work ahead of you to reach this level."

Abdullah of Bosnia was rubbing his hands together eagerly.

Master Ali set his sights on the boy. "Above all, you need to give the marble a good beating, so don't get needlessly excited."

The rest of the boys laughed. Abdullah knew he was being made fun of for his small hands, but he didn't pay any mind to his teacher's joke.

"You'll continue to draw the bow string sixty-six more times today. If there's anyone with a strong grip and trusts their muscles like a wrestler, then come on and string it up. Maybe this way you'll be on the way to becoming one of those *solaks* you're all gawking at."

A renowned archer in his own right, Master Ali unstrung the bow in a flash and it sprung back.

As he did every week, Hasan walked up to Master Ali, took the bow and tried to string it. His arms went limp without being able to bend the ends back even the slightest. He couldn't reckon how the men could bend the bows like a stalk of wheat. Helpless, he went back to his place. Iskender rose right after to give it a try, but he was no more successful than Hasan.

"Maybe we should all go back to the marble," Hasan said with a laugh.

25

The lowest-ranking janissaries were in a clear area in the middle of the training field. They wetted woolen matting for the winter bedding and tightly wrapped them one after another around the five iron wires they'd suspended over a wooden table. Then they tied up the center and the ends of the large felt cylinders around the iron wires and hung them from a beam, like rolled up carpets. They checked them over up and down to make sure they were sturdy and then went to join their regiments. Others were doing the same work in groups of ten, arranging the beams next to each other before they went off.

Iskender was excited for the day they would switch to real swords after they finished months of training with wooden ones. He looked over his hands that had become calloused from months of slapping the marble while listening to Vahdeddin.

"A janissary strings his bow, shoots arrows and wields a sword," Vahdeddin said. "These all rely on the strength of your hands and arms. The majority of the months of training you've done have been to strengthen your hands and arms. Now, though, you'll continue your training, but with real swords. Your first task is to hold it well and have a balanced swing."

Vahdeddin went over to the men preparing the felt rolls and

called Murad over to the group of twenty boys listening in rapt attention.

He gave one of the swords on the table to a boy. "Swing it," he said. "Try to slice the felt in two."

Murat swung the sword fast, thinking the large felt roll would be nothing more than a rag to the sharp sword. The blade slid down from where it hit the felt, not quite fully slicing off a little more than an inch from the bottom, out of his hand and flopped to the ground. It would have caught his leg if Murad hadn't pulled it back at the last moment.

Vahdeddin sent Murad back to his place. "Wet felt around iron is deceiving to a novice. This roll here is more durable than the thickest armor of a Genoese knight. A soldier who doesn't concentrate all his power on his arm swinging the sword and who doesn't keep a balanced guard will end up harming himself instead of his enemy."

Then he called Kara Mustafa over.

Kara Mustafa stood in front of the felt roll, drew his sword and swung down and across in a move the conscripts couldn't quite make out. He'd cut the roll through the center, with one half still suspended and the other on the ground. Vahdeddin then sent him away.

"A janissary does not draw his sword for nothing, and when he does, he does not sheathe it without giving it its due respect. You'll get to the level where you'll be able to cut these rolls through. The skill, though, isn't cutting through the felt—it is to swing the sword one hundred, two hundred times and reduce it to shreds."

Murad wondered how a sword could strike such felt a hundred times.

"There is not one enemy in battle. And a janissary who strikes down fifty men in battle is not considered triumphant."

He finished speaking and drew the sword that always hung at his left side. In ten seconds, he sliced the remaining half still hanging into twenty pieces before the astonished looks of the conscripts.

"Good God, that's impossible!" Abdullah said to Iskender.

"If he can do it, then we can do it. Nothing's impossible," Iskender said.

"I know how hard that thing is. There's no way those thin swords can cut it. There must be a trick to it."

Not winded in the least, Vahdeddin turned back to the boys. "Now it's your turn. We have much work to do. And when you can cut through these, maybe months, maybe weeks from now, we'll move on to felt rolls wrapped around ten wires, then twenty, then fifty.

"And don't forget to respect the sword."

BOOK TWO
The Sealed Letter

26

Kara Mustafa pulled on the reins when he saw men of Karaman in the plain stretching in front of him while he was on the one-day road to Manisa. They had surrounded a peasant and his plow. He knew this journey that began with the letter he got from the agha in Edirne three days ago would be trouble, but he hadn't reckoned he'd come across Ibrahim II of Karaman's infamous mischief-makers.

The agha had called for him at midnight. He received the letter with the sultan's signature bearer seal on it in a courtyard under the light of a crescent moon. His uneasiness increased when he heard what the agha said—*To the Chelebi,* son of the Sultan. With these three words he accepted his task and bowed his head. He saw the agha's eyes had gone bloodshot and felt he was receiving the most important charge of his life.

Marauders, he thought. He counted nine of them. He'd seen them as he descended a foothill of a long mountain that gave way to the plain and he knew he wouldn't be able to go back and change his route. He tried to set out a plan in his uneasiness.

The Karamanids immediately recognized a janissary on the open plain and made a move in his direction.

"Hey, yellow boots!" one of them yelled in surprise.

"Oho, look at this. So they wander through our land, too, now," another said derisively.

"What do you say, Jackal, are these palace dogs riding their horses right under are noses now?" Lame Hakan said.

Jackal was looking at the soldier on the foothill below the mountain. His eyes peered out angrily from under his scowling black brow, narrowed to the point where they were almost closed. He kept his eye on the far-off janissary as he talked with his companions. "Is this cur some advance scout for some coming army?"

"Murad gets on fine with Ibrahim. Why would he have a campaign here?" Chaka Bey said.

"Sultan Murad is good with everyone. He doesn't wage war on his enemies and they don't attack him. It's like they have some spoken agreement."

"It seems like that, Hakan, but now that Murad is gone and Edirne will be a bloodbath. Most of all, Ibrahim Bey is standing tall and maybe Murad sensed something."

"So is this dog hanging around on his orders, then? Is he scouting? And what if droves of them come behind him?"

"No, Chaka Bey, he wouldn't come to meddle with anything, riding there with a thousand Ottomans behind him to challenge us."

"He's right. He's not here to start anything," another said.

"He's not worth it," Sunger the Bear said clutching his ax. "We're nine men and he's alone. And even if more come, before that we'd already have gotten to him and given him a clobbering."

"Not so fast, Sungur. That's not just any man," Chaka Bey said. "He's a janissary. You shouldn't be so careless.

Jackal finally spoke up, "He's a messenger. He can't be a scout—his boots aren't red. And his horse is a Bulgarian—they use those to get messages out as fast as possible. His saddlebags are stuffed full, too, so he doesn't have to stop at any caravanserai. This dog's taking news somewhere, but where—and what?"

Jackal was quite familiar with janissaries. All the men were silent for a while after he spoke.

"If he's not a scout then what are we waiting for? Let's lop that pointy hat off his head," said Steely Tayyar, spear in hand.

He'd gotten his name from the stories of him striking down his target with a spear at great distance.

"Let's first find out where he's going and what his message is. Let's go, boys!"

They all spurred their horses on together and took off toward Kara Mustafa.

Mustafa knew the Karamanids were undisciplined, but he didn't expect they'd be this thoughtless. He took his bow from over his right shoulder, an arrow from the quiver over his left shoulder and took aim. He reckoned he'd be able to take out three of the men before they got to him, He'd also worked out which to target first and what he'd do once they got closer, as the Karamanids were debating what to do themselves.

His first arrow pierced the belly of the one on the far right in the back. The man fell to the ground as his horse spooked and kept running. He figured if he shot at the ones in the middle, then they would fan out, and he much preferred they come at him all together than from three sides.

Güral let out a scream as an arrow struck him in the eye before he'd shaken off the shock of his mate falling beside him. The remaining seven men arced around to the left as they bore down on Mustafa. He'd been waiting for this and let an arrow loose at the bulky man on the far right. He knew he'd need to shoot them down when he first saw them before he'd be forced to confront them sword to sword, but first he reckoned he could make it more difficult for the men coming for him if he got among the trees in the woods to his left. They'd gotten quite close already. Mustafa took aim again and shot another man straight through the heart, who then slumped and took his horse down with him.

Then something happened he hadn't expected as he broke for the trees.

He noticed something move from the left of the group, but he saw the steel-tipped spear coming at him much too late. Maybe he'd thought that a Karamanid wouldn't be such an expert spear thrower. There was only one thing to do, as any janissary would. He raised his left arm and in a split second twisted his body to the right. The spear struck his arm with its tip plunging in sticking out the other side.

"Attaboy, Tayyar!" one yelled.

"He's getting away to the woods! Cut him off!"

Mustafa drew his sword just before he entered the woods and tried to look at where the shaft of the spear met its steel head. He quickened his horse and tried to hold his left arm in front of him to control the reins as he waved his sword in the air with his other arm. The spear wasn't nearly enough to stop him, but his eyes were watering uncontrolledly from the pain in his arm and it was blurring his vision.

He was at the edge of the woods, and if he couldn't get rid of the spear sticking through his arm, it would catch a branch or bush and pull him from his horse. With just steps left to the trees he swung his sword down on the spear hanging out of his arm.

"Son of a bitch," one of the Karamanids said.

"Lousy Devshirme slave-rat!"

Mustafa thought he could try to lose them in the woods and continue on his way if it weren't for the peasant watching him anxiously, since he reckoned the Karamanids would go back in their rage and kill the man. The sultan tried to bring order to the land, and he'd heard the Karamanids would sometimes cause trouble close to the border, loot the villages and torment the peasants. His duty was to obey, though, not question. He knew the sultan wasn't at war with the Karamanids, but because of his duty, the murder of a peasant would disturb him. The task in his charge, though, also made him feel he shouldn't be delayed.

He decided running wasn't an option. Everything else aside, he figured the Karamanids would easily be able to track him from the blood flowing from his arm. It would endanger both his mission and, considering where he was going, jeopardize the peace. Even if he were to deliver the message after this, his work would get complicated out of nothing. It wasn't his duty to declare war—it was to end war and maintain the peace. He had no choice.

He dismounted where the plain met the woods and tried to hold his bow steady with his arm run through by the spear as he fitted an arrow to the string. He thought it would've been better if they'd cut off his legs. He realized he'd only be able to hold the bow long enough to shoot once more. Not being able to use a bow a was a great dishonor to a janissary.

The Karamanids slowed down as they entered the woods.

Mustafa was on the lookout for one of them. He'd hid behind a centuries-old plane tree and crouched down in wait.

Jackal and his men slowed more when they saw the Bulgarian horse with no rider. The only thing that broke the silence amid the towering trees was the horse stamping the underbrush. Steely Tayyar carefully took the second spear he had in his saddle as he eyed the peasant on the plain.

"We'll deal with you later," he grumbled.

An arrow pierced his neck as soon has shut his mouth and he fell. Mustafa had used his hidden ingenuity of aiming at the sound through the trees.

Jackal could tell from where the arrow had come from how Tayyar had fallen and ran his horse in that direction, crisscrossing back and forth. The others followed and Hasan quickly found the tree Mustafa had hidden behind. Not wanting to risk coming up against another spear, Mustafa used his last arrow for Tayyar—then his arm wouldn't be able to hold the bow any longer anyway.

Jackal and his men were seething with rage as they surrounded Mustafa. They'd flushed him back out to the plain to be able to handle him more easily.

"You've killed five of our men, you bastard!"

"Now we'll show you what's what. The first thing you'll want is to die."

Lame Hasan looked over his mates. "Slow, boys, we have time. Let's first find out what's so important that he's carrying."

"So, tell me," Jackal said. "What message do you have and who're you bringing it to, janissary? Is the Ottoman sultan tired of peace already? Is his fat ass uncomfortable in the beds of the palace so soon?"

After that, Mustafa decided Jackal must die. He looked the man in the eyes without a word.

Lame Hakan lurched his horse at Mustafa. "Speak up, you palace shit!" His sword was at Mustafa's throat.

"I don't know what I can tell you," Kara Mustafa said

How can a man carrying a message not know what it says? Maybe you'll remember if I tickle your brain with this ax here."

"Easy, Sungur. He's no use to us dead—for now. Wait for it."

"So, are you going to open your shit-eating mouth?"

"You know I'm a janissary, so you'll also know I'll carry this message to my grave. They call me Kara Mustafa. So far there hasn't been any treachery from me or any of my brothers. I'm in service to the sultan, I only answer to him, I only take orders from him and I'll only die for him. Killing a janissary would bring hell down on your chiefdom, don't forget. You lot can't make me talk."

Mustafa's mind was on the letter he'd hidden in his belt as he spoke—and he really had no idea of its contents. He wasn't trying to introduce himself to the Karamanids with his words of loyalty and service, though—he was trying to provoke them as much as possible.

Sungur the Bear had grown enraged by the end. "I'm going to hack this palace wimp to bits," he said as he stepped down from his horse.

Jackal knew the janissary wouldn't divulge anything and so didn't say anything to his man. Sungur walked up to Mustafa and lifted his ax. In the blink of an eye, Kara Mustafa wrenched the spear point from his arm and stabbed the man in the throat before he had a chance to bring down his ax.

Now there was only three of them. Two had swords and the other a flail. Mustafa had snatched the ax from Sungur's hand as he fell and flung it at Jackals' head. Lame Hakan was still gawking at the ax stuck in the forehead of his agha of forty years when Mustafa took Jackal's sword and ran him through.

"I hear they call you Chaka," Mustafa said.

Chaka Bey was the only one left, staring in fear at the janissary atop Jackal's horse.

"Go and tell your Karaman chief. His dogs aren't to meddle with the people. They aren't to bring trouble to Sultan Murad's realm. The sultan is gentle, wise and peaceful, but he'll bring terror to dogs like you, tear off your heads and rip you open like a lion. The infidels were just as heedless and they paid a heavy price in Varna. Do not incite the sultan."

Mustafa thought about the letter in his belt as Chaka Bey ran away as fast as he could. He felt an odd burning sensation in him as he'd spoken of Sultan Murad. He was tied to the sultan from the heart, and this man whom he served had grown quite old. His peaceful ways had given hope to his enemies—his good intentions and justice had been abused. His burning wasn't from any confusion, though. The message he was carrying had blood in it. He could feel it. Now he understood the janissary agha's bloodshot eyes. He got the meaning of the silence of the palace that night and where he was going. He sadly reminisced about the stories he'd told the inexperienced young prince about his father years ago.

The peasant was on his way back to his house as Mustafa continued on to the Chelebi's palace. He felt the pain even deeper that he wouldn't be able to shoot another arrow.

27

"So, is the world eternal or is it something with an end?" the prince asked his teachers seated at their reading lecterns on both sides of the room as he rose to put his copy of *The Iliad* back on the shelf.

He carefully put the ancient epic, which he read constantly, next to the other books and manuscripts remaining from the Library of Alexandria. The room was full of books and maps covered the walls—Ptolemy's map of the world foremost among them. On the opposite wall were astronomical tables from al-Khwarizmi's *Zij al-Sindhind.* He had stood opposite these maps countless times in unending discussions with his teachers.

"Mehmed, it seems the incoherence has started to have an effect on you," Mullah Gürani said.

It had been a while now that Mullah Gürani had been mentioning al-Ghazali's *The Incoherence of the Philosophers* and ibd Rushd's *The Incoherence of the Incoherence.*

Mehmed smiled. His teachers all enjoyed that he understood from the content which debate and philosophical problem they talked about.

"Everything with a beginning has an end, Mehmed. Only God is eternal," Mullah Hüsrev said. "This has been a matter of debate between philosophers for centuries since Aristotle and Plato." Mehmed took his seat and Hüsrev continued, "There are two schools at its foundation. One is the philosophy that the world is eternal, which relies on ibn Sina's Neoplatonism, and the other from al-Ghazali, whose work philosophers have asserted has great errors."

"*The Incoherence of the Philosophers*," Müllah Gürani said. "That work you've been trying to wrap your head around for days—is the book that debunks the philosophers' arguments one by one and started the school."

"What is ibn-Sina's philosophy?" Mehmed asked.

He would try to understand the topics at first, and then try to resolve his doubts and the questions that had stuck in his mind with his tutors.

"You need to understand Neoplatonism before you can understand ibn Sina," Mullah Gürani said. "Aristotle and Plato had different views, but then the philosophy of Neoplatonism developed centuries later in various line with Plato and his students. According to it, the entire universe in simply united in a single power, in an endless force they call the One."

"Even though the Greek philosophers don't so much ascsay there is God," Mullah Hüsrev said, "they agree on the existence of a single power. Ibn Sina also developed this philosophy of the One under the influence of al-Farabi.

"According to ibn Sina, there was nothing before the world and then the Creator decided to create it after a certain time. The Creator didn't have such a desire before, so that means after that specific time, the desire to create the world arose in the Creator. This implies that no desire penetrates other than the will of God, an insinuation that a desire does not exist from nothingness, which is a curse in itself. Everything in the world is perfect because God is the Shaper of Beauty and created everything in its ideal form, so it is an unacceptable idea that He thought about this perfection at a specific time and then that it later came to His mind. Multiplicity can take form from the One, but as a result, that multiplicity is the One. The One cannot create another One.

"Everything around us is in motion. Specks of dust, stones, dirt, water, air, mountains, the moon, the sun, the planets, the galaxy—everything—but everything is always a part of change. According to the physical laws, every movement has a starting point. A substance has a need for a potential to form itself. The only existent with no need for complementary potential is the Creator. Therefore, that the world exists, its actual reality and that it has existed since the beginning is its proof."

"Possibility and reality are at the heart of this philosophy," Mullah Gürani added. The reality of the world shows there was possibility before it. When we think that every reality is bound to a possibility, what comes out is that the only entity with no need for possibility is the Originator. So, as Neoplatonism argues, everything is in need of something and every result requires a reason. There are other entities around the Maker of Order, but they owe their existence to God at the center for all eternity. Outside the center, the universe is ordered according to its own rules—the relationship between cause and effect and the rules of logic. There is nothing in the world that is not mathematical or logical."

"And what was al-Ghazali's answer?" Mehmed asked.

"According to al-Ghazali," Mullah Hüsrev said, "the main problem is that the philosophers speak of the Creator as a person and tie it into the rules of logic. First of all, the concepts of space and time are entirely concepts of man, and whereas it may also seem logical and practical for the Creator to warrant these, it would not set one on the right path. That's why what the philosophers talk about as time is created time, which can't be used to quantify the Creator. That the world was not created from the beginning is not to say that then a desire for it arose later because the before and after in this proposition are only valid for man. The before and after can be completely different for man. Furthermore, that everything in the world is in a state of motion and change is also inconsistent with the rules of logic, because talking about motion and change can only be done by latching on to a fixed point. More so, the claim that everything in the world is in motion shows that it comes from a fixed point."

Mullah Gürani picked up from there. "Al-Ghazali mentions this example a couple of times in his book. Let's say you put two dates of the same type, same taste and same quality in front of someone. When you put the dates in front of someone who is hungry, they will always take one of them. Him preferring one date or the other does not mean he prefers one because he doesn't prefer the other, as he could've just as easily chosen the other, but somehow chose the one he ate instead. And so his choice for the one he ate and the one that wasn't chosen can't be explained."

"What does al-Ghazali say, then, to the rules of logic and the relationship between cause and effect?"

"This is where al-Ghazali's main criticism lies," Mullah Hüsrev said. "Rules of philosophy function with a specific logic and can be explained through propositions based on the relationship between cause and effect. According to al-Ghazali, though, the relationship between cause and effect cannot supersede the Creator, and the idea it can is blasphemy. As such, that the world does work within specific rules is a blessing to the servants of God. It enables people to live in peace and happily with specific expectations. Order passes before chaos, we live our lives and it can be rendered calculable. So then, according to al-Ghazali, everything in the world at every moment is within the command and desire of the Creator. As for the relationship between cause and effect, cotton burns when it touches fire. The cotton touching fire is the cause and the cotton burning is the effect. Man's expectations take this shape and they become real. It's the Great Will, though, that lights the cotton."

Gürani yielded to Mullah Hüsrev. "Al-Ghazali gives the miracles of the prophets as the greatest evidence. That Abraham didn't burn in the fire, that Moses turned his staff into a serpent and that Jesus made the blind see have their origin in an illusion of the relation between cause and effect. The Self Subsisting has the capability to bring into existence the events He wants in the way He pleases. It lies in that all causes don't have the same effect and different causes don't give rise to a single effect.

"What this actually means is that everything in the world is being brought into existence at every moment. Every speck, all beings on earth come into existence every second in new shapes, new times and new spaces. The concepts of continuity and movement, and time and space that we think we have are no more than illusions. That's why the Quran stresses so often that the world is an illusion. And so man needs prayer and worship more than anything, as the completion of everything that's done in one way or another isn't tied to us or causes, but is rather embedded in the will of God.

"Al-Ghazali relates a story a few times of how the rules of logic can't explain the Exalted Will. Let's imagine a boy and a grown man go to heaven on Judgment Day. The boy is in a lower level of heaven and the man is in a higher level. The boy asks God why He allowed the man to a higher level. God says it's because the man had lived longer and performed more good deeds. Then the child asks why God didn't allow him to live longer so he, too, could have performed more good deeds. God says because when the boy would have been grown he would've been a sinner and gone to hell, so that's why He delivered him. Then the wailings of a horde rise from hell asking why God hadn't killed them sooner, as well."

"How does ibn Rushd respond to al-Ghazali's sound argument, then?" Mehmed asked.

"His point of view can be taken as somewhere in between those of ibn Sina and al-Ghazali. In the Quran, God says he created the world and the entire cosmos formed in two days and that it took shape by His hand. According to ibn Rushd, all of these verses can be evaluated both literally and figuratively. The way one reads them depends on the person."

"There are three types of people," Mullah Gürani said. "The first reads the verses, believes in their veracity without question and continues with their worship. The second reads the verses, thinks, weighs them in their head and, believing, continues on their way, knowing a few things. The third always thinks, weighs and evaluates everything, and their doubts never cease. Sometimes, though, those who have read the Quran from beginning to end can't feel that they get it. The first and second types of people read the verses literally, and there's nothing wrong in that. The third type, though, always goes after beginnings and greater answers. What differentiates these different types of people can be their level of education, disposition or upbringing. What's important is to pay attention to these concepts while talking. According to ibn Rushd, the third type of person shouldn't try to explain what they know and feel to the first and second types of people—otherwise they'd be directed toward blasphemy.

"This is because the first and second types of people will be shaken if they see the true meanings behind their beliefs. They don't awaken to the metaphorical meanings and deeper interpretations and their beliefs will weaken and disappear in constriction.

"That's what ibn Rushd claims. It's the science ibn Sina did. Like mathematics, medicine and physics, sometimes true or false interpretations are reached, and this is also the nature of this science. Ibn Rushd believed al-Ghazali obstructed philosophical thought in Islam, fearing that it ossifies Islamic dogma as Christian theologians had their own and defends a philosophical thought against al-Ghazali in his *The Incoherence of the Incoherence.*"

"Do all these great thinkers not refute one another? I mean, wouldn't some of them have to be in heaven now and the others in hell?" Mehmed asked.

"No, Mehmed. Quite the opposite," Mullah Gürani said. "They all must be evaluated in accordance with their own times. Islamic scholars were confronted with Greek philosophy when the lands of Islam bordered those of Rome. Al-Farabi and ibn Sina demonstrated that Islam isn't in any conflict with this philosophical thought and that reason and logic don't contradict the existence of God. They brought it to a level so that now philosophers the world over still call al-Farabi the Second Master in the line after Aristotle. After a while, though, al-Ghazali felt it had gone too far and that the philosophers claimed there was no need for the book and tradition in order to understand the religion and man's only need is reason. That's why he tries to prove the incoherence of reason and the belief and metaphysics of faith. Ibn Rushd worked to restore the balance, believing in the road to dogma al-Ghazali had opened in Islam. He's accepted in both Persian and European lands as the one who best understands Plato."

"As a result," Mullah Hüsrev said, "Islam is a religion of reason and doesn't conflict with logic, but there is complete submission at its core. This is independent from logic—something beyond it. Islam is submission. People must see the Truth clearly and distinctly so they can choose submission through their own reason and will."

As he listened to his two tutors, Mehmed looked at the man with a white beard, wearing a white gown and holding a *tespih* who was reading the Quran in a corner.

"Sheikh Akshamsaddin, what do you think of this matter?"

Akshamsaddin lifted his head and smiled at Mehmed. Gürani and Hüsrev looked over at the sheikh.

"God's words are many, Mehmed. *And if whatever trees upon the earth were pens and the seas ink, replenished by seven more seas thereafter, the words of God would not be exhausted.* Islam has had such motley thinkers and philosophers and they all try to understand and explain God. Each is also the color and wealth of Islam. There is one Truth, but there are many roads to the Truth. The ink of the scholar is more precious than the blood of martyrs. The death of a scholar is like the death of humanity. The three men you've mentioned spoke of nothing other than God. The Self Subsisting sometimes choses people who see and understand what others can't and it's their duty to understand and explain. Others who are chosen have the duty to permit this and prepare the environment for it. Only a holy ruler can preside over God's divine order. Some are chosen to understand, others to produce and still others to rule it. God knows everything best.

"To understand why what has been chosen falls on which people is to serve on the path." Akshamsaddin paused for a moment and his face grew serious. He looked at Mehmed. "Life is short."

A knock came at the door as Mehmed was thinking about why the sheikh had said such a thing so abruptly.

One of the palace pages came up to Mehmed and whispered in his ear.

"Let him come," the prince said.

Kara Mustafa appeared at the door after a while. Blood was leaking from the cloth wrapped around his left arm.

He approached the prince and held out the sealed letter from his belt. He was having trouble standing. Mehmed carefully opened the letter without cracking the seal.

Your great father Sultan Murad Khan son of Mehmed the Victorious, by God's grace has attained paradise. It will be favorable for the perpetuity of the state for you to come to the palace forthwith.

May God bless you, my Padishah.

Your servant, Halil Pasha

28

Mehmed and Jafer Agha stopped when they came to half a dozen horsemen on the Gallipoli coast. Taking nearly no time for rest, they had been pushing their horses for two days. Their horses had galloped so swiftly that they'd halved the time for the journey from the normal eight days to four. They also kept their identities hidden to protect against any assassination plots by Ibrahim of Karaman or Constantine.

"What is it, gentlemen?" Jafer Agha said to the men on the road to the port. "What are you waiting for?"

"It's forbidden to cross," a brute of a man in the group said. "We control all crossings."

Mehmed looked over the men and their weapons. It was clear from their clothing they were Turks, as well as from how they spoke. Their swords were curved, however the two men at the back were carrying straight swords like those of knights. Mehmed couldn't make sense of it. The two men in front wore breastplates, which Turks didn't often use. Their turbans were ordinary and a couple of their caftans were eye catching—a sign they were veteran soldiers.

"Why have you cut off the roads?" Jafer Agha said.

"It doesn't concern you, sir. All crossings are prohibited, that's it."

"On who's order? The sultan's?

The man grinned. "No. And soon there will be a sultan from the people."

"What's happened to Sultan Murad?" Mehmed said, feigning ignorance.

"They say the sultan has died," one of the men at the back said. "Our chief Orhan Chelebi will take his place. We've taken hold of all roads to the city to stop anyone else from claiming the throne."

The situation became clear to Mehmed and Jafer Agha in all its clarity. These were the men of his uncle Orhan Chelebi who had been given to Eastern Rome as a hostage and lived in Constantinople. There was no doubt the news of the sultan's death had reached Emperor Constantine—and the Romans were trying to install Orhan on the throne. Sultan Murad had tried to secure his release for decades but had never succeeded. Constantine's father John VIII Palaiologos had paid sacks of gold in tribute while he was emperor to keep Orhan under his control. This Ottoman prince who now lived as a Roman lord was Constantine's greatest asset to holding sway over the Ottomans. And the time they'd been waiting for was finally upon them.

Mehmed and Jafer Agha couldn't reckon how the news of the sultan's death had reached Constantinople. As far as they knew, it had been secretly sent to Mehmed alone.

"So who are you?" the man at the front said.

"We're booksellers," Mehmed said. "We're taking books to the Edirne Madrasah."

"You have fine horses for booksellers," one of the other men said with a suspicious look.

"You have proof you're bring books to the madrasah?"

"Of course," Mehmed said. "It's in the saddlebag."

"Show it, then."

Mehmed turned around and reached for the leather saddlebag slung over his horse's back. Jafer Agha gently clasped his sword. Mehmed pulled his horse toward the middle of the group as he took out a thick manuscript.

"Here you go, have a look," he said as he handed it over.

The men looked uneasily at each other.

Mehmed then held it out to the other side.

"Look at these if you're still not convinced," he said as he slipped the hidden dagger from his saddle. He slashed to the left and the right, slicing the throats of two men, then threw the dagger at the face of a third as the first two fell from their horses. It plunged straight into the man's forehead.

Taking advantage of the remaining men's surprise, Jafer Agha pulled his sword and ran another through the belly and twisted it back out before he had a chance to strike. The two armored men took hold of their broadswords as Mehmed drew his blade.

Jafer Agha charged the one on the right and Mehmed went for the other.

They deftly wielded their blades amid the clatter of steel. The blows were flying so fast that the swords were sending off sparks. It was clear these two men who hadn't spoken since the beginning were from the knights Constantine had given to serve Orhan.

Mehmed held the reins in his left hand as he swung his scimitar. The knight swung his sword down on Mehmed from the left only to be parried away.

Jafer Agha fended off a strike straight to his belly with a quick upward flick of his scimitar.

The sun glinted off the steel of his blade as Mehmed deftly brandished his sword after what was already a long battle. The Damascus steel blade cut straight through the knight's neck and his lifeless head tumbled to the ground.

Jafer Agha had also cut down the other knight who was lying on the ground with blood flowing from his mouth.

Mehmed smiled and looked over to Jafer Agha as they sped along the way to the Gallipoli port.

"Didn't I tell you books are more important than the sword?"

29

A crowd formed as Giorgios Sphrantzes' retinue entered the port of the capital of the Greek Empire of Trebizond. Throwing themselves under the malicious cracks of whips, the crowd wasn't interested in either the retinue taking the renowned Venetian commander Aluvixe Diedo from the Black Sea to Trebizond or Diedo's eponymous and equally famous galley. They had seen the flags with the double headed eagle and stars of the imperial Constantinopolitan ships as they gathered at port. Where the ships were coming from was always a source of interest and curiosity whether it was Europe, elsewhere in Anatolia or the Caucasus. A ship arriving from Constantinople had the effect as if it were bringing news of the center of the world.

Two mendicants were talking, curious like the rest of the crowd, as Sphrantzes and his regiment made their way to the emperor's palace.

"Is that fatty Constantine's man, Giorgios Sphrantzes?"

"That's what they're saying."

"What—is there a war? Why'd they come to the realm of the *Komnenos?*

"Apparently they called for Emperor Constantine to come."

"He's married already, right?"

"Could he be married? They say he's cursed. He was young when he married his first wife and then she up and died a year later—we don't know why."

"He didn't get married again?"

"He did, but they say he tried everything to get a dowry from a Roman."

"Then what?"

"Those devilish Turks didn't give him any peace. They say the whole Turkish fleet blockaded the island when he went to get his queen and that the woman died of fear."

"I wonder if that's true."

"Constantine XI's bad luck is out there in the open—I bet it's true. They say Sphrantzes went to ask for the daughter of the Georgian king first and now he's here to take a look at Emperor Ioannes' daughter."

The two beggars noticed armored palace guards on horseback bearing down on the crowd as they were talking.

"Clear out, clear out!"

A few of the guards were whipping indiscriminately at those in front of them. A man was struck and fell into the mud. He wasn't so concerned about his dirtied shirt, but the whip had left an awful sting.

Sphrantzes and his retinue entered the palace of Ioannes IV Megas Komnenos as the crowd dispersed.

"Ah, Giorgios, my old friend!" Emperor Ioannes welcomed his guest from Constantinople with open arms. The gold wine goblet in his hand outshined his crown. "How long has it been? Three years?"

"Hospitable Ioannes, my thanks for this warm welcome. And yes, it must be three years now."

The two men exchanged a friendly embrace—one an emperor and the other the top confident of the emperor of the most important city in the world.

"I suppose it was during Easter the last time. We were at the service at the Hagia Sophia with the queen and your lovely daughter."

"Oh yes, I remember. I'm getting old, you know. Your memory is quite firm, though." The emperor took another sip from his goblet.

He made a quick gesture to his servants to bring more wine.

"It goes well before a meal, my friend. You have one, too."

Two, blonde, blue-eyed Greek servants brought wine for Sphrantzes and Diedo. Diedo couldn't pull his passionate gaze from the girl's eyes. Then his eyes wandered down to her breasts above the neckline of her dress. The servant girl also didn't leave his looks unanswered.

Ioannes laughed. "So, tell me, Giorgios, is it true what I've heard? Is the great emperor in Constantinople on the hunt for a wife again?"

"Your Majesty, as you know, the emperor still has no heir. He thinks of it more as he grows in years and he desires to marry posthaste."

"How old is old Constantine?"

"He'll reach forty-seven this year."

"And you say that's old, do you? I'm fifty-six and I can still sire children. Constantine shouldn't give up so quickly," Ioannes said with a laugh and a look around at the servants, falling on the girl who had just poured his wine as she smiled back at him. "And I'll be able to for the next fifty-six years, at least!" he said as he grabbed his crotch.

"My dear Ioannes, you're having quite the fun, but you know that despite his age, the emperor still hasn't had any children. He's thinking of the future of the empire."

"Giorgios, old friend, I know—how wouldn't I? There's ill luck with the Palaiologoi." Ioannes' voice lowered and grew serious. "The emperor hasn't been so fortunate when it comes to women. First, he was born under an ominous star, then the Palaiologoi had their endless strife and struggles for the throne and then finally his wives have died as if the angle of death flies over him. So, tell me, how can I help?"

"You're very close with the emperor, Your Majesty—like brothers, two rulers of the empires of Christendom. The emperor wishes to marry your daughter to strengthen these ties."

"My dear Giorgios, there's no need to play those Roman games and be roundabout to convince me. The only reason Constantine wishes to marry my daughter is so he has a queen worthy of him. To be honest, though, I shy away from Constantine's ill fortune."

"Your Majesty, I'd hope you're not one to pay heed to the nonsense from the rabble. It's quite obvious why his previous wives died. His first, Maddalena Tocca, was sickly from the beginning. I saw her illness myself. And when he went to collect Lord Dorino Gattilusio of Lesbos' daughter Caterina, the Turks literally scared her to death. Or is it that you don't want your beautiful daughter to be the queen of Constantinople? You won't have to worry about the Turks coming at you from all sides once your familial ties with Constantine become stronger. The emperor is thinking of making an alliance with you and Ibrahim of Karaman to put an end to the Ottoman's advances."

"Clever and shrewd Giorgios, it's not me who needs this alliance, but him."

Aluvixe Diedo had stayed silent since they'd arrived, but now he took two steps forward. "But to fight the Turks you need power on the sea and experienced seamen. Constantine has always been in good fitting with us Venetians and we are prepared to support him in any war against the Turk. My men and I have given our word to Constantine, and it's our word that rules the seas. The Turk has never had power on the sea."

"You must've meant you and the Genoese rule the sea," Ioannis said disparagingly—the contention between the Venetians and Genoese was no secret.

Sphrantzes stepped in. "And as you see, Your Majesty, Constantine has what you don't and you have what he lacks."

Ioannis stood opposite the two men, thinking of what they had said when voices started to come from outside and from the palace's lower floors.

"Murad!" a faint voice shouted from outside, followed by others.

Everyone in the royal chamber looked at the door as it opened and the emperor's messenger came through. He walked to the emperor and then whispered in his ear.

A smile spread across Ioannis' face as the messenger spoke.

As soon as he finished, the emperor raised his goblet and bellowed, "I declare a festival for three days and three nights! Sultan Murad is dead! Hurry and start the preparations for festivities—there's going to be great frivolity this evening!"

All the servants in the room began running around as the emperor spoke.

"Can you believe it, Giorgios? Sultan Murad had died!"

Sphrantzes, however, was quite the opposite of overjoyed. He had dropped his cup as he heard the news and his face had gone distressed.

"What is it, Giorgios? I never knew you loved Sultan Murad so—or is your bewilderment from joy?"

Sphrantzes' face was frozen for a moment as he looked at Ioannes. He pulled himself together and said, "But, Your Majesty, this isn't good news in the least."

"The death of any sultan of the Turks, especially one as dominant and proficient as Murad, is good news for us and our land, Giorgios."

"Sultan Murad was well-regarded and seen as a wise ruler in Constantinople and other European courts. Our relationship with him was quite good. He wouldn't wage war so long as he wasn't squeezed into a corner or goaded and he always came with a mind for peace. But I'm also thinking about his son who brought into his place years ago."

"What're you talking about, for the love of Christ? Get your head together! I remember it like it was yesterday how Murad defied the crusader armies from all over Europe in Varna, and how he debased our honor."

"But Murad actually withdrew to Bursa to recover. He was always watchful for the opportunity to worship and retire from the work of the state. The crusaders made a grave error when he left the throne to his young son and they chose to gather against him. And when Hunyadi Janos from the Kingdom of Hungary joined in—he broke the vow of peace he'd given to Murad."

"Since when do you believe an oath made to a Mohametan must be kept, Giorgios?"

"That betrayal cost them dearly, Your Majesty—and us, as well. What I will say is that Murad was a wise man. It was clear what he would do and when. But his son is mad. He was never able to get over that he was forced to surrender at Varna. It nagged away at him in Manisa and he's planned day and night how to take his revenge once he ascends to the throne."

"Is great Roman Constantinople afraid of a young boy—this inexperienced upstart?"

"He must be nineteen by now."

"Well, I'd say compared to Murad, this kid's nothing. There's no need for Constantine to worry. Orhan Chelebi will get the throne—and even if he doesn't, the soldiers will hold Orhan above his young nephew. Constantine will be able to handle this all very comfortably. And even more, now the Austrians, Hungarians, Venetians and Genoese, not to mention Ibrahim of Karaman and Hasan the Tall of the Aq Qoyunlu will either all together or piece by piece try to think of ways to wipe the Ottomans from the land. Such a chance doesn't come often, Giorgios. Let's plan what we must do to have a greater share fall to us. But now, see that you enjoy yourself—it's clear who the emperor's bride will be."

Sphrantzes looked at Ioannes curiously.

"Murad's now widow, Mara, of course," Ioannes said. "You know he married the daughter of the Serbian Despot Durad Brankovic years ago. Maybe you're right, Giorgios, maybe Constantine's ill omens hold no water. It's time now, though, to break the back of the Turk."

Sphrantzes began to thing about this suggestion as soon as he heard it. Ioannes could be right, after all. The daughter of the Serbian despot had long been renowned for her great nobility and beauty. Constantine would be able to strengthen his allegiances with the Serbian Despotate to the west and grow closer to the Ottomans by marrying a wife of the deceased sultan. Marrying one of Murad's widows was no small thing, though. He knew Muslims looked on widows like normal people and reckoned they wouldn't be met with anything adverse from the Ottomans from Constantine marrying Mara. It would behoove the emperor and seemed to be advantageous from every angle.

Sphrantzes' mind, however, was more on Murad's uncontrollable son. He wasn't sure what to think as the stories he'd heard about the prince ran through his head. It had been said that he'd minted his own coins in Manisa just the previous year with murmurings that he'd taken the leadership for himself while his father was still alive and that he'd gathered loyal janissaries around him. He was having difficulty in understanding what they were up against the more he thought about how Murad had sent special tutors who had somehow turned this young man who couldn't listen to reason as a boy into a man. But maybe the stories of this boy had been unduly exaggerated and Ioannes was right. Maybe the time had come to look to dealing with the Ottomans.

Beside all that, he had to arrange a secret meeting with the pasha in Edirne to find out what was going on. He should finish his work at once and return to Constantinople.

Everybody was merry as the festivities were underway at the palace. Aluvixe Diedo sipped from the cup stuck in the cleavage of the girl who'd served him that morning while men made nice with the other half-naked women as they snuggled up to them in the corners of the hall and amused themselves.

One man was showing a woman his deep scars from past sea battles while another flexed his swollen arms from rowing on the galleys. Another man had set a servant girl on a table in the corner and ripped open her gown as she attempted to fight him off and was trying to bite at her nipples, much to her displeasure. An old man looked at his daughter painfully as he brought around the wine and silently prayed for God to strike the men down.

30

Constantine XI Palaiologos turned his head as he looked up from where he was sitting at the centuries-old mosaic of the City of Constantine on the ceiling of the church, like the vault of heaven itself. He always felt a nebulous burning when he looked on the image of the great emperor for whom he was named presenting the city to the baby Jesus on the Virgin Mary's lap. His eyes wandered over and over the inscription on the gold mosaic—*Constantine, the Great Emperor among the Saints.* Then he looked with admiration at Justinian on the other side of the Virgin Mary, presenting the Hagia Sophia. It was often he would sit and look long at these figures with bitter envy.

A little hope welled inside him, though. The hope that the city would be able to return to its days of splendor now that the great Ottoman sultan had died, and he thoroughly believed he would be able to recapture the lands he'd lost to him parcel by parcel.

He'd grown accustomed over time since he'd become emperor a few years earlier to pull himself away by looking at the mosaics during the long church services he had to attend—and where he often found himself quite bored. It wasn't just impatience—the congregation filled the church. Everyone wanted the service to end as soon as possible, as Constantine was so thrilled and emboldened with the death of the Ottoman sultan that he ordered the races at the Hippodrome be reinstated after many years.

"Blessed is the kingdom of the Father and of the Son and of the Holy Spirit, now and ever and unto ages of ages," Patriarch Grigorios III Mammas chanted to begin the service as Constantine bowed his head and turned to look at him.

The patricians standing in the nave, the women in the upper galleries, the soldiers to the back and the guests behind them all stopped muttering as the patriarch spoke.

"In peace let us pray to the Lord and in greeting to Emperor Constantine of great Rome," he continued, facing the congregation and the dozens of mosaics of Jesus and the Virgin Mary. Mammas' long beard hung in tassels over his black robe wrapped around his ostentatious vestments with a gold cross on a chain around his neck. He was as close to Constantine as one could be.

"Lord have mercy for holy Rome and the people who dwell therein. The Lord is with us."

The patriarch raised and lowered his hands as he spoke, gesturing at the mosaics as he looked out over the congregation. Sometimes he would go up to the images and make the sign of the cross.

"There are those among us who have been influenced by the heathens who surround us who damn our icons and allege we are idolaters." The old clergyman had years of experience and would raise and lower his voice for points of emphasis, but was always stern, as he was now. "The heathen Turks who surround us damn our holy icons and the image of Christ. And this is where we are different from them. They venerate this Mohamet, whom they've never seen, never known and whom they can't even imagine. Their god is powerless—their god is misshapen and weak of heart."

Those in the congregation murmured their agreement as he spoke and laughed derisively at mention of Muhammad.

"But our Lord Jesus Christ preached his ministry among us, spoke with us, walked with us and wept with us. The Father sacrificed his Son become man for the sake of humanity.

"He was sacrificed for the sins of all mankind. Blasphemous Jewish executioners tortured him so that we would not see. He suffered so to save us from suffering.

"And people saw him and portrayed his form. These icons represent the descent of God to earth and His presence among man. The icons show that the Son of God was man, flesh and blood. Jesus as the divine human Son of God.

"Lord, preserve us from the blindness of the heathens."

"Amen," the congregation relied in unison.

"Lord, drive off the blasphemers and heathens."

"Amen."

"Lord, bless great Rome."

"As You are our shepherd, do not let us stray from the right path."

"Amen."

A monk among the congregation in the colossal church looked on the patriarch, perturbed and suspicious. Gennadios Scholarios gently leaned on his staff—he wasn't pleased with this type of speech that roiled the congregation. His disagreements with Giorgios Mammas only increased with these words of disgust. His rancor grew more apparent on his face as the patriarch spoke.

"We must be united with all Christendom against the Mohametans," the patriarch continued. "We must reconcile with the Latins for the glory of the Lord."

Scholarios had long been opposed to the unification of the Latin and Greek churches. He was adamant that it was unacceptable to compromise faith for political expediency. People should be sincere in their belief, free from influence, he thought. The grumbling in the church showed the extent to which the Greeks disliked the Latins for reasons great and many.

When the indignant monk looked at the emperor, he saw that Constantine was disturbed by these murmurings. He felt his guess wasn't mistaken that the patriarch had prepared this sermon with the emperor. Constantine had for years entered into all types of cooperation with the Latins in order to build an alliance against the Ottomans and other Turks, and he'd persuaded his clergy to direct the people to accept it. This was unacceptable for many who saw the Latins as enemies, like Scholarios, and they took the suggestion as worse than blasphemy.

Constantine took a deep breath as the patriarch came to the main point of his sermon.

A deacon brought out a baby born not but two days ago. He stopped in front of the silver basin in front of the patriarch.

"Every person is born in sin," the patriarch said. "And so this infant was born a sinner. But the Lord Jesus Christ sacrificed himself for this child's soul."

Constantine smiled at the man standing next to him—the baby's father, Don Francisco de Toledo. He was a leading patrician in the city and one of three men who never left Constantine's side. The baptism this day was specially prepared in his honor. His family was spread across Europe, and all the notable people in the city were in attendance for this special ceremony, along with representatives from Venice, Genoa, Hungary and many other kingdoms.

The patriarch submerged the baby into the baptismal font and held it back up three times as he performed the ritual. "The servant of God, Theon, is baptized in the name of the Father, Amen. And of the Son, Amen. And of the Holy Spirit, Amen."

"Amen," the congregation responded.

"For the love of God, he's going to kill the small thing," Marco Barbaro de' Piero from the Knights Hospitaller of Rhodes, one of the guests at the back, whispered in derision to the man beside him as the patriarch went through the stages of the baptism.

He gripped the hilt of the priceless sword at his waist as he did whenever he bristled at something. The large, red cross on his tunic made it clear he was a Knight of Saint John.

"Why doesn't he just drop the water on his forehead, for Christ's sake?"

The knight had expected the baptism to resemble the ceremony of his own Latin Rite.

"This is the Greek tradition, Sir," his squire said, stifling his laughter.

The patriarch competed the rest of the sacrament and sang, "You are washed clean, in the Name of the Father, and of the Son, and of the Holy Spirit. Amen," and handed the baby back to the deacon.

"He'd cleanse the whole world of sin if he dunked the poor thing one more time," the knight said with a snide smile between his mustache and goatee. His grumbling was barely heard, though.

Don Francisco breathed a deep sigh. The newborn of another patrician had died before being baptized, and so damned to eternal hellfire. The soul of Don Francisco's son, though, would remain forever Christian.

Constantine was moved as he looked on the infant. None of his wives had been able to give him a child, and now he didn't have a wife to be able to even expect a child. He'd been waiting excitedly for weeks for the news his trusted confidant Giorgios Sphrantzes would bring. Even though it had only been a few years since he had ascended to the throne of Rome, he felt those around him expected him to produce an heir, and the pressure was stifling. But he had a faithful servant in Sphrantzes.

The incense in the suspended censers continued to burn throughout the ceremony. The prayer of blessing and the smoke from the incense slowly rose up to the large dome of the Hagia Sophia.

The scent of the incense came to Megaduke Loukas Notaras—another of Constantine's men who was always at his side—and he fell into thought. He looked up at the Seraphim to the upper right. The highest of the angels in Christianity, the colossal wings of the two Seraphim covered the corners to the right and left of the great church. Known for falling to the influence of smells, Notaras looked as if he could see the angels flapping their wings and he felt the yellow, green and red of the ceiling falling into each other.

Notaras caught Gannadios Scholarios' eye from afar as his eyes wandered and he gave him a silent greeting. Notaras opposed the Latin Right like Scholarios and always favored the monk over the patriarch. As with many other issues, Constantine was unfortunately on the opposing side from Notaras. The emperor, however, wouldn't drive Notaras from his side only for this, and instead made use of his differing views.

Patriarch Giorgios took the olive oil and anointed the child with signs of the cross on his forehead, chest, back, feet, ears and mouth. The choir sang a Psalm and the patriarch continued with the rest of the ceremony.

Once it had ended, Constantine and his men exited the church behind the palace guards opening the way through the throngs of people.

They were off to the Hippodrome. A quarter of Constantinople had already filled the stands in the square for the chariot races that were soon to begin—the first to be held for decades.

31

A child was running as the greed flag in his hand fluttered in the wind. He didn't slow down a step as he plunged into the river of people all heading to the same place, wiggling and tearing through the crowd.

The towering men he passed had green, red, blue or white on their shoulders showing their allegiance to the racing clubs. The soldiers at the Hippodrome struggled to maintain order as the factions in the pulsing crowd broke out in fights. The child got to the entrance of the long racetrack. The din got louder as he rubbed past the bellies of the men around him.

He ran up the stairs in the open area past the gates and stared out from the stands at the thousands of people around the Hippodrome. It was the first time in his life he would see the chariot races. Even though the Hippodrome maintained little of its grandeur of centuries past, enough had been preserved to hold races. The walls had collapsed in places and parts of the stands were little more than ruins. It had fallen to disuse and decay after crusaders had sacked the city two hundred years before, but Constantine hadn't abandoned this powerful tool to keep the people under control in the empire's most difficult of times. More so, there was good reason for today's races.

The Walled Obelisk, Serpentine Column and Obelisk of Theodosius stood in a row down the center of the square. Between them, workers were busy making the final preparations to the seven bronze dolphins used for counting the laps.

The boy didn't understand why the roaring in the stands came to an abrupt halt. He turned his head to where everyone was looking and saw the emperor and his entourage taking their seats.

There was Theophilos Palaiologos to Constantine's right, Don Francisco de Toledo to his left and then Megaduke Loukas Notaras, all amid the prominent members of the Palaiologos dynasty.

Theophilos was sometimes known as the Greek for his pride in his people.

"What a glorious day for horseraces," he said as he smelled the air.

The emperor and his entourage were seated in the royal stands raised above the rest of the people and free from the disorder below.

"A terrific opportunity to celebrate the death of Sultan Murad."

"It certainly is, Theophilos," Demetrios Kantakouzenos said. "Murad was a thorn in our side. Our hands were tied, but that boy sultan will be a puppet in our hands."

"I still can't reckon how they survived Orhan's men, but it doesn't matter. Maybe it's better this way. A boy of nineteen," Theophilos scoffed.

"What damage did you see from Murad?" Notaras objected. "I always thought him to be a wise ruler who didn't harm us"

"But Murad wouldn't have sat so quietly if our allies hadn't checked him in Varna and Kosovo," Theophilos said.

"Absolutely," Kantakouzenos said, "And he strived to encircle the city since the day he took the throne, but Hunyadi Janos and the Karamanids never gave him respite."

"Thanks to us," Theophilos said with a laugh.

Constantine's eyes were on the racetrack as the charioteers passed by one by one and saluted him. He waved his hand for his entourage to be quiet.

Four competitors started to pass by in a row. Guards prodded them with their spears to force the—all slaves—to their knees in front of the emperor.

"We who are about to die salute you, Great Basileus," a soldier charioteer yelled.

Constantine quite liked this.

"It's clear who the emperor's man is," Theophilos said. "No one else has a chance."

Each chariot was teamed with four horses with one man behind in the narrow carriage. Reins ran from horse to horse, back around the charioteer's waist and then from his hands back to the horses.

A boy in the stands across from the emperor couldn't make sense of it and asked his father why the reins went around the charioteer's waist.

"It keeps them from falling from their hands throughout the race," he explained.

"And what if one of the horses falls?"

"Well, then the charioteer falls with it," the boy's father said with a smile. "That's the excitement of being a charioteer, after all."

They boy looked carefully at the chariots. The sharp spikes protruding from the wheel hubs caught his eye.

"Is the emperor with the Greens still?" Theophilos said at the other side of the stands.

"You know the Greens are selected from my most trusted palace guards, Theophilos. I would say no one else could win this race."

"Though I've heard the Reds have found a wonderful slave for a charioteer this time. The man's Jewish and grew up in the stables in Italy."

"The Jews don't succeed in anything but thieving," Constantine said with a grin.

Four gates suddenly swung open with the sound of the trumpeters and the race was underway.

The pain in Yehuda's back from the reins wrapped around him

grew as they dug in. He had dozens of wounds from being lashed with a whip and they needed much more time to heal. But with lashings every day, his shredded back could never heal. The reins dug in deeper and made his open wounds bleed even more, and the ones that had begun to heal felt as though they were being rubbed with salt.

Now, though, the last thing Yehuda could think about was his bleeding back. He lashed the reins against the horses again from the carriage. The charioteer from the Greens trailing him saw and whipped his horses on passed him. The cracking of whips and galloping hooves echoed throughout the stands.

"So, what is the Emperor thinking about to handle the new Ottoman sultan?" Notaras asked.

"He'll ruin our levity with all this seriousness," Theolphilos spat.

"Isn't it clear what we will do, dear Loukas," Constantine said, looking over at Notaras. "First we'll test the waters and try his patience. And, of course, we'll continue with Orhan's ransom."

"Why didn't we install Orhan right away? Didn't we have word he'd died?" Don Francisco said.

"They kept it hidden for days," Constantine said. "The Turks are very sneaky. Still, though, we got news from the pasha, but the young sultan acted faster than we'd expected."

Sphrantzes pointed to the entrance to the stands. "Speak and so he comes."

Orhan entered the Hippodrome accompanied by his knights and took his place among the patricians. His turban and caftan set him apart from everyone else.

Theophilos laughed. "Speak of the Devil is more like it."

"Look, look! The Greens is starting to overtake him!" a man yelled as he jumped to his feet.

The horses were at a full gallop and sending up clouds of dust behind them, nearly blocking out the race from the view of the hundreds of screaming supporters of the different factions.

As a slave taken from Italy, Yehuda was just desperately trying to stay alive. He didn't know, though, if he'd stay alive whether he won or not.

He'd heard more than enough of the torture he'd get if he didn't come in first. But then if he won, it means he would have beaten the emperor's favorite Reds—which was just another more indirect path to death. The more he thought about this impasse, it wasn't the pain in his back or the flying dust or the possibility of dying under the horses' hooves that distressed him, but the ridiculousness of it all.

Constantine wanted his own men to win, but the races were expected to be fair. On the other side, too, was the slave trader who held Yehuda's head with the dream of his slave winning him gold. Afterward, he wouldn't care one way or another if Yehuda died. Yehuda thought about the family he left behind in Italy and wondered if they were still alive.

"You said he's a boy, but he's nineteen, Your Highness," Notaras said. "And what's more, we shouldn't forget his wildness when he had the throne years before."

"The emperor here is forty-six, Loukas," Kantakouzenos said. "The new sultan isn't a boy compared to the Basileus, he's more like the baby we blessed today."

"I'm with Demetrios on this," Constantine said. "I respectfully disagree with your not taking our rival lightly, Loukas, but you're worried over nothing. Now, if you would, let me enjoy the race."

Notaras didn't say another word. He figured the emperor's sycophants had prevented him from thinking straight. He, however, was very curious about what kind of man Mehmed had become.

Yehuda saw the third of the seven dolphins next to the Obelisk of Theodosius have their heads lowered—there were four laps left. Then the Blue chariot sped past him and pulled alongside the Green. The Green charioteer swept his horses in front to block the Blue and, like Yehuda, instead of slowing down to let the Green pass, hung on the reins with more voracity. Yehuda was thinking the man was making a huge mistake as the Blue chariot stayed firmly between the wall and the emperor's man. All of a sudden, one of the Blue's wheels burst into pieces as it scraped against the wall. The charioteer was thrown to the ground and, with the reins wrapped around his waist, was dragged along the course only to be crushed under the hooves of the horses galloping over him from behind. Guards quickly came and collected the charioteer's bloodied and pulverized body and pulled it to the side as the chariots sped on their way. The driverless horses slowed a little farther down the track and were taken away.

When the fifth dolphin dipped, Yehuda was wrestling with whether he should try to win or not. The family he'd left behind in Italy nearly a year ago was going through his mind. He was the only one of three brothers Christian slave traders had bought. The trader who had bought him reckoned he could pique the interest of the wealthy in Constantinople since Yehuda had been a stable boy. Even though the races had waned with the ruin of the Hippodrome, the trader struck gold selling Yehuda to a Constantinopolitan patrician. Yehuda initially resisted racing, but couldn't withstand the whip unleashed on his back in the stables.

"I can't tell if the Red is trying to win or trying to lose," Notaras said.

"He must be afraid of the emperor—you know what happened last time," Kantekouzenos whispered in his ear.

"You're worried for nothing," Don Francisco said. "It looks like the White will win, not the Green or Red. Look at the man's ambition."

The White charioteer jerked the reins as he sped around the Serpentine Column, sending the chariot teetering to its side. He shook off the impact and regained his balance only for the coming horses to knock him back over. He was dragged by the reins for a stretch before he somersaulted to save himself and ended up sitting on the track shaken.

Now only Yehuda and the emperor's man remained with their horses nose to nose. Yehuda feared the wrath of his master when the Green pulled ahead, and that of the emperor when he gained the lead. Sweat was flying from his forehead and pouring cold down his back, making his wounds burn all the more. He had one lap left to make up his mind what he would do. Everyone in the stands was on their feet—half of them shouting for Green and the other half for Red. Constantine rose to his feet and leaned forward against the wall over the stands.

Yehuda's mind was set. He knew how far the emperor's rancor could go. He'd heard of how Constantine had tortured previous competitors in the vaults below the Golden Gate. He'd been born into a hopeless world, into the wrong religion and he and his loved ones—his mother, father, brothers and sister—had all suffered torment and persecution their entire lives. And whereas he was relieved to be delivered from the hands of the Latins, now he was a plaything for his Constantinopolitan master. He grew weary of overthinking as thoughts of torture and the whip passed through his mind.

He twisted the reins around his arms, whipped them against his horses one last time and finished an entire length in front of his rival. He crossed the finish line and drove his horses to the wall below the emperor. He panicked as his still-speeding horses ran straight for the wall. They stopped just short, sending the chariot smashing into the wall.

The crowd fell into a rapt silence.

The attendants looked at Yehuda lying on the track after he'd been dragged for yards and announced the results, "He's died! Green wins!"

The crowd erupted in shouts.

"Long live the emperor!"

"Incredible!"

"I figured that Jew would bungle it," Constantine said as he left the stands.

32

A young man was panting for breath.

He wiped the sweat from his brow and looked out over the long, straight crowd. He remembered what a dangerous undertaking this was when he saw the enormous regiment of soldiers in procession from the Friday Mosque to the palace.

Hundreds of palace dignitaries would go to the mosque for Friday prayers whenever a sultan ascended to the throne. The prince had taken the sword and strapped it to his waist, becoming the sultan and bringing the stately ceremony to a close. Now the procession was heading back to the palace.

The young man looked at the note he was holding one more time. He lifted his head and watched the slowly moving procession in the valley before him as he planned what he needed to do. The Royal Regiment had set up a wall of hundreds of janissaries with locked arms on both sides of the road to make way for the procession—impassable to the people scrambling for a closer look. They stretched for hundreds of yards, curving with the road and striking the image of a fallen rainbow. The individual men came into view as the young man drew closer and it became apparent from where he'd have to approach the crowd.

He recognized the group of a hundred conscripts at the very front with their tall, red, conical hats. Their robes were bluish, grey and sometimes red with upright collars and were tucked into their belts to keep them from flying about. Their red shalvar came to their knees with a brighter crimson ribbon wrapped below. The young man took special note of the swords hanging at their sides.

He could tell the man on horseback amid the procession behind the conscripts was the commander of the city's forces from the fan crest of his janissary headpiece. He reckoned the fifty janissaries walking in pairs in front of the commander in his long, blue, fur-lined jerkin hanging over a brown robe were in charge of maintaining order in the city. They were quite the sight in their navy and dark, bluish grey robes, the bands of golden embroidery around their janissary hats and their ivory staffs.

He guessed the mounted man in the middle of the group wearing a janissary hat, gold armbands and with a long spear in his hand was the rear-guard chief. The twenty pairs of soldiers on horseback behind him in the short, leather robes of the sergeants and plumes of grey rising from their hats left no doubt that they were the rear-guard water bearers. Their horses were draped with caparisons in dark colors that matched their shirts.

The young man knew the sultan was getting closer when he saw a banner emblazoned with a Zulfiqar blade and he started to shake with fear. He counted thirty men with lion pelts hanging from their shoulders, plumed hats, sandy robes and yellow boots walking side by side behind the janissary holding a three-pronged banner. He had begun to sweat as he counted them all and his eyes were on the janissaries' shining, metal armbands and the wide swords hanging from their waists.

He got a little closer and a strong wind began to howl in his ears. There was a group of men on horseback wearing green turbans and caftans who he reckoned were emirs, sayids or sheikhs. A brute *azad* was at their head, leading them in the cry of *Hu Allah* in a deep voice as they pounded their chests. If there was anyone in the crowd still not impressed by the spectacle, this was sure to bring them over.

A little behind the sheikhs was a camel carrying a dark-grey litter with a red door and green bands from where the Quran was being read. He knew when he saw this that the sultan had gotten very close.

He felt a burning in his chest when he saw another regiment with a banner of crescents followed by janissaries with crests of egret feathers and red quivers. He stood for a moment, petrified in place, and took a deep breath.

He gulped, convincing himself it wasn't yet time, and blinked his fogging eyes as he tried to compose himself.

Thinking that the viziers had come once he saw golden yellow shields on the horses, he started to try to make out who was whom. He reckoned the middle-aged man between the men with quilted turbans, each with a white plume, must be Zaganos Pasha. There were dozens of men with double-edged axes, thick blades and maces wearing red-crowned turbans and sky-blue robes before and behind him.

His heart started racing when he realized it was Grand Vizier Chandarli Halil Pasha—the bearded man sitting atop his horse with an air of dignity with three plumes rising from his quilted turban who was quite older than the rest. He was wearing a white fur caftan dappled in black, lined with light brown and undyed cloth that hung down over his horse. The young man made a special effort not to catch his eye.

Thirty janissaries with the sultan's hunting dogs but no swords then came—the kennel keepers. One of the dogs snarled and seized the foot of a man who had stuck it out between the janissaries in his excitement. His friends pulled him back and he was relieved to see that it was only his sandal that was missing and not his foot. None of them could hold back their laughter. The handler holding the dog's leash had known the man wasn't a threat and was just an overzealous commoner. He'd pulled the dog back, figuring the man had gotten enough of a warning—these dogs could take down a mountain bear, after all.

The dogs were far from the young man's mind, though, as he'd seen something that required much more attention. He thought the hounds were the least of his worries as they passed when he saw the sultan's page followed by six janissaries with golden embroidered headpieces each holding a crimson banner.

The lefty *solaks* with red, metal fixtures and black and white feather plumes in their hats, colorfully embroidered robes over florid shirts and, more importantly, daggers at their waists always walked immediately in front of the sultan with the pages. Following behind the horses of the head page and head *solak* were thirty archers marching in twos, their bows over their left shoulder and their quivers over their right, in golden belts and with fanned plumes. They took their name from their training to shoot on horseback while turned behind using their left hand.

He immediately recognized the sultan astride his horse from his long, thin face, light beard, aquiline nose and sharp, piercing eyes.

"Is that the sultan?" one of the men around said.

"Maybe it's not him—he's got a turban of an ulama. He must be someone else."

"Maybe we missed him. He was probably one of them with the quilted turbans who went by before."

"Or maybe he still hasn't come by."

The young man knew he wasn't mistaken. The sultan preferred the turban of the *ulema* as a sign of his love of science and esteem for scholars. He disliked the taller, more ostentatious turbans sultans usually wore.

The young man saw sheikhs, more viziers and a great many of what he reckoned were only the best janissaries all around the sultan.

He figured it would make more sense to approach from behind than to elbow his way against the flow.

The crowd all broke out in ebullience with chants of *long live the sultan.* The commotion drew the attention of all the janissaries and pages.

The young man struggled to push through the crowd as he headed farther behind the regiment. He found a good spot and stopped behind one of the janissaries forming the barrier. It was time.

He muttered *bismillah* and squeezed his right hand into a fist. Then he brought it to his shoulder and in a second, smashed his elbow straight into the back of the neck of the janissary in front of him, more powerful than any weapon. The janissary would've sworn a boulder had fallen on him if he weren't out cold.

The young man breached the wall of janissaries and threw himself forward into the middle of the procession. Two janissaries realized their fellow soldiers were falling and started looking for the man who had already been lost in the crowd stretching out before them. With the noise from the crowd, though, they had difficulty communicating with the other soldiers.

The young man tried to maintain his course, focused on the six plumes rising above the procession. He had turned into a reaper of life and tried to set his attention on the pages, janissaries and dog handlers. A janissary spotted him and knew right away that something was wrong. He drew his sword, but the young man grabbed another janissary's shoulders and spun him around as a shield and the blade came down on the janissary's shoulder.

All the janissaries were wielding their swords as if they were on a battlefield and were looking over the crowd, but there was no sight of the intruder.

A mounted sergeant a little in front of the regiment caught sight of the young man sneaking through the procession and threw his spear straight at his back. Even in the tumult, the young man heard the whistling of the spear as it flew at him and he quickly snatched the golden shield hanging from a horse and spun around. The spear hit the shield and glanced off, leaving a deep gouge.

The young man knew he was close to his target when he spied the quilted turban with a red crown. He quickened his pace and reached his right hand out for the sultan when he got to the black Arabian horse.

Then out of nowhere he felt a burning in his heart, and before he knew what had happened he saw an arrow sticking out of his chest, one from his outstretched hand and another from his forehead. A *solak* a little further ahead in the procession had sensed something in his vigilance and turned around. Seeing the hand reaching for the sultan, he had let loose three arrows in only two seconds. The first struck the young man's heart, the second his outstretched hand and the third was a direct hit to the man's forehead.

It flashed through the young man's mind that when a lefty takes aim, one's chances are nil.

Sultan Mehmed stopped his horse when he saw the man riddled with arrows lying on the ground. The entire procession stopped with him. Halil Pasha had already come to the sultan's side and ordered the janissaries to lift the man from the ground.

Mehmed dismounted a lifted his hand to the coming janissaries to signal them to stop. He looked at the man's face again. It was Burhan—his closest childhood friend with whom he'd grown up for years and whom he'd personally charged with being a spy in the heart of Constantinople.

He leaned over and saw a piece of paper in the young man's bloodied hand. He opened the man's fingers, took the paper and read it carefully. It was written in *Ruq'ah* script and he read it to the bewildered, curious and anxious looks of the *solaks,* viziers and Hilal Pasha.

Mehmed realized as he read the note that Solak Burhan, his friend from when he was a prince in Manisa, one of his best janissaries and spies who'd never revealed his identity in Constantinople, fitting in everywhere, hadn't died for nothing.

He mounted his horse, put the note in his pocket and ordered everyone back to their places.

The news Burhan brought was strictly for the sultan's eyes only.

33

Beyazit had spent hours in the Art Institute of Chicago's library and had finally been able to put Alberti Balbi's notes in order. The travelogue had no dates, which made it all the more difficult. He tried to put the pages in order by checking the events against the notes in his own file. He wasn't sure if some of the pages were in the right place, there were disconnects in places, but at least now they were in chronological order.

He started reading from the beginning.

The sea voyage was stormy. The sky turned a leaden grey and the sea jet-black a day out from Venice along the Dalmatian coast. We were buffeted by waves the whole time on the Adriatic. We certainly would've ended up on the sea floor had the ship not been under the command of a Venetian captain and if the crewmen weren't also Venetian sea hands.

The captain looked up and laughed when I came to him and asked if we should be worried. He said he'd rather be at the helm in this kind of weather than walking on dry land. It seems I've forgotten that many Venetians think this way. It's true, a ship might be safer at port, but ships are made for the sea, not to be anchored at port.

It's much easier to write about all this than to actually do it. At one point, I saw a crewman grab a sail rope in the confusion on deck and the power of the quickly unfurling sail ripped his hand from his wrist. His screams were more terrifying to me and his fellow deckhands than the storm. The men wrapped up the poor sailor's arm and brought him below to the animal hold. The captain spoke like a merchant and didn't say anything other than harm comes to those with no use.

I now realize I don't enjoy sea voyages as much as I used to. It's as if I feel myself more a stranger than one who's spent his life on ships. I can even say that it got to me and I got seasick. I'm comfortable in my cabin specially set aside for envoys, although I haven't left it for a while so nobody sees my paled face.

I also wasn't quite comfortable in my cabin. I felt I was riding an angry horse as the galley bucked up and down over the waves. At times I took out the *portolan* chart I have in my bag, spread it over my tiny table and looked to see where we were, tried to find the closest ports and how much further we had to go.

The white crescents on red and green flags I saw along the western coasts of Asia Minor from the Aegean are the most explicit sign I was heading to the lands of the Turks. According to the *portolani* from a hundred years ago, these crescents cover a great expanse. One shouldn't blame the Venetian and Genoese statesmen for the resentment of the Turks, and if they keep moving at their present pace, they'll be able to spread out over the east of Europe, all of Asia Minor and even as far as the north of Africa.

Fortunately, our voyage over the sea came to an end at a Hungarian port. We were going to make the rest of the journey over land. It would take much longer, but it was the most secure route in that weather. Envoys from the principalities along the way joined us, enlarging the convoy, and that's how we were to arrive in Edirne. We were all glad our time at sea had ended, but it was as if our troubles had just begun. We had to pay bribes at every border of Hungary, Serbia and Wallachia. Some said our money was no good and set their eyes on our goods. We were wary of Serb bandits and so tried to keep on our way without stopping, but the road was already narrow and not much more than a path in places, and we completely lost it. There we were instinctively finding our way through the forests and mountains like men wandering in the dark.

What made the Roman Empire so venerable was its great number of roads and their reliability. Now, though, where roses were once scattered beneath the hooves of the Caesar's horse has been overtaken by thorns and swamps. They say these roads would have completely disappeared if the crusader armies hadn't continually set out against the Mohametans.

We relaxed a bit when we got to Vidin along the Serbian, Wallachian and Bulgarian border. From here on out we were entering the dominion of the Turk and the roads and buildings along the way were significantly better tended. The dusty, muddy and vague paths gave way to newly stone-paved roads.

We arrived in Sophia as evening was falling and decided to stay in a large inn—what the Turks call a caravanserai. It's here in this caravanserai where I'm writing at these late hours of night. It's a large, rectangular building built like a frame. There's a large, open area in the middle to tie up and fodder the horses with rooms and a kitchen surrounding it. The rest of the place is a large hall where everyone eats together. I even saw a nest set in the walls for pigeons. They turn no one away, Christian, Jew or poor. I was amazed to hear that a room and food are given for three days to whoever comes. I thought about our captain and what he said about how harm comes to those with no use.

The word caravanserai comes from the caravans of travelers who stay there and the Turks' word for palace. This place is obviously no palace, but it certainly gives the feeling of a palace to those who've traveled for days, been shaken from side to side on a horse from morning to night and been rattled in carriages.

The food they provide is good and hearty. The only thing I recognized, though, was a gigantic honeycomb placed in front of me.

There's a reddish wheat they call *bulgur pilavi* and a hot soup called *tarhana.* First, they gave us the soup and then we ate the bulgur. I liked the piping hot bread more than anything. The big loaf was brown on the outside and firm, and the inside was a lovely wheaten color and pillow soft. Hot steam rose from it as we broke it open. It was delightful dipping it in the honey. And before I forget, they drink a sour milk they call *ayran.* They claim it drives off thirst and fatigue. I didn't like it. The icy spring water they brought in ceramic jugs was much better.

Everyone washed their hands after they ate, just as they'd done beforehand. Their hands, fingers and especially fingernails are exceptionally clean. I suppose there's something behind this hand washing. One pours water from a thin, long-necked ewer they call an *ibrik* while another reaches out washes his hands, rubbing away with a fragrant soap. I don't know why they haven't thought of putting the water in a bowl as we do and washing their hands in that. Maybe it's just the custom of the caravanserai.

I met a German man named Johannes Gutenberg once while eating. He was an interesting man, always haggling with the Mohametan merchants. He had recognized me as Christian from my clothing and came up to me. Like me, he also spoke Latin quite well and we could understand each other. I asked him why he was haggling with the Mohametan Arab. He said he needed more paper now than anybody had ever needed before. Then he explained at length how animal hide parchment is very expensive and that the Mohametans are the best at producing paper quickly and cheaply.

I asked him what he was going to do with that much paper. He said it was a big secret, but that it would be useless without paper. That's why he was traveling from land to land to negotiate with merchants. He said with a grin that he reckoned if he pushed the one from Hispania a bit more, he'd tell him how he could get the finest pulp to make the best quality paper. Then he said there would be hundreds if not thousands of Bibles. After the last scandal he'd experienced, the man was justified in trying to make this many Bibles. He'd polished metal plates to shine like mirrors and sold them to hundreds of people, telling them they could hold them up to saints' tombs and behold their spirits. The pilgrims started to get suspicious after a while, but by then, he'd already disappeared.

Now, though, I'm thinking of Cristina as I prepare for bed in the room given me. I don't need any of Gutenberg's mirrors to know that her spirit is with me. Evenings like this were one of the times we would make love. There was no time in our beautiful house in Venice when we hadn't made love. I miss her smell and her graceful sawn neck so much. All of that's in the past and now every moment is painful.

It's as if my past disappears with the sun the farther east I travel. Today in Sophia, leaving behind my world and entering Mohametan lands, made me feel thoroughly better. It seems as though it's not only Venice, the Adriatic and Latin Christendom I'm leaving behind, but my entire life. I felt like quite a stranger in this land this morning at the caravanserai when the men all stared for quite some time at my pointed cap, jacket—which they thought to be tight—breeches and hose and everything else. The more I think about my experiences, though, the more I'm convinced I'm a stranger in my own land.

I understand it better now—belonging isn't attached to land, but within a person. It's not the land, colors and buildings that change, but the person. I gawked at the merchant Turks with their turbans in many of the ports up and down Italy, but I'll be the one gawked at tomorrow when we get to Edirne. The sorrow of what I've experienced overshadows my excitement and curiosity for tomorrow. If what Bernardo says is true, then Mehmed is much more than the boy everyone wants to believe he is.

34

Happy that he was finally nearing Edirne, Alberti Balbi of Venice grew worried when the clattering carriage came to a stop.

After the days-long journey, the last thing he imagined was getting robbed by the infamous Serb and Croat bandits while only half a day away from Edirne. He reckoned that only getting robbed would be the best thing that could happen if he were to believe the stories he'd heard. Nightmarish tales of savagery here about the voivode of Walachia, Vlad Dracula, and his men had spread far and wide.

He had thought he would be a prime target for bandits when he set out in this desolate land due to his pointed, velvet cap, navy blue *cioppa,* breeches and hose that went passed his knees.

He popped his head outside the carriage to see what was happening and saw two men on horseback in clothing he'd never encountered before talking with the guide from his retinue. The harnesses on the soldiers' horses were of the type of beauty he'd only ever seen on the mounts of kings. He took careful note with his trained eye of an experienced envoy of the swords hanging from their red belts, their embroidered hats and daggers.

The guide came back to the carriage with two teams of horses after he'd finished speaking with the men just as Balbi was rising from his seat.

"These are janissaries, Sir," the guide told him. "They'll accompany us to Edirne. The Ottomans do this for all coming emissaries."

The two janissaries, Iskender and Hasan, looked solemnly back at Balbi with his head sticking out of the carriage.

The French envoy across from Balbi kept on with his conversation with Duke Francesco Sforza of Milan. "It's hard to believe—are these janissaries the ones we've heard so much about? They look so odd. And they only sent two men. Prince Vlad's men go around by the dozen—what could two janissaries do?

Sforza laughed. "You underestimate the janissaries. I've seen what these men can do many times with my own eyes. Prince Vlad's boors wouldn't be able to do anything to them—they've been raised as warriors since they were young boys. Even if they spot our convoy, they'll turn tail as soon as they see their strange hats. It's been a hundred years that the Serbs and Croats here have known that the sultan's janissaries aren't to be trifled with."

"They say the janissaries only come to heel in the presence of a powerful sultan, though. How do you think they'll look on this boy sultan of theirs, Francesco?"

"You're right. Sultan Murad had a strong position. It was he who gave the orders. They say the janissaries trembled even in the presence of his horse. Then again, the sultanate is very important to the Turks and the Ottomans' reign has been ongoing for a hundred fifty years unbroken. One can't question a sultan's power."

"Be that as it may, I heard the janissaries rebelled when Murad ceded power to his son years ago and wanted to see him back on the throne. What do you say to that?"

"That's true, but Murad was alive then. They have no choice other than Mehmed now."

"Does he not have any brothers?"

"He has brothers, but elder one died young. Murad loved his oldest son, Alaeddin, and always wanted him to be sultan, but the boy suddenly died one night. Some say it was an assassination. His death destroyed Murad. He'd neglected Mehmed up until then, but after Alaeddin's death, he sent the best tutors in the realm to train the young prince."

"Seems like there was some secret power working to install Mehmed on the throne, doesn't it? And what about Constantinople's man Orhan Chelebi?"

"He's Murad's cousin. New Rome has used him as a pawn for decades. He was always reminded about Orhan whenever he was away from the throne. The Ottomans paid thousands of gold ducats because of him while Murad was sultan."

Sforza heard a commotion and looked outside. "The peasants are greeting the janissaries. That means we're in the Turk's land."

Balbi patted his belly. "I'm starving."

"Well, that's the good part, Alberti. They have wonderful food. They cook meat very well. They also have this type of fermented milk they call yogurt, and they mix it with cool water."

"Ah yes, ayran. I had that at the caravanserai, although I didn't much care for it."

"You better not say that to them—they'd be destroyed. Pay particular attention to the order tomorrow. The Ottomans hold it very highly. It's torturous to go before the sultan alone. The story goes back to Murad's grandfather, Murad I. When he'd defeated the crusaders in Kosovo, a Serb named Milos—if I'm not mistaken—entered the sultan's tent on the battlefield with the pretext of kissing the sultan's hand. He took a dagger hidden in his boot and run the sultan through the heart right there as soon as he entered. Ever since then, no one can see the sultan so easily. Being in audience with the sultan is also torturous. Although they say tomorrow will be a general audience, so it'll be a bit more comfortable."

Balbi, Sforza and the other emissaries in carriage at the back of the delegation looked out curiously when they arrived in Edirne at noon escorted by janissaries to every side.

It was the first time Alberti Balbi had seen the Ottoman capital and he was amazed at the crowds. His brother Bernardo had said as much, but Alberti hadn't expected such a vibrant scene. There were the stands of a bazaar set up on both sides of a long street. He looked carefully at a Turkish woman in a violet caftan with embroidered flowers, white shalvar, yellow boots and a white scarf over her head who was shopping at the bazaar. A woman next to her was wearing a fur-lined, brocade jacket with sleeves that went to her elbows over a raspberry-colored caftan, white robe and red shalvar all cinched at her waist with a leather belt. The pinkish red pomegranates on the stand in front of her made Balbi's mouth water. He stuck his head so far out of the carriage that a peasant porting a tray full of peaches and strawberries on top of his turban would've run into it had the mounted janissary there not warned the porter.

He saw tiny bowls of something white in a tiny basket carried by a man wearing a light blue shirt, red shalvar and yellow boots with a quilted turban on his head, and asked Sforza what they were.

"I have no idea, but we can find out," he said with a grin.

He called out for the guide to stop the carriage and told him to ask the janissaries what the man was selling.

The peddler was surprised at what he'd run across and the janissary's strong voice, and immediately held out a bowl for the envoy.

Balbi picked up one of the little white pieces and put it in his mouth. His face immediately puckered and he spat it out.

Iskender, Hasan, the other envoys and the peddler all laughed.

"They call it *chökelek*—some sort of dried curd. It should be eaten in *börek,* though, not uncooked like this," Sforza said through his laughter.

"What's *börek,* then?" Balbi said, exasperated.

"You'll see at the reception at the ceremony tomorrow," Sforza said, still laughing.

The envoys called for the carriage to move on, but it didn't and so they asked the guide what the problem was.

"The janissary says you have to pay the peddler for the *chökelek.*"

Balbi took a small gold coin from his purse and tossed it to the peddler.

"That must be the difference between these janissaries and the knights back home," he said. "Our knights take what they please from the peasants. Here they make you pay even a simple peddler." *Maybe it's true equity,* he thought.

The convoy continued on its way through the bazaar.

Balbi looked out at all the bustling people—an Armenian woman wearing a peacock-blue caftan and a robe of dark plum purple, a Greek girl with a short caftan covered with stripes of green embroidery over a pink skirt, a Jewish woman with green boots and a scarlet shawl wrapped over her head and a Jewish man in a dark-grey caftan and wearing a violet cap. There were stands with gleaming silks; fabrics with floral designs; leather and boots in brown, black and burgundy; curls of gossamer and sheets that looked as if they'd been woven under the rays of the sun. Balbi had already started to think of what he had to get to take back with him.

He turned from the crowds in the streets around them back to the buildings as the carriage made its way through the city. He saw mosques with stone walls and tall, pointed minarets, tall towers of churches topped with crosses rising up and what he recognized as synagogues from their construction. Then he heard a noise—*Allahu Akbar*—coming from some of the buildings and looked at Sforza quizzically.

"That's what they call the *adhan,*" Sforza said. "It's the voice that calls the Mohametans to prayer."

The convoy came to a stop after a short while and, when the envoys looked out, they saw they were in front of a large mosque.

"The janissaries say they have to do their prayers," the guide said as he came to the carriage.

"How long will it last?" Sforza asked.

"Not too long. It'll be over by the time you get out and have a drink from the fountain."

Balbi hesitated before he stepped out.

Having grown accustomed to it all over years of service, Sforza and his men stepped right out and went to the hexagonal fountain.

Balbi found some courage from the others and stepped out into the courtyard festooned with variegated flowers. He walked up to the fountain and splashed his face with water. The cool water brought him some relief, then he drank his fill. The others in the retinue dismounted and did the same. Balbi liked the clean water, the stone-paved ground and the lack of mud in the garden. He watched with interest as the janissaries removed their boots and washed their faces. He looked at the inscription above the large, carved, wooden doors of the mosque, but couldn't read it. The Arabic letters had a strange form.

"It says Shah Melek," one of the janissaries said as he walked past into the mosque.

"It's the mosque's name," Sforza said with a smile. "It's what you were trying to read on the wall."

The janissaries all entered the mosque and took their place at the very back.

"Do you see that?" Balbi said to Sforza. "They're all the way in the back. These grand janissaries are at the very back."

"Don't be so loud," Sforza said. "I doubt the last thing these Mohametans want to see when they pray is a Christian blathering in the door to their mosque."

Everyone in the stream of men coming to the mosque all looked over the envoys out the corner of their eyes before entering.

Balbi admired the deep blue tiles covering the walls of the interior from where he stood in the doorway.

35

Janissaries met us an hour or two outside of Edirne. I've since learned many things about these soldiers who I've heard so much about. Their name comes from the Turks' words *yeni* and *cheri*, which together mean new soldier. They're called new because Mehmed's great-great-grandfather Murad I created the corps, so they're relatively new in the nearly two hundred years the Turks and Ottomans have been here.

They're not only renowned in the Italian states, but throughout all Europe to the west. I had thought I was prepared for these men known for their indomitability, but it's not so easy to distinguish the tales from fact in what people say and claim about them. Still, they managed to surprise me at first sight. It was how they looked more than anything else. How can I describe their incredible clothing?

What first struck me were their strange hats that hang from the back of their heads and down to their backs. I learned later that they have many names. They generally call this odd hat a *börk*. It rises over half a foot from their foreheads before it lays back and falls between their shoulders. Maybe I should relate the tale as strange as this headpiece's appearance so it makes more sense.

Some say the soldiers have their roots in the type of Mohametanism of the Bektashi order. The Bektashis' split is somewhat like the

Latin and Greek schism, but as far as I can tell, there's much fewer differences—only in the details of interpretations. Those who are Bektashis and those who aren't sit together and eat and drink and get along with each other just fine. Christians from the Latin and Greek rites, though, are always at each other's throats.

They say the founder of the order, Haji Bektash Veli, came and greeted the soldiers when Murad I created the corps and laid his hand on the sergeant on the head. Supposedly when the sergeant bowed in respect, the ample sleeve of Haji Bektash Veli's robe draped over his head. From then on to today they say the janissaries' tall hats have been fashioned in the likeness of Haji Bektash Veli's sleeve. It's as if Haji Bektash Veli's hand has remained on their heads, in a sense. Others, though, say this is nonsense, because the janissaries could never be as madly loyal to any other leader, even if spiritual, than they are to the sultan. The last part of Haji Bektash Veli's name has the meaning of what we would call a saint. Haji Bektash is only one of dozens of saints whose legends have passed from one language to another, and they come up with and add new details about them as they please. Just like Christians and Jews become holy when they go on pilgrimage to Jerusalem, so do the Mohametans when they make the pilgrimage to Mecca, and afterward they earn the right to be called haji.

The janissary hats have a pocket at the forehead. They put showy plumes and crests in them for ceremonies, but normally keep their spoons there, so they call it a spoon rack. This is where one of the most interesting features of the janissaries is hidden. The Mohametans cherish food as sacred and call it all a blessing, believing whatever they eat and drink has come from God. And so the janissaries, holding their food as sacred and a blessing from God, have made a crown out of the utensil used to spoon up their main dish of soup. With the same logic, they call the leader of every company a *chorbajibashi*, or head soup distributor, and they call the corps a hearth in the sense of a kitchen with ashes strewn about. When they have faith in a sultan, they are madly devoted to him, but sometimes it takes a little time and sometimes it never happens. They don't serve a sultan they don't care for and are obstinate to him. These are the times when they gather around the large food pot in the middle of the barracks, which they turn over and get to scheming. This is what the Turks call tipping the pot—a formal rebellion.

As a matter of fact, the janissaries revolted when Mehmed was years younger and his father left the throne to him when he was still alive. They set flames to the city, tipping the pot, so to say, and shouting that they wanted Sultan Murad back. It went so far that Murad took back the throne due to the danger of the crusaders who were quickly advancing from the west.

Now, though, the janissaries look to be completely loyal to Mehmed—after all, the sultan is their purpose in life.

A Hungarian envoy here related an amusing story about the janissaries' devotion. As a gesture, the sultan had given him a janissary for his service, who then escorted the envoy everywhere he went and waited at his door at the ready for orders. One morning, the envoy wanted a hot loaf of bread and told the janissary waiting at the door to go to the bakery and get one. The janissary had taken an oath to follow whatever order he got and he turned over all the bakeries in the city, but since it was still quite early, none of them were open and the bread hadn't yet been baked.

The janissary woke up one of the bakers, personally lit the oven, kneaded the dough and brought the ten big, piping hot loaves that came from it back loaded on his horse to the Hungarian envoy's door. The janissary explained what had happened as he held out the sack of bread when the envoy asked. The envoy told him it wouldn't have been a problem if he had just explained the situation. The janissary gave him a strange look and told him he didn't understand. He said that if he would've been unable to fulfill his request, he would've held the bakers responsible and the sack of loaves would've been a sack of their heads instead.

This story might seem like an exaggeration to those unfamiliar with this land, but it's not so hard to believe considering the many other similar stories around. Firstly, maintaining order in the city is the janissaries' responsibility. It's true that their essential duty is service to the sultan and they serve the sultan in battle—however a large portion of them look after the order of the capital. The janissaries are also a nightmare for tradesman and merchants here due to their fine sense of justice and uncompromising demeanor. A janissary could very well levy a heavy punishment on a baker who opens his shop late.

Second, these men aren't only the terrors of war that we know them as—they're skilled in many areas outside the arts of war. Their education starts when they're still young and goes on for years while they engage in may jobs such as woodcutting, leather working, gardening, cooking, tailoring, baking and many other trades, and they are all a master of one of them. The Turks also love the arts such as calligraphy—or the art of letters, as they call it—marbling, miniatures and poetry, and are likewise well trained in them. They even need to get a certificate to practice them, called an *ijazet,* from their masters.

Let me return to their dress for now, though. The robe they call a *dolama* is their main piece of clothing when they're not in battle. It covers the whole body and so is such named, meaning a wrap. It's narrow from the waist up and is tight over the chest and back. It also has many small buttons down to the waist. I've seen them in many colors, but generally they're dark blue, a greyish dark blue, red or sandy. I wouldn't know what to call some of the other hues. All of these colors have a meaning, according to the Hungarian envoy. They can't wear whatever color they please, either. For instance, if the wonderful boots they wear are yellow, it means the janissary is of a higher rank than one with red boots.

One of the Ottoman's most striking features for me, though, is the sensitivity they show to order. It is finely defined what everyone in the palace and the army is responsible for and their position in relation to everyone else. Considering the irregulars and mercenaries we see coming from far and yon for plunder and booty, one doesn't need a soothsayer to figure out the secret to the Turk's successes.

From the waist down, the skirt of their *dolama* robe widens. This part has no buttons and so is left open. I've also seen some janissaries tuck the ends up into their belts so they don't get in the way as they walk.

They wear a loose type of trousers, or shalvar, that go to the knee and are generally red. They have a winding from the knee down of either broadcloth, felt or coarse wool that goes down into their boots. These are either yellow or red, as I said before, and either come to the ankle or over the calf depending on the season. They carry ivory batons, have engraved daggers in their belts, swords hanging from their left and some have quivers slung over their shoulders. These well-built soldiers give off a rather imposing air with this regalia.

I see quite well now why our knights have struggled so against them.

36

"Hurry up, don't be lazy," Wolfman Dogan snarled.

He was walking about a palace courtyard holding a tasseled baton and raining orders down on the pages as they ran to and fro. His belly was slightly too large for his rich caftan to hold in and it was hanging out. His face was more charmless and beastly today than usual.

"Pull the throne over another foot!" he said as he slapped a page across the head so sharply it knocked his pointed hat off.

The courtyard was being prepared for the ceremony with the envoys the next day. There were hundreds of palace attendants throughout the courtyard, going over everything and where the representatives from which realms would stand.

Two janissaries at the side of the courtyard were standing upright and watching the commotion from afar.

"He's giving the poor wretches hell again," Iskender said.

"He's come over with the new sultan on the throne," Hasan said. "It's like the weight of some great authority's been lifted and he's eased up. The orders he's giving the janissaries are impossible to fulfill, too."

"I remember our first years at the hearth, though. He was fair."

"No doubt the position breaks a man. It's like he forgot he was once slapped upside the head now when he does it."

"You think he looks down on the sultan?"

"This is how I see it—him and Halil Pasha are thick as thieves. I'd say he regards the pasha higher. He's got an air about him that he believes he can make anything he wants be done."

"That's what I was wondering, Hasan. I'm getting more confused as it goes. We serve the sultan and he's the janissary agha who represents him. And so what if he revolts against the sultan? Who do we follow?"

Wolfman rapped his baton across another page's face.

Hasan looked over at Iskender. "You're asking me things I don't know the answer to, brother. We'll just wait together and see what happens."

"Maybe there's a point to what the sultan does," said Iskender.

"I've heard the sultan doesn't actually hold the agha in much favor, but he must reckon there'd be trouble if he got rid of him for someone else where we are now."

Two janissaries were pulling away a third with a bloodied mouth and eyes.

"Oh, he's going to get it now," Hasan said.

"Who's that?" Iskender asked.

"He's a boy from the fifty-sixth regiment. I heard he ran off last week. He's got a sweetheart in a one of the nearby villages and he snuck out to see her. He asked the agha for permission to leave the corps. He wouldn't ever let that happen, would he? The boy up and went one night and they've been looking for him for a few days."

Iskender's heart burned and sweat started to drip down his forehead from under his hat.

"What're they going to do to him?"

"That's up to the agha. Maybe beat him to death or string him up in chains. God knows."

They set their attention to what was happening farther off.

The two large janissaries threw the boy down at Wolfman's feet.

"Stand up, you cur!" he howled.

The janissary tried to do as he was told and struggled to straighten himself. His head was covered with mud and his face was bloody with a gash through one of his brows. It was clear the janissaries who went after him had beaten him soundly.

Wolfman looked the boy in the face in disgust. "Look at yourself. I can't tell if you're a janissary or a bandit!"

The janissary silently hung his head. He was in no state to speak anyway and his strength was spent.

"You know what comes to those like you? Two hundred lashes with the cane!"

"They'll kill the boy!" Hasan whispered to Iskender.

A hundred or even fifty lashes from the cane were unbearably painful, and two hundred was a death warrant, signed and sealed.

"We'll fix your feet so you won't be able to run off any time soon!" Wolfman went on.

Iskender couldn't stand it any longer. He'd already run out to confront the agha before Hasan had a chance to grab him or pull him back.

"Agha, it doesn't fall to me and I'm speaking without permission, but this boy's taken his beating. Forgive him this once. It seems like he's smartened up already."

The pages and janissaries in the courtyard were dumbfounded at the sight of Iskender up against Wolfman. They all dropped what they were doing and waited in suspense to see how the agha would react.

Wolfman knew Iskender very well as one of the corps' best soldiers, a master archer and swordsman, and someone who quickly fulfilled whatever he set to. He never liked Iskender's rebelliousness, though. It crossed his mind to slap him across the face and knock him down, but doing that to such a well-loved soldier would make him an object of contempt in the corps and it would weaken the power of his word. He decided to respond less harshly.

"Alright then," he said. "You'll take his two hundred lashings and it'll be done with!"

Iskender bowed his head in silence. It would be his head if he were to take another step, which is what the agha was hoping for.

"Now both of you get out of my sight!" Wolfman said, seeing he wouldn't get a reaction from Iskender.

The young janissary looked up at Iskender as they left through the door to the courtyard. "Why'd you do it?"

Iskender smiled. "You're not the only one with a sweetheart."

Iskender had a limp for the next two weeks from the beating he took.

37

Chandarli Halil Pasha was agitated as Mehmed sat on his throne. As was the custom, a walnut throne with mother of pearl inlay was placed in the palace courtyard. The sultan had started the ceremony in the crowded garden as he sat.

Halil Pasha had continued to act in congruence with the Ottomans—as a grand vizier like his grandfather, his grandfather and his father before him—but he was now pulsating with the thought that his time in his position would ultimately come to an end. Like his forefathers, he had served the Ottoman sultan for years. The Chandarli family had always played an important role in power. Now, though, he couldn't stop thinking of what happened years ago as he looked on the new sultan sitting just off from him.

When Sultan Murad relinquished the throne for prayer and peace to his still only twelve-year-old son, the prince's first order of business was to turn his father's policy of peace on its head and declared war on many lands, Constantinople first and foremost. He had signaled this policy of aggression his first day in power. There was also no shortage of viziers who supported him in this. If not for Sultan Murad's promise, Halil Pasha thought for days that this prince would have removed him from his position. However, with the centuries of experience of the Chandarli family's time as grand vizier, he cleverly used his influence to whip up discontent in the janissaries and forced the more experienced Murad to reassume the throne as the janissaries neared rebellion at a time when crusader armies were building up in Varna. Even though Mehmed was initially opposed to it, Halil Pasha convinced him it was necessary for the survival of the sultanate. In the end, Mehmed sent a message to his father that said, "If I am sultan, then I command you go to Varna at the head of your army. If you are sultan, then it is imperative you return."

The prince's anger with the grand vizier was evident when he had returned to Manisa so many years before. Halil Pasha felt his days were numbered the more he thought about what had happened as if it were only the day before. This grand vizier who had spent his entire life in service to the House of Osman, however, still faithfully sent word to Mehmed that his father had passed and delivered him to the throne without any unrest appearing in the capital.

"Why is my grand vizier standing so far away?" Sultan Mehmed said as he looked directly at Halil Pasha.

Zaganos Pasha and Shihabeddin Pasha, who had both never left Mehmed's side since his days in Manisa, looked over angry and curious at Halil Pasha waiting a little to the side. They were no less taken aback by this surprise from Mehmed as the grand vizier.

Halil Pasha, with his years of experience, immediately walked to the sultan's left. He thought maybe Mehmed had changed after all these years, that he'd matured and drawn closer to his own views, and so he felt relieved.

Perhaps Mehmed also understood the mistakes he had made as a child and grasped over the years that it was best for the Ottomans to follow a policy of defense.

"Start calling in the delegations," Mehmed said to Halil Pasha. "We have much work to do still."

The Venetians were the first to appear before the sultan. Girolamo Minotto, the Venetian *bailo* of Constantinople, wearing a pointed black cap, approached the sultan with his retinue. In constant competition with the Genoese for trade over the sea, the Venetians were happy they had been given priority. Having ruled the seas for years, the Venetians held trade above all else and conducted their trade ethically in all circumstances, domestic and foreign. They had always maintained a close relationship with the Ottomans, as they had with other lands, so long as business was thriving.

Minotto rose from bowing to Mehmed and said, "On behalf of the Most Serene Republic of Venetian and its people, I respectfully salute the great sultan."

The palace interpreter—the *reis ül-küttab*—stepped back, knowing there was nothing for him to do, when he heard the Venetian *bailo* address Mehmed in Ottoman. Since he had spent most of his time in Constantinople, Minotto was quite close with the Ottomans, and new very well how important cultural familiarity was in business relations.

He motioned to his retinue, which then presented the sultan with various gifts from Italy.

"Please accept these gifts even though they are not worthy of you. Our olives and oil are famous far and wide. It is my hope you will enjoy them."

With a look from Halil Pasha, two of the pageboys waiting at the ready by the sultan stepped forward and accepted the casks and crates.

"Our main gift for you, however, is this beautiful ivory," Minetto said. Two of his envoys stepped forward and present the sultan with the gleaming ivory in a velvet-lined box. Mehmed looked with interest over the warriors, archers and winged lions carved on it. He knew quite well that as much as these gifts were a necessity of foreign diplomacy, they were also a show of force from the powers presenting them.

Bailo Minotto waited to speak again until after the pageboys left with the gifts. "The Venetians lived in peace in your realm under the reign of your father Sultan Murad and conducted our trade without hindrance."

Sultan Mehmed continued to listen without speaking as he looked on Minotto.

"Our desire from the great sultan is for the continuation of our privilege on the seas and for the consolidation of friendship between our lands."

Zaganos Pasha looked over at the Venetian again when he heard the man mention friendship. He had always been wary of these crafty people who worshipped money and mixed friendship with self-interest. Especially in moments such as this, he reckoned the words from the Venetians should be given the utmost attention and that their interests were buried somewhere beneath this mention of rapport.

"The Venetians and Ottomans are close friends," Mehmed said. "All of your privileges from the time of my father Sultan Murad will continue."

Minotto breathed a deep sigh of relief.

The *bailo* had figured the new sultan wouldn't want to irritate the Venetians, but he also hadn't expected such affinity in this open environment. The smile on his face, however, turned into a look of astonishment with what the sultan asked next.

"I heard a plague has broken out in Italy. Is this correct?"

"There's nothing Your Highness the Sultan doesn't know. It is true. It hasn't spread much yet, though. It is in one small town and is under control."

"If there's anything my sultanate can do for you, you need only say the word."

Minotto couldn't tell if he should be pleased or worried with this offer.

"I and Venice are indeed grateful to you," he said, deciding it would be better to withdraw.

Minotto twisted his thin mustache as he passed by the Genoese delegation, proud of the interest the sultan had shown him.

The leader of the Genoese colony neighboring Constantinople on the northeastern shore of the Golden Horn—the *podestà* of Galata, Angelo Giovanni Lomellino —came before the sultan with a cross-shaped sword. "It is a great honor for me and all of Galata to present the new sultan with a sword of the renowned Genoese knights."

The pageboys only became aware of the sword's weight when they took it into their hands. Those who weren't knights couldn't easily wield it, and even with two people holding it, they still almost plunged it into a conscript's shoulder. The hilt was as thick as a man's fist and long enough for it to be held with two hands, one above the other. The elaborate metalwork on the guard and the crucifix on the pommel attracted their attention.

"The Genoese have always been happy to be a neighbor of the Ottomans ever since the time of Osman Bey. We wish for our amiable relations to grow also in the time of this great sultan. We also hope to show that Genoese galleys are every bit as convenient as those of Venice."

"They say Genoese knights are fighting against the English in France. What is your benefit in this war, Podestà?" Mehmed asked.

Lomellino tried to collect himself, not knowing how to respond to this unexpected query. "Is it not a knight's duty to always be at war, Your Majesty? They prefer to fight for glory on whichever side they deem justified."

Mehmed wanted to ask the man whether it is also glorious to wage war for profit, but he didn't want to offend his guest in his own land or go too far. Instead, he said, "Our neighborly relations will continue to improve as they had been in the time of my father."

The envoy from the Holy Roman Empire, Francesco Filelfo, presented the sultan with a silver chamfron and crinet. The armor was for a warhorse's face with overlapping plates for flexibility over the neck. The ears and holes for the eyes and nostrils made it look like the head and neck of a living horse with the plates of the crinet adorned with fire-breathing dragons.

Filelfo spoke to the *reis ül-küttab* in his own language. "I am happy to convey the greetings of King Frederick III to the young Sultan Mehmed."

Shihabettin Pasha knew quite well the mention of Mehmed's youth needed to be parsed. Frederick ruled over one of the largest empires in Europe and must have been thinking of removing this inexperienced sultan in his own way from the wars in Varna and Kosovo. The arrogance in what this envoy said was the most important heralder of it.

Filelfo, an Italian by birth, was a master of foreign diplomacy and word games. It was uncertain whether he meant that to be a sultan at such a young age suited Mehmed as it does so few and therefore was a great thing, or if he meant Mehmed was young and inexperienced. Either way, that was the point, and he had hit the mark.

Mehmed listened to the translation from the *reis ül-küttab* and replied, "Tell your aged king that I received his greeting," which put slight smiles on the faces of Shihabettin Pasha and the other palace dignitaries.

Filelfo couldn't quite tell, either, what the sultan meant by calling the king aged—Mehmed could have either meant experienced and wise or a doddering old man.

"Your king's entry into the French's battles with the English seem to greatly exhaust his empire. Who do you think has won the war, Filelfo?"

"Even though it has taken many years, of course, our king and army have attained victory," Filelfo said in an attempt to defend his king.

"It is obvious these more than a century-long wars have brought no prosperity to either kingdom. I hope your people find peace as soon as possible," Mehmed said.

The delegation from the Despot of Serbia Durad Brankovic then came before the Mehmed and first expressed their deep sorrow over the death of Sultan Murad. Brankovic's daughter Mara had been wed to Murad and so the Serbs felt a certain closeness to him. The old sultan had always preferred to expand his territory peacefully rather than by the sword. By wedding Mara, he ensured that one of the Ottoman's nemeses remained submissive for years.

Now, though, the Serbs announced that the despot's daughter must return to her own land.

"Mara Valide is free to act as she wishes," Mehmed said. "We will ask her ourselves and permit whatever it is she desires."

With their first request finding no resistance, the head of the Serbian delegation continued. "Sultan Murad had sent fifteen thousand gold ducats every year to the despot for the sultana. He would now like this price to be increased to twenty thousand on account of her bereavement."

Zaganos Pasha forced himself to not draw his dagger from his belt and cut the Serbian envoy's throat then and there. It seemed the Serbs had returned to their old, aggressive tactics.

"I understand this desire of your despot," Mehmed said to astonished looks from his viziers. "The sultana's mourning is great. Twenty thousand gold ducats will be sent off along with her."

Lazarus was next as the envoy from Austria and Hungary. Those in the garden had their interest greatly piqued with what he said, having found much courage after the indulgence shown to the Serbian delegation.

"Duke of Austria and King of Hungary and Croatia Ladislaus V's governor-regent Hunyadi Janos, along with celebrating your rise to the throne, believes to have suffered heavy losses in the time of Sultan Murad."

Hunyadi Jano was known across Europe for his violence and ambition, and no one had expected him to dispatch an envoy to the Ottomans. Rather than benevolence, it was more a sign of malice.

Sultan Mehmed's orders from that morning had been clear—all delegations would be shown in with no exception.

Ishak Bey had personally fought against Lazarus in Varna, and was now glaring angrily into the envoy's eyes.

Lazarus went on with his requests, wary to avoid Ishak Bey's penetrating glare. "If thirty-five thousand gold ducats are not paid every year, Governor-Regent Hunyadi Janos will not hesitate to gather crusaders and take action against the Ottomans."

The *reis ül-küttab* translated the demand and Mehmed responded calmly, "It seems Janos has not learned a sufficient lesson from his experience with his crusades."

"Misfortunes befell us in Varna and Kosovo," Lazarus said, "but the Hungarians' horizon is well open now. The future for our friends is bright, but it dark for our enemies."

"Tell Janos I will send the thirty-five thousand gold ducats. The Ottomans wish for the peace agreements from the time of my father to continue."

Shihabettin Pasha and Zaganos Pasha were by now well aware things were going entirely wrong.

"I will gladly convey your answer to the governor-regent," Lazarus said.

Giorgios Sphrantzes had been listening carefully to the new sultan and his answers since the beginning of the ceremony. He knew his turn had come when the pageboys approached him as the Hungarian envoy was speaking. The portly man with short legs wearing a long, rich tunic and with bare feet in sandals struck the figure of a typical Constantinopolitan diplomat. It was now time for the last and most important delegation of the day.

He and his eight-man retinue came before the sultan and bowed in salutation.

"The great Constantine XI Palaiologos, emperor of the sacred Roman Empire, has commanded me to congratulate you on your ascension to power." He caught the eye of Halil Pasha and then looked back at the sultan. "Your father Sultan Murad had always been seen as a friend to New Rome due to his policies of justice, tolerance, good sense and peace. With thanks to this understanding, our two realms have increased trade with each other and, as it was in the time of your great-grandfather Sultan Bayezid, neither of us have experienced any unpleasantries."

Zaganos Pasha noticed right away that the renowned diplomat's carefully crafted speech had something much weightier behind it.

Sphrantzes had been following the sultan since he had begun speaking, and now that he'd reached the end of is greeting, he took courage from Mehmed's behavior and announced his requests. "Emperor Constantine, the defender and preserver of our Lord Jesus Christ, wants the fifty thousand gold ducats paid yearly for the expenses of Orhan Chelebi—the famous Ottoman prince under his patronage—which were paid in the time of your father Sultan Murad, to be raised to one hundred thousand, as his empire is under a considerable burden concerning the accommodation of Orhan, his men, horses, equipment and many other expenditures."

Zaganos Pasha had reckoned Orhan would be used as leverage today as he had been continuously for decades.

"Emperor Constantine and the sacred Empire of Rome wish to renew the peace between our realms and thus foster even greater relations between us."

All of the palace dignitaries and other delegations in the garden were curiously waiting for the sultan's response as much as Sphrantzes and his retinue.

Mehmed remained silent for a moment and then looked at Sphrantzes. Constantine's confidant was disturbed by his sharp gaze and looked again over at Halil Pasha.

"Tell this to your emperor," Mehmed finally said. "The new sultan will observe the treaties of his father so long as he does, as well, and the annual amount mentioned will be delivered."

A smile spread across Sphrantzes' face. The emperor and *kom-*

nenos had been right—the Ottomans were going to be a thing of the past with this young man in the seat of power.

Mehmed rose from his throne after he had finished speaking and turned his back. Sphrantzes was looking at Halil Pasha's eyes as the sultan disappeared through the palace's wide gate.

He saw that the satisfaction in the man's eyes was not much different than his own.

Filelfo smiled with great pleasure as he wrote a letter to inform King Frederick—

Sultan Mehmed is young, passive and inexperienced. He is out from his father's shadow and easily manipulated. We needn't worry any longer about the scourge of the Turk. The King can easily manage the domestic affairs and the troubles in the west.

The other envoys were also sitting down to write similar messages.

The days of the Grand Turk were over.

38

Mehmed received all of the envoys in a large, palace courtyard today. The courtyard is surrounded by a stone wall two-stories tall with corridors leading to the inside. The order of the group of janissaries and conscripts that lined the walls of the large, rectangular courtyard was quite magnificent.

The thrones of the Turk are quite different from our own. It isn't raised with stairs or any other contrivance leading up to it and sits at the same level as everyone standing. There is no vestige of a stage and the Turk sultan stands on the same ground as everybody else.

Our thrones are also taller, with higher backs and more richly decorated. Those of the Turk, though, are wide enough for two or three people to sit side by side.

The most interesting thing, however, it the absence of a crown. It its place, Mehmed wears an ordinary turban. I think it's a white cloth wrapped around a red cap. If the young man hadn't been sitting on a throne, I doubt I would have recognized him as the sultan. He also didn't have a queen next to him, as in the kingdoms of Europe. They say the sultan's wife is busy having a very large mosque built in the city. It's a custom of the Turks for the sultan's wives to be involved in benevolent works of charity. It is, however, incredibly difficult to see them out in the open.

Despite his young age, this is Mehmed's second time on the throne. Sultan Murad had years ago left the throne to his son and was through with the palace. According to what they say, he was a calm man with no liking of war and conflict. It is hard to believe that he went so far as to abdicate the throne while other kings spin sundry intrigues in order to take each other's place.

All of the envoys and diplomats in the courtyard were at least as excited as I was to see this young sultan. It was as though representatives had been sent from the four corners of the world. At the head were those from Italy—the Genoese, Anconetanis, Neapolitans and, of course, us Venetians. Later were the Serbs, Albanians, Austrians, Hungarians and Germans.

As if a test of the sultan's patience, each emissary unhesitatingly conveyed his desires and requests to Mehmed one after another.

What was astounding was Mehmed didn't oppose any of the demands. He renewed the treaties and proclaimed he would consider the ordinances to the benefit of his fiercest of enemies. Seeing the pleasure of the Hungarians, Austrians and Constantinopolitans was precious.

I, however, feel something different about Mehmed that no one else has seen. Like Janus, his true face is in contrast to the one we see. Maybe because I'm here, I reflect my own feelings onto him. As I carry on with the thought that the pain deep inside me will abate, it seems to grow increasingly more. I see Cristina everywhere I look. I appear as an emissary from without, but my outlook is that of a traveler.

39

I was finally accepted for an audience with Sultan Mehmed. After the general audience with all the envoys, the sultan was ready to see me. I knew word from the palace had come when two janissaries appeared at my door with the first light of morning. It was apparently decided the meeting would be held today. Informing me so suddenly must have been the result of some intense safety measures. Mehmed is under threat of assassination at any moment since there is another who could claim the right to the throne. They say Mehmed's brother Orhan has been hidden away for decades in Constantinople and that if he finds the opportunity, he will rise up as the true leader of the House of Osman. With the passing of Sultan Murad, and with him his experience, it looks to some to only be a matter of time before the new, young sultan disappears from the scene. This is the view of many of the emissaries here.

When I saw Mehmed for the first time, however, I knew immediately that he was much more than a child. The first meeting was much more troublesome than I thought it would be, though. The janissaries who came to retrieve me first took me to one of the famous hamams of the Turks and I was washed quite nicely. They informed me that I would wear new, clean clothes—as if my own clothing wasn't suitable—and that I would be given a caftan and shirt according to my measurements straight away. I found myself in a moment of absentmindedness and told them I could wear my own clothes. It was much wiser to accept one of these embroidered caftans, and at no cost at that, for reasons I'll explain a little later. The smell of roses wafted around me as I got dressed.

There were hundreds of janissaries of various ranks at the palace. As their clothing was different from each other's according to their duty and rank, the surroundings looked like a field of wildflowers. The most dashing of them were the sultan's close guards of *peyks* and *solaks*. There were many statesmen young and old, most of them emissaries, going to and fro in stately turbans. Despite all the bustle, however, it was unbelievably quiet with a regularity that puts one in a strange mood. The doorkeepers delivered me to the pageboys who then brought me to the janissaries. My excitement increased with every step. The silence grew even deeper as we neared the sultan's chamber. We stopped in front of a door after passing through a wide corridor with *solaks* to both sides. I felt sweat pour down my back from the excitement and sense of being out of place that I wouldn't have guessed, and in that moment, I felt my body heat up.

Two head doorkeepers stepped to my right and left, took me by both arms and we entered as the doors opened. Emissaries being shown in to an audience with the sultan in this way had begun with Murad I. After a great victory against the crusaders in Kosovo, a Serb entered Murad's tent on the pretext of kissing his hand, but instead cut the sultan down with the dagger he had secreted in. Another reason is that emissaries have fainted and ended up crumpled on the floor due to the magnificence of the Grand Turk. If I hadn't passed through that corridor today and had an audience with the sultan, I would reckon this second reason was no more than a fabrication from the Turks, who are, after all, quite fond of boasting.

Mehmed was seated on a divan no more than a foot tall, that back of which ran along the walls. On the ceiling of the chamber directly above Mehmed was an eight-pointed star composed of two, overlapping squares carved from wood. There were a few books beside him, along with a few viziers and Grand Vizier Halil Pasha.

Mehmed is indeed as young as they say—maybe eighteen, maybe nineteen, but certainly not yet twenty. The look on his face, however, is much deeper than a young man of his age would be able to affect. There is a simplicity and elegance to all the lines of his face. His eyes are neither as large as those of the Arabs nor as small as those of the Mongols. His lips are thin and well-shaped. His aquiline nose seems to be emblematic of a stark contrast to the experiences of this young sultan. He has a slight, but not sparse beard. He looks weak at first glance, but his body is sturdy, neither a beanpole nor a dwarf juniper.

He was wearing a red velvet caftan with embroidered tulips. I had never seen such velvet, even in Venice, which is famous for it. I'm going to look into whether it was Italian tailors or Turks who sewed it. The sleeves and front of his pistachio green shirt were exposed from beneath his sleeveless caftan, which was open at the front.

The man sitting to the sultan's left and who never left his side was the formerly Jewish vizier and physician Yakup Pasha—he must have changed his name from its original Ya'qov to be concordant with the name found in the Quran. They say Yakup has reached thirty, although he doesn't look much older than Mehmed. This physician is much praised in the palace. Vizier Zaganos Pasha was just behind him. He looked to be forty-five or fifty. To Mehmed's right, standing perfectly straight and the eldest in the room, was Grand Vizier Halil Pasha. His black beard was strong and his brows bushy and scowling. He is from the Chandarli family, which, although not as storied as the House of Osman, has throughout centuries held the position of grand vizier as he does today. His grandfather Chandarli Halil Pasha the Elder had been Murad I's grand vizier, as this Halil Pasha was to Murad II. His arms were folded with his hands stuck into the sleeves of his tan caftan lined with fur. I learned later that it is not appropriate to show one's hands unnecessarily in the presence of the sultan.

These caftans of the Turks and their other clothing in general look much ampler and more comfortable than our own. I was embarrassed in my tight jacket and shirt, feeling as though every inch of me was visible as I was surrounded by these men in caftans. Their clothing is more functional, as well. Our bunched-up sleeves and hanging cuffs are both more expensive and get dirty after three days, they tear and then are no longer wearable without mending. Their clothing appears to have been made for comfort and also lends them an imposing air.

I straight off presented Mehmed with a gift of a case three feet by one and a half feet of colored stones, metal and wood covered with our much-vaunted Venetian lacquer. Mehmed rose to his feet when my attendants brought it into the chamber. He inspected the colorful stones, glass and designs, and then turning to me with a smile on his face and said in Venetian, "You've gone to much bother."

With these words, standing opposite the Grand Turk, I felt more as though I was meeting with a friend of forty years in an audience with an emperor. These few words from Mehmed were somehow enough to drive away the timidity and tensions I felt in that chamber. At that moment, I saw this Ottoman sultan before me, whom we have been conditioned to see in a specific way through rituals, tradition, protocol and regulations, to be as enthusiastic, accessible and common as the young painters I have encountered in Saint Mark's Square.

I mentioned my brother Bernardo Balbi a short while later, took a velvet pouch from my pocket—my actual gift—and handed it to him. He took the medallion in his hand—one side had his likeness and the obverse face had three eagle heads, just as he had asked of my brother years before. He inspected both sides of the medallion, looked up at me and with a smile, said, "Not bad." Then I gave him the names of the most famous medallion makers and painters in Florence.

He spoke with me much longer than I had expected he would. We discussed Venice, the situation of the Church in Rome, the Turks trading in Italy, the Venetian traders in his realm and many other topics. He was surprised when I told him I had visited Taranto in the Kingdom of Naples before I had come here, and I told him of the prince. Mehmed's knowledge of geography and history is vast, and not only of Venice, but of all the Italian republics, kingdoms and duchies. He speaks fluent Venetian, for which he constantly mentions Bernardo.

He was pleased with our conversation and so invited me to stay in the part of the palace for guests. From the look on Halil Pasha's face, I understood that he was not of the same mind as the sultan when it came to this.

Before leaving, I asked Mehmed what the meaning was of the three eagles. I told him there's no doubt that two eagles represent Europe and Asia—maybe his two capitals, with Bursa in Asia Minor and Edirne in Europe, as the back sides of these medallions are generally used to symbolize the great territories an emperor has taken. I told him that I couldn't figure out the third one, though.

Mehmed turned to the gigantic map by Ptolemy covering the wall and in a staid voice said the third eagle is the center—the center between the Orient and the Occident.

40

Evrenoszade Ali Bey wiped the sweat from his brow in the darkness as he remembered the days of fifty years ago when the land was soaked with the blood of Muslims slaughtering Muslims.

No one knew at first how to describe this lame Mongol from the frosty Central Asian steppes who burned and plundered to bring the entire world under his power. With extraordinary speed, the man swept through and left devastation in his wake, his soldiers warming themselves with fires made with pages torn from books and sleeping in the madrasahs they had turned to ruin. He was a man of solid spirit unable to be cowed and who bowed to no one. They said his name was Temur—*Iron*—later called Temir and Tamerlane. The great Ottoman Sultan Bayezid lost the Chubuk plain to him just as he was about to put an end to New Rome. The lands with most beautiful fortress the sultan had built on the Anatolian shores were divided among his sons and the Anatolian beys. This lame Mongol opened the path for a fight between brothers that time has rarely encountered.

Süleyman declared his sovereignty in Edirne, Isa in Balak Hisar, Mehmed in Amasya, and Musa in Bursa. With his unmatched faith, Bayezid had named his sons after four great prophets—Solomon, Jesus, Muhammad and Moses—and now his sons had signed their names to war for bloody domination. On top of that, the Karamanids declared their realm in Konya, the Aydinids in the west and the House of Dulkadir in the east, in addition to a dozen others. The order of the region had been upended.

Everybody wanted to forget this time when thousands were put to slaughter, but it seemed Ali Bey was remembering those days anew for everyone. No matter how much Ali Bey questioned it, he was trying to believe the order he had received was the most correct—*kill them wherever you catch them.* He walked silently through the narrow corridor in the darkness of night. *They will never turn from the war to turn you from your faith*—the thoughts at war with each other in his head had thoroughly done him in. He felt he had aged fifty years when he had first gotten the order that morning and was struggling to reckon where he could conjure the vigor to live again—*sedition is more violent and more harmful than killing.*

Ali Bey came to the doors of Little Ahmed's room and looked around once more until he was satisfied no one else was there before he grabbed the knocker. The door opened without a sound and he walked toward the center of the room where there was a cradle with shimmering mother of pearl and in it a baby sound asleep. He knew this little baby had expressly been used so the Ottomans would share power. He also knew as well as the one who had given the order that following a sudden assassination of Sultan Mehmed, this baby would be brought to power. He looked on the innocent child with the thought continuously running through his head of the chain reaction this incident would instigate.

Mehmed's own brother Orhan, who was in Constantine's hands, would not recognize an infant as the Ottoman sultan and would declare himself sultan. The janissaries also would most likely want to see a man at their head rather than a baby, and would foment unceasing unrest in the capital. This incident would lead to the second interregnum and be the end of the Ottomans—in any case, it would put an end to their rule. Ibrahim II of Karaman was waiting for the uprising and would most certainly try to take all of central

Anatolia under his rule. Osman's dream would turn into a horrific nightmare.

Ali Bey thought of the blood that would flow for decades to come and the mission of righteousness that would be torn to shreds as he removed the white silk handkerchief from the right pocket of his caftan. He looked at the baby's face and thought of his mother—the daughter of the Isfendiyarid bey, whom he knew well. He couldn't rid his mind of how word of this would affect his poor mother who had already stopped eating and drinking due to her sadness from the loss of Sultan Murad. He tried to think as he neared the right side of the cradle of how the Sublime State being in turmoil would lead to the deaths of hundreds of soldiers, the poor families ruled over by a false and lawless power, and the hundreds of children whose fates would be cut short before they were even born.

He gently pressed the silk handkerchief over Little Ahmed's face with his left hand and thought about how much easier it would be to face off a five-hundred-man crusader army single handedly. For the first time in his life, this old warrior who had spent his life wielding a sword and shooting arrows on the battlefield in service to Sultan Murad, challenging the brutish Slavs and defying ax-swinging Hungarians in the squares of Varna and Kosovo, felt his eyes mist over.

The next morning, when Sultan Mehmed would order his decapitation, Ali Bey would voluntarily lay his head down beneath the hair-splitting sword of Malik the Executioner. Little Ahmed's corpse would be sent along with his father Sultan Murad's coffin to Bursa. Come morning, Mehmed would be the only sultan in the capital. Other than him, only Orhan would be able to assert a claim to the throne.

41

Passing by the people in the crowded bazaar, an eagle-nosed man with thin lips spoke to his companion with his hand inside his caftan, "Jafer, your drawing everyone's attention to us. There's nothing to worry about."

Jafer Agha had devoted his entire life to the man he was walking with now and perceived every passerby as a threat, instinctively bringing his hand to the dagger in his belt.

"You're right, Sir, but I'm having trouble telling who could be friend and who could be foe."

The mass of people around was enough to truly worry the man. There were farmers from the villages who had come to sell their fruits and vegetables, sherbet sellers with jugs on their backs and glasses in hand to quench people's thirst and confectioners selling chewy candies to mollify the children's boredom. Men and women were doing their weekly shopping, all of them coming to Edirne's gigantic bazaar and making two or three passes through to find the cheapest and finest quality goods. This scene was making Jafer Agha constantly question what the young man he'd been accompanying for an hour was up to.

They entered an open area at the entrance to the market where the city's booksellers had gathered. The young man stroked his tidy beard and curiously started looking over the books on the stands.

"Please, I can help if there's anything you're looking for," one of the booksellers said when he saw the young man approach.

"I'm looking for Ferdowsi's *Shahnameh.* Do you have it?"

"I have an old copy," the bookseller said as he turned around and rummaged through his shelves before he held out the book.

The young man first looked at the decorated cover of the book full of miniatures and then in turn at the horsemen battling on green slopes, the archers, the dead lying on the ground, the mystical clouds in the sky and the colors overflowing the frames of the pages as he leafed through the book.

They say Keyumars brought the custom of throne and crown, and was shah,
And this splendor, order and magnificence came when the sun was in Aries,
And shone with such brilliance that the world at once grew young—

He looked to the side and saw a woman in violet silk who had just recited the verse—he continued with the verse without thinking.

From him came all progress, new clothing and cooked food, before unknown,
He reigned over the all of the world for thirty years, a sun shining in goodness from his throne—

"So, are you a scribe, too?" the bookseller asked the young man from behind the stand.

The woman took manuscripts out of her cowhide bag and held them out for the bookseller, "I brought the last two copies, Akif Efendi."

"Thank you, Nilüfer Hanim," the bookseller said. He bent down and pulled out a thick book from under the stand for the woman. "This should amuse you for some time. I want ten copies—twenty *akche* each."

"Alright, Akif Efendi. I'll bring the first copy in two weeks."

The woman turned to the young man as she put the book in her bag, "I beg your pardon, I didn't mean to—the verse just came out of my mouth. One doesn't easily forget a line one's written a hundred times. I suppose I couldn't hold myself back when I saw you holding the *Sahnameh.* But how wonderful, you continued the verse straight away."

"Don't worry about it. On the contrary, it's livened me up. It means there are others who hold Keyumars' story in their memories," the young man said with a smile. "I'm no scribe, though. I'm just a student of literature on my own accord."

"So, you really love Ferdowsi a lot, do you?"

"Ferdowsi, Homer, Mir Ali-Shir Nava'i, Ahmedi—everything that explains rulers, kings, emperors and the ephemeral world."

The young man had no idea what to say when the woman asked him what he did for a living.

Jafer Agha cut in, "We're book merchants. We buy and sell books."

"Yeah, that's right," the young man said. "That's what we do. You must be a book copier."

"Yes, it's a practice I acquired at my grandfather's library," the woman said as she turned back to the bookseller.

"May God grant you prosperous business—good day, Akif Efendi," the young man said as he started to walk away. Then to the woman, "I heard the new sultan is looking for talented scribes. Apparently, he has books he wants copied. It pays well, too. I heard it's something like one hundred *akche* per copy." Jafer Agha was staring dumbstruck. "If you go to the palace sometime, tell Zaganos Pasha's men that a book merchant named Mehmed recommends you. They'll tell you what you need to know."

"What a coincidence that your name's Mehmed, too," the woman said.

"His Excellency's name is very common—nothing to be surprised about. It was nice to meet you."

"God bless you for telling me about it. Maybe I'll have the opportunity to see the new sultan, as well," Nilüfer said before taking her leave.

Jafer Agha's satchel was full of books when the left the booksellers.

When they were going back through the market on their way back, an old woman buying apples from a villager caught his attention. The village man had arranged the bright red, plump apples in the crates in front of him so they could be seen, but was giving the woman crushed and rotten ones from the backside, every so often mixing them with the ones at the front.

"Come on, my boy, give me the good one's already. You think I don't see? Why are you giving me the rotten ones?" the old woman said.

"I am, ma'am—what more do you want?" the villager said.

He filled the bag and gave it to the boy next to him to weigh. The boy bent over the crates to throw a couple more apples in to meet the weight the woman wanted.

The seller slapped the boy across the head. "It's full already, you pipsqueak! Why are filling it more?"

The old woman held out the money, but the young man stopped the seller from taking it, "Hold on there, sir. Why do you cheat in your trade?"

Jafer Agha put the satchel of books down and threw his hands up in frustration.

"What cheating, boy—and why are you butting in anyway!?" the man huffed.

"Don't you know your ill-gotten gains won't bring any good to your business? You display your quality goods to draw people in and then you force them to buy rotten apples. If it's rotten apples you're selling, then display those. And then you don't even weigh them properly!"

"I'll sell my own product however I want and it's no one else's business. Now beat it!"

Having lost his patience, Jafer Agha was about to jump forward and rip the man's tongue out, but the young man surreptitiously gave him and elbow and stopped him.

"Aren't there officials to inspect this? You think the officials from the great Sublime State won't find you and arrest you?" the young man said.

"But where are they, my boy?" the old woman said. "Sultan Murad kept them in line, but now they're emboldened since he passed. They say the new sultan is green and doesn't know about anything."

"He'll learn, ma'am, they'll learn, and everybody else, too. Everybody will soon see the new sultan is like none before him!"

"Quit your babbling, boy," the apple seller said. "We have the work and the power—and who do you think you are anyway!?

Jafer Agha was glowing red by now, but the young man stepped in front of him and gave him an order, "Don't hurt him too much."

With one slap across the face, Jafer Agha left the man's nose and mouth bleeding. He grabbed the man by the collar and pulled him back up from the ground. He lifted the man up so his feet dangled above the ground, slammed him against the door of a mosque behind him and whispered in his face, "His name is Mehmed—Sultan Mehmed. Remember that slap the next time your hand slips on the scale. I'm giving your name to the city's keeper of weights and you won't be able to sell anything at market for a year!" Then he let the man flop to the ground.

The man, now half-conscious, would still be grateful years later that he was able to survive the slap from the empire's top janissary who had hit him like a sack of bricks.

The old woman looked at Sultan Mehmed. "My boy, who are you?"

"I'm a Muslim who believes in God, what is Just and the Truth, ma'am," he said.

The two janissaries in charge of public order at the bazaar approached the tumult and immediately recognized Jafer Agha as a high-ranking janissary. They couldn't make anything of Mehmed in ordinary clothing, but as soon as they figured out what had happened, they immediately flanked Mehmed and took him through the crowd.

42

After looking through books for a long while, the sultan's physician Yakup Pasha looked over at Mehmed, who was sitting cross-legged on a divan as he looked over various maps.

"You've found some very nice ones again, my Sultan," he said. "I've never seen al-Razi's work on measles before. Ibn Sina mentions it quite a bit in *The Cannon of Medicine.*"

Zaganos Pasha was sitting next to Mehmed. "So you're into ibn Sina like all the Italians, are you, Yakup?

"I've only read eight works of his at the Sorbonne, Zaganos. Ibn Sina is a medical student's bread and water."

"There's a lot the booksellers don't have, Yakup," Mehmed said. "I can't find anything I'm looking for. I've been having difficulty finding the Greek myths or even coming across the Persian poems I've heard. There's no sign of any astronomical treatises. Everyone talks of the observatory in Samarkand, but all of these resources and all the best institutions should be here."

"You're right, my Sultan," Yakup Pasha said. "But this undertaking of yours to translate and copy books you've started will speed that up."

Mehmed stood up, walked to the window and looked out to the horizon.

"What I've dreamed of, though, is a whole new world, a whole new center. An empire with its center where the whole world meets from both east and west. A city like Mecca for the prophet, Baghdad for the Abbadids, Aleppo for Alexander the Great, Jerusalem for Saladin and Rome for Caesar. A city under God's order, in service to the Truth, where everyone lives happily, where all the sciences are raised to the highest level, equal to heaven itself."

Halil Pasha entered the room as Mehmed finished speaking. He bowed in greeting to the sultan—his face was distressed.

"Sultan, Ibrahim of Karaman has said he does not recognize your supreme sovereignty. He has sermons read for his own behalf in Konya, Akshehir and Beyshehir, and burns Ottoman edicts in front of the people. He says it is his word that is valid in those lands. The Aydin, Germiyan and Menteshe Lordships have taken courage from him and they're creating discord among the people along the Aegean coast."

Mehmed turned to Ishak Pasha, "What do you say, Ishak? Is it time we show him a little teeth?"

This was the signal the seasoned Anatolian beylerbey—the lord of lords—had been waiting weeks for.

"At your command, my Sultan"

"I'll deal personally with the Karamanids," Mehmed said. "We have much to do, but it seems we first have to get rid of this burden on our backs first."

Mehmed went to retire to his private chamber, but turned around at the door. "Zaganos Pasha, I almost forgot. There's a woman named Nilüfer—she's a good scribe. She will ask for you at the palace. Have her be given valuable manuscripts to copy. Pay her in advance, as well. Also, call for Mullah Lütfi and have him come to me."

"At your command, my Sultan."

43

Mehmed has started a large undertaking at the palace to reproduce books. Today, I met Mullah Lütfi, the head of the palace library and the one in charge of it all. The jolt I experienced, though, has overridden all these developments.

The sultan was going to give me a duty in this work, as well.

I dropped my notes all of a sudden as I was leaving my new room at the palace. All of the pages flew everywhere in the wide corridor. I was hurriedly trying to collect them all when a man the same age as me—thirty to thirty-five—with blonde hair, not often seen among the Turks, and blue eyes bent down and picked up one of my notes that had stuck to his foot. If it weren't for the turban he was wearing, his mustache reaching down to a goatee, as some Turks find fashionable, and, of course, his clothing, I would have sworn he was German. His straight nose and light skin gave him a more European appearance than one from the Orient. If he were to take of his robes, long shirt and colorful boots, and replace them with armor, he wouldn't look any different than a Christian knight.

He greeted me in the way Turks do when they see each other. I was surprised, as they generally don't give this greeting to those who aren't Mohametan. It was also clear as day from my clothing that I am Venetian.

I told the man that I am not a Mohametan.

He said God's greeting embraces everyone. He also recognized me as Christian and said, as far as he could tell, there's a book that binds us together, and since I am well versed in books, books bring us together.

I didn't understand much, but I was also happy he didn't look on me with disgust as some Turks do. Then again, a Mohametan greeting was the last thing I wanted.

Then, out of nowhere, he said if I'd like, let him get me a caftan. I was thoroughly confused.

The man spoke in riddles. He could tell from my face I was confused and said I fuss about my clothes.

Then I realized he had read the page he had picked up from underfoot. He hadn't looked long, but it had been enough.

I asked him if he knew Latin. He smiled and said he reckoned if he didn't, the sultan wouldn't have him in charge of a library packed with books in Latin.

Mullah Lütfi is an interesting man. Mullah is the title the Turks give to their scholars. He could be called a scientist or thinker. He was going to show me to the library and introduce me to the people I was going to work with. I saw first-hand with him how the work that happens throughout the day in the palace's vast library. On order from the sultan, scribes reproduce books of which there are only one copy, or very few, and those that aren't in Ottoman are translated. A dozen groups of translators work on many works in Arabic, Persian and Latin. There are also a few women among the scribes. They usually take the books home and later deliver the finished copies to the palace, where they also collect their payment. The palace pays very generously for this work, as well.

One of the women came in when I was in the library with the mullah. I couldn't believe my eyes—it was Cristina, but in the clothing of a Turk, coming straight toward me. I first thought I was seeing a mirage from the delirium I've been experiencing. She was wearing a crimson caftan lined in green and violet, a white blouse and brocade shalvar tucked into yellow boots. The contrast between the gleaming white scarf over her head and the jet-black cosmetics around her inky eyes was so beautiful that I couldn't take my eyes off her for quite some time. The cherry-red of her lips was even more eye catching than her crimson caftan. I pulled myself together as she got closer, this Turk who resembled Cristina so.

It was clear she had writing sets and books in the leather bag slung from her right shoulder down to her waist on the left. Mullah Lütfi introduced her to me as Nilüfer—the granddaughter of the old beylerbey of Rumelia Ragip Pasha. She is also a skilled calligrapher.

Then Mullah Lütfi said we'd be working together. I was taken aback.

We were to examine the history of Alexander the Great in renowned Persian poet Ferdowsi's *Shahnameh* and compare them with the histories of Alexander in Latin. Nilüfer was to add these differences between them as annotations in the copies of the *Shahnameh* she would make. I told Mullah Lütfi that I hadn't brought any of those books with me and my memory wouldn't suffice for the work. Then he gave me a look as if to say I shouldn't worry and hurried me over to a section of the library lined with books in Latin.

We had the first meeting with Nilüfer among the books. I told her she might have difficulty understanding my accent, but it would only be a matter of time before she got used to it. She listened to me intently, squinting her eyes as she tried to understand. It isn't just her features that resemble Cristina, but also her gestures, the tilt of her head and her gaze. I don't know if it would be better to liken her long, beautiful lashes to the janissaries' arrows or the curved scimitars of the Turks. What I do know is they pierced my being. Her interest also raised when I mentioned I have the chance to meet with her a few times. For now, though, I told her I was off to the Karamanids and wouldn't be at the palace.

Despite having come to the palace several times, she had never encountered the sultan, and it seemed she was a little irritated by it.

I told her we could meet again in a few days after I read the books to refresh my memory, and we decided to meet at Ragip Pasha's house. I will find out where it is from Mullah Lütfi.

I immediately took the books from the library, laid them in front of me and set to work sitting on a cushion. My legs got quite sore from sitting cross-legged while reading, as I had never done so for so long before—my lower back started to ache, too. I don't understand how these Turks can sit doubled over like this with no chairs. It was a nuisance I could tolerate, though, in order to meet with Nilüfer as soon as possible.

I believe now that people are created in the world in pairs.

44

Wolfman Dogan was seething with rage as he was being beating across the soles of his feet. It was unheard of for a janissary agha to be given a thrashing like this. Having devoted his entire life to service to the sultan, he in no way could stomach receiving corporal punishment ordered by the sultan himself.

"Don't give me that dirty look, you filthy dog!" Malik the Executioner growled. Having been dismissed from his duty, the agha's feet were being set into with a walnut cane as thick as an ax handle in a rapid succession of one hundred fifty strikes.

Malik had done the same to countless high-ranking officers of the army before stepping to Wolfman. The meting out of ordinary discipline in the janissary corps was still conducted by janissaries. Those who didn't abide by the rules of the corps, who didn't keep their beds clean or those who were negligent in their duties easily mended their ways after a beating with a rod.

Special execution teams were assembled for the punishment of senior soldiers such as Wolfman—the head of the janissary corps until the day before—who now, however, was lying on the ground as he received blow after blow across his soles. He wasn't to receive more than half a dozen.

"I'll teach you what it means to cross Sultan Mehmed!" Malik thundered into Wolfman's face as he laid into him. "By nightfall you'll know what obedience is and what isn't. I've turned many lions like you into kittens here!"

"Hit me, you bastard—hit me harder, hit me faster! We don't beat men, we grow up slapping boulders. Is it not custom to reward janissaries on campaign with extra pay you prick?! You don't know, it's no game to play around with our reward pay!"

Wolfman's voice grew angerier as he was beaten, but it also started to tremble. His face was also turning bright red from the blood collecting in his head as he laid on the ground with his feet raised up.

"You cur—you were a great agha, you rose to the top of the corps, but you still couldn't be a janissary! The purpose of your life is to die for the sultan, to obey his every word and wage holy war in service to the House of Osman. If the sultan sees you worthy of a prize, he would award it—he'll bestow reward pay if he sees fit. Your function is to preserve life and order and ensure the sultanate advances in peace. But you—you've lost yourself to your own arrogance and pride. You've become the wellspring of discontent and indiscipline!"

Malik, his arms as thick as tree trunks, was now striking Wolfman's feet even faster.

"I ask you, great executioner, who doubts my obedience? It was I who became the wolf hunter called Wolfman, piercing the Serb wolves to the battlefield with my arrows and punching those still living as I walked among them. You were here beating the people with a cane, while I battled jackals!"

Malik threw his cudgel to the ground. "Let's see, then, how you wiped the battlefield with those wolves." He then ordered the two janissaries to his sides—both as well-muscled as he—to step aside.

He first jerked Wolfman up by the armpits and sat him in a chair. The now former janissary agha was well out of sorts by what was happening, and even if he were to put up a fight against Malik, his strength had been sapped by the two hundred blows he'd already taken. Wanting to resist the arms of the infamous executioner, he found himself sitting in a chair. Malik backhanded him across the face one more time. He fell to the ground only for Malik to again sit him in the chair and this time slap him across the face with his palm. Now collapsed on the other side of the chair, Malik again lifted him back to the seat.

"You are nobody—there is only the sultan!" Malik barked with every slap. "You are nobody—there is only order!"

His mouth and eyes bleeding, the day two months before that led to these lighting slaps to the face came to Wolfman's mind.

Sultan Mehmed had declared a campaign upon the Karamanid rebellion in Konya, and ordered the entire army to prepare. The janissaries, however, were grieving over the death of their beloved Sultan Murad and were constantly commemorating the seasoned sultan, as they considered the new sultan to be very young and inexperienced. Even though they didn't waver in going to war for him, they showed little respect. Above all, the janissary uprising years before when Sultan Murad abdicated the throne to the prince and their disobedience had created a chilly relationship between Sultan Mehmed and his soldiers.

"You are nothing—there is only the House of Osman!" Malik yelled as he slapped Wolfman again.

With the full army finally going on campaign under Wolfman's leadership, the janissaries started grumbling that since this was the sultan's first campaign, they wanted reward pay of a purse of *akche* for each soldier. Sultan Mehmed thought giving five thousand *akche* in reward pay for nothing would put an unnecessary strain on the Treasury balances. The disrespect shown him was unacceptable.

He had responded well to the janissaries' demands just before setting out on campaign, but then decided to bring the corps, which was underestimating him, into line.

"You are nothing—there is only God the Truth!"

Ibrahim of Karaman, as always, flinched, painfully realizing the new sultan had called his bluff, as soon as he heard the great Ottoman army would bear down on him and bowed in submission to Sultan Mehmed. With the army having turned back for Edirne the day before, Mehmed's first order of business was to remove the janissary agha and other troublemakers like him from duty.

"You are nothing—there is only service!" Malik yelled, landing another slap.

Wolfman found Malik the Executioner and his men surrounding him without a clue as to what had happened. He started to realize better with every blow across his head that he had underestimated Mehmed, overstepped his bounds and betrayed his service. He was coming to the aching realization that Mehmed was no longer the hotheaded child who had been seated on the throne five years earlier.

"You'll understand now," Malik snarled. "You'll all understand. You'll all understand that you can't mock the House of Osman!"

Malik stepped away and Wolfman collapsed, feeling as if he'd been crushed beneath a massive plane tree.

Order in the janissary corps had been restored.

45

"You still haven't forgotten how many years it's been," Hasan said. Iskender kept looking at the sky. The two janissaries were lying in a makeshift camp on a mountain slope, their hands behind their heads for lack of pillows, gazing at the sky through the blackness of night. There was nobody around other than them.

"The stars are gorgeous tonight, aren't they?" Iskender said. "Sometimes I think when I'm looking at the night sky that Mariam is looking at the same star and I see her in that star. She's grown up, her face is even more beautiful, no longer a child, but a young woman."

Hasan stayed quiet as he listened.

"But I get scared sometimes, too," Iskender said. "I'm afraid I won't recognize her at all."

"You're not the one who should be scared—she should," Hasan said. "If there's someone who's changed, it's you. What would you say she'd think if she saw a janissary facing her?"

Iskender sighed, his eyes still fixed on the stars. Their swords, shirts and vests were lying next to them on the grass. The sky was so clear all the stars sparkled in the inky night.

"You're right," Iskender said. "Sometimes I don't even recognize myself. Everything changed so fast. First the years at the shipyard, then my education—and it went by so fast. If it hadn't been like that it would've made me go mad. Always thinking of a girl and dreaming of her but not being able to see her face is the worst torment."

"Haven't you ever thought about running off back to her?" Hasan asked.

"I've thought about it. I thought about it for days, weeks and months when I was in Gallipoli. I planned every day to run away back to the city. What would've happened afterward, though? Theophilos' men would have killed me on sight and anyone who saw me in the city wouldn't waste any time ratting me out to them. I'd be mincemeat for the knights, and what's more, when they realized Mariam was with me, they'd make quick work of her and her family, too. There's nothing different now, either. Me going back would be the end for her."

"But what if you were to bring her here? What if we were to go to Constantinople and trundle her off?" Hasan knew his suggestion was impossible to do, but he couldn't help saying something to try to make his friend feel better.

"If I did that, then I'd be a runaway janissary and I'd have to live my whole life as a fugitive." He lifted up his head and looked over at Hasan. "And it wouldn't be so hard for you and the others to find me," he joked.

"So, what will happen?" Hasan asked.

Then a voice came from behind them. "A creature can't know what will be in the future."

Iskender and Hasan looked behind and saw Mullah Fenari coming toward them.

"I didn't want to listen in on you boys unannounced," Mullah Fenari said. "I just overheard the last part."

"But when you don't know the future," Iskender said, "then you can't figure out what to do in the present."

"And that's the great problem—it brings misery and despair," Mullah Fenari said, as if he knew what the next words out of the janissaries' mouths would be. Iskender slowly nodded in agreement.

"That's why we believe in patience. If a man believes his troubles are not in vain and has faith that the Creator provides solutions for those problems, then fate offers unexpected remedies at the most unexpected of times. The important thing is to believe in the benevolence of those remedies. He who believes in good is happy."

"Yeah, well, swinging a sword and shooting arrows is easier than what you're talking about," Iskender said.

Mullah Fenari smiled. "You're right, Iskender, they are. Battling with the sword is small jihad. The real challenge is the battle with the self. That's also why being a janissary is grueling and arduous—they must do both perfectly." He looked up at the stars. "A janissary must be as perfect as what you see above you."

46

I set off in the afternoon to meet Nilüfer, as I have been for the past few weeks. My interest in Nilüfer has been growing since the first day we met, like a snowball rolling down a slope. It's very difficult, though, for a foreigner to enter a Turk's house. They call the women's quarters in the house the harem, and they take it as sacred. I'm realizing now that much of the information in the travel accounts I read before I came is a product of a boundless European imagination, as it is nearly impossible for a foreigner to see the interior of these houses—the women's quarters most of all. There is always someone with us every moment when Nilüfer and I meet, and many of our meetings are in the palace library.

The maid Shushan opened the carved double doors of her house in the center of the city. I felt naked again when I removed my shoes and put them on the incredibly beautiful rug in the house. Turks never wear their shoes in the home since they attach great importance to a home's cleanliness and they pray with their foreheads on the ground. This is something a Venetian like me has had difficulty adjusting to and is a little uncomforting, as we are so accustomed to wearing our shoes throughout the day.

The maid brought me to another room, and even though I only saw her from behind as she went through the other, and only for a moment, I could tell it was Nilüfer from her figure. This was the first time I ever saw any Turkish woman's hair, not just Nilüfer's. I wanted to bury my face in it, smell its perfume and lose myself in it like an opium-smoking Turk. I so wanted to be alone in private with her for hours. I was embarrassed as soon as I felt this well up, as there in front of me was Ragip Pasha.

Even though he's eighty, the pasha looks quite healthy. He told me I was early. He could still speak Venetian very well, as his duty in earlier life was to meet with the emissaries from Venice, Genoa, Hungary, Germany and many other lands. His wife had died years ago. According what they tell me, he was one of Murad's most loyal men at one time. He always chats with me so he can practice his rusty Venetian and says every time we meet that he knows something regarding Sultan Mehmed assigning me this work. He says this because he personally saw how Sultan Murad had endeavored to prepare his son for the empire, repeatedly commissioning its best tutors for the boy. Ragip Pasha was also there when after the death of his son Alaaddin, Sultan Murad went to Mehmed in Manisa. The sultan had also brought with him his realm's best teachers.

Today, Nilüfer was wearing a black headscarf with black lace around the edges. I reckoned the reason why she so quickly ran out of the room when I came in was so she could cover her head. She was wearing a dress the purple of a damascene plumb that lightly wrapped down to her waist and then widened below her brown leather belt to her ankles. Its narrow collar rose half an inch up her neck on both sides, its sleeves were very wide and sometimes slid all the way up to her elbows.

I stood up and bowed my head when she entered the room, and in a moment of absent-mindedness, I at first nearly hugged her with pressed cheeks as we so often do in greeting in Venice. She also bowed her head slightly. Then she knelt down among the books scattered around the room and laid out her writing tools in front of her.

The sofas in the house all have slips with white embroidery and there is marvelous calligraphy hanging on the walls, all of which Nilüfer had done herself.

As she had to Ragip Pasha, Nilüfer also asked me about Sultan Mehmed and the air of the palace. I explained that the sultan is very busy these days and things are getting ever more heated with Constantinople. Nilüfer's eyes sparkled when I mentioned Mehmed.

My heart is wrapped in darkness when I think about this at night. What chance does a simple Venetian who the Turks call an infidel have with a Mohametan woman in love with the emperor, this Grand Turk?

Nilüfer neatly arranged her writing instruments over the low table where she was kneeling and started to copy the *Shahnameh* from an old copy with its moldered pages scattered about. Every once in a while, I thought about the high price it would fetch from a Venetian merchant. She quickly filled the pages with ink as her hand made swift movements like a swan splashing its wings in a pond.

It was quite amazing and I told her I thought calligraphers wrote slowly.

I was right, she said, but then told me what she was doing wasn't calligraphy, it was copying. For this, quantity is important, she said, and for the other, it's quality.

She both wrote and read out the part of the life of Alexander the Great she was working on. I listened to her and explained the versions of it I know. The main elements of the histories, or stories—as one sometimes they were more one than the other—were the same, but there were differences in the names of places and details. Sometimes there were events I'd never heard of. She wrote down notes next to the passage as I told her of these and would use another page to write out a longer annotation. As for Ragip Pasha, he sat and read a book without disturbing us in the least.

The maid of the house brought me some of the Turks' quite delicious baklava. She looked over me for a very long time when she left the plate and then again when she was opening the door. Next to the baklava was a bowl of raisin compote. They asked if I wanted more after I had gobbled down the baklava and slurped down the compote. Even though I said there was no need, as I was slightly ashamed, they were very insistent and so I happily accepted. I foreigner coming to the Ottoman realm should be ready for plenty at mealtime. They make you eat and drink no matter whether you're hungry or not. If possible, one should go hungry and parched—then both guest and host will be delighted.

Ragip Pasha got up, said he'd be back and went to another room a little after Shushan brought the second plate. I reckoned he had gone to pray when I heard the call to prayer on my way home. Then out of nowhere, Nilüfer asked me what Venetian women are like and to describe them a little.

I hadn't expected the question and so didn't know what to say, but I told her they aren't as beautiful as the women here. She quickly blushed and the maid opened her eyes wide in anticipation.

I was startled when she asked if all Venetian men are always so bold, but I knew she had liked it. When something strikes a woman's fancy, it must be a universal feature of theirs to turn it into a superficial huff. Cristina always used to do the exact same thing.

I told her I thought I had said something nice. I apologized if I had been rude and told her there are many aspects of her culture I still don't know.

Then after staying quiet for a while, as if she'd accepted my apology, she asked what they were and what things Venetian women busy themselves with. She's never asked me about these types of things before.

I explained I'd never seen dresses with figures as elegant and graceful in Venice as I have here and that the biggest difference is that Venetian clothing is a bit tighter and more open.

She looked me quickly up and down and asked if I thought tight, open clothing was more pretty. Then she said I should get one of their caftans.

I was ashamed of my tight breeches and shorter jacket, and knew I wouldn't be able to meet her again dressed like this. I'm going to ask Mullah Lütfi about that caftan.

47

"We should attack as soon as possible already and finish this when they're not expecting it!"

Sofas upholstered in red and gold velvet wrapped around the room where the meetings of the Imperial Council of the Divan were held. The design on the carved wooden ceiling radiated out from the center of the room into larger and larger derivations. Other than this, the room was simple and modest with calligraphy and miniatures hanging on the walls. Right behind the sultan was a piece of calligraphy declaring *ya haqq—long live the Truth*—from its frame.

Mehmed was seated erect at the center of one of the walls of the narrow, rectangular room with his viziers arranged along the long wall to his right and left. After the viziers in the far corners were the treasurer, the signer of the sultan's *tughra* and the *reis ül-küttab.*

Sitting just to the left of the sultan, Zaganos Pasha continued speaking, "If you'd come to the throne one day later, maybe it would have been too late. Constantine would have declared Orhan sultan."

Next to him was Shihabettin Pasha. "Since the reign of Sultan Murad and those before him, the Romans have never ceased badgering us and try to raise an army of crusaders against us at every opportunity. There is no point in waiting any longer, my Sultan."

"You want me to declare war on no grounds, then?" Mehmed said. "Have the Romans attacked us? Have they persecuted any Muslims or other people in my realm? Have they acted wrongly against any Muslim in their own? As far as I know, the Romans have for years been faithful to the treaties from the time of my father."

"They say Constantine has the priests in the city who want to convert to Islam secretly drowned," Shihabettin Pasha said.

"I don't need rumors, I need truths," Mehmed said.

"My Sultan," Zaganos Pasha said, "we've long known the Romans always have a foot on each side. You also know these men have more than a thousand years of experience in diplomacy and that they have a tradition of settling accounts fifty years later with deceit rarely seen elsewhere. Are we supposed to sit here with our arms crossed and wait for their secret meeting with the Karamanids, Hungarians and Genoese to come to light?"

Mehmed then turned to Halil Pasha to his right, who until then had remained silent. "Grand Vizier of my father, what do you think of it?"

Halil Pasha had been listening to Zaganos and Shihabettin as he peered out from behind his thick, greying brows. "Your honorable father always got along with the Romans because he knew well that the slightest attrition would result in another crusade. He avoided wearing down the state and chasing military adventure as if they were Satan himself and always chose the path of peace. I favor maintaining this policy, my Sultan. The state needs stability, not adventure."

"This isn't the Rome of old any longer," Zaganos Pasha said. "It can neither gather crusaders around itself nor see the support it asks for from its closest allies. The Venetians think only of trade anyway."

Mehmed looked over at Yakup Pasha—his physician originally from Venice.

Zaganos Pasha went on, "Constantinople is dealing with Hungary, Austria, Albania and the Slavs."

"England and France have been at war over power for decades," Shihabettin Pasha said. "The situation in the west of Europe isn't much different as in its east."

Halil Pasha looked derisively at Zaganos Pasha and Shihabettin Pasha. "You two weren't in Varna or Kosovo, and so must have quickly forgotten. Constantinople still has the power to turn all of Christendom against us when it feels itself in danger. The janissaries' blood spilt in Kosovo not but five years ago still hasn't even dried yet."

"You don't have to remind me, Halil Pasha," Mehmed said. "I was there. But I'll give you that. Even though Constantinople's voice isn't heeded as was of old, I believe it is still seen as an unshakeable fortress of Christianity and could easily gather together its followers."

"You're right, my Sultan," Zaganos Pasha said, "but we are still able to go up against such a power—it is the never-ending, never-tiring jihad of the Sublime Ottoman State. We have grown ever since the time of Osman to now by means of holy war. Wouldn't you say it's the perfect time to take action again and give the soldiers some excitement?"

"You know well enough yourself, Zaganos," Mehmed said. "The Ottomans never declare jihad just to excite the soldiers and never declare war just to increase our lands. What we have fought for is for justice to rule, to proclaim to the people their rights and to save the oppressed from the claws of tyranny. I know, as well, that this state is on the right path, but this action requires valid reasons." He paused for a moment. "We'll wait for now. If Constantinople is the city I know and Constantine is the emperor I know, then they are already squirming. We'll continue to strengthen our power in the meantime. This inveterate fortress deep in our hearts, surrounded by our cannon will one day come to an end."

Realizing the topic was closed, Halil Pasha continued on to the council's next discussion. "There's a movement that calls itself the Hurufis. They're growing increasingly in number in Anatolia and Edirne, and they could pose a threat if they're not dealt with."

Mehmed looked over at his *tughra* signer—an old man in a black robe wearing a black turban and with an inky beard sitting across from the viziers. Mullah Fahreddin-i Ajemi knew it was his time to speak.

"What kind of threat?" Mehmed asked.

As of now, Mullah Fahreddin had been the most competent authority concerning Islam in the time of Sultan Murad II.

"They believe in the mysticism of letters and numbers and their glory," he said. "They ascribe many different meanings to words and numbers."

"Hasn't the cypher of the abjad and numbers forever been a tradition in quite many religions, as well as Islam?" Mehmed asked as if he already knew the answer.

"Yes, although these Hurufis are different. They want to continue the teachings of Fazlallah Astarabadi of Persia. He also called himself Naimi. Their nonsensical beliefs cloud Muslims' faith."

"Are Muslim's beliefs shaken so quickly?" Mehmed asked, his voiced tinged with sarcasm.

Mullah Fahreddin didn't care for the response. He thought Mehmed wasn't acting as harshly as was required when dealing with other religions.

"These Hurufis smell like they're going the way of Sheikh Bedreddin" Halil Pasha said. "They're steadily gathering supporters."

"Do they use force or oppress anyone?" Mehmed asked. He went on when neither the mullah nor the pashas could answer. "Are they deceive? Do they incite violence against the people or create unrest?"

Mehmed had looked over the pashas and mullah as he spoke. None of them had answers to his questions.

"If Muslims don't have answers to these questions," Mehmed said, "if they're confused, then all the better for the Hurufis. Whether they descend from Sheikh Bedreddin or believe in Fazlallah's teachings, so long as these men don't provoke unrest or disturb anyone, they are free to live in my realm. Is it not incumbent on a true Muslim to give satisfying answers to them?"

Mullah Fahreddin had now gone cross. "My Sultan, Your Highness, people greatly underestimate superstitions."

Mehmed's response was weighty enough to end the council meeting. "The illustrious mullahs also greatly underestimate Islam's tolerance and confidence."

48

All empires have a culture of giving names to nearly everything, and this one is no different. I haven't arrived at this from nothing, either. What I've learned from the Imperial Council, what they call the Divan, and the janissary corps haven't led me to any other conclusion.

I had the opportunity to tour the janissary corps today on special permission from the sultan. The day started with much bustling about. The Divan met in the early hours of the morning. It's the highest-level political body in the palace, much like the Council of Ten we have in Venice. Maybe we started using them in Venice and got the name divan for soft cushions against the walls where the council meets after seeing it among the Turks. With the sultan at the head, the top officials here are the grand vizier, other viziers, the signer of the sultan's tughra—the *nishanji*—the shaykh al-Islam who is the Mohametan's religious leader, the janissary agha, and the Anatolian and Rumelian beylerbeys.

Although the content of the meeting is kept very secret, everyone knows they reviewed the relationship with Constantinople. Zaganos Pasha spearheaded the warmongering faction of the palace and made incredible arguments for going to war. Emperor Constantine's threatening posturing and soldiers targeting the Turks are the greatest motives for the faction of warmongers.

I somewhat entered the council's conversation on this topic, which they had begun when I was counting its members. The Turks have assigned names and have well-defined jobs for each rank. What one does and their titles are marvelously set. This is the same art of naming there was in the amazingly organized system of Old Rome. The names here seem very complicated at first, but it's simple enough to make those who know the language laugh.

For example, *nishan* means *sign* or *mark*, like a signature, and so the *nashanji* is the man authorized to sign the sultan's *tughra*—their own type of signature. Another name for the sultan is *padishah*, which comes from Persian and means master of kings. Just as many of the languages in Europe have so much from Latin, like affixes and roots, so too is Arabic and Persian mixed in Turkish. The title *reis ül-küttab* comes from Arabic and means chief of the scribes. He is the man who sees to the work of the sultan's writing and interprets for foreign guests. The Persian title *defterdar* means *bookkeeper*—he keeps the records of the finances and is, naturally, the treasurer. The title *mirahur* is Persian for stablemaster, and is the man responsible for the sultan's horses.

The flood of titles in this culture of naming, however, is best seen among the janissary corps. I wrote earlier about why the leader of what they call the hearth is called the *chorbajibashi*—the head soup cook, but I didn't understand then why such a silly name like soup cook was seen fit for a high-ranking military leader. The janissaries spread out over a wide field going this way and that in regular groups like ants and have maybe a hundred identifiable titles. I drew a very large schema of their structure, but it only reflects one-tenth of the corps' composition. A commanding officer by the name of Chorbajibashi Vahdeddin gave me a tour of his regiment and spoke at great length.

At the core of the Janissary corps is the regiment—what they call an *orta*. Each regiment has seventy men, and the man at its head is the *chorbaji*—the soup cook. Another name for them is *chavush*, or it's used for others—I don't fully get which is which. The barracks where the regiments stay are divided into rooms and the janissary at the head of the room is given the simple name, *odabashi*—head of the room.

Far from taking offence at the titles the Turks have created for themselves, they take pride in them, as every position has hefty responsibilities and rigorous demands. These positions, too, aren't bestowed based on pedigree or preference, but rather to those deserving of them based on merit and competence. For this reason, they believe the further one's original station is from their position, the more successful they will be and they also never stop giving thanks for the great blessings they believe God has bestowed on them. I was surprised to hear recently that one of Mehmed's viziers is named *Ashchi* Mamud—Mahmud the Cook, that is—which I heard from a German emissary.

Mehmed one day went as an ordinary person to inspect the city and get a feel for the people. I reckon the doges of Venice wouldn't do such a thing in their lives. There was one man yelling and screaming angrily at everything around him while Mehmed was walking through the bazaar. Mehmed walked up to him and asked what was the matter. Apparently, the man was a cook and said that despite having looked through the entire city, he couldn't find one *okka*—about two and three-quarters of a pound—of meat, that the state wasn't managing it and that the inspectors do as they like. The inspectors are supposed to keep an eye on sales at the bazaars and ensure they are fair. The man said if he were an inspector, he'd perform the job fairly and dutifully. Mehmed called the cook to the palace the next day and told the man he had appointed him as an inspector. He straightened out the markets and bazaars, and thus Mahmud the Cook became a vizier due to his meticulousness and meting out of justice.

I've heard many similar stories at the palace. It would be very difficult to explain that these people here who have risen in station to the lords who are born and die noble or the peasants condemned to the fields and cooks to the kitchen. Migrants to Venice, for example, can only acquire full citizenship after twenty-five years of residence and only if they aren't manual workers. It seems the Ottomans' liberalism in this will bring more harm than good. What other explanation can there be, though, for the peace in their lands and rapid expansion of their territories?

Returning to the janissary corps, however, it has many units and regiments, and their numbers are maintained under strict control. The *saksojubashi* trains the sultan's hunting hound, *zagarjis* look after them, so too do the *turnaji*—or crane men—who go out hunting with the hounds and also keep cranes. There are the gunners, the *sekban* third-rank mercenaries, the *slolaks* who make up the sultan's guard and the *peyk* armed footmen, just to name some. Each guild of sorts receives a new member every three or five years. Each regiment has its own symbol, which are constantly fluttering on their standards. One of the symbols that most interests me is that of a forked sword, what the Turks call *Zulfiqar*. They believe this is the sword Muhammad gave to his nephew Ali during the Mohamatans' fist battle at Badr, and is holy to them. Of the other symbols I've been able to note, there are the bow and arrow, spear, tent, ax, mosque, minaret, upturned crescent from the mosques, lion, elephant, camel, wolf, eagle, hawk, galley, anchor, crescent, date palm, ewer and broom. Arrows have an intangible value like that of swords, if not more so. For the parts of the army outside the janissaries, they say the cavalry archers from the fiefdoms called *sipahi* must wait decades before they are accepted so as to maintain the best force. Some have supposedly even waited seventy years.

Commander Vahdettin also mentioned the education they get as he showed me around. Each young recruit receives an incredible education in the corps as well as at the palace so they become well-rounded men. He claimed nobody but they can draw their bows, which they practice daily along with slapping boulders, target shooting and sword lessons.

The Turks' swords are very different from ours, as they do not run straight out from the hilt, but rather curve with a blade on only one edge. Vahdettin said that unlike the straight, double-edged swords of knights, their scimitars are lighter and require higher mastery to wield. The speech and manners of the janissaries are also at the level of Christian nobles. Among them are poets, musicians and calligraphers. They never turn their backs on guests and will always offer food. An account of travel I read before coming explained this very well, as it said they are demons in war and angles in peace.

49

I managed to meet with Mehmed again today, but something unpleasant happened as I was leaving my room. I saw that grim-faced bigot again— Fahreddin the Persian—or Fahreddin-i Ajemi as they say—the shaykh al-Islam himself. He is the highest Mohametan authority and what he says can easily become law, of course with the sultan's blessing. His face is foul and sour every time he sees me and it seems he's always cursing me. He is never without his black robe and black turban. His bulbous lips underneath his nasty beard are relentlessly mumbling something or another. He ordered me to stop as soon as he saw me and wailed about who let this infidel into the palace. And then, having heard his remonstration, a few janissaries immediately surrounded me.

Fortunately, at that moment Mullah Lütfi came and explained that I am here on special permission from the sultan. Fahreddin was fuming and turned beet red. He furiously stroked his beard and said something to the effect of may God rain down ten thousand calamities on infidels and their friends, and that crowns are being placed on men who should be beheaded. The man's job is to be despotic and damn others. He left after giving me one more look-over in disgust. People like Shaykh al-Islam Fahreddin-i Ajemi can be found everywhere here, and escaping their nastiness warrants a separate talent entirely.

What Mullah Lütfi brought me, though, is of the type of thing that greatly eases all of the unpleasantness. This time I accepted the handsome indigo caftan, crimson shalvar and blue waist wrap. I wasn't going to refuse these clothes again. He also provided me with a pair of yellow leather boots. I put them on with a pleasure I hadn't expected. I would have looked over myself in my room for longer if the janissary at the door hadn't said we were running late and hurried me along. This is how I dream of myself never leaving Nilüfer's side.

Movement in these clothes is more comfortable—walking, sitting and standing up—as they give incredible freedom to the arms and legs. If I weren't ashamed to do so, I would go out to the palace gardens and as children do go running and flap my ample sleeves like a bird. I suppose I understand better now why the Turks appear to be so confident when they walk. The jesters at the Doge's Palace would think themselves to be an Ottoman grand vizier if they were to wear this clothing.

This style of dress also lends much to the streets of the city. The different peoples of the city wear different colors, making the street appear as one of the sultan's gardens. The Armenians wear robes of a hue Mullah Lütfi once told me during a walk through the city they call peacock blue. The Moldavans wear robes of grey, the Tatars wear green waist sashes, Greek women caftans the color of damascene plums, Jewish men shades of blue, Jewish women red shalvar and then Turks, Albanians, Kurds and Bulgars in dozens of various colors. Mullah Lütfi mentioned a few of the laws, but it seemed to me everyone wears what they please. The Jews here don't wear a distinguishing marker like the yellow circle those in Venice must don.

Mehmed could only spare me a little time. I am surprised he was able to see me at all at a time like this, but he wanted to be informed of the progress I had made on the work he'd assigned me. I had to summarize it all as concisely and effectively as I could manage.

I told him of the main discrepancy between the Persian, Macedonian and Greek historians. Not all of them, but a great many Greek historians say Alexander the Great conquered the Persian Empire. I explained to him that due to Persian culture's great interest in Alexander, they disagree and these histories are a product of religious perversion. In his *Shahnameh,* Ferdowsi claims Alexander was sired by the Persian shah before he sent his mother back to King Phillip of Macedon, and so had always been Persian and heir to the throne in the first place. According to Ferdowsi and his sources, his time in Macedon, or Rome, as Ferdowsi says, was a time spent in exile and his conquering of Persia was just him regaining his true lands.

He listened to me intently and didn't interrupt. Then with his permission I asked what he thought of these differing accounts and who he thought the true Alexander was. He seemed surprised with my question at first, but I could tell he enjoyed it.

He looked at me and said Alexander is a shadow. I stayed quiet, as it seemed he wanted to explain.

He said he is like Plato's Allegory of the Cave and that the world is a pale version of the actual truth. What historians speak of is the shadow, or the illusion of truth, two steps removed from the actual truth. That's why, he said, it's of great import to record history as it happens.

I earlier met some of the historians who reside at the palace and now see better why they are so diligent in their charge.

The Turks understanding of the deficiencies in this resembles that of the sultan. Mehmed says that words fly away but writing remains and is one of mankind's greatest abilities.

For me, though, writing is the way to keep a record of the ever-shifting form of my spirit. There isn't a night that passes when I don't question my past, my personage or my individual self, and don't think about what I do that makes me who I am. When I compare texts on the same subject but that describe them differently, such as Ottoman writings and Latin histories, I feel somehow stuck between two great cultures, and these great pages, like walls pressing me from both sides, even drive away my sleep. I sometime also feel a strange reprieve—a feeling as if I straddle the border of two lands with a foot in each one.

I see no other way a man can feel when having been amid so many different people and their languages.

50

Theophilos smiled when he saw the Muslim peasants on a hillside of the Marmara coast. There were quite a few simple peasants plowing their fields as he counted them, but more importantly, none had weapons. He thought these rustic, ordinary peasants were parasites on the land.

He was in full armor and his cloak bore the imperial double-headed eagle emblem of the Palaiologos dynasty of New Rome. This eagle with its heads looking away from each other had come to more represent the squabbling aristocracy and battles for the throne.

He turned to Kantakouzenos, who was riding next to him. "What say you? Would this give Constantine the war he desires?"

Kantakouzenos nodded in satisfaction. "Exceedingly."

Theophilos and the battalion of two hundred fifty men under his command drew their weapons and started to quickly draw nearer.

This territory, miles outside the city walls, was like a buffer between the Ottomans and Constantinople. Constantine, like his predecessors Ioannes VIII Palaiologos and Manuel II Palaiologos, very much wanted to take this land and the land beyond, but they had remained passive as they had all feared Sultan Murad. Murad's success at Varna had also always frightened the emperors. Constantine, in his turn, also didn't want to upset the old sultan's policies of peace. Now, though, was the perfect time to start taking back land from the untried new sultan, and this coastline was the perfect place to start.

The first blow from Theophilos' sword struck a young man across the face as he carried water to his elderly father. The young man fell to the ground with blood gushing from his cheek and mouth amid the shattered pitcher. The Constantinopolitan soldiers cut down everyone who crossed their paths. One clubbed a man over the head with a mace, pulling it out covered in the man's blood-soaked hair and pieces of his scalp. Another trampled over a boy in the village square with his horse. The boy's mother turned to run as the boy was crushed, but fell victim to another soldier's sword.

They spread out to the village square, between the houses and the fields behind them. Theophilos had been waiting for this day for years and, now that it had come, was swinging his sword with great relish. It had been painful for him to sit with his hands tied for decades while the Ottomans were within reach.

"These lands are ours—all for holy Rome!" he cried out. He believed he was recovering something with every piece of flesh his sword sliced through.

Constantine had spoken with Theophilos in the days prior and decided that such an attack would be the best way to determine the impotence of the new sultan. If the plan were to go well, then it would set off confusion in the palace in Edirne with the incitement of the pashas. Then Constantine would put forth Orhan. Constantine had also given thought to the possibility of attacking the sultan's territory. He reckoned, as had happened to many rulers before, that Mehmed would retreat in failure and his weakness would be born out for all to see. Constantinople, after all, had been surrounded dozens of times throughout its millennium of existence by the land's most powerful kingdoms and empires, and yet none had been able to take it.

Theophilos signaled his archers to leave no one standing. They lit the ends of their arrows and shot at the houses, their roofs, through the windows and into the doors. Another contingent of soldiers went through the village and set alight all the buildings with torches. One peasant burned in his house while another tried to put out the fire with water from the fountain. A sword caught him in the neck before he could empty his bucket.

Theophilos' face was still spattered with blood on their return to the city with his regiment.

Constantine would be pleased.

51

The entire palace had a somber air. There was talk of how Constantine attacked Muslims in his own territory along the Marmara coast. Many had been killed and hundreds had been taken prisoner. I had seen Theophilos by happenstance years ago in Naples, and had heard stories of his cruelty then. The Latins have disgust for him as much as he hates the Mohamatans. He sees his own people as so superior that some call him Theophilos the Greek. He believes he will restore the former boundaries of the Roman Empire, and so occasionally goes on tours of Europe to collect money from all the Christian monarchs with brazen duplicity. His talk of superiority does very well to gather idle mercenaries and he easily keeps many soldiers under his command. The riches he's collected, though, he uses for a life of luxury. If anyone speaks out against him, he has them found and tortured as he continues his tyranny. For Constantine, the enemy Turks are too great a treasure to give up.

I have my own bedevilment.

My interest in Nilüfer has also created a desire in me to learn more about women and marriage traditions among the Turks. It is true Mohamatans can marry four women, as there are many examples of such permission and what should and shouldn't be done in their holy book. Nilüfer, however, says this permission is given conditionally and that when one considers the difficulty of the conditions, then polygamy is more discouraged than encouraged. For example, she says it is a condition for a man to treat each of his wives equally and show each of them equal love. She showed me a passage in a book that says as much.

When I asked her why this would be such a difficult condition to fulfill, she looked me in the eyes and asked if I could love two women equally.

I stayed quiet for a moment and then told her that I could one after the other, but not at the same time. Then I said I wouldn't have believed it myself before, but my thinking has changed since coming here.

She blushed and silently looked down at her notes. Then she said there is also polygamy in our lands.

I was confused and said I didn't understand.

She said if I could show her even one Venetian man who throughout his entire life was ever only with one woman at a single time, then she'd drop it.

There's a certain degree of truth to what she said. There is nearly no Venetian man who at one time hadn't also laid with a servant or a slave as well as his wife.

I pointed out that we aren't married to those we lay with.

She said what we do is even worse—whereas we do it secretly as if using the women, the Mohamatans have clear rules according to their religion's principles and she claimed no one succumbs to licentiousness. She said what we do is unlawful whereas the Mohamatans act within the law and afford women their rights.

I protested and said that we don't sanctify men's bodily cravings with religious law.

It is true here, Nilüfer's mention of privileges for women, and is no trifle. If these laws were to be enacted in Venice, I personally know much of the aristocracy would be furious and rebel. For example, when a man dies, the inheritance stays with his wife. Especially if she has no male children, then all the man's assets pass to her. This would be unacceptable in Venice. Women also have the right to apply to the court the same as men. There are many Christian Armenian women here who seek their rights from the Mohamatan courts and judges. The Mohamatan judges, what they call *qadis*, having been educated at the renowned Ottoman madrasahs, are the meticulous men who bring voice to law. The court admits all the people of the empire, Mohamatan, Christian and Jew, and those from all classes to dole out verdicts.

The sultan got his due from one of these qadis on one occasion, as well. Mehmed wanted to embellish the borders of his lands with amazing architecture and brought in monolithic marble columns from around the empire in order to build a mosque of uncompilable splendor with high ceilings. Among these they say there are two columns of red porphyry sent by the Mamluks in Egypt as a gift. The architect did the calculations, cut the columns shorter by one-third and thus built the mosque. Seeing his dear columns cut and the mosque ordinary, Mehmed flew into a rage and had the architect's hands cut off. When work isn't done right, everyone would agree this young sultan cannot withhold his fury. I'd say it was nothing short of barbarity if it had stopped there, but what happened next tells a different story.

The architect went to a qadi and pleaded his case. The qadi also called the sultan to the court. Mehmed came the next day, stony-faced and surrounded by his imperial guards, and stood before the qadi in all his majesty.

He said the architect has spoiled the columns he had had brought from around the empire with much labor, that he had wasted the toil of hundreds of people and that the materials for the earthly and spiritual sources for the construction of the mosque, which went on day and night, had been frittered away. He said that a slippery path would open if such crimes were to go unpunished.

The qadi then turned to the architect after taking the sultan's statement. The architect said he made his living with his hands and now he couldn't support himself.

The qadi then gave his decision. He told the sultan that the columns were stone, and it wouldn't make a difference even if they were gold, as they can be replaced. The man's hand's, though, were flesh and blood. The man had a wife and children to care for, and so ordered the sultan to pay the man a salary to more than cover his livelihood.

Mehmed agreed and said the architect would be paid a monthly salary from the Treasury.

The qadi refused this. He said Mehmed was at fault, not the state, and declared the salary would come from the revenue afforded to the sultan.

Mehmed found the qadi's just decision to be appropriate and gave an approving nod. When the case had finished, he walked to the qadi holding his scabbard and said that if the judge had favored him because he was sultan, he would have taken his sword and lopped the man's head off. After this, the qadi stood up, pulled a war mace from under his green robe and said that if Mehmed had challenged him because he is sultan, then he would have caved his head in without another thought.

I thought about the aristocracy in Venice, and the lords and dukes and barons further afield as I listened to this story. The justice of the Ottomans is in stark contrast to our own. After all, how could the qadi hurt a simple man who hadn't hurt the sultan?

Divorce is also unrestricted for the Mohamatans here. Unlike us in the Latin Rite for whom divorce is forbidden, the Mohamatans can divorce due to any discord, and both the men and women can supposedly remarry with ease. Maybe the polygamy here should be understood this way, as this city has many men who have divorced and remarried rather than being married to multiple women at once. Monogamy, for its part, is common among the lower classes, like farmers and the shopkeepers of the middle class. Polygamy, is mostly seen among the wealthy higher classes, such as the pashas and commanders, and even then, is still low in number. The largest difference between the aristocracy of European realms and the upper classes here is that whereas European aristocracy passes down by blood from generation to generation, here, the Mohamatans have no right to the station of their fathers. For example, a bookkeeper who is found to be taking bribes can be dismissed immediately, have all of his possessions confiscated and be left more destitute than a pauper. In the same way, one in desperation—as the people here live to fill their bellies for a day—can prove himself in battle and find himself to be a pasha the next day. And so, because of this, movement between the classes is common among the Mohamatans.

Considering inter-religious marriages, however, foreign men coming to the Ottoman realm must be resigned to their fate, since whereas the Mohamatan men can easily marry women from any religion they please, Mohamatan women are not allowed the same freedom and can only marry a Mohamatan man. When I intimated that this law is an example of discrimination among the Ottomans, who say they hold justice so high, Mullah Lütfi retorted that the law is the result of logic. He said that if a Mohamatan man warries a Christian woman, since the bloodline and lineage passes through the man, then their children will continue to be Mohamatan, but if a Mohamatan women were to do the same then it would break the patrilineal line.

They say the sultan will set out on campaign with an army of thousands of men in a few weeks. Apparently not for war, though, but for a building project. Mullah Lütfi believes the sultan has decided to go to war with Constantinople, but isn't telling anyone yet.

52

Patriarch Grigorios was worriedly looking out from a small window in the Hagia Sophia's highest gallery. He couldn't at first make sense of those gathering at the Sphendone stands at the highest point of the Hippodrome. When he squinted and focused, he saw a mass of people stretching back to the horizon, moving like an ant colony about a mile from the walls of Galata. He couldn't make sense of the smoke rising from the Asomaton area, where other than a few villages and ruined Greek columns and churches, there was nothing. Just as perplexing were the dozens of tents pitched there and the ships along the shore. He reckoned the Venetians or Genoese must be setting up a new colony across from the Ottoman's Anatolian Fortress in Amikos.

As if sharing his curiosity, a hawk took flight from the grand church's dome and soared over the city toward the commotion north of the city. It circled over the shore and haughtily opened space through a flock of seagulls feeding along the coast. Its sharp eyes spotted the only thing a hawk could have need for in such tumult—spilled blood. With a sense of smell as acute as its sight, the hawk could tell the blood was still warm.

A butcher with a well-honed knife said *bismillah*—in the name of God—and slit a ram's throat in one swipe as he held its left forelock to let it convulse as its life slipped away. He pressed his knees lightly on the ram's back so blood wouldn't splatter and slowly wiped the blood off his knife onto the ram's thick wool. This was the third ram he'd slaughtered today and there were four more to go.

Having started early in the morning with the butcher's first slaughter, a little farther away a mason held a stake with his left hand as he pounded it with a mallet to set it in place. The part of the plan that fell to him was to rope off the boundaries by noon and ensure it was possible to begin excavating the foundation by mid-afternoon. Unlike the ease with which the earlier stakes had sunk into the ground, this time it hit a stone and he couldn't figure out how to proceed. He pounded at the stake with increasing force, each time making the veins in his forehead bulge with exertion.

He remembered well the drawings spread out beside him that he'd looked over and over the day before as he tried to drive in the stake exactly where they indicated. If he didn't and they were a yard or two off, then the strange shape of the construction, which he was already struggling to understand, then it would be his head. The last thing he wanted to do was create problems in the area he was responsible for.

He had been excited when the qadi of Iznik had said when leaving Friday prayers that when winter began its thaw, the sultan wanted to have built an unrivaled fortress on the Bosporus, and so the qadi was looking for masons. The sultan would give everyone more than their due, but the work had to be done with masterful precision. The mason had reckoned it was going to be a large task, but he never thought while on the road with his team that he'd be part of an army of five thousand builders. He was given a portion of the construction that wasn't even one-fiftieth of its total and told the qadi that it would take a year to complete. The qadi, in return, told him it would be better if he didn't start if he couldn't finish within three months. The mason had calculated the time to be much too short even with three shifts at work. He couldn't figure why the sultan was in such a hurry to build a new fortress when there was already a relatively new one on the opposite shore.

Time was running short. He spit into his calloused hands, rubbed them together to keep the mallet from slipping and with a final *ya Allah—by God*—swung down on the stake and split it down the middle. The stake in the mason Hajji Ibrahim's hand had given up the ghost, but the stone beneath the turf was still quite solid. He was just one of hundreds of men performing the same task.

A little up the hill from Hajji Ibrahim, another mason was shaping stones to be fit in the wall. The man was knelt down in front of a large stone that came a little passed his waist as he chipped away at its edges with a hammer and chisel. Stones had been collected from the surrounding ruins week before and piled in place, but when it was clear they wouldn't be enough, ships were sent loaded with stone from around the Ottoman realm, mostly out of Eregli on the Black Sea and the port of Gallipoli. Like the hundreds of other masons around him on the craggy and rough terrain, he was shaping the rough blocks to be used for the fortress' towers and walls.

The clamor of hammer and chisel on stone and mallets driving stakes into the soil created a din among those still unloading timbers and boards from the lush Black Sea forests off the ships that had sailed from Eregli and Izmit along the coasts and depositing them where the foreman instructed. With the construction still in its preliminary stage, those watching the lime kilns paid special attention that the timbers were piled far enough away to not catch alight. Once the lumber and stone had been unloaded from the galleys, the countless tools the laborers would use to starts digging the foundation—pickaxes, shovels, chisels, stakes, hammers and wheelbarrows—created a scene that looked as if all the building tools from all of Anatolia and Europe had been brought to this one place.

Muslihiddin the Architect walked through the laborers both looking over the structures taking shape around him and checking them against the plans he was trying to unroll as he went. He was ordered to halt when he came to a golden cord in front of a red tent to the side of the site. With the plans obscuring Muslhiddin's face, even if they could guess who he was, the janissary guards wouldn't permit him entry without being certain. Sultan Mehmed had ordered from the first day of construction that this man was to be allowed in without question whenever he pleased and added the firm warning that he shouldn't have to repeat himself.

Muslihiddin entered to the sultan looking over piles of drawings and, having asked permission, spread out his plans before him.

"We're at this stage, Your Highness," he said, pointing to the plans. "There is a very large stone beneath the surface and it must extend farther back. The mason driving the stakes there is a master from Izmit. The others tried, but the stone can't be broken up. If we move the boundary three yards in, then it will just barely make it."

Mehmed had listened intently and then looked up at Muslihiddin. "My esteemed architect, don't you know that if we take the boundary in then the tower on that corner would end up between the walls? Can a tower be between two walls? Would the tower guard the walls or the walls guard the tower?"

"You're right, Your Highness, but excavating that boulder could take days. It would dely the finishing of the fortress at least a month, since with this part unfinished, then the construction of the remaining foundations, walls and bulwarks also can't continue."

Mehmed rose to his feet. "Who is responsible for this tower? Is it Saruja Pasha?"

"Yes, Your Highness."

Mehmed went to the door and waved for Jafer Agha to bring the pasha.

Jafer Agha came to Saruja Pasha's site, but almost didn't recognize him. Saruja Pasha was facing away amid a group of laborers trying to dislodge the boulder and calling out in unison to his lead.

"One, two, three!"

Their muscles tensed and they pushed with their entire, combined strength against the monolith.

Saruja Pasha turned around to wipe the dirt and grit from his hands and arms. He saw Jafer Agha and knew right off the sultan had called for him.

He looked over the coast just below the valley and could sense Halil Pasha even from that long distance.

"The sultan calling for me doesn't bode well," he grumbled, "but at least someone is enjoying it."

"Did you say something, Saruja?" Jafer Agha said.

"Just that my back is killing me."

"Look, Saruja," Mehmed said. "We are trying to build something to attain God's approval. Don't you know the difficulties we face fuel our desire, raise our service and increase our good deeds? Don't you know these things that appear as obstacles actually are in effect the steps that will lead us to our aim?"

Saruja Pasha listened in silence as the sultan spoke. When Mehemd finished, Saruja Pasha reckoned it was time for him to speak. "You're very right, my Sultan, but we've tried everything that can be done. There's a boulder nine feet around right where this pile has to go. It won't budge. I reckoned that if we spent any more time on it we would lose time."

"Saruja, the architect will explain why the stake must go there, but I'll show you something else."

Mehmed took a sheet of paper and a reed pen from the sofa in the large tent. He dipped the reed into an inkpot and made one shape that took up the entire sheet to the curiosity of everyone in the tent.

Mehmed asked Saruja Pasha to come to him with his plans. "Now let's look at the scheme. You haven't seen it in its entirety," he said. Mehmed spread his arms and opened the building plans all the way out. "Now, take a look at what's in this hand."

Saruja Pasha looked with surprise at the part the sultan was holding. Then he looked it over again. The fortress was in the shame of a gigantic letter *mim*.

He looked up from the plans at the sultan. "Please grant pardon to your humble servant, my Sultan. I didn't appreciate your pious devotion and didn't fully comprehend your noble dreams."

He looked up from the plans at Mehmed. "Please grant pardon to your humble servant, Sultan. I didn't realize your pious devotion and hadn't the full picture your noble dreams."

"I don't want an apology, dear Saruja—I want work. Now, go and get thirty stonecutters and you will sink that stake. Don't we need more stone anyway? Well then, we'll use the stones we find underground for the foundations and the walls without any of it going to waste. Hence, we won't lose time or manpower—it's already these men's job to shape the stones. Isn't that correct, Muslihiddin?"

"It is, Your Highness," the architect said.

"Then your man will drive in that stake," Mehmed said. "This matter will be over by noon."

Saruja Pasha and the Muslihiddin deplored as they left the tent that they hadn't been able to come up with such a simple solution.

"Don't worry, Saruja," Muslihiddin said. "I also didn't understand when the sultan first asked me months ago to turn his drawings into a construction plan."

Mehmed was left in his tent with Beylerbey Ishak Pasha of Anatolia and Beylerbey Karaja Pasha of Rumelia from whom he inquired about any expected or impending dangers. "Is there any unrest? The Greeks could attack from Constantinople at any time. With this many Ottoman ships in the Bosporus for the first time, even the Venetians and Genoese could be uneasy."

"There are no problems yet," Ishak Pasha said. "We have the soldiers prepared for all possibilities."

"The Greeks in Asomaton and the surrounding villages are just surprised and trying to make sense of what will be when construction ends," Karaja Pasha added.

"Continue to keep the soldiers and laborers informed," Mehmed said. "Don't molest the Greeks in their fields and gardens, and be tolerant if anyone says something cross here or there. Also have the soldiers help the laborers so long as there isn't need for them to show their teeth."

Ishak Pasha and Karaja Pasha left the tent after the sultan was finished and Mehmed was left, as he often was, with Yakup Pasha.

53

"What say you, Yakup? You think Constantine will send an army?"
"I've never been able to predict what Constantine would do, or any other Greek basileus for that matter. I'd expect anything from him. What I would say, though, is the best thing he could do for us is send an army here to this expansive, open plain. The janissaries would rout them like lambs to the slaughter."

"Very true. I think the same. I'd also say they're likely to send an emissary within a few days to try and figure out what is happening. With that excuse, they'll nose about and take a good look at us."

"The sooner the better, otherwise they'll find themselves run up against a grand fortress," Yakup Pasha said with a smile. "What is it, what are you thinking, my Sultan?" Yakup Pasha asked, seeing Mehmed disappear into another world entirely.

"What you said is precisely correct—if they come later, then they will see a fortress. Maybe they won't find anything other than a fortress here for centuries to come, Yakup." Mehmed stood up, lifted the thick curtain at the door to the tent and looked outside. "The Persian Shah Darius the Great built a bridge here a thousand years ago."

"I remember something like that from Herodotus' *Histories,*" Yakup Pasha said.

"He took everywhere into his realm—Egypt, India, Babylon, the

Mediterranean and Anatolia. The Scythians in the east of Europe and along the northern Black Sea were a thorn in the great shah's side and so he came here to the shores opposite us now with an army of seven hundred thousand men."

"Seven hundred thousand?"

"I think Herodotus may have exaggerated a bit. Let's say maybe fifty thousand for a journey of that distance. Darius looked long over the Bosporus, and Herodotus explains how he made a bridge over it."

"How can you be so sure it was right here?"

"Herodotus says it was where the two shores are closest. But you see now, there is no bridge nor any Persians."

"So it would seem then the old Persians weren't as skilled builders as the Romans. The Theodosian Walls still look like they were built yesterday."

"That, I wouldn't know, Yakup. What about the Ottoman walls and what we have built?" Mehmed walked over to the other corner of the tent. "The mark I will leave here will be so great that even when everything on earth is razed to the ground, it will still stand."

Both men didn't speak for some time.

"And what happened to Darius," Yakup Pasha finally asked.

"What would happen in that situation? There were revolts, his armies were defeated and only a few could return. Ferdowsi says there was constant strife for Alexander the Great, as well, in these lands but he still easily conquered Persia and Mesopotamia."

"Have you started to speak with Halil Pasha?"

Mehmed smiled, sat down on the sofa and pore over the construction plans. Yakup Pasha also busied himself with reading al-Razi's work on measles.

54

The sound of a pair of feet hurriedly pattering through the long corridors of the Blachernae Palace broke the silence. The palace guard walking at full stride and almost breaking into a run, had to keep hold of his sword to stop it from swinging as his cloak fluttered behind him.

The palace and its church formed a gigantic complex of stone towers, villas, chapels, dungeons and dozens of gleaming white columns giving it the appearance of temples Roman Greek emperors such as Anastasius I Dicorus, Alexios I Komnenos and Manuel I Komnenos had built in their names.

The labyrinthine corridors of the complex had provided passage between its vast area for the emperors of New Rome, their lords and patricians for five hundred years. Very few in the palace other than the imperial guards—who knew their every inch—could find their way through these corridors alone. Every new addition to the complex throughout the centuries had made the web of corridors more complicated and the palace was the embodiment of two thousand years of winding and sly Roman diplomacy.

Emperor Alexios I Komnenos had left the thousand-year Great Palace beside the Hagia Sophia in the center of the city for this palace to the northwest, which, along with its church, was built on the spot of a legendary apparition of the Virgin Mary. It had also served as the preferred residence for the Palaiologos dynasty.

The guard knew he was close when he saw steam spreading through the corridor. Just as he was going to knock on the door, which had steam billowing from the threshold, it opened and out ran a naked boy, his hair wet and face and lips a glowing red, who then disappeared into the corridor. After a moment, the guard thought it better to not proceed and rather call for the emperor from where he stood. All he could see before him were fleshy shadows amid the noise of water that drowned out all other sound.

"Come in," Constantine said.

The guard walked to where the voice had come from and found Constantine soaking naked in a large bathtub. His attendants were carrying buckets of hot water and pouring them over him. The color drained from Constantine's face and he lost his gaiety as the guard bent down and whispered in his ear.

Loukas Notaras had been right—they had greatly underestimated the young sultan.

Theophilos Palaiologos grew more heated and animated as he spoke from the black and white checkered marble floor of the Hall of Alexios I. "This man is undertaking building works with fifty thousand men right under our noses. He must be mad. What is he doing there—building a mosque, building a bridge? It's not clear. Whatever it is, it's unacceptable!"

"Why would he build a mosque on land with nothing other than Christian villages?" Demetrios Kantakouzenos said.

"I can't make sense of it, either," Theophilos said. "He's abandoned his capitol in Edirne and his lands in Europe and Anatolia to amass thousands of men in our land with nothing other than a handful of bandits."

"I warned you all not to underestimate this new sultan," Notaras said.

Constantine had remained silent so far as he looked on the icon of the Virgin Mary above the fireplace and listened. "Don't fall to desperate thoughts so quickly, gentlemen," he said as he turned around. He walked over to the ornate chessboard on a marble table in the spacious hall. He put his hand on the white king and slid it over in front of the black pawns on the other side. "Early egress is condemned to result in frustration. What we need to ask ourselves is not what the sultan is looking for so near us, but rather how we can benefit from it."

"I say we send a couple emissaries straight away to ensure a thorough inspection of what's going on there. We'll also learn the sultan's intentions this way," said Giorgios Sphrantzes

Constantine nodded his approval.

55

I had a very strange dream last night. It wasn't so much eventful, but the main images I remember were so vivid I can still see them.

Mehmed was wearing Venetian clothing—tight breeches, a jacket that came just below his waist and a silk scarf. He had a chaperone on his head and an unforgettable, thin mustache pointed up at the tips with a beard coming to a point at the chin.

More interesting was that Mehmed was an artist standing before me and painting my portrait. I was wearing my own clothes and standing motionless. I got up every so often to look at the painting. When I did, though, I didn't see a Venetian emissary, but a stately, Ottoman grand vizier with a full beard whose face was somehow familiar.

After looking, I went back to my seat and waited for Mehmed to finish the painting. I got back up to look at it again and saw that same Ottoman grand vizier. The thing, however, was Mehmed hadn't taken his eyes off me while painting.

I thought long about whether or not to tell Mullah Lütfi about the dream. I wanted to tell him since the Mohametans have their own aptitude when it comes to interpreting dreams. The Mohametan religion has no prejudice to this practice. The strange thing, however, is they both interpreted dreams and at the same time say one cannot act on dreams. Some claim some dreams should never be told. The reason I haven't told Mullah Lütfi of mine is because I fear it might disturb him.

I nevertheless much prefer to dream of Nilüfer rather than Mehmed, and I forced myself to that end. My mind is always playing some type of game with me, though.

Sometimes a silently lie down and close my eyes to visions of the house on the pier in Venice where I lived with my beloved wife. I don't only think of it—I try to feel as if I'm there. I conjure up the bedroom around me, the sea outside the windows, the city and all of Venice. Then I imagine Cristina lying beside me. I make myself believe it so deeply that I think if I could hold her hand if I were to reach out.

My time spent and experiences with the Ottomans and Nilüfer also all seem like a dream in those moments between sleep and wakefulness when I sometimes feel as if I'm in Venice with my beloved.

But what if it really is so?

What if what I experience here is a dream, a fleeting dream that is merely a fraction of the night? And as for what Mullah Lütfi has told me about dreams, does this not point to what will be?

He told me once that the entire world is an illusion. When I asked him what he meant, he said it's a recurring message in the books he reads—that what we call life is as short as the blink of an eye and just as insignificant when compared to the eternity of creation, and true life begins afterward in a different realm altogether. He said it is dreams that are the mysterious link between that other world and the spirit.

These Mohametan Turks have much to say about belief in the hereafter. I also intend to write something on their beliefs about the afterlife.

Now it's best if I lie down and dream of Cristina—or should I say Nilüfer? The palace is empty, as the sultan's building works have yet to finish.

56

Fabruzi Corner was a skilled diplomat with one foot in Venice and the other in Constantinople. Constantine always kept him near to both maintain relations with farther west in Europe and ensure friendly interactions with the Ottomans. Corner acted marvelously with Sultan Murad, just as he had with many other kings, emperors and shahs. Despite as inherently distasteful it was to be sent as an emissary to the new sultan in such a way, he felt lucky to have the chance to get to know this ruler whose latest actions were so puzzling. He hoped he would return to Constantine with good news as he thought about his good relations with the previous sultan and how he could use them now.

He reached Asomaton after an hour on horseback and saw two janissaries there to meet him.

"The Turks are always so humble," he grumbled to Nicolo, one of the men in his delegation. "They send two people to meet a delegation of ten." Then with more derision and to the laughs of his men, "Considering the value they give to those not of their Mohametan religion, and us being ten infidels, I think they do us a great compliment."

"Aren't you exaggerating a bit, Sir?" Nicolo said. "We outnumber them five to one and, including me, we have knights with us from noble Venetian families." He looked at his sword, its guard lending the shape of a cross. "It would only take me two seconds to lop off their heads."

"You worry about nothing. The Turks love heaping respect on emissaries. We're their guests. As long as you aren't nonchalant when speaking with the sultan, then your life is the same as theirs."

Corner and his delegation followed the janissaries into the building site and saw that it was on a much grander scale than what their spies had said when they came up to the rising structure. A gigantic fortress with defense walls had already begun to take shape in only a few weeks' time.

"For the love of our Lord and Savior Jesus Christ," Corner said as he looked around. "The sultan must have gathered together every master builder from his entire realm."

"And they're in such a rush. Why do you think they're in such instant need of a fortress?" Nicolo whispered.

"I don't know, but we'll learn something about it when the opportunity arises."

The astonished delegation was led to the sultan's tent through laborers carrying timbers, masons mixing mortar and shaping stones, and thousands of other men seeing to their work.

"I bring greetings to the great Ottoman sultan in the name of the exalted Basileus Constantine of Rome," Corner said.

"It is clear you haven't come from Constantinople only to extend the emperor's greetings, my respected emissary," Zaganos Pasha said with dripping acrimony.

Having started with confidence, Corner was slightly taken aback by Zaganos Pasha's bald lack of diplomacy. He then reluctantly looked at Halil Pasha to the other side of the sultan, his arms folded in his caftan of forest green and the turban of the grand vizier atop his head. He couldn't make sense of why the grand vizier was so silent now, as he had always talked on end in their meetings in the time of Sultan Murad. Halil Pasha looked straight back at him, his face betraying nothing behind his grey beard and mustache.

"These old pashas who have known us since times past know we always endeavor to buttress a constructive relationship with the Ottomans," Corner said. He turned to the sultan, "The viziers of your departed father—Halil Pasha, Saruja Pasha and Ishak Pasha—all bore witness to our conversations with Sultan Murad. The Ottoman sultans and Roman basileis have had long-established and close cooperation and acted together concerning the goings on at each other's borders, and shared information mutually."

Zaganos Pasha leaned over to Shihabettin Pasha, "Does he mean like killing Muslim peasants?"

Fabruzzi reckoned the passive and calm days of the previous sultan were now no more than a dream and that he should get to the point without further ado.

"Some periodic attrition, of course, due to the close proximity of our lands, and what you speak of is the land of the basileus. The Turks rebelled and the emperor acted as any ruler would to protect his territory and existence."

"Peace is not a game of diplomacy," Zaganos Pasha shot back. "Peace means the servants of God living happily and in tranquility under their ruler."

"Very well, dear vizier. So what kind of peace is one to interpret from the building of a gigantic fortress at this very moment with thousands of laborers?"

"The communities want governance and governance wants order. The communities are as happy and strong as the power of the forces that protect them. However, I have difficulty understanding why the emissary so wants me to explain this when the largest fortresses and walls, three thick, nonetheless, the world has seen protect and surround his city."

Corner swallowed carefully so those around him wouldn't sense his nerves and then looked back to the sultan. "Even when your great-great-grandfather Sultan Bayezid had the magnificent fortress built on the other shore of the Bosporus, he first obtained permission from the emperor. He knew diplomacy well. Before and after that, as well, the sultans and emperors have always informed each other of such grand ventures. Emperor Constantine wants to learn of the motivation behind this colossal undertaking for me to tell him why he was not informed of it."

Having remained silent, Mehmed now rose to his feet. "I'm curious, Fabruzi. When was the last time you were in Venice?"

Corner couldn't make sense of the question. "I was there last month, Your Majesty," he said, curious as to what Mehmed was getting at.

"I always hear your city is quite lovely, but which do you like more, Constantinople or Venice?"

"Both cities are home to me, so I can't make such a distinction."

"Ah yes, your home. It must have escaped my mind that Venetians ruled Constantinople for not but sixty years. Your people loved it so much that they carted off everything of value back to Venice after the last campaign of the cross, didn't they?"

Corner didn't much care for this mention of this crusade two hundred years earlier.

"Your reticence must be a product of ignorance. From what you said earlier, you know the history of my father and great-great-grandfather quite well, but you should know that of your own better. The four bronze horses from Constantinople are still at Saint Mark's Cathedral, are they not?"

"You are correct, Your Excellency, and your knowledge of Venice is striking. Although I have difficulty in trying to understand what it is you want to say. The relationship between Venice and Constantinople is their own affair, which I'm certain you also appreciate."

Mehmed paced slowly through the tent. "That is exactly what I am saying, my dear emissary," he said as he stood before Corner. "The bronze horses the Venetians looted from Constantinople are their own business. Me building a fortress on my land is my own business. Constantine knows very well the boundaries of his land, and if he doesn't, the gigantic walls around his city should serve as a reminder. You remember the relations between Sultan Bayezid and the Greek emperor, but you forget that it was the emperor who invited Timur into Anatolia. You mention your conversations with my father, but you look past the Palaiologos emperor's armies in Varna and Kosovo."

Corner felt himself having trouble breathing.

"Give the emperor this message," Mehmed continued. "I am unlike all the sultans who came before me. The days past are just those. Your dreams cannot attain what I can do. Now go back with your delegation to the safety of your city walls. And if you come again asking of what I do in my own lands, then I'll send back your heads."

Corner looked out over the Bosporus as he left the tent with his delegation. His gaze stretched over its waters to Bayezid's fortress on the opposite shore. The teaming laborers in front of him and the enraged sultan he left behind told well that Mehmed had entered a different path from his modest predecessors.

Constantine would not be happy.

57

Something very interesting happened yesterday as I was about to leave after drinking the ice-cold water from a fountain in a square with Mullah Lütfi. I reckon I've found a solution to put an end to my troubles.

Mullah Lütfi noticed a white kerchief that had fallen to the ground beside the fountain. I should add it is was a beautiful kerchief with lace along its edges. He stooped over to pick it up and, thinking there might be someone looking for it, wiped it off and put it on top of the fountain. Just as he was doing this, he noticed a small piece of coal inside it. Very odd this, a piece of black coal in a folded, white kerchief.

He smiled and placed it on the fountain. I asked him why he chuckled and what a piece of coal was doing in a kerchief. He said it was a love letter, or more a message.

It seems this is a common mode of communication between young men and women in public. He explained at length that certain articles have particular meanings according to what their names rhyme with. For example, coal—*kömür*—is a message saying the person wants to spend their life with the other, life being *ömür*. This is often used between lovers. A pearl—*inji*—means you are the pearl of beauty. A pear—*armut*—means give me some hope—*umut*. Of course, flowers also all have their own special meanings.

A white flower symbolizes purity and cleanliness, lilac trust and a secret. Young men who want to get married have these messages sent to their sweethearts. It's as though every flower and plant has some attached meaning.

I asked him how they get the communication across to each other. He said they either leave them on fountains like the kerchief or pass them on to the servants of the house.

When I asked if they write an accompanying letter, he told me sometimes they do and sometimes they don't, and that it changes depending on the situation.

He explained everything one by one to my questions as I grew more interested. I was carefully noting in my head everything he said and anxiously repeating it all to myself so I wouldn't forget. I thought about taking out my book to write it down, but I didn't out of embarrassment.

As soon as I took my leave for my room, I found some white carnations in one of the palace gardens and carefully placed them in between the leaves of the *Iskendernameh* I had with me. According to what I remember, white carnations show that the giver has fallen in love with the recipient.

I gave the book with the carnations to Nilüfer today when we met. Of course, I also made long preparations for it, as Ragip Pasha shouldn't be any the wiser.

We finished our normal work and our comparisons of the different books, and then as I was getting up to leave, I left my book next to her notes and headed for the door. Then right as I was through the door, she spoke up and said I'd forgotten my book, calling me Signore Alberti.

I stood at the threshold looking at her and said it wasn't important. I'd be back tomorrow and maybe she would find something that interests her. Then I turned on my heels and quickly walked away. I never would have said such a thing in my life if I hadn't known I was going to run away right afterward.

I'm certain she understood what I wanted to say and will look in the book.

For now, though, I'm waiting and wondering, but I'm also afraid. What if she rebuffs me or complains about it to Ragip Pasha? What would happen if word of such a complaint got to Mehmed? I truly regret what I did. It has even crossed my mind to collect all my things, board a Venetian ship and run from Constantinople back to my city.

58

Iskender pulled up on the reins two hundred yards off when he saw a ship frame at the shipyard and dozens of laborers and crewmen working along the shore amid stacks of boards and timbers. Hasan and Abdullah stopped along with him. Iskender looked around and sighed.

"It's been a full five years," he said. "Five long years. I used to hold myself back from crying at night in those first weeks after I left the city."

"I was sent to a family of farmers," Hasan said. "We were so close we nearly ate off the same plate. I was comfortable and it was really nice."

"I missed my mother dearly," Abdullah said.

"You still miss your mother. You still haven't grown up," Hasan said with a laugh.

"I never thought I'd come back here," Iskender said.

Baltaoghlu Süleyman—the head of the Gallipoli Shipyard and a sea captain of renown—seemed to recognize the young janissary flanked by two others in front of him. As he was known to do before he fully recognized someone, he turned his left eye toward the janissary in the middle and squinted with a smile.

"Alexander—my Greek boy from Constantinople! I would know

you anywhere." He looked over at Hasan and Abdullah. "He was one of my best deckhands. He never laughed and was always ruminating on something, but he'd take to any job like mad and worked harder than everybody else. It was a little difficult for him to learn Turkish since he never talked. That's fine though—we need workers and warriors, not scribes. Isn't that right?"

"You're embarrassing me, Captain," Iskender said. "But tell me, though, why is the sultan running you so ragged?"

Iskender took out a letter from his belt and held it out for the man. The captain looked at the janissaries as if a thought was crossing his mind, took the letter and began to read.

The sultan sent the order to increase the workers at the shipyard tenfold, get timber and boards from the southwestern Thracian forests and built a fleet of dozens of ships as fast as possible. Baltaoghlu Süleyman thought over what the sultan would do with this many ships. No sultan had ever had a fleet so big before.

"Is it that the sultan's decided to attack Venice and I don't even know about it?" he joked.

"Even better," Hasan said.

Iskender smiled. "Don't you think the time's come for me to return home, Captain?"

BOOK THREE

The Ottoman Dragon

59

Sweat poured from the foreheads of Master Orban and the six men with him as they lowered a gigantic, bronze church bell to the stone floor, its muffled clang ringing in their ears as it hit the floor.

"For the love of Christ, how many times do I have to tell you—go slow, slow!" Orban said.

Orban had been left forced to complete the work with apprentices and novices since all of the laborers had given up before a month was out due to the arduousness of the task. The work was going worse by the day as he struggled with undisciplined men and he missed the pleasant days he'd had with his father over ten years ago. He had grown up intimately with ore—what he called gold from stone—ever since he had opened his eyes for the first time just behind the furnace. The sound of hammers on iron was his music, the bellows firing up ore dust was his air and the furnace's flames in the dark foundry were his only light.

"You can say we cleared another one," he said as he looked at the gigantic bell and let out a deep breath.

The abundant copper mines in the Kingdom of Hungary had led to the training of many master foundrymen under Regent-Governor Hunyadi Janos, but very few of them had followed their fathers into casting cannons as Orban had. With the Chinese invention of gunpowder centuries before and its transmission over the Central Asian steppes, Hungarians had been casting bronze cannons in their foundries for nearly a hundred years themselves. The constant floods in the kingdom would fill in each mine one by one, rendering them unusable and taking the charm out of the work. Dozens of master foundrymen had been forced to shutter their furnaces every year, the workers decreased and only a few keen workmen like Orban remained. The previously invincible Hungarian kings of great renown had given up their aggression after Hunyadi Janos' defeat to the Ottomans and had shut themselves off in their own lands.

Due to the shuttered mines, Orban would take what iron and bronze he could find in the city, melt them down and produce cannons. He was one of the kingdom's master foundrymen and was having trouble fulfilling the regent-governor's demands for bombards. He also couldn't make sense of why he had been getting constant orders for cannons so suddenly.

"Come on, come on! Don't just stand there with your lead feet. The furnace is dying down. Hurry, get more charcoal, hurry!" Orban yelled. The gigantic, elongated, arch-shaped furnace constantly needed feeding. The fire had been burning for days after reaching temperature and the molten metal would later pour from the hole at the bottom into crucibles that were then emptied into yard-long molds.

Orban, already in his forties, ran out to the charcoal stores beside the foundry, filled his copper bucket, ran up the wooden stairs and emptied it into the furnace. On his second trip up the stairs, an apprentice popped up in front of him in the narrow passage and they both tumbled to the ground.

A piece of charcoal circled around on the ground toward the door and bumped up against a boot that had just stepped in.

He looked up with his charcoal-blackened face to see two soldiers standing in the doorway.

"We're done for—again," he whispered to himself.

"Master Orban, it would be much better if you fulfilled the regent-governor's latest order rather than playing with the children on the ground," one of the soldiers said.

"But I told you before, gentlemen," he said as he straightened himself up, almost imploring. "I don't have enough materials. On top of that, you see what conditions I'm working under here."

"We wouldn't know one way or the other, Orban. Do what you will, but the cannons will be ready when we come back next week."

"There's no way I can finish them in a week. I beg you, allow just a few more days. Don't you see what I'm working with here?"

"Look, Orban. We're under great strain, too. The Turk has declared war on the heart of Christendom. The order for shot was increased for the aid of Emperor Constantine."

"You know well enough what happens to those who don't follow Hunyadi Janos' orders," the other soldier chimed in.

Too much charcoal had been added to the furnace and now the flames had started to lick out.

Orban thought about what the soldiers had told him without a further thought to the threat to his life levied at him. A war between the Ottomans and Constantinople meant only one thing to a master foundryman—quality materials and quick gains.

Maybe this was the only way to get out of his years-long mire anyway.

He had no intention of waiting a week for his death with the unskilled laborers around him. He decided that come nightfall, he would get on his horse with however much money he could gather and head straight for Constantinople. He had no doubt Constantine would reward him and give him an army when he offered the emperor his services. He was growing more excited to be able to do his work among soldiers rather than scrounging churches for what metal he could find.

60

"So, you're telling us you make higher-quality cannons than our Greek, German and Varangian master foundrymen?" Constantine said with a scoff as he ate grapes, seated on his throne.

"If you provide the necessary material and manpower, Your Highness, I can produce cannons that would pulverize an army outside your city walls even if it were of every man alive," Orban said from his knees before the emperor as he nervously crumpled his strange Hungarian hat.

"Slow down, Master Orban," a man of the same age said as he approached the foundryman.

"If you don't know, let me introduce him—Johannes Grandi," Sphtantzes said. "He is the commander of our preeminent war engineers and head of the cannon unit."

"There's no need for fanfare," Grandi said as he put his hand up.

Originally hailing from Germany, he had spent a large portion of his life in the Eastern Roman Empire. His hair was tussled, but it wasn't only this and his military uniform that set him apart from the other palace officials in their ornately patterned robes and tunics, he was also a man of few words who didn't lay unnecessary praise. This German-born man was said to be the best war engineer alive.

"There are neither furnaces nor molds for how you say you

would cast cannons. Aren't you exaggerating your talents just a little bit?" he asked Orban.

"New molds and furnaces can be made."

"But at that diameter, you would need to cast them in one piece to prevent cracking as they cool. It's also almost impossible to maintain the sulfur and saltpeter ratios in the black powder for cannons of such size."

"You leave the ratios to me," Orban said. "The rest is easy."

Grandi looked pensively at Orban before he silently withdrew back to the side.

"Even if we had time to waste on your experiments, we can't give the gold you ask for," Constantine said.

"But Your Majesty—"

"You should be thankful I made time to speak with you and that you're leaving this audience in one piece. Now go back to your trash heap in Hungary. We've seen quite well already how you Hungarians deal with the Turk," Constantine growled as he angrily hurled a bunch of grapes at the man's face.

Orban had no intention of going back, though. The journey to Constantinople had already taken a week, and the week he'd been given would be well over by the time he got back. Hunyadi Janos' soldiers would certainly be waiting for his head at the foundry. There would be no salvation once in their hands.

He decided he had no other choice than to give it one last chance.

61

"Don't double over, sir," Mehmed said. "We respect our scholars and artist, and your craft is also an art."

Orban looked up in surprise at Mehmed after the *reis ül-küttab* finished the translation. He thought maybe something hadn't been translated correctly.

Mehmed leaned slightly toward him as if to say he had heard correctly and to stand up.

Orban slowly rose to his feet.

"Since my engineers find you worthy of coming before me, you must have something to say." Mehmed looked over at the palace's head engineer and waited for Orban to speak.

Orban collected himself before he began to speak. "If you provide the necessary material and manpower, I can help you cast cannons that can crumble Constantinople's walls."

He told of his troubles back in Hungary and the response he had gotten from Constantine.

Mehmed had been listening carefully to what the man had to say. "And what has possessed you to think I would provide you my patronage?"

"I have always heard the Ottoman sultans value one's skill over one's religion or origin and that many scholars have come to your lands."

"You've heard correctly, Master Orban, but competence also has a price in consideration of our expectations." Mehmed turned around the ruler in his hands. "We demand discipline and the highest performance from our men. We care not for lethargy. When promises aren't kept, our clemency becomes manifold rage. Have you also heard of this?"

"Your Majesty, there would be accidents every day and catastrophes with every cannon if what you ask for isn't minded at a foundry."

The *reis ül-küttab* translated for the sultan.

"And so what do you ask for in return," Mehmed said.

Orban thought for a moment. "Enough wealth to never fall into hardship for the remainder of my life."

62

Mehmed twirled the ruler in his hand as he looked at his engineers lined up along the wall. They also seemed satisfied.

"I will give you what you ask for, Master Orban. But you will cast cannons according to my own design. These will be cannons unrivaled the world over. They will be larger than you have ever seen, louder than anything you have heard and will fire shot the size of a small world unto themselves. Can you pledge to that?"

Orban wasn't about to hesitate. "With the necessary material and men, I could make cannons to bring down the walls of Babylon itself if you so desire. There is one problem, though. I don't know how you would transport cannons with that big a bore to Constantinople."

Mehmed smiled. "Master Orban, you get to work casting the cannons with my men and don't worry about how to move them."

Halil Pasha turned to Mehmed after Orban, Muslihiddin and Saruja Pasha left the audience hall. "The Sultan would know best, but are we not putting ourselves in danger trusting this man?"

"What is there for us to worry about?" Mehmed said.

"He could be a spy from Constantine. He could report about our tools of war and munitions."

"I thought of that, Halil. The man will be in sight day and night. He will also be alone with nobody to bring word to. You have as much of a possibility of being a spy as he does."

Halil Pasha didn't care much for Mehmed's needling. He ignored it, though, and continued, "And so what if he has given us misinformation to drive us in the wrong direction and it puts our cannons out of commission on the battlefield?"

"Something of that sort would mean the man putting the lives of the Greeks before his own. And he knows it will be his head if we sense any trouble. If he is such a dreamer to die for Constantine, then let it be. He would deserve to fight among my men. But, with that belief, I'm unlikely to get anything out of them. More than that, the openness and honesty in what he said show he is a simple tradesman who's not accustomed to verbal trickery. If he can do what you say, then I'll give him more than he asked for."

Mehmed looked out the window as he finished speaking, out toward the mountains extending to the horizon. What he saw in his mind, though, weren't mountains, but the imposing city walls of Constantinople. He very much needed to listen to every idea to aid in his tearing down of these walls that had stood for a thousand years.

Orban realized how generous the sultan had been in accepting his offer when he entered the munitions foundry behind the palace with Muslihiddin. There seemed to be no need for a foundryman like himself in the gigantic foundry spreading out before his eyes. It was the first time he had ever seen such a large area used for casting cannons. Three separate furnaces were continuously belching flames, and each with dozens of master foundrymen at work around them. Everyone around the furnaces seemed to know what they needed to do in a system and understanding Orban was unaccustomed to.

At first glance, he felt as though he could live out his days there. He told himself from that day forth, he would show much more gratitude to the sultan.

63

I decided it was time to visit the sultan's famous armory, which I had been putting off for weeks, when I heard a Hungarian foundryman had newly arrived. I wake up early like the Mohamatans who rise for the morning prayer and quickly get to the foundry, its continuous fires become tiny suns. If I had known the fires of the foundry would allow me to pass Edirne's cold winter days as if it was summer, I would have gone much earlier. The foundry's flames oddly calm the fires raging inside me. Master Muslihiddin, the head of the foundry, has set aside a pleasant place for me in his own room. I sit there and order my notes as I watch the foundrymen as they go about their work.

The Turks' diligence is easy to see at the weapons foundry. They work in three shifts per day. One shift works from morning until late afternoon, the second from late afternoon until the night prayer and the third from then until morning in a constant rotation. Their times of prayer always dictate when they start and finish their work. This system of rotation ensures the furnaces are always stoked and increases the speed of the work threefold. Whereas in Venice it's common for a couple men to keep night watch to stoke the fires, here, even the apprentices who sweep the floors change and there are always dozens of men on the job. As far as I can tell, it looks as if there are two hundred men working at any one time.

There are three large furnaces that are the foundry's skeleton around which everything else is attached. The furnaces are essentially the same as I have seen in the lands of Italy, England and Denmark, but they differ in two aspects. The first is that furnaces here are incomparably large, at nearly the height of three men. The second is the bellows are run by a large waterwheel. It is constantly churning from the water of the stream next to the foundry, and as it turns, it blows air through the channels connected to it and distributes it equally to the three furnaces. I plan to draw plans of this particular water mill and its intricacies in the coming days for my notes. This apparatus makes slaves unnecessary to constantly pump the bellows.

Mehmed drew the rough plans for the water mill, as he had for the rest of the foundry, and then had Muslihiddin and Saruja Pasha design the details. It's the same for the cannons. Bernardo always said that the prince never when anywhere without his drawing book. I now see the same thing years later. He's always calculating something, drawing and showing them to his engineers.

Master Muslihiddin showed me around his small library. He said the sultan has every manuscript written on water mills and mining found and translated, and then has schemas drawn up based on those. There are many manuscripts in Arabic, Persian, Chinese, Latin and Greek. It's obvious from the illustrations that they're all works on mechanical subjects. Muslihiddin's table is stacked with drawings and record books. He says he keeps accounts of what they've done every day, the reserve materials they've used, the results they've gotten and ratios for black powder.

Each of the three furnaces has its own master foundryman in charge of its operations. Muslihhidin has one, the middle furnace is run by Saruja Pasha, who has been a vizier since the time of Sultan Murad, and a Genoese foundryman named Dognano runs the other. Saruja Pasha works in coordination with Dognano so as not to hinder his other diplomatic work. Orban is responsible for the furnace on the near side. His men are the many-skilled janissaries. The sultan ordered that a certain number of janissaries concentrate fully on artillery and munitions, and they follow their masters very well. Those among the janissaries who know Hungarian and Genoese do the translating and facilitate the communication between the master foundrymen and the foremen.

The head foundrymen scurry back and forth between the foundry and the black powder works. Care was taken that these two buildings be far from each other so one would stay safe if the other goes up in flames. The masters in these two buildings complicate their work, but as always, the Ottomans take security above all else. The entrance and exit of the powder works are always under guard. I was easily able to enter the foundry since Muslihiddin and Saruja Pasha know me, but the janissaries at the door to the powder works wouldn't let me enter without a tughra from the sultan. The production and storage of black powder is under strict control, according to what I've heard. Mehmed is trying to increase the production of black powder as much as possible. With the edicts he's sent to every corner of Edirne, powder production has been set up in areas where saltpeter is present, and places where it isn't were ordered to explore for areas where they can increase production.

At the moment, the best areas of production are Gallipoli in Rumelia, and north of Kayseri in Anatolia. Ibrahim II of Karaman to the south of Kayseri taunts Ottoman soldiers, but has been careful not to go beyond that. The books Muslihiddin has explain in detail the use of black powder mixtures after saltpeter passes through its stages of refinement. I haven't been to Gallipoli or Kayseri, and also haven't seen how it's produced here in Edirne. It's also difficult to understand their particular process just by reading it. Muslihiddin has been explaining they boil the saltpeter at specific levels at each stage, leave it in pools, wet and dry it repeatedly, pack it in barrels and many more of the procedures.

What I have been able to see, though, is Orban constantly arguing with Muslihiddin about the powder mixture. Orban always estimates the sulfur and charcoal mixture whereas Muslihiddin tries to write down every experiment in his records. He showed me a book by Hasan al-Rammah on black powder and engineering when I asked what the best powder mixture is. He claims this book, which was written two hundred years ago, is the best source and gives the most accurate powder mixture. He says it's as good as the composition of his own mixture. This is the mixture of the best type of black powder he showed me from his records.

Saltpeter74 percent, or 3/4
Sulfur11 percent, or 1/8
Charcoal13 percent, or 1/8

He gave me the fractions when I asked if there wasn't any easier way to do it than with percentages.

They meticulously determine the weight on their odd scales, mix all the parts thoroughly and pour cattle urine and water over it. After it dries, it's then beaten for a continues twenty-four hours. They work in three shifts at the powder works, just like they do at the foundry, using very big, wooden mortars and pestles. Even I know any spark from metal could send the entire building into oblivion. Afterward, the finely ground grains are sifted into powder. This also gets rid of any small pebbles or sand in the mixture. Then for the last step, they pack it into barrels.

Muslihiddin said that whereas black powder has been known of in China for centuries, they were unable to purify it correctly and the ratios of sulfur and charcoal were off. He showed me books by scholars from the past five hundred years, such as al-Razi, al-Hamdani and ibn al-Baytar, and said Arabs had developed the original mixes and developed on them.

This is the mixture for bronze he has in his records.

Copper1/3
Tin1/4
Brass1/7

He says bronze is both easier to cast than iron and cannons made of it are more durable. It naturally costs more than iron, but Mehmed has left the revenues of a few fiefdoms to Muslihiddin and Saruja Pasha's disposal. Having come from the region with the world's richest copper mines, Orban provides great help to them. It wouldn't be presumptive to say all of the engineers here are under much strain to create physical cannons from the sultan's drawings. They always thank God and are happy when they receive good results. Those not of the Mohamatan faith, like Orban, continue their work quietly. I don't sense they have any complaints or grievances.

Muslihiddin explained with wide eyes at what high compression the correct mixture of black powder would fire a shot. Rather than the powder firing the shot, I'd say it comes from the fervor of these men.

I heard they will try a new cannon in a few days. Like everyone, I'm also curious to see the result.

64

"Slowly, slowly, slowly," Orban said—one of the dozen words he'd newly learned in Turkish.

Two master foundrymen slowly collected the molten bronze pouring from the hole at the bottom of the furnace into a crucible. They carried the crucible with a set of six-foot-long iron tongs with handles extending in opposite directions, which made moving it easier and minimized the advent of accidents. Their thick, leather gloves protected their hands against the heat of the red-hot iron tongs, even if only a little. The molten bronze had been heated in the furnace for three days until it reached its melting point of nearly two thousand degrees as janissaries continuously alternated stoking the flames with charcoal and adding ore. Mehmed had ordered five janissary regiments to solely work at the foundry's furnaces, which, owing to their lives of tremendous discipline, had increased the foundry's output even more when they began.

Master Muslihiddin had been working to prepare the molds to take the molten bronze since the morning prayer. He along with the Genoese mold maker Dognano and Saruja Pasha had decided to prepare the nine-foot-long and half-foot wide clay mold vertically instead of horizontally so it would be easier for the bronze to fill it fully. They were all eager to see the result from this method, as it was the first time they had used it. Orban was against the idea when he first heard it, but was convinced when Muslihiddin showed him the mathematic ratios and geometric drawings, which showed the molten bronze would be under its own weight and would therefor ensure the breech of the cannon was sturdier. As the breech takes the highest impact from firing, the sturdier it is ensures a more durable and long-lasting cannon. Every time Muslihiddin came with drawings and calculations in hand, Orban told him he'd won and set back to work.

After the mold was fixed in place with thick timbers and ropes, iron rings were placed inside toward the bottom and the top to ease the molten bronze to take the correct shape at the most important places and meld with the bronze to further increase its ability to withstand the wear from firing.

Iskender and Murad climbed up the scaffold that had been built days in advance as they carried the crucible of molten bronze. They coordinated their movements as they began to tip out the glowing, molten bronze from the crucible. When it was empty, Hasan and Abdullah brought more from Saruja Pasha's furnace and ascended the scaffold as Iskender and Murad climbed down the other side and started filling in the rest of the mold.

"This is where I get nervous," Muslihiddin said.

"You mean the second crucible?" Orban asked.

A janissary who knew Hungarian made communication between them easier. Sometimes Orban would speak with Turkish words here and there, and Muslihiddin would sometimes get himself across in the language of his fellow foundryman.

"The bronze poured first has to take to the second round before it starts to cool. If not, even if it comes out of the mold in one piece, there'll be a seam that will show it didn't bind."

Orban had a good handle on Muslihiddin's concerns. "Even more," he said, "the two parts would have different strengths if the two alloys aren't exactly the same."

The two master foundrymen knew they had to find a solution to this problem.

65

There wasn't even the slightest difference with Nilüfer or the maid when I got to the house today. I had a short conversation with Ragip Pasha before we started our daily tasks. I saw the book in with Nilüfer's notes. Everything was so ordinary that I started to think she hadn't opened it and seen the carnations.

Then I asked her for the book with the excuse of wanting to look over a chapter. I looked at her face to see if she would give any sign as she held it out, but she just handed it to me.

I was surprised, though, when I opened it—the flower I'd put between the pages wasn't there. I started to flip through it like mad and Nilüfer asked me what was wrong and if I could find the chapter.

She looked me in the eyes. That's when I realized she had gotten my message and I blushed from self-consciousness. I stuttered a bit and said I somehow couldn't find the chapter I was thinking of.

I caught the maid with a sneaky smile on her face. They both knew what was going on and were expertly hiding it. The maid took such pleasure in my surprise that she went to the kitchen so Ragip Pasha wouldn't get where her smile came from. I couldn't wait for the prayer time to come.

I was relieved when I finally heard the call to prayer an hour later. As soon as Ragip Pasha went to the other room, Nilüfer looked up and told me she'd gotten my message. She said she sees that I've gotten used to their customs, but only with those I work with.

Her sharp tongue was like a slap in the face.

Then she said she didn't understand what I wanted to say. She looked over at the maid and said that, more correctly, they didn't understand.

I explained the kerchief I had seen earlier with Mullah Lütfi and explained with my face flushing ever deeper that I was trying to make use of this custom, as well. I added also that I apologize if I'd been indelicate.

She thanked me for my honesty and said she reckoned I'd chosen the wrong flower.

It turns out a white carnation isn't the symbol for love. She explained that when two lovers who have known each other for a long time have drifted apart and remain separate, it has the meaning of deep longing.

She and the maid both laughed at me sweetly. I felt I was sinking into the floor.

Then Nilüfer went on and said it's a pink carnation that's for love.

She said a rose means I weep when you smile, but she couldn't remember which specific color it was. She also said soap has the meaning of saying one will wash the other's troubles away.

I gathered myself and told her to let it be so, as a white carnation suits my feelings. I told her that she looks very much like my departed wife and every time I see her, I feel as if we already met years ago, which is why I feel I've been separated from her. Then I asked if it isn't true that the Turks always say there is good in every misfortune.

They both drew quiet and serious when I said this. The maid made an excuse and quietly went to the kitchen. Nilüfer told me I am a good person, if not a little too bold. She said she didn't know if it stemmed from naivete or if it's how I conduct myself in Venice. She called me a smart man, but there's one thing I should know, that Mohamatan women are forbidden from marrying Christian men, but if it were the other way around, maybe I'd have a chance.

Indeed, it was the response I had been inspecting, but I hadn't expected her to say it so openly.

I could have told her I'm actually not that deeply religious, but I was breathless.

Nilüfer was about to say something more when the maid came back and looked at her. We realized what she was getting at when Ragip Pasha returned and we got back to the texts.

The remaining hours of the day seemed as if they were years. I didn't want to read or write anything. I was terrified Ragip Pasha might have sensed something.

I said I had a headache and left early for home.

I don't know how I'll be able to look Nilüfer in the face again. I'll find Mullah Lütfi tomorrow and tell him I've told Nilüfer everything I know, so there's nothing left for me to explain, that my work has come to an end and there's no need for me to meet with her anymore.

66

The mold was broken open three days after the cannon was cast to the enchanted looks of the janissaries, dazzled by the bronze piece twice their size. None of them, however, could figure out how to get it in place and move it to the firing range.

Muslihiddin had four timbers placed around the cannon, forming a square. Then with the help of the scaffold, he assembled a system of ropes and pulleys with the ropes hanging down over the cannon. It was then moveable with the aid of the master craftsmen from the janissary catapult regiment.

He put a ring around each of the ends of the cannon and gave each end of the ropes hanging down from the pulleys to groups of thirty janissaries. He gave them the sign to start pulling and warned them to be careful, otherwise the smallest slip could send the cannon spinning and get it tangled in the ropes.

He had a carriage made of timber planks with a carved-out area for the cannon to rest brought close by. The janissaries on the ropes first worked to slowly position the cannon's breech over where it would lay. The ropes suspending the other end were putting great strain on the timbers above. The janissaries were baffled for a bit as to what to do with the cannon hanging in the air. None of them could see how this ten-ton hunk of bronze straining at its ropes level to the ground would be lowered into place onto the carriage. The sound of cracking coming from the timbers overhead also started to worry everyone.

The artillery crew was accustomed to moving cannons one-fifth the size of this one and had no idea how to tackle this behemoth. Muslihiddin and Orban decided to roll the carriage closer in place rather than trying to shift the cannon. The men moving the carriage into place ran the risk of ending up underneath ten tons of bronze if the janissaries let up on the ropes or if the rafters splintered to pieces.

One of the janissaries offered himself to push the carriage into place. The master foundrymen agreed and the janissary removed the chocks from the carriage's four wheels. He looked up at the cannon and then put his entire weight into the carriage to try to inch it forward.

"Slacken the lines!" Muslihiddin ordered, and the two teams on either side dropped one hand below the other at the same time.

"Again!" Muslihiddin shouted, and the janissaries again dropped one hand below the other on the ropes as their fellow soldier tried to move the carriage into place at the same speed.

Muslihiddin was about to call out again when one the rafters holding the ropes let out a crack and wrenched in two from the weight, sending the ropes whirring up through the pulleys as the cannon crashed onto the carriage in a rain of splinters.

The janissary at the carriage had tried to escape, but its timbers tumbled onto one of his feet along with the cannon. As the other janissaries tried to pull his right leg out from the wreckage as he wailed in pain, Muslihiddin and Orban were only thinking of one thing. They would need to find another solution for moving these mammoth cannons if they didn't want to waste the sultan's janissaries before the battle even started.

Moreover, this cannon, which was to be finally brought to the battlefield the next day, had split in two at the joint before its first trial, confirming their worst fears.

Muslihiddin felt the answer he'd been looking for spontaneously come to him when the cannon split cleanly in the middle as if it had been cut with a knife.

67

The people leaned out their windows, left their houses and gathered in the squares to get word of what was happening as palace criers walked through the streets of Edirne pounding davuls and hollering.

Each crier had the same message, which they repeated again and again. "Hear ye, hear ye! The sultan's new cannon will be tested tomorrow after the morning prayer. The cannon will be extremely loud. Do not be afraid. Do not worry. Do not think it is a battle. Do not fear, thinking lightning has struck!"

As they did for all news the palace announced to the public, the criers wended their way through every neighborhood as they beat their davuls. Orban had specifically told the sultan that the sound from a cannon this large could terrify anyone who had never heard it before and could spread confusion and panic among the city folk.

The next day, it looked as if the entire city had turned out at the drill field outside the foundry. Muslihiddin told Mehmed the field should be cleared of people up to a little over a mile, otherwise the firing wouldn't be able to take place. Janissaries then started to clear people from the field on order from the sultan and moved them to the wooded areas to the side.

This setback, which they hadn't accounted for, had annoyed Muslihiddin, who was now ill-tempered and exasperatedly looking at Orban. He had told Orban the day before that cannons fire better in the morning and evening, but the noon-day sun heats the bronze and distorts the calculations. Orban had told him there was no need to worry since it wasn't summer, but Muslihiddin took out his notes and tried to explain that it wasn't the heat itself that would be a problem, but the angle of the sunlight.

After the janissaries had cleared the field, they formed two lines, one on each side of the range, to ensure no one entered anywhere the cannon ball might fall.

The cannon was finally unveiled after the two-hour delay to the wonderment of the buzzing crowd. The high palace officials looking out the windows, janissaries and diplomats couldn't hide their amazement.

The hulking, seventeen-foot-long cannon, three feet around, made the gunners at its side look miniscule, not even visible to those farthest away in the crowd. Its brilliant bronze, however, was impossible for anyone not to see. A triangular scaffold had been arranged beneath the barrel, which pointed out at thirty degrees over the empty field.

In consultation with the sultan, Orban and Muslihhidin had decided to forge the cannon in two pieces after the unsuccessful attempt with the first, unwieldy cannon. This second cannon was both easier to move and forge. Muslihiddin had spent many sleepless nights trying to work out a system of screws to fasten the two sections together. He at first thought to use very small screws, but it posed the risk of leaking. In the following days, he decided to make the cannon itself a screw. He had a small model made first, which had the breech end screw into the muzzle, and when screwed together, was no different than a cannon forged in one piece.

Getting the muzzle and breech ends of the nineteen-ton cannon to screw into each other had been the second problem Orban and Muslihiddin had to overcome. To do so, Orban had suggested the reinforce rings have raised holes so ropes could easily pass through them and timbers could be fitted in to screw the two ends together. His solution made it easier to both move and assemble the behemoth. Mehmed had encouraged them, saying there is nothing man can forge that manpower cannot move. He had looked through books and every other source he found that describe wheel arrays and carriage contraptions. He also led the way with his own drawings, which he showed Muslihiddin.

It had taken days to move the cannon the hundred yards from the foundry to the field and assemble it.

Orban used a long-handled shovel to personally load the massive amount of black powder into the barrel. Muslihiddin used a ramrod to pack the powder well in the breech and then added some straw to hasten the ignition of the powder. Iskender and Hasan directed the granite cannonball and into the muzzle. Muslihiddin then added more straw and Orban at the breech end loaded the shaft stemming from the touchhole with a narrow slat. All of this took some time in order to ensure the barrel was neither obstructed nor left with space for air to escape. If it were blocked, there would be no air and the powder wouldn't ignite, but if too much space was left, then the explosion into emptiness would lessen the force needed to propel the cannonball.

After everything had been readied, Orban and Muslihhidin warned the janissaries nearby to stand clear before they exchanged glances. They then turned to Mehmed and waited for his signal.

Muslihhidin said *bismillah ar-Rahman ar-Rahim*—in the name of God, the Gracious and Merciful—lit the touchhole and took three steps back as the crowd of people screamed from the terrifying explosion. The smoke emanating from the cannon made it impossible to see the cannonball or surroundings for a while.

The smoke lifted and they saw the pit the cannon had created from its recoil. After they had recovered from the deafening sound, they jumped on their horses and followed after the sultan with the gunners toward where the cannonball had fallen.

They couldn't find it despite the nearly mile and a half long line of janissaries, and so thought maybe the cannon hadn't actually fired and the shot was stuck at the breech. Orban and Muslihhidin were anxiously looking at each other, sweat pouring down their backs from this debacle they'd caused. The looked and searched, but there was no sign of a cannonball anywhere.

They proceeded three hundred yards further.

Muslihhidin was about to say there had been a mishap when Iskender pointed to the distance and shouted, "There ahead, where the trees are shredded!"

They all brought their horses to a gallop until they reached an area where some of the trees had had their tops sheared off and the trunks of others were splintered. There was a six-foot hole three feet around in the soil.

Mehmed pulled up on his reins, gave a smug smile and shouted, "*Ya al-Jabbar!*"—God the Irresistible.

Orban and Muslihhidin hadn't expected the cannonball to travel this far. While they were still in awe, a Venetian traveler had already likened it to a dragon.

68

I would like so much to be able to share my feelings with someone and pour out my grief. My heart is as strained as that new cannon the Ottomans have—that dragon. These Mohamatan men don't much care for talk of women, though. They speak with each other, but consider discussing their wives to be immoral. I was able to share my love with myself, though, and at least got to sleep last night, even if but for a short time.

What else can I do? These lines are also of myself.

Writing is becoming more than ever a way for me to speak with myself and deal with my own despair. I feel as though I becalm myself as I write. Sometimes I wish I had started this work when Cristina had died and so would have been able to disencumber myself from this grief.

I waited for morning throughout the night. I won't wait for this work to end and hold out hope for something that won't be any longer. Nilüfer is not Cristina, and I must accept that. I won't be stuck fooling myself any more.

I told myself this over and over as I waited for morning.

Then with the light of dawn, I went to the library in search of Mullah Lütfi. He always goes there to read after the morning prayer. He wasn't there, though. The others in the library said he was with the sultan.

Mehmed likes to spend every moment with his scholars and talk whenever given the opportunity. They say it's a habit he formed as a child.

I went to find him again after noon. I had fully intended to go tell him that the work had finished and I wouldn't be able to meet with Nilüfer any longer when I heard her voice.

She told me that since I hadn't come to the house today, she thought I was ill and so decided to come and see.

I was surprised and didn't know what to say.

She took a manuscript out of her bag and handed it to Mullah Lütfi. She had to come to the palace to deliver it anyway. I swallowed hard when he asked me why I was looking for him. Nilüfer gave me a look, her eyes fraught as if trying to say something.

I told him I wasn't feeling well, as Nilüfer had thought, and was going to tell him to give her word that I wouldn't be able to meet with her today. Then I said the problem had been solved.

Then, as Mullah Lütfi left us, Nilüfer asked me if I wouldn't be coming any longer, as if she had sensed what I was feeling. She said we had much more work to do and the sultan didn't like work left half done. She recounted how he rewards good work but levies heavy punishments on those who work indiscriminately. I should know this much better than her after all, she said, since I know him better, to which I agreed.

She looked around as if she were making sure everyone was far enough away from us and then said she hadn't been able to sleep a wink last night. She asked me to forgive her for what she had said before—she didn't want to give me false hope, but then said she shouldn't have been so crude about it.

I told her it wasn't important and that it is rather I who apologize since I shouldn't have taken it to that extent.

She told me again that I'm a good man who has experienced much suffering and that she could have been more understanding. When she said this, I so strongly wanted to take her in my arms, kiss her and caress her neck as I had done with Cristina.

We compared the last chapter of the book until mid-afternoon as if nothing had happened. It was a strange feeling, since we went on with our work very seriously, but it was also as if we both understood that a gigantic wall between us had been torn down. She hadn't actually said anything different from what she had said yesterday, but I felt like it was all the exact opposite. All she did, however, was restate what she said yesterday in softer terms.

She said she almost forgot something when we were parting. Then she pulled a book from her bag and held it out for me.

I flipped through the pages with an impulsive urge, and there between them was a red rose. What does it mean, though?

How would I be able to find out what a red rose means here?

69

Antonio Rizzo was relieved to see the foggy skyline of the city from the helm of his ship as it sailed down the Bosporus. The dome of Hagia Sophia twinkled indistinctly in the distance. He had set sail three days earlier from Caffa on the northern Black Sea coast and, like his men, was looking forward to resting in the city.

As he looked over the land, however, an imposing fortress along the coast caught his eye, as he had never seen it before. The Bosporus' swift current and stiff winds brought his ship nearer the fortress. He was trying to make sense of the men moving about on the thick, tall bastions when his first mate, Piero Davanza, came running up to him.

"Captain, Captain! The Turks are yelling from the shore for us to lower our sails and lift the oarts."

"Since when do we lower our sails here, Piero!" Rizzo growled.

The captain was thinking about the passenger he had below deck.

Dominigo of Morea could tell something was wrong. He pulled a small cylindrical case from the pocket of his crimson jacket and looked at it anxiously. Held closed with iron rings, he clenched the leather case and put it back in his pocket.

The crew had piled up at the starboard gunwale to try to make sense of the fortress, its walls, ramparts and towers at the corners becoming more visible as they drew closer. Rizzo knew there had been no such fortress there when he had left the city three months earlier as he looked it over again.

"Piero, am I not seeing straight or is this a fortress?" he said.

"I can't make sense of it, Captain. None of us can."

Then the lookout in the crow's-nest called out, "There're cannons! There are cannons on the ramparts!" spreading commotion over the deck.

Rizzo took hold of the wheel and cranked it as far port as possible. The ship then drew away from the European shore toward the Anatolian side.

After a while, Rizzo realized they were pulling near the Anatolian Fortress off portside.

"Why do you think they want to stop us, Captain?"

"It's certain those curs don't want to give us flowers."

The crew heard a janissary call out from a crenel when the ship pulled beside the Anatolian Fortress. His hands cupping his mouth, the janissary cried out, "Lower your sails and lift your oars for your own good!"

He kept yelling the same warning repeatedly.

"Maybe it would be better if we do as they say," Davanza said.

Rizzo looked at his first mate. "Don't be so afraid. What can they do anyway? The current and the wind are in our favor. We'll be in the city before they even know it."

Davanza had no response.

They heard a violent explosion of the portside before a cannonball careened into the water fifteen yards from the ship. Rizzo looked confidently at Davanza as the cannonball sent up bubbling foam on its way to the bottom of the Bosporus.

"You see, I told you. I know the firing range of that fortress quite well. There's no way they can reach us."

Davanza took a deep breath along with the rest of the crew and was more at ease as the ship sailed toward the middle of the Bosporus. Before he could ask about the guns at the new fortress, they heard the rumble of a second cannon off starboard.

In seconds, the cannonball careened through the starboard balustrade and tore through the crewmen there.

The ship was quickly taking on water and the surviving crew threw themselves into the water. Not knowing where they should swim, some took off for the Anatolian shore while the others swam for the European coast.

Davanza and Dominigo swam toward the new fortress as Antonio Rizzo's lifeless body sank with his ship through the cold waters of the Bosporus.

70

"Why didn't you follow the order to lower your sails, Captain?" the commander of the fortress, Firuz Agha, asked in Ottoman. Davanza knew the language of the palace and so there was no need to speak in Venetian.

Davanza, his hair still wet, was sitting in a chair with his knees up to his chest, wrapped in a blanket. He was glad to be alive even though he was in the fortress' dungeon. Still in shock, though, the voice of this man with a curled-up mustache standing over him sounded more terrifying than it actually was.

He shook as he answered. "We've passed here many times transporting goods from the Venetian and Genoese colonies to the city. We've never before been ordered to lower our sails here. We were surprised."

"Do you not know the new order of things? The sultan's decrees are absolute. Every ship, no matter its provenance, must obtain permission from this fortress to pass before continuing on its way. It is the same in both directions."

"We didn't know."

"But we warned you from the watchtowers before you pulled along the coast by the fortress. You heeded neither call from either side."

Davanza hung his head and thought of Rizzo as he looked at his trembling feet.

"Don't fear, Captain. You'll be better after a good sleep."

Davanza, now captain of a sunken ship, still couldn't believe he was still alive.

"You don't seem to understand." Firuz Agha said, his hands clasped behind his back as he paced back and forth. "Things have grown serious now. We are at war with the Greeks in Constantinople, and we don't know which side you sailors are on." He stopped beside Davanza. "Things will get messier if you don't mind your actions. Do not start to provoke us as Constantine is. Now I have to give an account to the sultan about why I sank a Venetian ship. You also have lost dozens of men and a valuable captain."

"Are you going to let me go?"

"Don't worry. Once you've pulled yourself together and gotten a change of clothes, my soldiers will bring you to the city. Make it known to the Venetians there and the *bailo* that this is no trifle. Your crew, however, will stay as our guests for a while."

71

I met the palace astrologer today. They call him the *qadizade.* He's had much work to do and no time for me since he's been trying to determine an auspicious date for the sultan's coming war campaign. Mehmed doesn't do anything without first consulting his astrologer. A large building in the palace complex is completely set aside for him and his work. There are star maps everywhere on the walls and spread out over the tables. I personally didn't know these maps could be so detailed.

I was surprised to see that Mehmed plans his future according to the astrologer, since I didn't think the Turks believed in soothsayers and divination. Mullah Lütfi has gotten angry and said he has no time for such nonsense whenever I've asked him about such things. The astrologer was just as offended and said he was no such thing as a soothsayer and tried to rebuke me.

I told him, though, that he reads the future.

He agreed, but said it is I who says he reads the future and he insisted he makes no prophesies.

When I asked him to explain, he said that divining the future is done without any data and claims to predict the far-off future whereas he only interprets signs.

As an example, he asked if it is divination if one says it will rain after seeing grey clouds.

I said it wasn't. And to that he said that is precisely what he does, and then set back to work.

The astrologer believes the stars have a bearing on people and affect their moods. This practice, of course, is long established ever since the times of the ancient Greeks, but the Ottomans seem to think the line between the Greek myths and science has been broken. They don't discount the ancient astrologers out of hand, though. The palace astrologer knows Ptolemy's *Geography* from cover to cover. He did, however, wrinkle his nose and say Ptolemy was wrong on a great many topics.

Here I should write a few lines about the differences between Mohamatan understandings and our own. Whereas the Church forbids doubt, questioning and free thought, with clerics conducting their research behind closed doors, the Mohamatans believe they better understand God's order and attain greater devotion through study. That is why here in the Ottoman lands many clerics are men of science and many men of science are clerics. Mullah Lütfi always says science is not religion. For example, the astrologer's library at the palace has books by Hindu mathematicians, tables of star names from Cathay, astronomical tables from the ancient Greeks and Persians, and works from many other places and people. On this topic, Mullah Lütfi told me of a saying of their prophet Muhammad—*seek knowledge even if one must go to China.*

I don't only write down the astrologer's astronomical theories in my notes, either. There is a sundial on a tower adjacent his building in a courtyard of the palace. It's the most interesting I've ever seen, as it shows the five times for prayer throughout the day.

It's a waist-high platform with many lines on it and a triangular piece of metal like a bird's beak rising above it. When the astrologer was boasting about what it could do, I said a straight rod could do the same in clear weather.

He smiled and said it was clear how much I didn't know of astronomy. He recounted how every day is longer or shorter and how all time changes according to the time of the rising and setting sun. That's why, he said, this instrument gives the correct time every day throughout the year. He said the time also changes depending on longitude and latitude.

I, of course, know that the days grow longer and shorter, but I hadn't thought that their prayer times changed depending on longitude and latitude.

The astrologer's room is full of interesting instruments—incredible nested, metal globes and different types of astrolabes. The sultan's main design was to gather the world's finest astronomers in his lands.

72

Iskender was excited when he entered the Privy Chamber of the Edirne Palace. Constantly under his command, the possibility of coming face to face with the sultan would make any janissary tremble from head to toe.

This day, however, he was in search of Jafer Agha. Iskender had been charged with delivering a leather case to him. He had been told the sultan was meeting with his commanders, and so Jafer Agha should be there. There was nothing in the beautiful and simple room, however, other than a quiet air. Iskender looked around carefully at the folded prayer rug by the wall, the books scattered about and the maps on the walls.

The carved, wooden star on the ceiling, as intricate as embroidery, caught his eye. His gaze was drawn to it every time he saw one.

"It's the *Rub el-Hizb,*" a voice said from behind him.

Iskender turned around and saw Mullah Fenari. This teacher would show up in the janissary corps at the most unexpected of times, put Iskender's spirit at ease with a few words and then disappear just as quickly as he had come.

"It's the name of the star you're looking at," Mullah Fenari said. "There's a circle in the middle and two squares surrounding it. It's also called the eight-pointed star."

"I've seen them in many places," Iskender said as he looked down from the ceiling. "In houses, at the palaces, the mosques, on doors. I've always wondered what it's meaning is."

"There's a time for everything and nothing is coincidence. This is what the star explains. Everything in creation moves according to an order—the perfect order a supreme will has created."

As always when he found himself with Mullah Fenari, Iskender started to think of the things he could never open up about to anyone anywhere.

"I don't believe my fate is so perfect," he said. "Or maybe more correctly, I have trouble understanding what it is." He was thinking of Mariam as he spoke. He wanted a life together with her, for his fate to include her.

"A servant of God will at times have want for something," Mullah Fenari said. "This want is so lofty and precious that God consents to His servant and bestows upon him something of even greater value—the uniting of eternal bliss in both this world and the next. What is important is for a servant of God not to accept his fate as a fetter chained to his neck, but for him to create his own fate by honoring the dignity of man and believing that his fate takes shape along the line of destiny the supreme will has drawn. This is the star of perfection."

Iskender looked back up to the ceiling and thought about what the mullah had said.

"If you ask me, though," Mullah Fenari said, "in this room, the circle at the center of the star is the sultan himself. He is the shadow of the supreme will on earth and the frames around it are his servants."

Iskender looked down again to ask another question, but saw Mullah Ferari was no longer in the room. He looked behind as the door was about to close when it opened again and in walked Jafer Agha.

"The sultan is about to return from the garden. What do you want?" Jafer Agha said. As the sultan's head guard, he preceded the sultan everywhere and made the final inspections himself.

"I was told to deliver this to you," Iskender said as he held out the leather case.

"Alright," Jafer Agha said as he took the case. "Now get out of here."

"It would be good for you to see this," he added as he walked into the vizier's room. He held out the leather case for Zaganos Pasha. "They found it on a man from a Venetian merchant ship after sinking it."

Zaganos Pasha knew as soon as he saw it that it was the type of case the Constantinopolitans used to carry secret messages.

"It's a case for a secret message, Jafer," he said.

"It was on a man named Dominigo who was pulled from the water. Could its contents not have gotten wet?"

"Water can't penetrate these. They use them specifically for messages carried from sea to sea—" he looked over at Karaja Pasha "—on spy ships."

"So then, the Venetians weren't carrying foodstuffs as they claimed."

"They were, but apparently they were up to other work, too. The Venetians like to kill two birds with one stone."

Zaganos Pasha pulled the engraved dagger from his belt, placed the leather cylinder on the table and sliced off the end.

"This coded message is in such a simple case, Jafer. Whoever was carrying it must have thought no one would be able to work it out if it were to fall out of his hands."

"A commander by the name of Piero Davanza requested the man carrying it return with him to Venice, but Firuz Agha said he wouldn't release him until he knew what the case held."

Zaganos Pasha held the two ends of the piece of rolled up paper he'd pulled from the case and carefully looked it over. He went in front of a mirror on the wall and looked at the paper's reflection. The curiosity on his face gradually turned into concern.

"They're readying themselves, Jafer," He said. "The entire world is preparing."

73

“To the north!” Geronimo shouted from atop his horse.

It was already difficult to track prey through the dense trees of the forest, and the falling snow and mud was further complicating the matter for the knights and their companions.

The wild boar in the mountain forests outside Genoa could be over four feet long and two feet at the shoulder. It was a demonstration of ability for the famous Genoese knights in their spare time to hunt these boars, which sometimes were over six-feet long, as it required exertion and attention nearly beyond that of man. It was the beast for which these crusader knight most strived when they weren’t at war and they hunted boar at risk to their lives.

Three hundred yards in front of Geronimo, with the word from his companion, Leonardo pulled his reins to the right and sped in among the trees. The hounds in the lead headed in the same direction.

Leonardo saw something dark appear and then vanish as it ran through the green of the forest. He held the reins in his left hand and a spear with a cross-shaped point in his right. The spear was made to pierce the under part of the boar’s neck only so far so it would hold the beast back and leave the hunter out of reach of its tusks.

Waiting at the other side of the forest, Maurizio thought that maybe they had choses the wrong day for the hunt as he watched the snow pile up on his horse and his shoulders. The increasing barks from the hounds showed that his three companions were on the trail of a beast after two hours in the forest. His horse was accustomed to the barking of dogs and stood motionless as steam billowed from its nostrils with every breath. Maurizio saw a man on horseback approaching from the horizon and could tell from his clothes that he was foreign to this place.

"Damnit! What in God's creation is this?" Geronimo said when he caught sight of the dark shape Leonardo had seen just moments before. He clenched his spear and spurred his horse on again. He heard the boar's grunts and knew he was quite close.

The three hounds had cornered the boar against a stand of trees, but when Geronimo saw it, he would have just as easily believed it was an aurochs.

"Leonardo, do you see what I see?" he yelled to his friend who was approaching the beast from the other side.

"Stay back and let the hounds have a go at it for a bit," Leonardo yelled back.

The hounds snarled and barked as they gnashed their teeth at the boar. Geronimo and Leonardo were waiting for them to spook and wear the beast down. Slobber flew from their mouths in the frenzy of growls and snarls. None of the hounds had the courage to attack the boar, though, and didn't much know what to do. By instinct, they were merely trying to keep the beast from moving an inch.

With a thick coat of black hair and small eyes, the boar threateningly thrashed its long snout and thick, curved, spear-like tusks. Well-known for the danger they posed when defending themselves, the two knights were watching curiously to see what the boar would do.

Each of the hounds keeping the boar at bay looked more like puppies against its bulk. It lowered its eyes at the middle hound and stamped its front hoof into the forest floor a few times before it suddenly lunged forward. It raised its forehooves and struck one hound's skull with such speed and force that the hound crumpled to the forest floor unable to get back up. The bore then flashed its tusks at the hound to its left and caught it in the throat. It thrashed its head and sent the hound crashing into a nearby tree. Still alive and whimpering, the hound didn't dare set on the boar again. The boar set its sights on the hound to its right, and with an instinctually involuntary swing of its head, sent its tusks plunging into the dog's neck.

The hounds' continued taunting from pools of their own blood served only to further enrage the boar. It took off for Geronimo's horse, which was standing just a short distance away. The knight raised his spear and waited in fear and suspense. The boar, at nearly the length of the horse's neck, lunged forward to escape as the horse bucked, its forelegs stamping the air. The boar's skull, hard as steel, struck the horse's flank, sending both horse and knight tumbling to the ground.

Leonardo found himself with only the one option to go for the beast about to tear his friend to shreds. He launched his spear at the boar and drew his horse closer to the beast. The spear was stuck half a foot into the boar's back, but didn't seem to have much an effect. Leonardo winced as he began to pull away.

Geronimo let out a deep sigh and they both agreed to let the animal escape.

The hulking, black boar's hooves were flying. It felt cold steel over the back of its neck as it was about to cross between two trees. Giovanni Giustiniani Longo, the leader of the group, had hefted his sword through the boar's spine, down its back and through to its belly.

Giustiniani had realized which direction the boar and his companions had gone and so jumped from his horse and drew his sword, his back pressed against a tree in wait to catch the beast he'd been tracking since the hunt began. He always preferred his trusty sword over a spear. The boar was passing right by him as he waited in silent ambush. He had leapt from behind the tree and cleaved the boar's spine with his broadsword as a bullfighter would in the arena.

The boar convulsed as the Genoese knight continued to push down with both hands on the hilt of his sword engraved with a cross. With even the slightest wrong move, the boar would erupt in a ferocious attack. With great strain, the boar brought its head forward, its tusks brushing against Giustiniani's waist. He was roused by the stories running through his head of the hunters who had been torn to shreds by boars after landing a spear. This experienced knight, however, kept firm hold on his sword, his brow furrowed. The tips of his curled mustache had been encased to ice.

The boar looked up with its tiny eyes, the same color as Giustiniani's, before it collapsed to the snow-covered forest floor.

74

The boar's front legs were bound together and attached to a tether behind Leonardo and Geronimo's horses.

The four knights and Constantine's emissary, who a little earlier had found Maurizo, headed out back on the road on their horses.

"So, why does Constantine have a need for me and my men?" Giustiniani asked. "Can't grand Constantinople defend itself against the Turks any longer?"

"The emperor knows very well that you are a master commander in the defense of your city. He believes your experience would be beneficial to the defense of his city."

"I thought the walls of Constantinople were impenetrable," Maurizio said, slightly mocking the whole idea.

""Our walls are stronger than ever. The new Ottoman sultan is a bit audacious, though. He's having an incredible fortress built and cannons forged of which man has never seen. The emperor has full belief he will be able to overcome the new Turk just as we have previous Ottoman sultans, the Arabs, Adjarians and Avars. He wants to teach the new sultan a lesson with certain victory. The Turks won't meddle with us anymore once they see all of Christendom behind us. The young sultan's failure at the base of the city walls will be the end of the House of Osman."

"Is it that Constantine's confidence has come from his spies among the Turks?" Giustiniani said. "We know well enough Constantinople's knotty diplomacy." He looked at his fellow knights with a grin.

The emissary ignored the biting comment for a while before saying, "The emperor also knows Sultan Murad's janissaries put your father to death in Varna."

Hearing this, Giustiniani halted his mount, drew his sword and leveled it at the emissary's throat. The others followed suit and stopped. Giustiniani stared furiously into the emissary's eyes as he waited for an explanation.

The startled emissary collected himself. "You misunderstand, signore," he stammered. "Constantine wanted me to let you know particularly of this opportunity to avenge your father. The death of your father—kin of the old and noble Doria family of Genoa—was mourned in our land as it was across Europe.

Giustiniani sheathed his sword, even if but a little reluctantly, and spurred his horse on again. "Please keep your famed word games to yourself, ambassador," he said. "I may not be so tolerant a second time."

He was angry, but knew Constantine was right. He had never forgotten how Murad's janissaries had massacred his father and the knights who had gone to war by their own volition on the battlefield fifteen years before in Varna. He had liked the idea of taking revenge on the Ottomans ever since the moment the emissary had first mentioned it, but he knew he couldn't trust the Greeks, and so was feeling out the emissary to learn of Constantine's true intentions.

"The emperor knows you and your order of knights enjoy battle against the Mohamatans. We still remember your order's victories in Jerusalem, Hispania and the east of Europe."

It is every knight's noble duty is to destroy these Mohamatans and their defiance of our Lord and Savior Jesus Christ. It's hard to say, though, that those in Constantinople believe in the Latin Church. Am I wrong, ambassador?"

"It's true, there are slight differences between us, but the emperor's emissaries are in Rome as we speak to reaffirm the union of the Latin and Greek Churches. Constantine continues his negotiations with the pope. These little problems will disappear shortly. You leave that part to us."

"I wonder, signore," the emissary said as he looked at Leonardo and Geronimo dragging the boar behind their horses. "How much do you get for these beasts?"

"My men don't hunt for money," Giustiniani said.

"Still, though, its tusks and hide fetch a nice price," Leonardo said as he cracked a smile.

"They even make bristles for paintbrushes with its hair," Geronimo said.

"T wild boar eat anything they find."

"You shouldn't doubt it, ambassador. They'll even eat parts of the skull of anything they find. They're in their rut now, the time when they're at their most furious, and it's impossible to get near them."

"Of course, that is if you're not so daring a knight as we are," Maurizio said.

"What do we get in return for helping to save your city?" Leonardo asked.

"In addition to preserving the greatest fortress of Christendom, Constantine will cover your pains many times over." He then looked to Giustiani. "He asked me to let you know he will speak with you personally when you come to the city."

Constantine was planning to offer him the island of Corfu in return for his defense of the city.

"The differences between the Latin and Greek Rites don't interest me," Geronimo said after the emissary had left Giustiniani to his men. "Let's go and make war on the Mohamatans. It's our principle duty."

"Constantinople has always been a city of wealth, Giovanni," Leonardo said. "Do you think we would return empty handed?"

"It would certainly be more enjoyable than hunting boar in the snow and mud," Maurizio said with a chuckle. "We've gotten soft around the middle being here for so long. Let's go and liven ourselves up. I wouldn't doubt your men spread far and wide in the Genoese colonies would jump without a thought when they hear of this worthy task."

Giustiniani sent the emissary off with his answer. "Tell Constantine that Giovanni Guistiniani Longo and his men will be in Constantinople in one month. I only have one condition."

"I'm listening, signore."

"The city walls shall be under my command."

The emissary looked at Giustiniani. "I have no doubt the emperor will accept your condition."

Guistiani thought of only one thing as the emissary took his leave—to exact his revenge on the son of the sultan who slaughtered his father and regain the honor lost in Varna.

After seeing off the emissary, he turned and walked to his men, his fluttering cape emblazoned with a black boar with white tusks.

75

Paolo Bocchiardo looked through the narrow slit in the visor of his helmet at his opponent a hundred yards away. What he saw was a reflection of himself on black earth. Opposite him was a mounted knight in full armor, carrying a nine-foot long lance, like himself, from the Knights of the Brazen Serpent. The sun was shining from behind him and glinting off his opponent's armor. He cocked his head slightly to the right to escape the glare—if the brilliance caught his eye in action, it could cost him his life.

For this tradition reaching back centuries, the city of Compiegne in France was overrun by knights of renown from across Europe and thousands of spectators who came to watch them. King Charles VII of France had ordered a tournament be held to celebrate his victory over the English in expelling them from his lands at the end of the Hundred Years' War. Hearing the announcement of the tournament after a long hiatus, Europe's illustrious orders of knights flocked to Compiegne, which had long been a center for these duels.

Rather than following the tournament, two men in the royal stands wearing crests of the double eagle were there to extend their emperor's invitation to the Bocchiardo brothers, whose fame stretched across Europe and along the Mediterranean coast. The people were celebrating with the tournament after over a century of war, eating and drinking amid laughter and games with the merriment of a feast. The crowd was eager for the last joust between two groups of three knights to finally start after waiting for nearly three hours. The famous knights had been waiting for some time for the emissaries to arrive, as was the code of the tournament.

"The white lion on a black field—that must be them," one of the emissaries said when he saw the crest on the tunic over a knight's armor.

The emissaries knew they hadn't been mistaken when the herald announced the final group of knights to the royal stands from the side of the tournament field.

"And finally, for the joust with two groups of three. On the right, France's pride, the Knights of the Brazen Serpent! On the left, those who know no defeat, from the Republic of Genoa, the renowned Bocchiardo brothers!"

"The first should be Paolo. They say he always goes first, followed by his older brothers in order," one emissary said to the other.

"Pray they leave the joust unscathed."

"If they take a lance, then it would make more sense to talk with the victorious knights," the other emissary said with a grin.

"This order, the Knights of the Brazen Serpent, was the one led by Joan of Arc when she expelled the English from Orleans and Bourgogne, isn't it?"

"The very same."

The emissaries exchanged an anxious glance.

Paolo's destrier warhorse was much larger and heavier than the swifter and more agile coursers more often used on the battlefield. These prized mounts lent their riders' lances deadly force.

The herald gave the signal and the two knights spurred their horses on. Paolo lowered his upright lance parallel to his horse. They reached a trot, with which the knights could maintain their balance. Like their riders, both horses had armor over their heads and down their necks. The overlapping steel plates of their chamfrons and crinets where both beautiful and imposing, and would deflect any blow from a lance or sword.

Paolo brought his horse to a cantor with a kick of the spurs jutting from his armored boots as the two knights drew closer. Looking through the narrow sight in his visor, he first tried to aim for his opponent's shoulder, but the glare from the sun was blinding. He lowered his lance for a more certain strike.

When the two knights met across the list, Paolo's lance struck his opponent over the heart with such force that the knight's armor dented in. The cheers and cries of surprise from the crowd wove into a great clamor. The other knight's lance had caught Paolo in the center of his chest. With his years of experience, he clenched the reins, leaned forward and managed to splinter his lance while deflecting his opponents' blow. The high back of his saddle also helped him stay in place.

Paolo looked back after passing his opponent to see the knight lying motionless on the list.

When his time came, Troilo Bocchiardo knew his opponent would be brimming with fervor to get even. He had run second in tournaments for years and, after their inevitable loss in the first course, he was well accustomed to the indignation of his opponents.

The herald signaled the start and he spurred his horse toward his opponent. He focused on the tip of his opponents lance rather than his own and shifted his body to withstand a blow to the gut. He pulled back on the reins in a way so the spectators wouldn't notice as the lance struck him and was able to slow down his horse in an attempt to lessen the blow.

The knight's lance landed and Triolo found himself lying on the list. The crowd erupted in cries of disbelief. The emissaries continued to watch with interest. Troilo knew the best course of action when up against a knight charging with this much fury was to fall to the ground as lightly as possible. He readied himself to show his true mastery when his squire handed him his sword.

The other knight dismounted, received his sword and charged. Triolo parried his opponent's strike just as it was about to come down on his helmet and launched a counterattack. He swung his sword deftly and struck the knight in the arm, but it glanced off his armor.

Troilo knew the only way to down his opponent was to strike at the open joints of his armor. He ducked under a swipe, found his footing and plunged his sword into the chainmail just below the knight's helmet and through to his collarbone.

The crowd jumped to their feet in cheers for Troilo as his opponent fell bleeding to the field.

76

"I heard the oldest brother is a boulder of a man. This should be much easier for him," one of the emissaries said, having lost himself in the excitement.

"You wouldn't say that if you saw his opponent," said the other as he pointed to the third knight from the Brazen Serpent.

The emissary turned to look and saw a knight the size of two men clad in a jet-black harness of armor.

"Is it a man in that thing, isn't it?"

They looked to the other side of the field and saw that the oldest of the Bocchiardo brothers wasn't much different. They both took a deep breath.

"It'll be a close contest."

Antonio Bocchiardo's bascinet came to conical points at the crown and visor, lending it a terrifying look and his black, plate armor made him seem more a monster than a man. There were raised pauldrons above his shoulders and small, articulated steel plates to close the joints. With steel around his wrists, elbows, knees and neck, and this being the first time they'd seen such a thing, the younger spectators wondered how a sword could fall him.

Antonio took his elaborate shield embossed with a lion in his left hand and took hold of the reins of his horse, which was as exceptionally bodied as himself, and straightened his helmet. The other knight also readied his shield and furiously spurred his horse on as they both lowered their lances, vowing to himself to not let the blood of the two great knights of his order on the field go unrequited. Both their lances splintered off each other's shields as the two knights met. They halted their horses and dismounted for ground combat.

Antonio waited for his squire to hand him his weapon. The spectators broke out in gasps and cries of astonishment when they saw the weapons brought to the field for the duel. In front of Antonio was a mace with a spiked ball hanging from a chain attached to a foot and a half, iron handle. In front of his opponent was a long-handled battle ax.

Antonio started swinging at his opponent's head as soon as he took the mace in hand in an attempt to intimidation. The knight came fearlessly upon him, able to stay out of reach and still attack with his long-handled ax. The half-circle blade at the end of the two-foot handle was so well honed it reflected the dazzling sunlight. Antonio swung for his opponent's head, who despite his bulk, nimbly evaded what would have been a crushing blow and proved himself to be no easy target. As soon as he found his footing, he swung his ax at Antonio's chest without allowing him to collect himself for a second attack. Antonio jumped back and the ax tore through his armor, narrowly missing his flesh.

The two knights seemed hesitant to make the first move as they circled each other in search of the right moment. The knight from the Brazen Serpent spun the ax in his hands as he proclaimed his expertise with the weapon to both Antonio and the stands. He abruptly swung down on Antonio's head. It glanced of the pointed helmet in a rain of sparks and struck his shoulder plate. Knowing a good opportunity when he saw one, Antonio swung his mace so fiercely against his rival's back that it left an imprint of its spikes in the armor.

The crowd all jumped to their feet and waited for Antonio to strike the finishing blow. Antonio raised his arm and brought the mace down on his opponent's head as he lay prone on the field, caving in his helmet in what could have been a deadly strike.

Constantine's emissaries were left with no doubt the emperor had chosen the right men as the crowd cheered on the spectacle and applauded the knights. The emissaries were going to extend the same invitation to many of the orders of knights at the tournament, just as they intended to do to the Bocchiardo brothers.

77

"No matter what's on the table, we must take care not to eat or talk too much," said Constantine's emissary as he and his delegation approached the castle of Prince Vlad Dracula of Wallachia. "The prince doesn't care for those who talk too much, nor for those who stay quiet."

"Do you think there's any truth to what they say?"

"I don't know, but what I do know is his intense hatred for the Turks stems from his childhood spent as a hostage with them. Several years ago, his father Vlad II sent him as a hostage to Sultan Murad as a sign of his loyalty. He stayed for a while with Mehmed in Manisa, and they say he holds a particular spite from those times.

"He is highly respected in the Order of the Dragon for his torture of heretics and all enemies of Christendom, Jews and Mohametans alike. He's what Constantine wants, after all."

"Well, won't it just be lovely if we can take our leave from this bastard and get back in one piece."

"You forget that if he refuses then we can kiss our lives goodbye back in Constantinople."

"I'd rather die in my own city than at the hands of this cur."

The emissaries stopped their carriage in front of the castle.

"What in hell is this place with this troupe of beggars?" one of the emissaries said as he stepped out from the carriage to the sight of a group of elderly peasants being admitted to the castle through a side door.

As the emissaries entered through the main gate, an old peasant turned to them and said, "Our thanks, sirs. May our Lord and Savior Jesus Christ preserve you."

The emissaries looked at each other, not knowing what to make of it.

"I beg you, I didn't do anything! They're lying, I didn't cheat anyone! Please, I beg of you!" a woman cried.

Two of Vlad's men took hold of the struggling woman and forced her to the open area in front of the table where there were two dozen stakes placed a yard apart in a half circle. All of them had someone placed at them, except for one.

The woman's screams bore down on the others who were weeping quietly, already exhausted from their own cries. Each of the prisoners—men, women and some children—had a soldier holding them in place.

"Ha, another traitor," Vlad said as he chewed a piece of meat. "There's no difference between these Jews and Muslims who betray Christianity." He spat a bone onto the table. Vlad's grotesque torture for unfaithful wives had been made known to all the guests.

Vlad was seated at the head of a long, wide table as his guests continued with their meals, seated on each side. Vlad often held banquets in one of the courtyards of his castle, and some of his guests' hands trembled as they ate their dishes of stewed pork. Most of them hungrily asked the servants for more and drank their wine with relish. Among the guests of Serb, Croat and Hungarian nobles was a boyar from Transylvania at the banquet for the first time.

"You've forgotten one of the stakes, dear Prince," he said with a smile. "Why is it empty? If you'd had said, I would've brought a traitor from my lands."

The nobles accustomed to these banquets all stopped chewing.

Vlad looked over at the man. "One of the stakes at my banquets is always left unoccupied, my dear boyar. Whoever speaks indiscreetly or tries to teach me my own work, well then, that stake is for he with the loose tongue."

He motioned for his soldiers.

"This, this is madness—madness!" the man stuttered, not knowing what else to say. "I am a boyar of Transylvania, you can't do this to me—you can't, I say! Leave me be!"

The soldiers bound the boyar's hands as he struggled and then hauled him to the empty stake among the others.

Since the voivodship of Wallachia wasn't hereditary, similar to the many small principalities that comprised much of the Kingdom of Hungary, such as Transylvania and Moldavia. A boyar would influence the others, declare himself voivode and try to come to power through domination. The voivodes who ruled these regions later came to agreement and supported each other so no other families would come to power. When a voivode died by any reason, either other boyars would want to subsume the land into their own or claim power for themselves, inevitably leading to bloody, years-long power struggles.

The main reason for Vlad's reign of terror, however, was not to intimidate the boyars around him with his passion for power, but his determination to fulfil his duties as a member of the Order of the Dragon—the defender of the Church—in which his father had also been a member.

"I hear not enough taxes have been taken from the field in the Danube region, Danesti," Vlad said.

The rotund boyar of the Volga cut off another piece from the pork butt. "I do my best. The only thing left for me to get out of those peasants is to work them at night. Unfortunately, much of the population there is quite old, Your Excellency. You give them two lashes of the whip in the field and then they're spent," he scoffed.

"You see, that's why our people must only be young, healthy and well-bred," Vlad said. "The old and sick suck the blood of the people. We need to rid ourselves of them. They weaken us and pilfer what power we need to fight our enemies."

As he spoke, an old peasant in rags from head to toe off from the table dropped to his knees and said, "We are grateful to you, dear Prince. You have filled our bellies. May our Lord and Savior Jesus Christ preserve you."

The guests at the table all turned to him in surprise.

Vlad angrily looked to his soldiers. "What is he doing here? Go and take him to his place!"

"I—I just wanted to thank you, but I couldn't find the dining table. Help me," the peasant said as the soldiers took hold off him and marched him out. They brought him next to a building that been burning and was freshly extinguished with smoke still rising from its roof. Then they through him through the wide doors of a barn where, as they shut behind him, he found himself among dozens of sickly and elderly men and women.

"The man must be mad," one boyar said to the laughter of the rest.

"A real churl," another said.

"Which would you prefer we start with?" Vlad said as he looked over at the emissaries at the table. We have dear guests with us today who have come from Constantinople itself. The Turks' new sultan is giving them quite a bother. Let this meal be in honor of the final war we enter against the Turk!"

"Constantine will appreciate your cooperation," one of the emissaries said.

"Let's start with this one in the turban," said another.

Vlad ordered his men to bring the man wearing a turban across the table from him.

"Do you not know you mustn't wear a hat in my presence? Remove your turban," he said.

"I prefer to die with my turban on my head," the man, wretched from the beatings he'd taken, said.

"I've never actually seen one of these Mohamatans going around without a turban," one of the boyars said with derision.

"They're insolent!"

"Do you know what I do to those who so love wearing hats?" Vlad said as he looked over to his soldiers.

They brought him a long, thick nail and hammer. He approached the man, whose arms were bound behind his back and who had a soldier on each arm. They shoved him to his knees. Vlad stepped up and calmly pounded the nail three times through the man's turban and into his head as he screamed in pain and collapsed.

Some of the guests at the table were merry and laughing while others continued to eat the platters of meat brought to the table. Others, though, held their tongues.

"Let's continue now that we've started with the enemies of the Church. Do you know the easiest way to tell if a man is a Jew," he said as he looked at those around the table.

"Well, they don't eat pork," one said, "so make them eat it."

"There's an easier way."

Vlad signaled to his men, who then cut the clothing of all the men in front of the stakes and stripped them naked.

"And there you have it—their trimmed pillicocks!"

"Marvelous, Your Excellency."

"What type of pig is this, Your Excellency?" asked one of the guests who had noticed something off from the beginning of the meal. "It has a very different taste."

"Why yes, I noticed that, as well," another said. "And there's also an odd aroma coming from the kitchen.

All of them had tried to forestall their curiosity and fears.

Vlad smiled and looked over his guests. "It is meat prepared for the exsanguinaters who eat the bloodsuckers of this land."

Considering the old and sick to be a burden on the land, Vlad had first had them rounded up and then brought to a large barn with a table featuring a banquet, as he said there would be. Then he had all the doors and windows locked and set a torch to it. It was their meat he was specially having served to the boyars.

Vlad Dracula—still yet to acquire his epithet of *the Impaler*—turned to Constantine's emissaries toward the end of day as the last prisoner was being placed on the stake.

"Go and tell your emperor all the knights of the Order of the Dragon will be at his side in the battle against Mehmed when the time comes. I will send my best men, my best archers. Also, though, don't fear Mehmed too much. He's not much more than a tempestuous lunatic. My only condition is that his head be brought to my land."

Vlad was delighted with this opportunity now at hand to go up against this sultan he remembered so well from his childhood. As for the emissaries, they now understood on their return journey why his name, Dracula, means son of the Dragon—a devil in the flesh.

78

The messenger felt a deep pang of sadness when he saw the statue of two knights riding one horse atop a tall column at the entrance to the Temple Church, up from the banks of the Thames in London.

The church, having been the Knights Templar commandery in England from where they set out on crusade against Muslims far and wide until just over a century before, was a symbol of the fallen order. For the English, as in the rest of Europe, when word of the Knights Templar was spoken, it wasn't their victory against the Muslims in Jerusalem that came to mind, but Salah ad-Din Yusuf ibn Ayyub's capture of the holy city and their eventual loss of favor with the monarchs of Europe and excommunication by the pope.

The statue, however, with two knights on a horse, was erected as a symbol of the order's modest origins. The order took its name from the Temple of Solomon on whose ruins they believed Al-Aqsa Mosque had been built. The order began as the Poor Fellow-Soldiers of Christ and of the Temple of Solomon to defend Christian pilgrims and attained the support of all the Christian kings of Europe. Its wealth, however, quickly grew. The order used part its riches to build its commanderies in the capitals of Europe and the Orient, in addition to magnificent cathedrals, churches and chapels.

With mounting losses to the Muslim armies, the order changed its course and began wielding its power and wealth against the kings in Europe. After centuries, King Phillip IV of France and Pope Clement V collaborated to put an end to the order. Its grand master and precepts were accused of heresy, thrown in dungeons and tortured, with some burned at the stake. It was the end of the order. Its temple churches were both taken over as property of the crowns in the lands they were in and turned over to its rival order of the Knights Hospitaller.

Everyone knew this at least, and didn't want to speak word of the temple. The messenger, however, standing in front of the circular church, brought testament to the contrary and entered with the message that would bring new life to the successors of these knights, put to rest over a century ago.

The night winds whipped up the cassock of the priest at the Temple in Paris as he shut its large, wooden, outer gates.

"Wait there," he said to a boy standing with a torch at the threshold of the inner gates. The expression of obedient anxiety on boy's face came from being accustomed to do exactly as the priest told him.

It became an insurmountable castle once the outer gates were locked, which is what it had been built as. Jacques de Molay, the last grand master of Knights Templar, had had it built up into a castle-church as accusations of heresy mounted against him. The four round towers at the corners of the inner Temple Enclosure made it even more impervious to sieges.

The priest looked at the boy and smiled as they walked through the courtyard and closed the inner gates. He put his hand on the boy's shoulder and pulled him close. The boy's torch illuminated the frescoes of saints and the Virgin Mary as they made their way through the compound.

They stopped when the light of the torch fell on a statue of Christ on the cross in front of the church.

A man stood there looking at the priest, his face obscured by his cowl.

"Who are you? How did you get in here?" the priest said.

""Send off the boy," the man said. "I bring word of the antichrist."

The priest shook of his moment of confusion and told the boy to return to the quarters.

He had just heard the secret code he had been waiting for his entire life.

With its headwaters in the Swiss Alps, the Rhine wound its way through the French and German kingdoms and through the Low Countries to the North Sea. At one time drawing the boundary of Caesar's vast empire, it now linked the cities of kingdoms large and small. It carried the blood of the Jews massacred in Strasburg during the Black Death, the ashes of those burnt at the stake as witches in Rotterdam and the bones of the pagans who fought Christian conversion.

Having been expelled from the Holy Lands in the twelfth century, the Knights Templar had built one more of the citadels they had established throughout the river basin in German lands to protect themselves. The Knights Templar came to the aid of peasants who were unable to hold land in territories fragmented by conflict and plays for power. When their grand master was burned at the stake, the remaining knights first dispersed throughout Europe and then secretly returned to their castles and churches, now in the hands of the Knights Hospitaller, once the dust has settled.

In this line now with the Hospitallers himself, the priest listened to what the visitor who had come with their common code had to say in the confessional.

"The time has come," the man said from the other side of the lattice. The time to take revenge for the loss to Salah ad-Din has come, Father. Our wait of two centuries will finally come to an end. We will revive our lost honor and fame, and will once again declare the glory of our Lord and Savior Jesus Christ. The Turk sultan is preparing to attack the city of Constantine the Great—he who first brought us into the fold of Christendom. We will not allow this to happen—we will not allow the fortress of Christendom to fall."

The priest listened to the whispered message in suspense and firmly held the crucifix hanging from his neck.

"The French and the English are weary of fighting against their Christian brethren and your knights are waiting for your order to march on the enemies of the Church."

"Has word gone out to the other commanders?" the priest asked.

"All of them. Every commandery has received word."

"Who will provide the transport."

"For that we have Venetian and Genoese captains and their ships."

The priest broke the momentary silence in the confessional. "May our Lord and Savior Jesus Christ preserve you. Slaughter this antichrist."

Throughout the month, the messenger from the grand master carried the same message to the five priories and more than two dozen commanderies across Europe.

79

Like all Venetian captains, Piero Davanza felt relief when he saw the Doge's Palace from the deck of his galley. There was no better feeling than returning home, and the best sign he had of being home after his weeks-long journey on the sea was the faint red and white geometric patterns of the palace on the seafront. He breathed deeply the air of his city and stood stark still as he looked out over the bay toward the palace. He always believed its name—the Most Serene Republic of Venice—came from these tranquil waters. He was delighted to arrive at the peaceful harbor after his ship had been sunk in the Bosporus in a rain of cannon fire. Firuz Agha had almost not released him from captivity.

Above the waters of the Adriatic, the palace rose on slender columns as if there was no land underneath. The architects built the Gothic palace to be the sole representative of the republic and it was in constant and rapid renovation. Whereas the colonnades of a loggia would normally rise on top of walls, those of the Doge's Palace began with short columns topped with arches leading to a second loggia above from where the walls rose to the roof. The quatrefoils of sculpted stone set in circles above the capitals of the upper columns gracefully led to the upper walls.

More a diplomat than merchant, Davanza's sea voyages began and ended at the palace. He gazed over the upper loggia of the waterfront façade. In the ceremony of the Marriage of the Sea, the doge of Venice would throw a ring into the sea from this *Bucintoro* barge with the words, *I wed thee, O Sea, in token of true and lasting dominion.* Venice dominated the seas, from the Adriatic to the Ionian, over the Sea of Crete to the Aegean and Sea of Marmara, through the Bosporus and to the Black Sea.

Davanza's hopes began to rise as he looked out on the palace that appeared as if it stood on twigs above the water, but his face fell when he saw smoke rising from the adjacent square. He thought maybe he'd chosen the wrong time to return to his city and was indecisive about whether he should immediately go to the doge or not to give the news he brought from Constantinople.

The crew started to move the sacks full of silks, a multitude of spices, indigo and many other exotic products from the Orient and India as the ship pulled broadside to the city's large port.

"What's this smoke about?" Davanza asked a merchant on the dock to whom he was going to sell a portion of his freight.

"It's the Council."

Davanza bristled at the mention of Venice's clandestine Council of Ten. It had the authority to oversee the doge and Senate, and was a potential nightmare for every senator and seaman in the city. It began preoccupied with the offenses of treason and counterfeiting, but eventually assumed the charge to singlehandedly guarantee the republic's two essential aspects of independence and dominance in trade.

"They've convicted more than thirty people—three of them senators. They say Claro Contarini is among them and the rest are nobles and city folk."

"Claro?!"

Davanza was greatly disturbed to hear the name of his close friend with whom he had met before setting off for Constantinople. Like all captains, he knew what had occurred between Claro and Nicoleto Marmagna, who was from a great seafaring family. It was astonishing, though, for someone he knew so closely and who happened to also be a nobleman, to be among the convicted.

"Was it treason or counterfeiting?"

As he inquired about his friend, he saw one of the crewmen put the sack he was carrying in a puddle to take a rest.

"Be careful, you idiot! If you spoil the spices in that sack, you wouldn't be able to pay for it even if you worked for me the rest of your life!" he yelled, taking out his anger on the man.

"I beg your pardon, Signore. It won't happen again."

"It wasn't for treason or counterfeiting, Piero." The merchant lowered his voice and leaned toward Davanza's ear. "It was sodomy."

"Since when has the Council of Ten preoccupied itself with such things? What happened to the *Signori di Notte*?"

Piero was at a loss. The Lords of the Night oversaw the nocturnal patrols that searched through the neighborhoods and Senate, which liked to show itself as more pious than the Church, for the offences of sodomy, pederasty and many others along the gamut of crimes.

"Word is the Signori handed over their duties to the Council of Ten. The Senate is also waging a war against heretics, Piero. After all this that happened, two men can barely stand together and talk. On top of that, no one will say a thing if they mete out the prescribed punishment on the accused deviants, otherwise they themselves are easily be accused and tossed in the dungeons. Carlo's case went on for two months and they say he confessed his crimes."

"Who could claim their innocence after that torture?" Davanza said as he thought of the terrifying room in the Doge's Palace he had perhaps passed by a hundred times.

"How are things in Constantinople? They say Constantine lowered taxes. Is that true?"

"It's no good, my friend. Not good at all. The Turk is about to besiege the city. Myself and many other sailors barely escaped the emperor."

"Where'd you get the goods, then?"

Davanza gave a short laugh. "How quickly you forget that a Venetian sees to his business no matter the conditions he finds himself in."

He instantly felt guilty for the joke as the acrid smell of smoke swept passed his nose.

One of the condemned prisoners, his hands bound behind him, walked toward the dozen scaffolds set up next to each other in the square between the Doge's Palace and Saint Mark's Basilica. Before him was a priest holding a large cross and flanked by two of the city forces. Blood seeped from the young prisoner's eyes, nose and mouth.

The city folk who had come to watch the executions yelled out with derision.

"Filthy perverts!"

"Heathens!"

"Sinners!"

The executioner was waiting on the scaffold.

The convicted man was pulled up to the scaffold and the priest turned to him, holding the cross before his face.

"Our Lord and Savior Jesus Christ will forgive you, but you must admit your guilt. You must call to Him to fall into His embrace."

The man, without the power to even hold his head up, jerked and spit at the cross—the spittle mixed with blood sprayed it and the priest's face.

The priest's anger hardened along with the gasps from the crowd. It was of great importance for the condemned, who had confessed at his hearing, to do so again before the people. The people's belief in the power of the Senate hung on the legitimacy of the executions. The priest knew that if it weren't to happen, it would create folk heroes out of the condemned, who had endured countless torture to ensure they beg forgiveness from the Savior before the people.

One of the city forces struck the man on the back of the legs and brought him to his knees as the priest furiously descended the scaffold. Then with a kick to the back from the *forza,* the man's head laid out on the block.

"I'm innocent, I'm innocent! I'm married and have children. This is slander!" the man cried with the final power he could muster between his convulsing sobs.

The *forza* kept his foot on the man's back to keep him from trying to raise his head.

The crowd continued to debase the man.

"Answer to your Maker!"

"Sinner!"

The executioner raised his ax and brought down its circular blade, lopping off the man's head.

Half a dozen people ran from the crowd for the man's freshly severed scull now gushing with blood. The belief that a heretic's crushed scull—*cranum humanum*—was a cure for the falling sickness was widespread in Venice, as it was throughout Italy.

The headless corpse was then carried to a pile of wood next to Saint Mark's Basilica and thrown on top of the five bodies of the people executed throughout the hour. The city forces ignited the kindling as the pungent smoke from the neighboring pile burned their noses. This second part of the execution process was almost theater.

Even though the punishment for sodomy was to be burned at the stake, the wailing of the condemned had disturbed the palace officials and so the doge and bishop had decided a few years earlier that there was no harm in first beheading the offenders. The bishop found the punishment adequate according to faith and the palace officials could continue their work in peace.

The billowing flames rose past the four bronze horses above the entrance to the grand cathedral. Having been brought to Venice from Constantinople two centuries before, their constant exposure to soot and smoke left no trace of the glories of Constantine the Great's New Rome.

80

Commander Gabriele Trevisano led his men up the marble stairs of the palace, playing for time, as he knew the meeting had already begun. He passed the statue of Neptune—the symbol of Venice's dominion on the seas—and beneath the carved marble arch at the entrance to the palace.

He took his place in the large Senate Hall for this emergency meeting being held after receiving the news Davanza had delivered the previous day. Trevisano hated the Senate Hall—its walls covered with paintings of famous senators seemed childish to his warrior's spirit. The gilt ceiling and colorful walls gave him a headache and he waited impatiently for the meeting to end so he could get respite from the riot of color. He only felt at ease on the sea, on ships and amid forces boarding enemy ships. He couldn't suffer the political speeches now being made.

"We have no quarrel with the Turk," Doge Francesco Foscari said. "Why would we fight against him with no rhyme or reason?"

The doge was wearing his ducal hat of gold, white and saffron brocade raised at the back and a waist-length cape emblazoned with jewels.

Foscari had been doge for decades and, appointed for life, he never rushed to choose sides.

"I can't help but agree with His Excellency," Davanza said, sensing this was the best moment to speak out against going to war. "We have many ships in Ottoman ports and the Grand Turk has always facilitated our trade in his realm. We sell the raw silk, rugs, olive oil, grapes and figs we buy in his territories and sell them throughout Europe. Our relationship with the Turk is indispensable for our commercial life."

"Who knows," a senator said. "If Constantine loses control of the seas to the Turk, then it could put an end to his deceit."

"I respect your faith in trade, dear senators," said Battista, clad all in black.

He wore only black or red like all members of the Council of Ten. His black robes were a contrast to the colorful paintings behind him on the wall. The painting of the decapitated Doge Marino Faliero, done so because of his betrayal, lent an even more terrifying air to the already frightening man.

"But you forget our faith in Christ," he continued. "It is incumbent upon us to come to Constantine's aid and that of all Christendom."

"True, but we can hardly say that Constantinople shares our faith, dear Battista," an elderly senator said. "We know Constantine keeps many enemies of the Church around him even though he tries to maintain a good relationship with us and his holiness the pope."

"We hear Constantine has sent emissaries to Rome," Admiral Alviso Longo said from among the Senate's military commanders. "There's also word he has accepted to praise the pope in their Greek liturgies. It seems this time the pope is ready and willing to come to Constantine's aid. We, too, should stand with Rome."

"We also mustn't forget the large Venetian colony in the city and that our people could be in danger," another captain said, his voice raising with fervor.

"I understand your enthusiasm, Captain," Doge Foscari said, "but Rome still has outstanding debts for the nine ships it received from us. If his holiness the pope so desires a fleet, he must first review his accounts in Milan."

"The sultan also always has many men from Italian lands." Davanza said. "His physician is said to be a Jew from the Kingdom of Naples. Rome is jealous of our independence in trade and power on the seas whereas the Turk often lowers the taxes he levies on our goods."

Pizamano, a powerful merchant, spoke in direct opposition. "Dear Piero, you always talk of profit, but you never think of the complete control over trade the Turk will have if he takes Constantinople. The Turk's good humor toward us is only so he can use Venice to play against Constantinople. If the city falls to the Turk, so too does the Bosporus and the way from the Mediterranean to the Black Sea. This will disrupt our connection to our colonies on both seas and will cost us dearly. We sail freely by and control the islands of Crete, Corfu and Caffa due to Constantinople. The loss of Constantinople means the collapse of our slave trade of Russians, Tartars, Circassians and Armenians. Have you not heard that Admiral Rizzo's galley was sunk by the Turk's cannons? Who knows how many more Venetian ships would suffer the same fate."

"And the Genoese are said to be quite ready to come to Constantine's aid," Battista said as his voice grew louder. "One need not be a soothsayer to know that Constantine will show favor to the Genoese if the Turk is defeated in battle. We mustn't hand Genoa this advantage."

"You know I don't like these kinds of conversations, dear senators," Trevisano said at long last, unable to hold back any longer. "But you overstate the scourge of the Turk. As always, with the order of the Senate, my fleet of thirty ships and more than a thousand men is at the ready to wage war to the death."

After hours of debate, only seven senators voted against sending aid to Constantine while the other seventy-four senators agreed to defend the city. Doge Foscari announced the decision—a large fleet would sail shortly for Constantinople under Admiral Trevisano and the command of Alviso Longo. Foodstuffs, such as sacks of wheat and other grains, would also be sent along with the weapons and men. In order to stay on the right side of the sultan, however, Venetian traders would try to remain neutral and take pains not to incite him. Emissaries would also be dispatched to the courts of Aragon and the Kingdom of Hungary to secure additional fleets.

Pope Nicholas V would personally see to the Holy Roman Empire.

Davanza had absolutely no intention of returning to the city anytime soon. He knew Trevisano would not take the sultan so lightly once he saw his new fortress crawling with men.

81

The papal guards opened the grand doors to the basilica with the rising of the sun.

One of the six reliefs on the bronze door, towering at over twenty feet, was of Saint Peter handing over the keys to heaven Its six panels depicted Jesus enthroned, Mary enthroned, St. Paul with the sword, St. Peter giving the keys to Pope Eugene IV, the beheading of St. Paul and the crucifixion of St. Peter. The basilica and its large square were today to host a historic coronation.

Constantine the Great had begun construction of the basilica over a thousand years before. Opposite the Roman Empire to the east, the fracturing kingdoms of Europe gathered themselves under the pope's leadership as the successor to Saint Peter to challenge the fortress of Christendom to the east. With New Rome's power growing with each passing century, Rome became jealous and made agreements with the kings who desired to regain their past glory. The interpretation of Christian theology in the west was increasingly at odds with those in the east in New Rome, and led to the schism of the Latin and Greek Rites.

A dozen of Constantine XI's emissaries sitting in the basilica's crowded reception hall before noon looked around with disdain as the founder of their city came to mind. They had come to get the pope's response to the call for support against the Ottomans that they had been making for weeks.

They had to wait a little longer, though, as before the splendid altar, Pope Nicolas V was to crown King Frederick IV of Germany for him to become Emperor Frederick III of the Holy Roman Empire.

If what the emissaries had heard was correct, Pope Nicholas would speak with Frederick about going to battle against the Ottomans.

"They apparently blew a Venetian merchant ship to pieces with a humongous cannon just last month," Pope Nicholas said, facing a full-length mirror framed in metal relief with his back to Frederick.

His attendants were making his final preparations for the coronation ceremony. They placed his mozzetta of red damask over the shoulders of his white cassock, falling to his elbows, with care as another began to fasten it.

"What is Venice telling its people caught in the middle? Wouldn't they have to answer to the Turk?"

King Frederick had on a white shirt, loose trousers over white breeches and a midnight-blue belt around his fur-lined cloak. The cloth around his neck was squeezing his throat and he tried to loosen it with his gloved fingers.

He also had one eye on the gold crown set with pearls and gemstones sitting next to the pope. Once it was placed on his head, he would be the lone sovereign of a vast empire ruling over all other kings and dukes in nearly the entirety of central Europe. He had worked for years to gain support from the pope to this end.

"My dear Frederick, don't you know the Venetians? They think only of trade. Although I suspect the Senate will agree to lend aid. But I'm also sure they don't want to provoke the Turk too much."

"Your Excellency, I hope they also know that my armies are worn down from the skirmishes along our borders with Hungary."

"Don't worry about Hungary," Nicholas said calmly. "Be patient for a while longer. All its lands will be yours when Hunyadi Janos is gone."

"And what about the increasing rebellion in the Duchy of Bourgogne?"

It seems Charles is getting closer to betrothing his daughter to your son Maximillian. My cardinals are in negotiations. Leave this business to us just as we secured your daughter Kunigunde's marriage to Duke Albert IV of Bavaria. With it, the Habsburg dynasty will be strengthened.

"The empire will always be indebted to you, Your Excellency."

The attendants wrapped his red cincture around his girdle and placed a red camauro on his head.

"As you see, we bring land under your domain without need for war."

"Marriage is much easier than war, Your Excellency," Frederick said with a smile.

"How is Queen Eleanor?" Nicholas asked of the princess from Portugal he had introduced to Frederick when she was eighteen.

"Her father Alfonso is impatient to receive the edict he desires from you."

"I'm working on it with my cardinals. The king of Portugal will see more than his reward when he keeps his promises to us. We must stop the Turk in his tracks before he treads on our feet any more. If not, then both Portugal and your empire will suffer."

Frederick thought of what had transpired twelve years earlier.

"I know you remember what happened in Kosovo and Varna, dear Frederick. But Sultan Murad was an experienced commander. The new sultan, however, is only eighteen. The Turk will immediately stop the siege when he sees the mighty armies of Christ. We will take this opportunity to put an end to Mehmed's ambition at the foot of Constantinople's walls. Then, I suspect he won't cause us much more trouble."

"But those of the Greek Rite don't show due respect to our Lord Christ, Your Excellency. Sometimes I have my doubts as to whether they are Christians or heretics. Why should we help them?"

"Never you worry. Constantine is prepared to make any concession to get our support. I am seeing to that. They will know the superiority of Rome."

An attendant then gingerly placed the bejeweled, gold papal tiara on his head. The pope reached out to another attendant for his scepter while a large, gold cross was placed around his neck.

"All is ready, my son," he said as he turned around.

Hundreds of people were still jostling to kiss the feet of the statue of Saint Peter at the other end of the basilica as Frederick and his ceremonial retinue came before the altar. After centuries of wear from kisses and passing hands, the statue's feet were well polished.

One of Constantine's emissaries was looking at Giotto di Bondone's gigantic *Navicella* mosaic on a far wall with a haloed Saint Peter kneeling and holding the right hand of Jesus. Behind Peter was a ship—the Ship of the Church—carrying the apostles, blown forward by angels. It was only one of the many mosaics and frescoes covering the basilica's large interior.

"They say the pope will demolish the rectangular roof along with the rest of the basilica and in its place build a large dome," one emissary said to another. "He's having stone brought from the Colosseum and they say word's been sent to all the architects and sculptors throughout Italy."

"Is this an attempt emulate the dome of our holy church of Hagia Sophia?" another said to the laughter of his companions.

The cardinals took their places, lining up to the right and left of the altar, each of them wearing a black cassock and red biretta with gold crosses around their necks. Pope Nicholas stood in the middle with candles in tall candelabras flickering behind him, the shafts of light lending him a more mystic air to those at the far end of the basilica.

Statues of the Virgin Mary, Jesus and many saints carved by sculptors from near and far lined much of the walls.

Dukes, princes, counts and barons of the Holy Roman Empire stood in their places as part of the ceremony. Following the hymns, Frederick walked up a red carpet to the cross in front of the altar. The Cardinal Bishop of Ostia rolled up Frederick's sleeve. He anointed the new emperor's right forearm and the nape of his neck with the Oil of the Catechumens, after which Frederick made the sign of the cross.

Nicholas then girded the imperial sword on the emperor, placed the imperial orb in his right hand and imperial scepter in his left before Frederick bowed and knelt to the red marble. Frederick leaned forward as Nicholas placed a splendid miter on his head, his power now completely buttressed by the power of the Church. He was now an emperor to be a personage of respect across all of Europe.

The legendary Charlemagne had knelt on this same stone as he received his crown six and a half centuries before.

The emissaries became even more confident seeing the power behind the rituals of the ceremony. They were to set out on their return journey the following morning with Cardinal Isidore as the pope's legate. Nicholas was pleased with his growing influence as Frederick's fingers inscribed the relief of Christ handing Peter the keys to heaven.

None in the Holy See could have known that day that this would be the final coronation in Rome.

82

Monks and priests who had heard of the meeting from the monasteries throughout the city flocked to the Senate. Those entering the arched doorway next to the Forum of Constantine filled the rectangular, column-lined courtyard of the Senate House. Guards with spears and shields were stationed to maintain order over the murmuring crowd.

Constantine looked anxiously out the window of his room on the top floor of the Senate House at the growing crowd. He thought it must be the work of the monk Gennadios Scholarios. The shouts coming from the dozen statesmen and theologians in the ongoing meeting in the hall below, however, wasn't a good sign.

"I will never betray my faith for the sake of aid. This is not possible. I will not, I say!" Scholarios, an influential theologian in the city, said as he pounded his fist on the table.

The monk, in a simple cassock with a *skoufos* atop his head, hadn't been able to withhold his anger any longer, leaning on his staff to stand up before finishing and sitting back down. Despite having been given a chair at a corner of the long table so he wouldn't be able to meddle in the debate too much, he had been making known his disagreement with every point since the meeting began.

"His Holiness the Pope is prepared to send his fleets to the city contingent upon your emissaries signing the agreement in Florence," Cardinal Isidore said.

Pope Nicholas had sent his best theologians to the city for the process of uniting the Latin and Greek Churches. Nicholas had given strict orders to Isadore, who was also the metropolitan of Kiev and all Rus, to accept no compromise. The pope wanted to use his upper hand for all he could.

"His Holiness the Pope will also increase the aid coming from the Italian republics and the Holy Roman Empire," he added.

"Like you did in the crusade two hundred years ago?" Scholarios said, sending a chill through the hall as he mentioned the one thing nobody there wanted to remember.

"Your armies didn't leave a stone in place when they set their eye on our empire while they were supposedly marching to Jerusalem. It was no Mohamatan army that conquered the city, but the pope's own armies!"

"It is of no use to anyone to bring up the unpleasantries of centuries past," Isidore said as he started to lose his composure. "It makes little sense to lay blame on the Church for the misguided sacking by the army of a Venetian doge and his personal ambition."

Loukas Notaras spoke up in an attempt to calm the situation. "I understand your concerns, Gennadios, but one must also give the cardinal his right. His very presence here should indicate the good will from the pope."

Nobody on either side of the table opposed the megaduke.

"We must think of our city as we do our faith," Patriarch Gregorios III said from the head of the table. "Aid from Pope Nicholas can benefit us. Mehmed had assembled soldiers from across his realm as we have never seen before. None of us had expected an army of this size. His avarice against us also grows with every day."

"What we ask of you is your fundamental conditions of faith," the archbishop of Mytilene, Leonardo of Chios, said, having been selected by the pope to accompany Cardinal Isidore. "It is a small think for you to see and say that the Father, Son and Holy Ghost are of the same essence. If you do, then like the Genoese in the city, so will everyone else be under guarantee."

It was no secret that Leonardo held rights of the Genoese, who controlled the island of his birth and diocese, above all others.

"What you ask of us is blasphemy!" Scholarios erupted.

"Gennadios is right," another priest said. "The creed from Constantine the Great's First Ecumenical Council at Nicaea and then the later creed from the Council of Constantinople is quite clear—*We believe in one God, the Father Almighty, Maker of heaven and earth, and of all things seen and unseen.*

"*And in one Lord Jesus Christ, the only-begotten Son of God, begotten of the Father before all æons, Light of Light, very God of very God, begotten, not made, being of one substance with the Father; by whom all things were made; who for us men, and for our salvation, came down from heaven, and was incarnate by the Holy Ghost and of the Virgin Mary, and was made man; he was crucified for us under Pontius Pilate, and suffered, and was buried, and the third day he rose again, according to the Scriptures, and ascended into heaven, and sitteth on the right hand of the Father; from thence he shall come again, with glory, to judge the quick and the dead; whose kingdom shall have no end.*

"*And in the Holy Ghost, the Lord and Giver of life, who proceedeth from the Father, who with the Father and the Son together is worshiped and glorified, who spake by the prophets. In one holy catholic and apostolic Church; we acknowledge one baptism for the remission of sins; we look for the resurrection of the dead, and the life of the world to come.*"

He quickly finished reciting the creed, quite familiar with it, to the impulsive *amen* from those seated around the table.

"But you with your *filioque* say the Holy Ghost *proceedeth from the Father and the Son.* You've changed the thousand-year creed in which we all believe!"

"You talk of a faith of a thousand years, but you forget the much older archives in Rome," Isidore said. "We know that in many of the Gospels and earlier edicts the Father and the Son are side by side, one and the same. You are wrong to defy the authority of Rome."

"And would Rome bestow the grace on us and release these Gospels for us to see," the priest asked, barely veiling his acrimony.

"Permission for you to examine the archives is the decision of His Holiness the Pope alone. You can't expect us to permit these ancient records to be degraded."

Scholarios and his fellow clerics all smiled scornfully.

"There is no need to see the records to believe the Father, the Son and the Holy Ghost are indivisible where each proceeds the other. Now you say the thousand-year creed is blasphemy itself," Isidore said, lowering his voice to a grumble. "You have done so with this perversion in this city in opposition to Rome for four hundred years."

"I couldn't quite here you, Cardinal Isidore," Notaras said. "If I were you, I wouldn't go on much further. Please don't forget you are in Constantine's city. You haven't been able to recover from the fall of your city so many centuries ago." He turned to address the entire hall. "It seems it would be best for us to reconsider this issue in our later negotiations. Let's move on."

"We hope you will mention the name of His Holiness the Pope in your services," Archbishop Leonardo said.

"In that is the death of our city," Scholarios shot back.

It was one of the main conditions for the pope to send aid and a way to make the city's patriarch and other leaders a simple extension of the papacy. Thus, all power other than the pope's would be eliminated and the priests in Constantinople would become clerics of the Latin Rite.

"The power in Constantinople comes from our centuries of independence from Rome. The pope wants to bring us under his purview," Patriarch Gregorios said.

Sphrantzes tried desperately to soften the conversation. "How would our independence suffer if we were to mention the pope in our services? What will truly break our independence is if we can't deter the Turk from waging battle against us."

"But, head chamberlain, such a decision to honor the pope in our services and ceremonies would mean giving him voice over all theological matters concerning us," another priest said.

Those on both sides of the table were raising their justifications.

"There is one thing you don't understand, Georgios," Isidore said. "Your Church will disappear along with your city if you set against the Turk alone. His Holiness the Pope is bestowing upon you a chance for survival. All he asks is for recognition of his benevolence."

"There is trouble with the Holy See if the pope so desires recompense for protecting fellow Christians against the enemies of the Church," Scholarios said, his anger unabated.

Notaras had known the talks wouldn't produce any consensus and the confrontations would continue to stiffen, but he hadn't expected them to worsen to this degree.

The debates and arguments continued for two hours, to little consequence.

"Do you really believe the pope will send aid?" Scholarios asked Notaras after they were left alone in the hall.

"I see no other way than to hope he does, Gennadios."

"What is hope for us, Loukas? We must pray to the Lord. Pope Nicholas wants us to turn from our faith and bow to him. I see no difference in falling to the Turk or bowing to the pope. Either way, it's an end to our faith. How have the people forgotten what the Latins did to this city? How can Constantine be so blind?"

"I know, Gannadios, I know," Notaras said thoughtfully. He knew the monk was right and that rather than coming to save the city, Nicholas' only desire was to have them respect his power. "I agree. I would rather see the turban of the Turk in the city than the Latin miter."

83

"If this disrespect continues, then I will have to inform His Holiness the Pope that you have not complied with the conditions for union," Cardinal Isidore said to Constantine as they stood in the emperor's room at the top of the Senate House, looking out on the restless crowd.

The room was just below the dome of the five-floor building. The leaded frames in its full-length windows prevented those outside from seeing in.

"Your emissaries agreed to the conditions for union and said they had your full approval, Your Excellency," Isidore continued.

"My men spoke correctly, dear Isidore," Constantine said. "I will observe the conditions for union. I will not deprive my city of the pope's armies over these small details."

"Scholarios and his ilk don't think as much."

"Gennadios is nothing more than a monk overly attached to the fine points of his faith. He cannot prevent union no matter how much resistance he puts up."

"And what about the heated crowd below? I would do something about it if I were you, Your Excellency. We want union fully under the pope, not only for show. If this doesn't come to pass, then I don't reckon we can help you."

This angered Constantine. He recognized Isidore's scarcely

veiled threat, but knew the slightest opposition would mean the fleets from Rome would drop sail.

He looked out behind the milling crowd and over the forum extending from the courtyard of the Senate House. At its center was the Column of Constantine. Its seven porphyry cylinders surrounded by the remnants of toppled and ruined statues of Athena, Artemis and Poseidon.

He motioned for Isidore do join him at the window. "In days of old, there was a statue of Prince Paris in judgement in the middle of the others next to that column. I never saw it, but I've always heard of it. Do you know of it, Isidore—the Judgement of Paris?"

Isidore didn't respond.

"Let me tell you of it. Zeus gave a banquet in celebration of the marriage of Achilles' parents Peleus and Thetis. Eris, the goddess of discord, wasn't invited and, as revenge she threw a golden apple from the Garden of Hesperides into the middle of the celebration. The goddesses Hera, Athena and Aphrodite all claimed the apple. They then went to Zeus for him to judge who was fairest. Not wanting to anger any of the goddesses, Zeus said the mortal Trojan Paris would judge. Each wanting the apple for their own, they set about trying to deceive and bribe Paris with their powers. Hera said she would make him king of Europe and Asia, Athena offered him wisdom and skill in war, and Aphrodite said she would give him the most beautiful woman in the world—Helen of Troy, the wife of King Menelaus of Sparta. I reckon you know the rest of the tale. The mortal who refused sovereignty and skill in war chose love and brought about the whole tragedy.

"Do you know what happened to that statue?" he asked, not pulling his gaze from Isidore. "Like so much of my city, it was plundered by the pope's armies." His face grew flushed. "You are mistaken, Isidore, if you think I will sacrifice my city over a few details. I made my decision long ago. You, also, don't ever tell me what I should do again. His Holiness the Pope will get what he asks for and the union will pass within a week."

Constantine squeezed the handle of the dagger at his waist and looked back at the crowd below.

"Pay me heed!" Scholarios yelled to the crowd as he lifted his hands. The crowd was delighted to see him after growing restless after having waited for hours. He continued after the crowd's murmuring died down. "The defense of our faith will continue against the Latin blasphemers in Rome. We will not bow our heads to the pope!"

The monks, priests and anti-unionists in the crowd broke out with cries of *long live Constantinople, long live the Greeks.*

"We have no need for anyone else to defend our city from the Mohametans. Our own power and faith are enough to save our beautiful city, as it has for centuries!"

"Damned be the pope!"

"We need nothing more than follow the teachings of our Lord Jesus Christ. Now, all of you, go back to your monasteries and your churches and pray—pray for God Almighty to give us strength!"

"Amen!"

"May our Lord and Savior Jesus Christ preserve us!"

"Amen!"

Scholarios and his followers left the courtyard unaware they would be stripped of any influence before the ceremony to confirm the union that would take place at Hagia Sophia in no less than a week. Constantine's men would also see to some of their deaths personally.

84

I heard it again this morning.

There is a lofty turret at the Mohametans' mosques where they worship. They call this tower a minaret. A singer of sorts ascends the tower five times a day to call the Mohametans to prayer. The first is just before dawn. They call it the *adhan,* and it is what the palace and the rest of the city starts the day with. I hear the opening and closing of doors and the sound of the footsteps of the newly arisen on the way to the mosque break the silence of morning. I am here with my notes while the Turks prepare for their prayers, what the Arabs call *salah* and the Persians *namaz.*

Here let me translate what the singer in the tower, who they call a *muezzin,* calls out.

At first, he repeats *God is great* four times, or *Allah* as the Mohametans refer to Him. Then he twice says, *there is no god but God.* Again, twice he calls out, *Mohamet is the messenger of God.* Then twice repeated, *hasten to prayer.* Again twice, *hasten to salvation,* although one could instead easily say, *hasten to success.* Then to finish, he again twice repeats, *God is great,* and closes with one intonation of *there is no god but God.*

For their morning prayer, there is an extra line after the one about salvation, which is, *prayer is better than sleep,* again repeated twice. Here, let me relate the tale behind this that Mullah Lütfi explained to me.

The first reciter of the call to prayer for the Mohametans, Bilal ibn Rabah, apparently made this addition when he saw Mohamet was still asleep one morning. Immediately awaking, Mohamet said it was good and that Bilal should continue with it.

Of course, I never heard Bilal's voice, but the voice I hear now penetrates the flesh. The deep voice used particularly for the morning call and its husky affections breaks the silence of dawn. The words are not plainly recited, but sung to a melody—what they call a *maqam.* According to what they say, every Mohametan land uses a different melody, and those in Mecca, Edirne and Egypt are all different from one another.

There is more open space in the Mohametans' mosques than in our churches with their narrow aisles and pews. The interior of the mosques is empty and spacious, and one can go in any direction one so pleases. I said the Turks go to their mosques with the sounding of their call to prayer, and whereas that is true, it could also give a false impression. Whereas many men go to the mosques, so too, do many perform their prayers at home. They believe they receive divine recognition for the good deed if they pray in the mosque, but that they still fulfill their obligation from praying at home. Of course, we pray at home as well, but Sunday Mass is obligatory.

One thing that might surprise my fellow envoys back in Venice concerns the rugs we hang on balconies—as is so often seen around Saint Mark's Square—lay over tables and floors, and hang on walls. Here they have similar, but quite small ones they call *sejjade,* which they don't' think of as rugs, but rather a mat of sorts on which they pray. Usually kept folded, they spread it on the floor when they pray at home and prostrate on top of it. I have seen both Ragip Pasha and Mullah Lütfi use many types. Merchants, travelers and envoys from the Italian republics and kingdoms have been taking stacks of these miniature Oriental rugs back with them, as they are easy to transport. I reckon a Turk in Venice might find it strange, laughable even, that we place them on balconies and tables in addition to the floor. The description of the flying carpet in the *One Thousand and One Nights* actually fits these prayer rugs very well. I asked Mullah Lütfi if he knew of these tales. He said they're true and that he who prays properly rises to Seventh Heaven, so what else can that be other than flying.

It's not enough, though, to only lay out a prayer rug. The Mohametans' preoccupation with water is maybe a reflection of their faith, or maybe it's the other way around and their faith makes them take pains for constant washing and cleaning. It's very important to them that the place of prayer and their person be spotlessly clean. Maybe the rooms of their houses and the palace are so sparkling because they pray everywhere. This is also the reason why they remove their footwear when inside.

They wash their limbs before prayer in ablution, what the Arabs call *wudu* and the Turks call *abdest,* which comes from the Persian words for water and hand. They are always mumbling something as they do this. Only after imploring dozens of men that I would be grateful if they would say it louder was I able to make out what they said during their ablutions and write it down. First, though, let me say that they always use colorful and fragrant soaps when washing. I had heard of these soaps from Edirne when I was still on the ship before I arrived.

They say *bismillah*—in the name of God—as they do before they start anything, before they pull up the sleeves of their caftan, shirt or inner robes to their elbows and start with the ablution. I was told one must state their intentions for purity inwardly before starting, as well. They wash their hands up to the wrist three times, first the right and then the left, then they take water into the mouth three times and spit it out. After that, they snort water up their nose from the right hand and use the left hand to blow it out. This they also do three times.

The Mohametans always use the left hand for filthy tasks and always step first with the left foot into any mire. The next step in their ablutions is to wash their face three times and then the arms up to the elbow three times, first the right, then the left. Then they take their wet right hand and run it through their hair under their turban, whichever type it may be, and they have quite a few, and back to the nape of the neck. They then clean their ears with the index finger and behind the ears with the thumb. At long last, they wash their feet up to the ankle, again first the right and then the left.

To finish, many then recite one of the verses from their holy book three times.

I haven't yet been able to fully learn what they say and do for prayer. To tell the truth, I'm hesitant to enter a mosque and observe them. I also worry I would make them uncomfortable with too many questions about their worship.

I'm relieved to write today. There is a tremendous crowd out in the city today. The sultan's announcement of his campaign has brought people from all quarters of the city. One could say this capital is a vast sea into which all rivers flow. The soldiers gathering here have been holding evening feasts as if they've come to a wedding instead of about to go off to war. They say the cavalry and the sultan's janissaries will play a stunning game of javelin tomorrow. The sultan himself sometimes even joins in, so they say. Supposedly, the emissaries and ambassadors in the city will also come to watch the games. I'll try to learn more details about these cavalrymen coming from the Ottoman provinces.

85

Conscripts loaded blunt javelins from the barracks warehouses onto horses and brought them to the field of play. The stands running two hundred yards along the field were filling to the brim as the final preparations were being made. No one wanted to miss the javelin games between the janissary regiments and the cavalrymen from the fiefdoms who had flocked to the city upon the sultan's call for jihad. Locals of all ages, soldiers, envoys, statesmen and the emissaries in the city had created such a large throng in the spacious square next to the Justice Pavilion that the guards trying to maintain security were on edge. Responsible for public order, Chief Garden Guard Dincher was struggling from where he stood at the base of the tower to keep his men in place. The crowd reminded him of the first time he entered the city in a procession years ago.

Added to the crowd was the wail and pounding of zurnas and davuls along with the shouts from sherbet sellers and other peddlers.

"They say the sultan will join in," the Genoese ambassador said to Alberti Balbi as he took his seat among the foreign dignitaries.

"I've seen so many oddities since I've been in this city that such a thing wouldn't surprise me in the least. What if something happens to him and he's injured? Do you think he could chance such a thing?"

"Is it certain he will, though?" the Genoese ambassador asked with a chuckle.

"But which team will he join? They all make up his army, don't they?"

"In theory, yes, but the sultan is above all considered a janissary and is their supreme commander. It stands to reason he'll take his place with them. That is unless he embarks on something truly mad. I personally don't think there's a possibility for that, though. He wouldn't be that out of his senses."

The teams began to take their places on the large field before the stands. To the right were the janissaries, sporting their headgear falling to the back, yellow boots and red sashes. To the left, a group rode to the field wearing browns, greys and black, identifying them as the fiefdom cavalry, taking their place with thirty yards between each of them.

"I don't get these Turks at all when all is said and done," Balbi said. "Right now, in Constantinople, there are most likely many knights from dozens of kingdoms swearing an oath to honor their swords with Mohametan blood whereas here they play games before going on campaign."

"Come now, Alberti. Javelin is much more than a game for these Turks. It's a part of life both for themselves and for the horses they so love. It points to their close relationship with their horses. No European knight or warhorse would be able to do what you're about to see. Only Arabians and the horses of the Bulgarians and Tatars can be trained for such feats after years-long relationships with their riders. These javelin games also keep them war-ready and bodily fit. With these men constantly playing javelin games, there's no need for any other battle training. It has everything a soldier needs for battle—horsemanship, marksmanship and agility. And, as you can see, they're well aware of it."

"And I would suspect cooperation, as well, right?"

"Precisely. For instance, at no time are brothers allowed to be on opposing sides. They also pay attention so no animosity arises between the teams. If they're vengeful and attempt to injure a soldier on the other side, then they are straightaway tossed from both the game and their team."

"You're most probably right about the sultan," Balbi said. "Look, he's taking his seat now with his viziers."

The ambassador looked to his left and recognized the young sultan and his viziers in the royal stand a little farther from where he and Balbi were seated.

"At least he showed up on time. I was worried we'd have to wait quite some time."

"You've forgotten how punctual these Turks are."

Once Mehmed took his seat, twelve cavalrymen in two rows from the left lined up on the field to come before him. The janissaries to the right did the same.

The mounted arbiter waiting at the middle of the field off to the side called the two team captains, Vahdeddin and Karaja Pasha, to his side. The spectators broke out in cheers as the two men ambled their mounts forward. Both men had fought in famous battles and had their own rolls in victories. They were known by name and exploit by many on both teams.

"Look, Alberti, how beautifully they handle their horses," the ambassador said.

The arbiter took the two captains, one to his right and the other to his left. "You know the rules. Let it be known the target is not the horse, but the rider. I javelin thrown from within fifteen yards will not earn a point and I will send off any player who deliberately throws his javelin to injure a player."

More so than explaining the rules, which he did with seriousness of voice, the arbiter's performance was to somewhat maintain the traditional character of the ritual. He was also trying to ensure that the players knew the rules were strict and that they were on the field to play a game. Karaja Pasha and Vahdeddin both nodded in recognition and returned to their places.

"Alright, men," Vahdeddin said just loud enough for his team to hear. "Let's show these janissaries what it means to handle a horse."

As was the rule, the youngest member of the janissary team started the game, and Sinan of Bosnia brought his horse to a trot toward the opposing side. In his right hand was a yard-long, blunted oak javelin slung at his side. He had already chosen an opponent by the time he crossed the center of the field, and if he could manage to strike this famous warrior from the victory at Varna, he would win one point for his side.

"Hajji Ali!" he shouted when thirty yards from the cavalrymen as he lifted his javelin and threw it to the back left of the players.

Hajji Ali was delighted with the challenge. Then the javelin came hurtling down on him like a bolt of lightning, and if he hadn't ducked to the right before long, the narrow miss would have instead cocked him in the middle of his forehead. The lad was young, he thought, but certainly skilled and well trained. He took off at a gallop to the cheers of the crowd as the javelin whisked passed his head, in pursuit of Sinan retreating to his team's area.

Sinan was nearly back in place and thirty yards away. Hajji Ali lifted his arm and flung his javelin at a full gallop. It flew through the air and struck Sinan in the back, earning the cavalrymen a point. Hasan had already taken off from the janissaries' area after Hajji Ali while the crowd was still cheering. He flung his first javelin before fully exiting his area and hit Hajji Ali in the shoulder, winning the first point for the janissaries. He loosed his second javelin as he reached center field. Hajji Ali slung down to the left of his horse as the javelin flew by and reached the waiting cavalrymen.

Hasan sped his mount when he saw Blind Abdullah in pursuit. He'd heard Abdullah had gotten his nickname not from any lack of eyesight, but because he had thrown a javelin and hit his target with his eyes shut. He pressed himself against his horse's neck as Abdullah's first javelin came down toward his head and was able to evade a hit. With the second javelin, he swung down and hung below his horse's belly to the crowd's amazement. Abdullah's third javelin glanced off his arm and the arbiter on the right of the field recorded the point.

"I wouldn't have thought the cavalrymen would give the janissaries such a run," Balbi said. "Aren't the janissaries the sultan's most skilled soldiers? They're taking quite the beating."

"They are, but you forget the game of javelin comes from the cavalrymen in the fiefdoms. They have iron rods in their hands from the time they're children. After those, their arms are strong once they grow up a bit more. Then these wooden rods are light as a feather and they can fling them incredibly far. Of course, they don't only play games. Their arms are strengthened as children and they're also adept with a sword. They spend their entire lives on horseback, but the janissaries are actually foot soldiers."

"What's their place in the army?" Balbi asked.

"The lords who hold the fiefs are obligated to maintain an army that they form from the best young men at the beck and call of the sultan. When a decree comes from the sultan, then thousands of soldiers are quickly assembled from throughout the territories." The ambassador took his eyes from the field and looked at Balbi. "A tremendous system, is it not?"

"They're certainly more organized and disciplined than our own knights."

The two men turned back to the fierce action on the field as the crowd suddenly jumped to their feet and broke out in cheers.

Abdullah returned to the janissaries and Iskender took off with such speed the spectators thought the horse was wild and trying to buck off its rider. His first two javelins easily struck his opponent as he galloped across the field, one on the shoulder and the other on the back. His third throw landed on his opponent just as he was about to enter the cavalry space and the crowd roared for the three hits for three points.

Hayati the Hawk then furiously took off after the janissary to close the difference. He'd earned his nickname in battle by those who claimed he had nearly taken flight on his horse. He took aim for Iskender's back, but the javelin flew by as the janissary swung down and dangled below his horse. Iskender let loose of the reins and clung to his horse's back, face down as the second javelin whisked passed him. Hayati was readying his third throw as he rapidly approached the janissaries' area and, thinking it wouldn't be fair to throw from such close a distance, pulled the reins and turned around in retreat.

"I would have thought the janissaries could only fight on foot," Balbi said.

"It defies reason to suppose the janissaries are untrained when it comes to the full art of war."

Vahdeddin galloped after Hayati, and with his years of experience, was able to get off three throws in quick succession. Hayati's nickname, however, wasn't just a flight of fancy, and Vahdeddin was quickly reminded of that as Hayati slung beneath his horse, dodging the first javelin, and clung on as it galloped across the field before pulling himself up from the other side. Seeing his second two throws evaded, with the deftness worthy him, Vahdeddin reckoned Hayati's position, released his reins, firmly fixed his feet under his saddle and leaned to the side. He then slung a javelin directly against Hayati's head to the bated breath of the spectators. Still in pursuit of Hayati, who was hanging below his horse, and without missing a beat of the hoof, he leaned to the other side and, as so few men could, flung another javelin with his left hand, striking his opponent and winning another point for his team.

The game was growing heated, and in the next go Selim the Yogurt Seller managed to strike Davud from the janissaries in the head to bring the cavalrymen back in the lead. Iskender and the other janissaries immediately called for the physician when they saw blood seeping through the white fabric of Davud's hat. Davud dismounted by the physicians waiting at the ready at the side of the field who, seeing the wound, were surprised to see how little affected the janissary was.

And with this, the first half of the game came to an end.

86

Alberti Balbi and the Genoese ambassador were sipping the sherbet they had bought from a peddler as the second half started.

"Mehmed must have gotten bored. Look, he's not in his seat," the ambassador said as he looked to the empty seat in the stands.

"I'd say otherwise," Balbi said with a grin as he looked back to the field. "He's right there in the middle of the janissaries."

Surprised, the ambassador looked over the janissaries, but at first couldn't make out Mehmed in the front row. It was the first time he'd ever seen the sultan wearing the janissary hat. The crowd was no less confused. On second look, however, his tawny beard, sharp eyes and aquiline nose made it clear it could be no one but the sultan.

"One certainly can't belittle his courage, that's for sure. He's rising against Constantinople and paying no heed to being injured on the eve of battle."

Mehmed had wanted to join in from the start, but hadn't wanted to offend either side. For him, though, merely watching the game from the stands was torture. He wanted to be among his soldiers and share in their excitement. He reckoned Davud leaving the game was the perfect excuse for him to join to keep the two sides even. There were hundreds of janissaries in line to replace an injured comrade, but he had no intention of staying in the stands another second.

Mehmed rode to the other side as the arbiters were about to start the second half. The cavalrymen all tensed in their saddles in wonder of what the sultan would say as he came so close.

"Today, on this field, I am an ordinary janissary," he said. "If you forget this and give me pass, indulge me or deliberately miss your throws, you can be certain the rest of your life will be spent in a dungeon. I've given my men strict orders and they're watching you closely. They will let me know if they think you show me any favor."

The cavalrymen all understood what they were told and bowed their heads slightly in obedience. They were all proud to go to battle under the command of their daring sultan, and him there on the field made them all the more so.

"Alright my lions. Let me see what you've got!" Mehmed said, reveling in the scene. "We are each other's equals. Our enemies can't match us. We are enough for ourselves. Our proper friendship and our battle are among ourselves."

Halil Pasha grumbled that Mehmed hadn't listened to him as he watched the sultan take his place among the janissaries on the far side of the field. No matter how long he explained the danger and unnecessary risk the game posed, as always, the young sultan was stubborn and did as he pleased. Halil Pasha was annoyed as the arbiters started the game. Zaganos Pasha, however, had a wide grin on his face. He thought it was precisely this that made Mehmed different than the previous sultans.

Jafer Agha ordered his men on the edge of the field and in the stands to keep watchful. His eyes were concerned as he peered out over the teaming crowd rather than watching the field, as the man for whose life he was responsible was now playing a game before thousands of people. It was madness, but he also took pleasure in the sultan joining in the game he himself had mastered.

Karaja Pasha had decided whose name he would call as he galloped forth holding five javelins in his left hand and one at the ready in his right. He wouldn't forget his throws today. It was certain he wouldn't play javelin again. How could he pick up another javelin after striking a hit against a sultan, after all?

"Mehmed!" he shouted as he flung his javelin at the sultan in the middle of the janissaries.

Mehmed pressed against his horse's neck as the javelin whipped over him and spurred Al-Khamsa on as the crowd grew louder. The davul players started to pound their drums with deafening vigor, with the shouts and cheers from the crowd added to the clamor. After their years-long relationship, Mehmed's horse could feel his heartbeat and was moving with him, instinctively sensing his commands. Mehmed had already raised his javelin, ready to throw as Karaja Pasha galloped away. He knew Karaja Pasha was too skilled to be beaten by a strike to the back. Karaja Pasha kept looking behind to try to see where the javelin would hit. Mehmet splayed forward on his mount and threw from below. Karaja Pasha hadn't seen the javelin, as it had come from below, and so had no opportunity to evade it. Then Mehmed brought Al-Khamse to low to the ground, nearly all the way, loosed another javelin and struck Karaja Pasha as he slung off the other side of his horse. Mehmed's third javelin hit Karaja Pasha on the shoulder. He picked up speed to evade the next throw, but couldn't pull his horse up in time and left the field of play, giving up three points.

"It looks like Mehmed doesn't stay idle in his free time," the Genoese ambassador said.

Ömer Bey went galloping after Mehmed and trained his javelin at the sultan's back. Mehmed slid his entire body down the left side of his horse and concealed himself. He spurred Al-Khamsa to such a speed that Ömer Bey didn't have time to get off another throw. The crowd's cheers raised to a din. The janissary Murad, his life having been devoted to the sultan, brought his horse to a trot as he passed Mehmed. Ömer Bey swung down and hid behind the right side of his horse as Murad threw his second javelin. The crowd held its breath as he hung on with his left foot under the saddle, his right pulled next to him with both knees bent and hands clasping the saddle. He evaded two throws and then pulled himself back up. Firmly seated again, he reached out with his left hand and snatched the whistling javelin from the air, earning three more points for the cavalrymen with the catch. The crowd again cheered on the feat.

"Long live the Sultan!" the cavalrymen and janissaries shouted all together as the evening sun painted the sky in reds at the end of the game.

The players were exhausted after the long match and looked forward to sitting down for some cold ayran, kababs and plates of baklava. Before, though, they had to clean at the glistening marble baths and change their dusty clothes.

Sitting in his room that evening as he formulated his plans, Mehmed reckoned his army was ready for the campaign. In three days, they would march from Edirne.

87

Iskender broke his head out from the water, surrounded by darkness. With a thin rope in his mouth, he took hold of the loopholes in the wall rising from the water and pulled himself up.

He quickly tied a knot in the rope where it met the water's surface.

"All set," he whispered to the janissaries on the other side of the moat, signaling them to come.

Holding the other end of the rope, Hasan slowly slipped into the water and started to swim across.

He reached Iskender on the other side and the two janissaries laid flat on the ground when a guard in a watchtower along the outer walls poked his head out from between the battlements and surveyed the area.

"All of the towers are crawling with guards," Hasan whispered. "We'll have to be really careful."

"Don't worry, I know this place like I know my own garden."

It had been years, but Iskender hadn't forgotten.

He scurried along the base of the wall with the rope after the guard disappeared behind the edge of the tower. He tied another knot in the taut rope at the base of the wall. He tugged on the rope twice for Hasan to follow.

"Now, this is where the hard part starts," Iskender whispered.

They edged along with their backs pressed to the wall and heard two guards talking as they walked above them. They could easily have been spotted if the guards had only looked a bit lower.

Iskender waited for the watchmen to pass before he turned around and started climbing up the wall, wedging his fingers and toes between the stones. His teeth were clamped down on the rope.

He slowly ascended the towering wall and was quite high up. Hasan waited below, ready to try and break his fall if he lost hold while he also kept an eye on the guards.

Iskender clambered up, using the footing of the vents and grooves, and had just reached the top of the wall when a small part of the stone under his right foot gave way. Iskender hung on with his right hand, swinging from the height. The crumbling stone and dust fell onto Hasan's face as he looked up through the darkness. He forced himself not to cough.

Iskender tried to pull himself up, now with the entire weight of his body straining his right arm. The sinews of his arms strained and tightened.

He reached out and grabbed hold of a loophole with his left hand, panting for air as sweat poured over his body. He pulled himself up over the battlements and tugged twice on the rope again to call for Hasan after tying another knot.

Hasan scrambled up the wall with the same agility. Once he reached the top, he saw two guards on the ground next to Iskender and then looked back up to his friend.

"I didn't think they'd be so happy to see you," Iskender said with a wry grin.

"I thought you were going to fall there for a moment."

"I was. Thank God Vahdet Agha made us do those archery drills from morning to night. If I hadn't drawn a bow a hundred times every morning there's no way my arm could've held me."

They marked the width to the second wall with the rope and then approached the other side.

Iskender pointed at a tower rising up twenty yards down the wall. “There should be a ramp down from one of these. That’s what we need to find.”

Hasan looked down the wall to both sides and tried to reckon the distance between the towers.

“We need to get into one of them.”

“Leave that to me,” Hasan said. “Wait here.”

He crept to the closest tower and went in.”

Iskender heard muffled yells and looked at the watchmen farther along the wall. No one else had heard. Everything was shrouded in darkness.

Hasan emerged from the tower a while later. “The ramp isn’t here, that’s for certain. All I found was a couple meat sacks for soldiers.”

They then went to look in the tower up the other way. One of the guards leveled his spear at Iskender as soon as they entered. Iskender shot out his hand and took hold of the end of the spear. He snapped off the point as he wrenched it to his side, turned it on the guard and stabbed him through the throat. With no chance against two janissaries, the guard farther back dropped his weapon.

“Please, don’t kill me. I beg of you.”

Iskender looked over to Hasan. Hasan unwrapped his red sash, tore a piece off and tied it over the man’s mouth. With the rest, he bound the man’s hands and feet, and sat him up on the ground.

The guard watched them in a daze as they went through the door and descended the ramp on the other side.

Later that night, underneath the light of a crescent moon, they would go over the exit from that part of the inner walls and the features of the octagonal towers.

Iskender felt all the power in his arms drain away as the city stretched out before him while he climbed up the imposing inner wall nearly twice as tall as the outer one. Waiting for him at a loophole, Hasan gathered his strength, took hold of him under his arms and pulled him up.

"You alright, Iskender? Pull yourself together," he whispered as he shook Iskender, who looked on with bloodshot eyes.

Hasan could feel Iskender's heart pounding as if it would burst through his chest. Iskender felt as though he was under a burden greater than the entire world. Seeing the paths he had run as a child winding into the city made him want to go on over and beyond the wall. He wanted to run straight to Mariam's house and hold her. He had no idea what had become of her over the years and a thousand possibilities came to mind—all of them bad. Had she married? Was she still in service to the patricians like a slave? Maybe the lecherous lord had taken her. More than any of these thoughts, though, he wondered if Mariam, the love of his life, was still alive.

There hadn't been one night since he left Constantinople that he hadn't thought of her as he laid down to sleep or woke up in the morning without seeing her. Now, though, with the city extending from the walls, all of his memories came flooding back and it seemed as if he'd never left—as if it had only been a day ago when he had been working with her in these fields. He hadn't been able make sense of his ordeal and how he had escaped, but he came to his senses as Hasan shook him and he saw the crescent moon shimmering over the city.

"We should go back already," Hasan said.

Hasan hunched down as he felt the air hiss as they walked back up the ramp they had taken from the outer ramparts. An arrow wedged itself between the stones of the wall next to him. He and Iskender turned and saw a group of soldiers running after them.

"There they are!" one shouted, a red cloth dangling from his hand.

Hasan ran up the ramp with Iskender following closely behind.

"He must not think much of our belts," Hasan said. "I'll give him a piece of my boot the next time."

Iskender cracked a smile.

A rain of arrows and spears continued behind them, some barely glancing off their shoulders, as they quickly slipped through the loopholes to the other side of the wall.

Halfway down the wall, they realized all the guards had swarmed above them and so they let go. They rolled as they hit the ground to lessen the impact and then threw themselves through the loopholes into the moat.

Arrows flew into the water, but lessened as they hurriedly swam across.

They knew as they pulled themselves from the water and disappeared under the cover of night that Muslihiddin would be pleased with the measurements they'd made with the rope.

Be patient, Iskender thought to himself. *Just a little more patience, and then Mariam.*

88

I was at that wonderful house again today. Nilüfer, Ragip Pasha and I talked much more than we wrote. It seems Ragip pasha sees me as part of the house. He said I'm very different from the other Christians he's met. We sat in the salon—me on a divan in one corner, Ragip Pasha in another and Nilüfer across from him. Their servant Shushan kept bringing that lovely savory *börek* pastry and sherbet.

These Turks are quite insistent when it comes to treating a guest and fill one up to the brim. They think because of being a guest, a person can't ask for something to eat if hungry. Obviously, they're mistaken. What's more, they find it a discourtesy if one refuses. Once I came to the house after a meal at the palace, and when I didn't eat the sweet baklava pastry, I felt Ragip Pasha get seriously perturbed. They simply don't take no for an answer and think it disrespectful if one doesn't eat the food they offer. This is widespread among the populace. If someone has something to eat, then they will break off a piece for whoever else is with them.

The conversation went from topic to topic and then came around to the sultan's impending campaign. Ragip Pasha was troubled by it. He and I think the same, more or less. He says Mehmed is still quite young and inexperienced, and that soldiers only show loyalty and devotion to a sultan who has accomplished great things. When he asked me about the goings on at the palace, I explained there are two perspectives. There is a faction of Mehmed's soldiers, the janissaries foremost among them, that are quite wedded to the idea, but there are just as many who oppose it—particularly the pashas.

The conversation descended into politics when Nilüfer interrupted and asked if they should give me—Signore Alberti—the gift they had of a swan. I was happy that she changed the subject. Being amid all the palace politics and intrigue has been wearing enough.

I was surprised—how could there be a swan? They laughed and Nilüfer said it wasn't that kind of swan. Then she knelt in front of her writing set, placed a sheet of paper on the small table, dipped her pen into the ink and started to write large letters as I looked on curiously. She wasn't writing normal Arabic letters or drawing. I was excited to see what it was and looked on silently as her right hand carefully and gracefully glided over the paper. I couldn't make sense of the lines, curves, points and circles that began to fill the sheet at first. But then a head, the elegant neck of a swan and wings began to take shape as she continued.

I told her I'd never seen anything like it.

She said it wasn't just any normal picture. There's writing there for those who can see past its appearance, she said, and the important thing is to be able read the meaning beyond its physical manifestation.

I was at a loss and asked if there really was writing there.

She said there was and that knowing the language wasn't enough to be able to read the calligraphy.

I looked over at Ragip Pasha for some hint, but he offered none. All I could see from the peculiar lines was a splendid swan.

Some Turks consider writing to be a sacred act. They also have great respect for the paper it's written on. If they find a piece of paper with writing on the ground, rather than throwing it away, they pick it up and put it somewhere high up. I thought of this habit of theirs when Nilüfer told me there was a divine message within the swan before me. Even the ordinary people can read and write. They consider it compulsory for all Mohametan men be able to read their holy book, as they constantly read it as part of their devotion. Whereas our priests are nearly the only to read the Gospels and interpret them for the illiterate people as they see fit, here, people read the books themselves and act accordingly.

Nilüfer then gave me the swan as a gift. There it was in front of me, but I couldn't make any message out of the lines and swirls—not even a single letter. I'll work at it a few nights longer before I ask Mullah Lütfi.

89

Muslihiddin rushed down the corridor leading to the Divan council, pushing a table on wheels and laid over with a sheet. The janissary Hasan had been tasked with accompanying him and he was curious about what under the sheet covering the large table. The uneven contours, rising and falling, made him wonder all the more. Muslihiddin was looking at his drawings as he went, leaving the table to go astray. Hasan reached out and stopped it in place right before it careened into the wall and the two men stood looking at each other.

The janissary Abdullah stood waiting with his back to the door to the Divan, spear in hand. His orders from Halil Pasha had been clear—no unauthorized person was to enter the chamber and the council was by no means to be interrupted.

After receiving his orders, Abdullah had started to wonder what was being said behind the door he guarded as the sultan's most senior pashas filed in one after another.

The Divan hall was adorned with satin and red and yellow cushioned sofas along its walls. Rather than the old Roman Senate of old with men in seats facing one speaker at the dais, the Ottomans sat cross-legged and subdued to discuss their issues as they moved the beads of their *tespihs* through their fingers.

No one had any intention of sitting down this time. The sultan was going to explain for the first time his plans for attack and everyone was standing at attention.

The palace engineer Muslihiddin, again in his usual haste, explained what he had been working on to Mehmed at the head of the table and the pashas standing around it.

He had just removed the sheet from the massive table to reveal a scale model of Constantinople's city walls.

"The moat in front of the walls is twenty-yards wide and fifteen-feet deep," he said, pointing to the trench in the model. "This moat extends continuously along the more than four miles of walls."

"It's been one of the main reasons for the failure of every siege thus far," Halil Pasha said. "They always clear out every part that gets filled with earth and keep the water high. It's insurmountable."

Muslihiddin pointed at the wall abutting the moat. "Rising from the moat is a six-foot breastwork. Between this and the second wall is fifteen yards." He looked at Mehmed, the viziers and the pashas to be sure they had all understood. Then he brought his hands up from behind the model and put them on the first wall. "This wall is twenty-six feet. There are square towers every forty yards that are generally thirty feet tall."

"Sultan Murad's cannons couldn't break those walls," Halil Pasha said as Zaganos Pasha became more annoyed with each of his points of contention.

Mehmed gave Muslihiddin a nod to continue.

"The inner walls are the largest and thickest at forty feet. There's a nineteen-yard gap between them and the outer walls. They call this the inner terrace. It's like a pen between the two walls."

"Where did you get such detailed information? If we have Greek spies in the city, I suggest you not trust them too much. The state of the walls might also be different now than from any information from a few years ago. They repair them every year."

Muslihiddin smiled. "No. The information isn't old and it didn't come from Greeks."

He framed the towers along the outer and inner walls with his hands and explained how at a height of sixty-five feet, the positions of the inner towers pen in the terrace in between. The model itself was a precise replica, even down to the color. In addition to being built to scale, great care had even been given to the lines of red brick in the stone walls.

He paused for a moment before continuing.

"To tell the truth, I must admit these walls are a wonder of engineering. They extend underground nearly as far as we see them above. These foundations both make the walls as stable as a mountain and prevent excavations." Muslihiddin again looked at Mehmed and the pashas before returning to the model. "As you can see from above in the model, the passageways from one wall to the other aren't in straight lines. The walls are a labyrinth with doors opening to various levels, ramps parallel to the walls, hidden stairways, vaulted passageways and barred pipes."

"Their weakest point is in the Lykos Valley," Zaganos Pasha said as he turned to the large map on a table next to the model and pointed to the region in the northwest.

"There are also additional points in the northern part due to the work on Blachernae Palace. The walls there could be more susceptible," Muslihiddin said.

"You're right," Halil Pasha said. "Sultan Murad and Sultan Bayezid before him thought the same and attacked this section, but they couldn't breach the outer walls. All of the city's soldiers and people mass there and put up a formidable defense. It seems we've already trained them well for this."

"You speak the truth, Halil Pasha," Mehmed said, taking a step forward, "but there's something you haven't considered. My armies are larger and more powerful than they ever have been before. My father and grandfather attacked the city at a single point with the power they had. We, however, won't give Constantine's soldiers and the crusaders coming to their aid the opportunity to breath.

We'll attack the city from all sides at once. Constantine will have to spread his defenses thin."

He then began to instruct his five main commanders where they would be stationed.

"Zaganos Pasha, you will have your soldiers right here around Galata, where you will wait," he said as he indicated with a pointing stick the area at the north of the Golden Horn on the large map of the city.

The map depicted the city on the peninsula, the sea bounding it to its north, south and east, and the land to its west. Zaganos Pasha was to command the area to the northwest of the Genoese quarter, which was surrounded by walls with the Galata Tower rising at its center.

Mehmed slid his stick down the map to the northwesterly most point where the city walls met the Golden Horn. "Karaja Pasha, you will be responsible for the area from Blachernae Palace to the Lykos River with the Rumelian forces under your command."

Karaja Pasha bowed his head slightly as he looked out from beneath his dark brow with a hand on the hilt of his sword.

"Ishak Pasha, you will be directly opposite this in command of the Anatolian forces along the walls from the outlet to the Marmara Sea to south of the Lykos Valley."

Mehmed then pointed to the southerly most point of the city where the walls began from the Golden Gate to the Rhegium Gate.

He explained that the Karaja Pasha would be stationed to the west and the Ishak Pasha to the east. He then explained he would command his janissaries from the Mesoteichion area just north of the middle of the land walls to above the Lykos Valley.

He explained that the Karaja Pasha would be stationed to the west and the Ishak Pasha to the east. He then explained he would command his janissaries from just north of the Mesoteichion middle land walls to above the Lykos Valley.

Then he turned his attention to Baltaoghlu Süleyman—the commander of the fleet. "Süleyman, you will hold your ships north of the Golden Horn and at the *Diplokionion.* From there you will be able to see any ships coming from the Venetian colonies on the Black Sea and cut off the crusader fleets coming up from Gallipoli. You will try to attack the sea walls when the chance arises. Your main mission, however, will be to attack the southern part of the city leading to the Golden Horn."

"But Your Excellency, our fleets are too week to take on the Venetian ships in any case," Halil Pasha said.

"If they have better quality ships, then we will have superiority in number," Zaganos Pasha cut in. "We've been building ships of all sizes at the Gallipoli shipyard."

Mehmed finally called over Tursun Bey and ordered him to take a small fleet and attack the Morea to blockade Constantine's brothers, Thomas and Demetrios—the despots of Morea—and prevent them from sending reinforcements to the city.

"There's something I am having difficulty with, Sultan," Saruja Pasha said as he stepped beside Halil Pasha. "Even if we gird the city on four sides, these thousand-year-old walls are masses of stone. How are we going to breach them?" He walked over to Muslihiddin's model. "The moat along the walls is twenty yards wide—nearly a small lake. How will we get across that? Let's say we fill it up somehow. Still, how will we breach the walls? Even if the entire army scales the first wall, the enemy will slaughter them all the moment they pinch them off in the terrace between it and the second wall."

"Saruja Pasha," Mehmed said, "since when have we waited for cities we have taken to be handed over on a silver platter? Concern yourself with fulfilling my orders and leave the breaching of the walls to me."

Saruja Pasha quietly stepped back in place.

90

I paid a visit to a Venetian merchant at his house today. He maintains a house here, as well, because of his constant business with the Turks. Every time he sees me, he tells me of an Egyptian magician and says I must see him. I've never been one to pay much attention to superstitions and magic. So many of the Turks believe in this nonsense, but this Egyptian magician's main source of income is from entertaining the foreigners who come to the city, and for a pretty price at that. I heard of his reputation from quite a few foreign ambassadors, as well as Turks, though, and my curiosity eclipsed my reason, so I decided to see him.

My Venetian friend Marco, whose home I was going to visit, had told such fantastical stories that I didn't entertain the idea for a moment that they could be real. One occasion, the magician told Marco he could make him drink a bowl of sherbet. Just to spite the magician, Marco asked for the sherbet to be in one of the colored blown glasses back in Venice he'd inherited from his father. The magician went to the kitchen and came back a little later holding a glass of sherbet. Marco has always sworn it was one of his fathers' glasses. He watched the magician perform the same trick for a few pashas and looked on with his own eyes as the pashas drank the sherbet that came from supposedly so many miles away. I've read of this famous magic with ink I will see today in other travelers' writings.

This magician by the name of Ismail ibn al-Zuhur once asked a visiting emissary to write a letter to someone he missed in his own land. The emissary wrote a letter and the magician put it under a cushion of the sofa. Then after a moment, he reached in and pulled out a different letter. He recognized the handwriting and was astonished to read a letter from his sweetheart.

Al- Zuhur also has an interesting story of having come from Egypt and settling here. A Mamluk pasha was dismissed all of a sudden. He suspected something when someone else took his position, so he wrote a letter to the vizier to explain the situation. He fell ill before receiving a response and was bedridden. The pasha felt it was the work of the man who replaced him and claimed to the vizier that the man had employed a sorcerer to afflict him. The vizier then extracted a confession from the newly installed pasha. He said they would find the sorcerer and lock him in a dungeon, and then if the old pasha didn't recover, then he could choose how he wanted to die.

The vizier wanted the sorcerer to be under constant watch in the dungeon and so posted two guards. One was to sleep while the other kept watch. One night, the guard keeping watch saw the sorcerer mutter something in the middle of the cell. Then the candle in front of the sorcerer disappeared and four candles appeared in the four corners of the cell. The sorcerer stood up and hit his head against the wall four times. Every time his head struck the wall, a dark-faced person entered the cell from behind each of the candles. As the men circled the cell, the sorcerer dropped to his knees again and muttered again. The candle reappeared in front of him and the four men disappeared.

The next morning, the ailing pasha woke up perfectly fit. He immediately did his ablutions and prayed in thanks. The sorcerer was released after months in the dungeon and reckoned he could no longer live there, and thence came here. That sorcerer is al-Wazahhir. Marco says he can't stay here long, either, as the men of the palace are waiting for him to make the smallest mistake, and when they find one, will either throw him in a dungeon or exile him. This is because the scholars of the Turks don't care to see these swindlers among them.

Al-Wazahhir seemed a little distressed when he came to Marco's house upon invitation. He stood at the window, staring at the clouds and complained that the weather wasn't as he wanted it. Marco asked him to perform his best trick of magic ink. Al-Wazahhir looked back at the sky and, slightly annoyed, acquiesced. He turned to me and asked for a sheet of paper, a reed pen and ink. I asked him what it was as he was writing something down. He unhaltingly said it was writing to call two *jinns,* which are beings in the Mohametan book in which they all believe but cannot see. They are somewhat like angels, but they believe *jinns* are wholly different than angels.

He told Marco to put a chunk of charcoal in a pan and prepare some frankincense and coriander next to it. When all was ready, he said that for the magic to work, it needed a child not yet come to maturity. We called out to a boy of about eleven or twelve in front of the house. He drew a square diagram on the palm of the boy's hand. He divided it into nine squares, leaving the middle square larger, and then filled them with Arabic numerals from one to nine. He poured ink into the large, middle square until it formed a circle. He told Marco to put the frankincense and coriander into the pan with the charcoal. Then he tore a piece from the paper with the writing and placed it on the charcoal. He looked at the boy and asked him if he'd seen the reflection of his face in the circle of ink. The boy said he hadn't. Al-Wazahhir got annoyed and said the boy wasn't young enough. I wasn't surprised in the least and was convinced this was all a misadventure. I soon understood, though, that I was quick to judge.

The second boy we called from the street was eight or nine. Al-Wazahhir said small children can see realms no one else can. He drew the same diagram on the boy's hand and again poured ink into the middle. The burning frankincense gave the room an intense aroma. This time when al-Wazahhir asked the boy if he saw his face in the ink, the boy said he had.

Then he placed some of the paper he had on the boy's head and some of it in the pan.

He asked the boy if he saw anything in the ink.

The boy was quiet for a moment. Then his eyes shot wide open and he said he saw someone sweeping the floor with a broom. The boy looked frightened when I looked closely at his face, but as if he was forced to obey and answer the question.

The magician tore off another piece of paper and put it on the coals. He also told Marco to add more frankincense. The smoke enveloped the room and the smell grew thicker.

Al-Wazahhir told the boy to tell him when the sweeping stopped, which he did a while later. He then asked the boy if he knew what a flag was. The boy said he did. The magician then told him to bring forth a flag, which he did. He asked the boy what color it was—the boy said it was red. Al-Wazzahir asked for the same thing again and again, and each time the boy said it had come and said its color. When the seventh flag came, he said it was green. The boy was stiff as he looked into the ink in the palm of his hand. Al-Wazahhir then muttered something and threw the pieces of paper in his hand onto the coals.

Al-Wazahhir then told the boy to bring forth the sultan's tent and to set it up. The boy said it happened. The magician asked him what color it was, to which the boy said it was red and lined in yellow. Al-Wazahhir told him to now have soldiers come and surround the sultan's tent with more tents. After a while, the child said it was done. The magician then told him to bring forth a bull, and the boy said he had. Next, he told the boy to have the soldiers slaughter the bull, cook it and eat it. The boy then said each was done. Finally, he asked the child whether or not he saw the sultan. The boy said the sultan was on his horse. With this, he told the boy to have the soldiers serve the sultan well. The boy said they were. The smoke and aroma of the frankincense was so thick in the room that it was unbearable. It burned my eyes and offended my throat.

I suspect if one were to do some similar trick in Venice, they'd be denounced as a witch and find themselves burning at the stake in Saint Mark's Square before sunrise the next day. Marco said the Turks wouldn't burn the man and that their laws were gentler in this respect. Al-Wazahhir also never dared to go beyond his tricks that had no effect on anybody.

Al-Wazahhir then turned to me, said the concoction was ready and asked me if there was anyone deceased I wanted to see. My heart started to pound. The first thing out of my mouth was Cristina. The boy was having difficulty to pronounce the name, but was able to say it correctly after a few attempts.

After a moment, he asked the boy whether he saw a woman. He did. I jumped to my feet when he said she had large, dark eyes and wavy hair. Then the boy said she had a very slim waist. I knew instantly he was trying to describe Cristina's bodice. I felt I would faint right there and cold sweat started to drip from my brow. I didn't ask the boy or al-Wazahhir anything else. Then in the same way, Marco also saw somebody no one there had ever had the opportunity to know. I watched the boys face in amazement as he gave the description.

91

"Murad and Bayezid couldn't even breach the outer walls when they laid siege to the city, so I don't much suspect this boy sultan will be any more successful," Theophilos said.

Seated around a large, square table were all of the city's dignitaries, commanders, head knights, the Venetian *bailo* and Genoese *podestà*, patricians and representatives from the crusader armies of Europe. Sitting at the head of the table was Constantine, thoughtfully looking over the walls on a map of the city that bore his name as he tried to turn the debates between the different groups around the table into an advantage and resolve the discord between the Venetian and Genoese governors.

"I wouldn't speak with such assurance if I were you," Notaras said. "We've been getting information that the Turk has been preparing the siege for months. They say he's had cannons forged the likes of which we've never seen."

"Let him forge as many cannons as he pleases," Theophilos said. "No danger from land is enough to surmount the three walls."

"You're right, Theophilos," the Venetian Bailo Minotto—long considered by many as a subject of the city—said, "but we are also getting word that Mehmed has been having ships built one after another at the Gallipoli shipyards. These definitely won't be used for fishing, either."

"If fleets were just ships made from trees then woodsmen would be admirals," the renowned Venetian captain Gabriele Trevisano said with a laugh.

"There's honestly nothing to say to you Venetians' arrogance," a Genoese captain said as the two glared at each other.

"Forgive me, I didn't know the Genoese were frightened of the Turk's sailors," Giacomo Coco interjected.

With this, the Venetian and Genoese captains began shouting back and forth, as had happened since the beginning of the meeting.

"Friends, friends!" Constantine shouted from the head of the table. "The last thing we need right now is quarrel."

He tried to appease everyone, but his attempts to dispel the animosity between the Venetians and Genoese didn't seem to come to much.

"Enough!" the renowned knight Giovanni Giustiniani Longo shouted from the opposite head of the table, his hand on his broad sword, its hilt engraved with a coat of arms bearing a boar—having listened and remained quiet until now.

"There is most likely an army of fifty thousand men heading straight for us at this very moment and you here are bickering like women."

Silence fell on the hall and everyone hung their heads. Two of the Venetian knights reckoned to put the Genoese knight in his place, but then thought better of it.

Guistiniani continued speaking as he strode around the table. "My men and I didn't come here to quarrel with fellow Christians. If the Turk has numbers, then so we too have experience. And I don't much suspect his numbers are much more than our own.

We have a fellowship here, today, that is more than enough to repel the Turk. I also see today Venetians here in this city, which no one has been able to blockade for a thousand years, sinking to shouting and pathetic squabbles. I see here today the flags of the knights who battled the Mohametans in Jerusalem. Among us are the sons of those who fought and spilled Turk blood in Varna and Kosovo, and died while saving the dignity of their men in defeat." He stopped and turned back around the table. "We have every power and experience in our hands to make the greatest graveyard for the Turks ever seen. It is my duty to defend the land walls and neither Mehmed nor any other Turk shall pass as long as I live. The Venetians and Genoese—those who are born and die at sea—will play with the Turk's inexperienced fleet as a leviathan plays with minnows."

He then faced Constantine. "I am Giovanni Giustiniani Longo of Genoa, and I and all the other knights here today in Constantinople await your orders."

Constantine and everyone else in the hall were impressed by the Genoese knight's mettle. Not wanting to miss the opportunity, Constantine stood up without losing any time and continued to explain everyone's duties over the map.

"Mehmed is most likely to attack the city from here," he said pointing to the Mesoteichion in the middle of the land walls. "The pasha says the same. Guistiniani and I will command from here. Theophilos and the Bocchiardo brothers will be in our right wing. Contarini, Manuel of Genoa and Kantakouzenos will take the southern walls."

He placed Venetian and Genoese knights at the gates of the city walls for support. He then placed the protection of the Golden Horn in the hands of Aluvixe Diedo, Giacomo Coco and Gabriele Trevisano.

Cardinal Isidore was to defend the city's eastern-most Acropolis Point with his archers while the Catalans of the city took position on the sea walls along the southern coast.

Orhan Chelebi stepped forward clad in a turban and caftan when Constantine came to the Marmara coast. "These walls will be under my watch, Your Excellency. The Turks at my command will route Mehmed's soldiers."

Having waited for years, Orhan was happy to see the end of the sultan and he was prepared to spend all he had so Mehmed wouldn't emerge from the siege alive. Constantine agreed and put him in charge of the area he asked for.

Diedo approached Constantine. "We could have some trouble if the Turk's fleet pushes on the Golden Horn all at once," he said softly.

A confident smile spread over Constantine face. "Don't worry, Captain. I've known of those galleys since before the first tree was even felled." Diedo realized he had underestimated the reach of Constantine's spies. "I've thought of a solution. You'll learn of it when it's time."

Constantine then looked over to Bartolomeo Soligo of Genoa, his head engineer. Those who were to come up against his unmatched invention would see once again why this city had not been captured by sea for a thousand years.

BOOK FOUR

War and Love

92

Does man always proceed with his head turned around? Leaving Nilüfer behind in Edirne as I proceed on my way to Constantinople has hardened my belief that the future has become the past. My mind is always on the crimson horizon behind me as I move from the center of one empire to another, toward the rising sun. There are thousands of men marching determinedly and dogged outside my carriage, which is rattling along as I try to write.

The janissaries know well enough that a careless process detached from the past is senseless and harmful. How else could one describe the departure from Edirne days ago to a grand ceremony with them looking back with every two steps. They believe at least as much as I do that new empires will be built on the bridges of the old and that as they proceed, they are searching for the past more than the future.

Traveling through the night, when I step out and look around me, as if in a dream, I feel like I am in a river of men rushing to the sea. I see the vague images in my mind mingled with the masses of men before and behind me, like a child seeing what he wants in the clouds. I resemble the river of men I see in the dark of night sometimes to the frothing waves I saw on sea voyages years ago, sometimes the gigantic dragons of the tales of Cathay Marco Polo described and sometimes the hidden *Shahmaran* with no beginning or end from the legends of Anatolia.

The sultan's preparations for the campaign began with the planting of a standard with a horse's tail, what they call a *tugh,* in a courtyard of the palace off a large square. The horse means much to them, and has for generation upon generation stretching back to their nomadic forefathers of the steppes.

The horse tail standard is placed throughout the sultan's realm when he is to go to war as a call for men to come and join his army. There are even those who reckoned until the last moment that they would be going to war against the Karamanids. It requires great skill to be able to read Mehmed's mind. They say he sometimes doesn't even explain his plans to his closest viziers. There is no doubt now, though, about the target of this unprecedented army.

Karaja Pasha began assembling his Rumelian forces and Ishak Pasha his from Anatolia with this planting of the standard in the palace courtyard. The people have come from their houses and villages with the call to war more as if they are going to a wedding. The stragglers think they've somehow been wronged. Those who received word of the campaign set out on the road on their horses, whose harnesses have been passed down through the generations, in their finest clothes and with their most prized weapons. The men of Anatolia had come to assemble in Bursa from as far and wide as Evdokia, Kastamone, Kamakh, Erzurum and Bayburt, while the Rumelians came to Edirne from centers such as Sofia, Kavala and Skopje.

The sultan's army can be divided into four parts. First are the *azaps,* or the foot soldiers, made up of peasants, and which are the least orderly or disciplined. They carry axes, knives and sickles with the purpose to raid and loot Christian villages. Most of their shirts are left open and they have no armor or uniform. The only common thing among them is their red turbans. They listen to the janissary aghas responsible for the order of the campaign, and so they're also called the *bashibozuk* irregulars. They have a hunger as if they'd waited for this war for years and cannot stop.

The second part of the army is the cavalry, what they call the *sipahis.* These are the forces the fief holders in Rumelia and Anatolia are required to maintain for the sultan. The lords are given fiefs of arable land in exchange for a specific number of horsemen at the ready to be used on campaign. And with this, the sultan can speedily gather thousands of mounted soldiers with a single decree. They come ready for battle with armor and helmets, weapons, shields and well-groomed sable horses. Each unit is headed by their lord.

There aren't only Mohametans at the sultan's command, either, as many of his vassals are Christian, and soldiers come from them, as well. Bulgarians, Serbs, Hungarians and Greeks are the most prominent. For those who think this odd, the Christians are allowed to pray and worship as they so please. Unlike the fanatical crusader armies wrapped in hatred for the Mohametans, Mehmed's army, like this one marching to battle, has soldiers from many religions. I've been talking with Mulah Lütfi as we travel, and I was surprised that he'd never thought about it when I asked. He said war cannot be waged against a people or faith, but rather to bring peace and justice to the people. He mentioned the sultan's target is those who persecute both his people and their own. He pointed out that in the end, the new emperor will still rule over the same population.

I always think of what he said the more I see Greeks on this campaign running to go fight against their own people.

Of course, the main part of the army, and what holds it together, is the janissaries. These formidable soldiers, who they say number around five thousand, are the unique center of the army, churning like the cauldron of Mount Etna on Sicily. I saw it erupt myself once while on the island. I was terrified as I watched the blazing lava fume and slowly flow down the mountain slopes in the dark of the night. A regiment of hundreds of janissaries carries the same glory and impending doom. It's as if the fire in their bellies spreads to the rest of the army as those who see them take heart and fall into line.

The Ottomans' march on campaign is a world unto itself.

There are advance units of engineers, architects and carpenters that stay hundreds of yards in front of the main procession to clean the roads and repair bridges. There are oxen, porters and soldiers who transport chests, sacks and baskets of arrows fashioned throughout the winter, spears, swords, armor, shields and many other implements of war. There are also swordsmiths and other weapon makers along with blacksmiths and founders who can make arms according to need. In addition to them, there are dervishes, sheikhs and descendants of their prophet who pray from morning to night and whip up the soldiers' fervor. Porters carry the tents and their accoutrements and the bakers, butchers, cooks and sherbet makers try to keep everyone's bellies full. There are physicians and caretakers to treat those who will inevitably be injured in battle. There are even tailors. And to complete the picture of a city on the move, there are merchants doing business as normal. It is breathtaking the amount of people who have joined in the campaign.

There are also animals spread out along the miles-long procession of so many types one might think it a scene from Noah's ark. There are camels heaped with crate upon crate of arrows and cannon balls, mules with bundles of spears slung over their backs. The horses are as grand as the army—Arabians, Tatars and Bulgarians in black, roan, grey and chestnut. The oxen pull the carts loaded with cannons and there are also sheep and goats for slaughter to provide the meals when the procession rests.

Mehmed is moving cannons one might think could not be ported over greata great distance. Carts pulled by thirty, fifty and sixty teams of oxen slowly roll along, hauling the many sizes of cannon Muslihiddin and Orban have produced over the past months.

The largest cannon has three hundred oxen pulling it along at such a slow pace that it trails a week behind the main procession. The bridges and crossings along the roads won't be able to bear the weight, so there are around two thousand laborers, carpenters, masons and framers who stay a few days ahead of the procession to repair and reinforce them with supports.

I saw for myself the uselessness of cannons during the German siege of Cividale northeast of Venice, and then later the English siege of Calais. When I think of these, I have difficulty understanding Mehmed's faith in his guns. These cities' walls are dwarfed by those of Constantinople, and the stone cannonballs had as much effect as a fly trying to escape a shut window. Of course, the cannons weren't as monstrous as those Mehmed has had made. It's not clear, though, whether loading and firing these hulking cannons will be more trouble than they're worth.

The soldiers, said to be somewhere between sixty thousand and eighty thousand, have their minds on anything but this. The procession is as happy as a young, indulged Turk the day before his circumcision, bursting with glee amid the merriment without thinking or knowing of what will befall him the next day. Many of the soldiers will inevitably fall in battle, but they believe their prophet awaits them on the other side. They see all obstacles before them favorably and challenges as opportunities to increase their rewards in paradise. Even with the rains over the past few days turning the roads into a mire, they still trudge along singing songs together.

The *mehter* musicians marching in front of the janissaries and other places in the procession beat their davul drums and wail on their zurnas with such a clamor that the peasants in the villages we pass think Judgement Day has come and pregnant women even miscarry.

Despite the horde of people and commotion, everyone's place is known, where they are to proceed, where they are to set up for the night and were they are to gather in the morning. There is no sign of chaos. The janissary regiments march under the leadership of their commanders to the bobbing, pronged standards. The cavalrymen under their lords are also in rows as orderly as a field of crops. We passed by a mosque and the prayer caller in the minaret was stricken dumb as he stared at the riot of color passing below. There's no doubt from his view high above, the foot soldiers' red turbans, the cavalry's pointed helmets, the clothing of the Balkan Christians and, of course, the janissaries' unusual white felt hats looked to him as a sea monster would to the lookout in the crow's nest of a galley.

This is the pomp of the Ottoman expedition. The world moves when the sultan sets out on campaign and only stops when he does.

93

Children waited in wonder and joy over a pot of boiling red water and vinegar over a fire. They were knelt in a circle around the fire, looking over the rim of the pot with their eyes fixed on the reddening water and the eggs roiling in it.

The skies above Constantinople were clear and bright. Easter celebrations of Holy Week were underway in every quarter of the city. The spring air was fresh and crisp—neither oppressively hot nor chilly. The balmy winds off the Marmara Sea in the early morning buffeted the faces of the people filling the streets.

One of the children couldn't wait any longer after the yellow onion skins had boiled and then a further fifteen for the eggs to take on the red tint. He used two slats of wood to fish out one of the eggs and blew on it for a while to cool it down as he juggled it still piping hot from hand to hand.

When he realized the other children were jealously staring at his egg, he jumped up and ran off into the crowds between the buildings.

He raised the egg up amid the throngs of people and shouted, "Christ is risen, Christ is risen!"

A mass of people sung out the same in Greek as they passed by Hagia Sophia on the city's main street—*Christos Anesti, Alithos Anesti, Alithos o Kyrios!—Christ is Risen, He Has Risen Indeed, Truly, the Lord!*

Those at the front of the procession held the *Epitaphios,* richly embroidered tapestry with the scene of Christ being prepared for the tomb and edged with golden fringe laid over the Holy Table.

People had tied ribbons to the table for their prayers to be answered. The embroidered fabric fluttered in the wind as it progressed down the street.

Musicians led the procession in front of the priests and other clergy accompanied by their young altar servers flanked by soldiers and chamberlains, followed by city folk singing hymns in praise of the resurrection. Patriarch Gregorios III was at their lead.

Holy Week had begun with the first full moon following the vernal equinox. The people had been celebrating and singing hymns in the churches for days, and the celebrations had this day reached their peak. The administrators and wealthy of the city were in their villas and palaces eating cheesy *en tyritas plakountas* pastries and roasted lamb—the symbol of Jesus' sacrifice.

Far from the center of the city, a watchman atop a tower of the city walls sighed peevishly that his duty fell on such a holiday. He peered out over the horizon and saw a dozen horsemen galloping toward the city. He stood up and leaned between the battlements, recognizing from their clothing that these men were janissaries.

He raised the alarm. "Turks, the Turks! They have soldiers to the northwest!"

The Fourth and Fifth Military Gates swung open to the watchman's cries and a dozen mounted soldiers galloped from each to descend on the janissaries in two flanks. More soldiers armed with lances and shields in groups of four quickly followed through the gates and over the wooden bridges over the moat.

The janissaries split into three groups, as if they had planned for the small contingent of soldiers coming at them. The middle group maintained a straight line while the four to the right broke for the Golden Gate to the south and the four to the left rode toward Blachernae Palace to the north. Not able to reckon what the janissaries were up to, the Constantinopolitan soldiers also split off after each group. The janissaries pulled up on their reins a half mile from the city walls and sat waiting in a line, their horses' heads perked up. Two hundred yards remained between them and the soldiers from the city. The janissaries sat motionless, as if no one was bearing down on them.

The soldiers lowered their lances in preparation for attack.

Back in the city, the procession carrying the *Epitaphios* felt a rumble. The people fell silent and stood in place, looking around to try to hear what it was. They were terrified as the roar and rumble continued like an earthquake. There had been dozens of destructive earthquakes throughout the thousand years of the city and the people were well frightened. Some of the cauldrons full of eggs—a symbol of the resurrection—tipped over from the tremors and spilled out their boiling red water and vinegar, with the eggs cracking on the ground.

Outside the city walls, the soldiers descending in attack on the janissaries pulled back on their reins to halt their galloping mounts. Their faces were the picture of horror from what they saw before them.

"For the love of Christ!" one said.

Units of soldiers on the ramparts ran past the watchmen in suspense as they looked out over the land to the horizon.

It was clear from where the rumblings were emanating.

Thousands of Ottoman soldiers began to appear over the horizon onto the plains in a thick, dark line. The green of the plains and blue of the sky a few miles away were shortly cut by a continuous black line growing wider as it neared.

The soldiers on the city walls were tongue tied, their mouths gaped open as they stared out to the distance.

The men in the army began to take shape the closer they got. There were hundreds of standards fluttering above the soldiers stretching the over four miles from the Marmara coast to the south to the northern reaches of the Golden Horn. The embroidered crescents, Zulfiqar swords, bows and arrows, horseshoes and fire-breathing dragons waving in the April breeze signified where each of the janissary regiments, companies of cavalry and foot soldiers were. The pounding davuls and screaming zurnas of the *mehter* band below the standard rose to an even more fevered pitch with every step, sending the soldiers on the battlements and the people of the city into bouts of terror.

Realizing that the janissaries they were after were the scouts, the soldiers shook off their daze, turned their horses around and rode back for the gates.

Each of the city's gates were shut one after another after the soldiers flew back over the bridges and behind the walls. The bridges over the moat were then raised with thick chains and some were set fire to as planned. Hundreds of soldiers braced and locked the doors from behind with gigantic timbers.As Constantinople had been beset by sieges throughout its thousand years, its soldiers were adept at completely sealing the city off to the outside. It was now impossible to enter.

Giovanni Giustiniani Longo, Constantine, Theophilos, the Bocchiardo brothers, Contarini and Kantakouzenos looked out from the towers with their men waiting at the ready behind them.

Mehmed's army flooded the plains running from the city walls a half mile away and left no space open.

The siege had truly begun.

94

The janissary gunners Hayati and Hüseyin loaded a cannon with black powder and rammed it down with a long staff. They then inserted dry grass and straw and rolled a heavy cannonball down its barrel. Finally, they again inserted straw and packed it around the shot to prevent leak before they stepped away.

Orban then filled the powder chamber at the breach end and stepped back with the gunners under his command. He took a long stick, its tip smoldering, and covered his ears as soon as it touched the powder hole. The rest of the gunners turned their backs, knelt down and covered their ears.

The cannon recoiled with a terrific blast, sending the cannonball hurtling through the air away from the army of thousands watching it on its flight. It howled sharply toward the thousand-year-old city walls, arched slightly and careened into the wall near the Gate of Saint Romanos south of the Lycos River. A small part of the wall crumbled as the stone cannonball broke into pieces.

The soldiers near the wall thought a lightning bolt had struck the city from the clear skies.

"We're under attack!" Giustiniani yelled from within the walls.

The fourteen cannons lined up along the four miles of walls followed the first in a volley.

Mahmud and the other three thousand janissary archers all

pulled arrows from their quivers and fitted them to their bows, taking aim at the heads of any soldier they could make out on the ramparts. Mahmud accounted for the arrows arc of flight and released it a foot and a half above his target.

Thousands of arrows rose through the air in a foreboding cloud, reached their peak and fell on the soldiers along the battlements. Very few of the soldiers were caught unprepared, as the rest raised their shields to fend of the attack. Some of the arrows ricocheted off the shields and fell to the ground and others half lodged themselves into the cracks of the battlements. A few pierced the shields to the thunderstruck looks of the watchmen while a couple held their faces too close to their shields and were pierced through the eyes and cheeks. The majority, though, stood up after the volley in a challenge to the Ottoman army.

Constantine watched the first attack transpire from a fortified tower above the inner walls.

"You see, Cardinal?" he said with high spirits to Isidore standing at his side. "We don't even have to move a hair to defend ourselves from the Turk."

"Very true, Your Excellency," Isidore said. "I must have forgotten about Constantinople's grand battlements and defenses."

"The machines are ready, Your Highness," a soldier said as he approached the emperor.

"What machines might these be?" Isidore said.

"You'll see shortly."

The barrage of cannon fire and salvo of arrows continued, but neither could open a crack in the walls or inflict casualties on the soldiers behind the battlements. Some of Mehmed's commanders had started to think in these first hours that Halil Pasha had been right and they would not be able to overtake the city. Perhaps it indeed was impossible and madness—the folly of an inexperienced, twenty-one-year-old sultan.

Mehmed grew troubled as he saw the ineffectiveness of the cannons and arrows as he looked on from his black stallion in front of his large tent adorned in red and yellow in the middle of the janissary regiments.

"I told you, neither Murad nor Bayezid were able to breach the walls and conquer the city and you thought you, of all of them, would succeed. You're wasting both the army and the treasury," Halil Pasha said from beside him as if asking for the sultan to answer for his decision.

As if this wasn't already enough to break his army's moral, a gigantic stone came hurtling over from behind the city walls and pulverized the middle of the Rumelian units to the south. Then following soon after, a second monolithic stone careened into the middle of the Anatolian units to the north.

Constantine had for months been preparing new mangonels to launch stones great distances. Theophilos laughed as he relished the sight from the tower above the Gate of Charisios. Two cannons had also been rendered useless when the gigantic stones broke apart as they pulverized dozens of soldiers in their wake.

Thousands of the city's archers were able to shoot arrows farther from their more advantageous position protected by the crenels along the ramparts. Much of Mehmed's cavalry had lined up along the moat across from the outer walls, ready for a charge, and many of them were lying in piles with their horses with arrows sticking out from their bellies, necks and heads. The still-mounted cavalrymen started to come to the painful realization that maybe the charge would never come to pass.

"It looks like Constantine has all his units at the land walls," Jafer Agha said to Mehmed.

"I see that, too," Mehmed said, grave and distressed. "We need to disperse them."

His expectations had come true. Even if his army was the most powerful ever seen, an attack on the city only from land was doomed to defeat.

In a week's time, he would see the aid he was waiting for upon the Marmara Sea. For the time being, though, he stormed into his tent.

95

The people of the city saw sails approaching from the Marmara Sea as they looked out from the upper stands of the Hippodrome, the top galleries of the Hagia Sophia and from atop the city's hills. At first, they thought it was another crusader fleet coming to their aid. Word had passed before the siege that armies from the pope, Venice and many of the Genoese colonies would come to the defense of the city.

As the fleet of ships small and large drew nearer, they dolefully realized as the crescents emblazoned on the multi-colored flags flying atop their masts became clear that this was Mehmed's new fleet that had been spoken of for months.

Constantine came to Captain Aluvixe Diedo, who was waiting with his fleet in place at the Prosphorion Harbor at the mouth to the Golden Horn, where he informed the emperor of the number and types of ships in the Ottoman fleet.

"The biggest of the ships are smaller and less equipped than our own, but they are great in number. We'll be in a difficult position if they all attack the Golden Horn at once," he said, nervous of the possibility.

"You leave that to me," Constantine said from atop his horse.

Bartolomeo Soligo was in a tower at the entrance to the Golden Horn at the northeastern most point of the city directly opposite

Galata. He rushed down the narrow, winding stairway. The smell of damp and mold had gotten to him after weeks of working with the engineers. He finally reached firm ground where there were two soldiers waiting on each side of a gigantic, wooden wheel.

"Alright, it's time," he told them.

The men each took hold of a handwheel and began rolling the cylinder, which was as tall as both of them together. Their arms strained as a boat with a dozen oarsmen waiting just offshore began to stroke for the Galata coast.

A chain with gigantic links slowly rose to the water's surface behind the boat as is it made for the opposite shore. Groups of soldiers on land at the base of the tower and in boats rolled barrels and pushed wooden apparatuses beneath the iron chain as it stretched along the water to prevent any kinks and ensure it created a stronger barrier. The oarsmen paddled the boat along while the men at the tower turned the wheel, relieving the tension of the ton of hulking iron for all of them.

The Genoese defenders waiting in a tower on the Galata coast reached out large hooks for the chain as the boat drew near and pulled it in just as the Ottoman fleet was approaching the mouth of the Golden Horn. Captain Baltaoghlu Süleyman bristled along with his hundreds of crewmen when saw the thick chain from where he stood at the helm of the large, center ship. He couldn't accept his fleet of a hundred fifty ships being stopped by such a ruse and ordered them all to attack.

Without paying mind to the chain, the Venetian and Genoese fleets under the commands of Aluvixe Diedo and Gabriel Trevisano pulled broadside each other as if to haul up another barrier in front of the ships. The ships were taller than the Ottoman galleys and their crews could look down on the enemy mariners and easily make out their movements inside.

The arrows sinking into the backs of the oarsmen pulling the chain was the first sign of the Ottoman sailors' rage. Ten galleys, five under Trevisano and five under Diedo quickly broadsided thirty of Baltaoghlu Süleyman's ships. One of Diedo's galley's with tall gunwales fired the first shot and splintered one of Baltaoghlu's smaller ships in two. The janissaries aboard the ships then followed with volleys of arrows at the decks of the Venetian and Genoese galleys. They towered over the Ottoman ships, however, and their arrows either lodged below the gunwale or sailed completely over if they aimed higher.

With Trevisano's order, cannons fired from the gun ports one after another. His ships were now nearly abutting Baltaloghlu's and were close enough for the crews to rain down stones attached to water buckets on the Ottoman mariners from ingenious rigs on deck. They screamed in pain as they fell, their heads and bodies beaten by stone and shot, and riddled with arrows. The crewmen on Diedo's galley were well-handed with their rigs. A rope passed through a block on the mainmast with one end attached to a bucket lowered to fill with sea water while a net at the other end was full of stones. The Ottoman sailors were caught unaware, having never seen or heard of such a contrivance used for close battles at sea. The falling stones cracked their skulls open as chaos and confusion broke out on Batlaoghlu's deck.

The Ottoman commander ordered some of his men to lay out the ladders and try to board the enemy ships. Men in groups of tens and twenties scrambled up the ladders they placed against the hulls above them. Some of them were met with spears and arrows from above before they could get the ladders in place, driven down and nailed to the deck while others where killed climbing up. The Venetian sailors leaned over the gunwales and cut down the few who made it to the top.

Baltaoghlu kept sending more soldiers to replace those lying on deck and who had fallen into the sea. They readily took up their orders and tried to scramble up the ladders, but they were no more successful than those before them. Diedo's seasoned gunners hit the enemy ship at its vital points and, before long, it started to sink in the turbid waters.

Seeing that his ships were being sunk one by one and his men slaughtered by the dozen, Baltaoghlu grabbed a flaming arrow, leveled it at one of Trevisano's galleys and was finally able to hit his mark. Trevisano, however, was for no lack of experience as a Genoese captain and immediately distanced his ships from the one going up in flames to save them from the same fate. He and Diedo saw the janissaries fitting more flaming arrows to their bows and increased the barrage of cannon fire and arrows.

Baltaoghlu had lost more than twenty ships and hundreds of men, and had only been able to destroy one enemy ship. Even with that, the ship now in a raging blaze had floated near his own and any jumping flame could set them alight.

He ordered his ships to retreat as the city folk watching the bloody battle from the battlements cried cheers of victory. Diedo and Trevisano congratulated each other, boasting that the Ottomans would have to do much more if they wanted to bring a challenge at sea.

Mehmed realized he had suffered his second defeat after the one on land when he got the bad word of the sea battle. He was hemorrhaging hope, men and ammunition while Constantine was stockpiling moral and manpower.

96

“Zaganos, we must try the cannons from here so we can press on the Golden Horn!”

After the failures on both land and at sea, Mehmed went to his viziers in the Valley of the Sweet Waters behind Galata to inspect the army and exchange ideas and tactics.

“But Sultan, Galata Tower and Galata’s walls cut off our cannons.”

“Can we not aim the cannons higher as we would arrows and ensure they don’t fall on land?”

Zagonos found the idea unusual, but realistic. “You mean shoot over Galata’s walls?”

“Exactly.”

“I don’t know if it’s been tried in any other siege of the city,” Zaganos said, “but I reckon we can do it.”

“I’ll draw up the plans and give them to you. Prepare the master founders.”

“Give me a week and we’ll forge them in the encampment here.”

Mehmed turned around as he was leaving Zaganos’ tent. “One day,” he said. “You’ll have the drawings by evening and we’ll try the cannons the next day in the mid-afternoon.”

The crews from Venice, Genoa and the city had spread along the Golden Horn when they heard a short whistle. Then the water heaved with rings of foam bubbling to the surface between the two shores to the confused looks of the mariners as if something had fallen from the sky.

Five minutes later, they looked up to see a second shot come screaming overhead and land directly in the middle of the deck of a ship under Giacomo Coco's command. The galley wrenched in two from the impact and began to sink. The survivors screamed as they threw themselves into the water and thrashed their arms as they tried to swim to the nearby ships and the shore.

"They're coming from behind Galata!" one of the crewmen shouted.

"To the base of Galata, to the shore!" Coco ordered to shelter his ships off Galata's walls along the coast and get out of reach of the cannon fire.

Diedo and Trevisano set the same course in an attempt to maneuver the entire Constantinople fleet out of range at the base of the walls.

Sultan Mehmed and Zaganos Pasha stood behind a gigantic cannon perched on the hill in front of them aimed up and over Galata. The cannon sat on a raised, triangular carriage of timbers with a crank to raise and lower its angle of fire. Zaganos had gotten additional materials and had been able to bring the sultan's drawings to life without having to forge a new cannon. Mehmed called it a mortar—short and able to fire at a steep pitch.

Watchmen who could see beyond the walls to the cannon's target from a tower farther back were there to alert the gunners to raise and lower the pitch, as they couldn't see past the battlements and were firing blind.

The people and soldiers on the opposite shore inside Constantinople's city walls sank into despair, thinking the Venetians and Genoese had gone to Galata's ports in betrayal.

Taking the cannonballs falling from the sky as a sign of Mehmed's diabolic forces, the people of the city lost hope for the first time since the beginning of the siege. This desperation, however, would soon abate the next day with the appearance of the flags of Christian reinforcements on the horizon over the Marmara Sea.

97

I woke up this morning to a roar and reckoned Sultan Mehmed was conducting another attack. Everyone was running back and forth when I stuck my head out from my tent. I quickly got dressed and stepped out. Rather than taking on the city walls, though, they were all either running to the northern stretches of the Golden Horn or to the south where there are no walls on the Marmara coast.

I heard them shouting about the Genoese, Latins and Christians amid the commotion. I jumped on my horse and followed when I saw a pack of *solaks* in the distance around the sultan galloping from the Golden Horn.

I got to the shore in the shadow of Galata, and like Mehmed and his men, was astonished to see half a dozen large Christian galleys had come to the city's defense. The Turks were alarmed when they saw ships sailing up the Marmara. Mehmed had gone to Baltaoghlu Süleyman who had anchored up from Galata. Some of the soldiers followed Mehmed while others flocked to the coast to watch the sea battle that would soon unfold.

The people of the city were so elated by these reinforcements that they thronged up the battlements, almost as if it were another wall of people. The city's church bells were also tolling to celebrate the coming defenses. Thousands of people had their heads stuck out from between the battlements atop the ramparts as they anxiously awaited the ships' arrival.

A mass of Mehmed's soldiers gathered in the area of the *Diplokionion* behind the sultan and stared out in astonishment at the galleys. I knew at first glance the Turks had no chance. Each of the flags whipping in the breeze over every galley presaged the coming of these old-hand Genoese captains renowned for their mastery of battle at sea. Foremost among them were Maurizio Cattaneo and Aloixe Navaier as well as the flag emblazoned with a shark of Francesco Lecanella, whom I know personally. The fleet must be the work of the pope's vast organization across Europe. Besides the chance to win fame and glory, His Holiness Pope Nicholas knows well how to finish a job by offering famous commanders land and treasure.

The Turk's gawked at the flags and billowing, white sails adorned with black crosses.

On Mehmed's order, five dozen ships under Baltaoghlu Süleyman's command sailed in front of them. They surrounded the Genoese fleet of gigantic galleys off Acropolis Point at the far end of the city. The Ottoman ships were so tiny next to the Genoese galleys they looked like ants swarming around an entire loaf of bread.

Süleyman's galley, which was slightly bigger than the rest under his command, tried to cut in front of Lecanella and hem him in. Crewmen in dozens of rowboats around the galleys tried everything they could to board the massive ships. They threw up grappling hooks and struggled to climb up. A group of archers was also shooting endlessly at the vessels.

Lecanella and the other commanders had no trouble weathering the attack, however, as the size of their ships allowed them to easily pass by. These Genoese captains have entered and emerged from many a battle, and responded readily to the attack with nets full of stones, spears, pikes and arrows. The masses of city folk watching the course of the battle from the sea walls overlooking the Marmara cheered in support of the Latins, and archers among the crowds aided the Genoese by shooting upon the great many Turks below.

The clashing soldiers were so fierce at one point that we could even hear their curses and howls from where we were. The Ottomans couldn't match the power of the Genoese galleys and the Genoese had underestimated the Turks. Thus, the battle grew quite heated. The Turks climbed up their ropes to board the galleys as the Genoese met and cut them down with swords and spears. The Ottoman mariners who fell into the sea were lost amid the violent waves of the Bosporus. Mehmed's soldiers were tenacious, though, and those behind pushed forward to try to board the galleys as their fellow mariners before them were killed or fell overboard. The Turks were steadfast and came in waves, yet still lost many soldiers. Süleyman's pitiable men were pierced with spears, decapitated and constantly falling into the water.

At one point, the crew on Süleyman's ship looked to leap onto Lecanella's galley, but fate seemed to be on Constantine's side rather than with Mehmed.

The Notus winds were whipping powerfully up the Bosporus and swelling the cross-clad sails of the Genoese. The commanders aligned with the wind and quickly picked up speed. The small Ottoman ships were so many it looked as though the Genoese galleys sailed directly over them.

Mehmed couldn't respond, but I saw him at one point ride into the sea. He had ridden so far out as he screamed at Süleyman that the hem of his caftan was floating on the water.

Süleyman had his fleet retreat when a dozen galleys under the commands of Trevisano and Diedo behind the chain stretched across the mouth to the Golden Horn came to greet the Genoese defenders.

It was clear the Genoese had brought many knights for the defense of the city along with sacks of wheat and other foodstuffs, but what they truly brought was hope. Superiority of morale is now again with the Greeks.

Whereas the Ottomans consider their siege a divine mission, the transpiring events don't show that to be the case in the least. Mehmed's soldiers must learn that with battles at sea, chance and experience are just as necessary as men and rigging. These Ottomans don't believe in chance, though.

The beliefs of many of the soldiers have been shaken after today. How can the Ottomans put up a fight with the larger Christian fleet with more men and which can enter they fray at any moment when they don't even have enough power to man four of their great many ships at once? Süleyman paid the price for the defeat at sea today, and they say Mehmed has replaced him with another commander named Hamza Bey.

Mullah Lütfi is calm as always and says a great victory requires great patience. He says everything good in the world has a price and that their faith is being tested. He is right, and I should know by now better than anyone what price every beauty has.

98

Two peasants from Anatolian villages who had answered the new sultan's call to the siege were confused as they cut down trees far from the city walls behind Galata while the war continued, still in its early days.

Thousands of laborers like them were frantically felling trees in the area around the *Diplokionion* two miles up from where the Golden Horn meets the Bosporus. Amid the sounds of thousands of axes chopping and the cracks of falling trees, the peasants only complaint was that they were here as woodcutters rather than in the battle.

One of the peasants at the top of the hill stood up and looked to the southwest. He saw a road ten-yards wide slowly cutting through the forest below. The road began at the coast, wended to the top of the hill and then back down to the southwest toward the Golden Horn. Ropes had been strung in straight lines the previous day to show where to cut the trees for the road. Mehmed had determined the route himself.

The peasant looked enviously at Zaganos Pasha's cannons and soldiers nearly two miles away. He could see from the smoke billowing into the sky that the battle at the far city walls miles away was raging in full swing. The last thing this young man cared to do was chop down trees.

Overseeing the woodcutters, Zaganos Pasha had said, "For jihad, some take up the sword, others forge cannons and still more have oars in hand. The wise man has his pen and the archer his bow. The woodsman, however, ably swings his ax."

The young man thought it was one of the best explanations he'd ever heard. It had given him confidence and he swung his ax with more vigor.

He would realize only a day later, however, when the course of the siege would change, that he had played a role in it without firing arrow or cannon.

99

I had a long chat with Mullah Lütfi again today in my tent. This siege, somehow not ending, has finally begun to wear on me. I miss Nilüfer dearly, our work together and our conversations. I wouldn't be able to escape my troubles if it weren't for these chats with Mullah Lütfi.

He saw the word Turk written in the notes I was holding and said I refer to them incorrectly. Whereas I write and ask about the Empire of the Turk, he said, they refer to themselves as the *Devlet-i Aliyye*—the Exalted State—and that their empire is not based on any one people.

I countered and said that the sultan himself is a Turk. He said I was correct, that Mehmed is of the House of Osman, whose founder, Osman Bey, was a Turk. He said every sultan since him has been a Turk, but that this doesn't mean that all of the people in the empire are Turks. He asked if I hadn't noticed the many peoples in the army, the Jewish converts to Mohametanism who are viziers or the Armenian, Arab, Genoese and Venetian merchants. He said it's absurd to call it the Turkish Empire.

I said that an emperor rules over an empire and asked why he is called a sultan instead.

Mullah Lütfi said whether it's emperor or sultan is unimportant, but the correct word for the empire is sultanate. The Greeks in Constantinople mostly use the word emperor.

I asked him that if the sultan were really to take Constantinople, would he not then inherit the empire. It didn't seem too likely this would come to pass considering the course of the siege, but of course I didn't say that.

I was right, he said, but what he was getting at was that an empire is a culture rather than the name of a system of administration—a culture composed of many peoples and faiths living in a land of differences governed by justice. He again said that is why calling it the Turkish Empire is absurd, what is important of the sultan, and what I should know already, is not his blood, but his merit.

I can't say he's wrong. This is a Turkish Empire in which its Turks have no special privilege. As he said, one of the sultan's viziers, who is also his head physician, was originally Jewish, those who make the arrows in the janissary corps are Gypsies and many of the merchants in Edirne are Jews and Armenians. There are many Kurds among their religious men and scholars.

Perhaps this is what makes calling them Ottomans more accurate. And perhaps that is why the lands of Italy are divided into small republics and kingdoms and Mehmed sees over a vast empire. They have virtue over our own. They are disciplined and work tirelessly compared to our laborers. They have justice where it would seem we have nepotism and bribery. One need not think much to understand the primacy of the crescent over the cross. Mullah Lütfi is a Turk, but he told me today that it is not what holds importance and the main distinction of empire is its spirit and order. If only the Italians, too, could form an empire.

This matter of names is not so simple to change, though. We in Europe have called them Turks for near on a century. When a Venetian or Genoese refers to a Turk, what he speaks of is a Mohametan—all of them from beyond Anatolia to the eastern reaches of Europe. I know many travelers and merchants from further west say the same. According to Mullah Lütfi, however, this is also wrong, as not all Turks are Mohametans and not all Mohametnas are Turks.

I don't much reckon I can leave this habit behind, but I'll try. That is, of course, if a sultanate still exists after this siege.

100

Work went on under cover of night as the winds swept up through the Golden Horn.

With four hours until dawn, the first of nearly eighty ships waiting in the Bosporus had approached the shore of the *Diplokionion.*

Mehmed had ordered Zaganos Pasha to increase the cannon fire so as not to give the enemy fleet in the Golden Horn and soldiers on the battlements any respite. Taking bombardment, their attention was on the shores of the Golden Horn and they didn't notice what was taking place in the valley and beyond the hill farther up the straight. The Genoese in Galata couldn't raise their heads from their walls as Mehmed had ordered the gunners to pound its southern walls at regular intervals to distract the people there. Many of Constantine's soldiers and Genoese defenders had noticed the road cutting up from behind Galata, but reckoned it was only to facilitate communication between the Ottoman soldiers or some other war preparation. Mehmed had designed the plan early on and had placed Zaganos Pasha on a ridge over the Golden Horn.

Mehmed had brought workers from the Galliopli shipyards who were now placing a sledge as big as the ship itself in the water and under the first to run close to shore. They swam out to the ship and fixed it to the sledge with ropes and girders. Dozens of ropes rose from the sides of the sledge, out of the water and over the shore where they were yoked to oxen. Some of the ropes were also slung over the shoulders of a hundred laborers.

The laborers and oxen began to push forward on Zaganos Pasha's command and climb the slope. The vessel slowly rose out of the water and landed on the road. After clearing the trees, the timbers had been split into planks and fitted into an enormous cradle thirty-feet wide to hold the ships.

Zaganos Pasha saw the ship start to lean starboard and called out for the laborers on portside to pull faster. Once everyone on both sides fell in line, the ship slipped into place with a thud that put everyone at ease. The boards of the road had for hours been slathered with olive oil and tallow, and no one could have guest how easily the ship would glide along. Watching the small ship being pulled up, Mehmed then signaled for Zaganos Pasha to haul out a larger one. The workers lowered another sledge into the water as the first ship was thirty feet up the hill. The shipyard workers again fastened the small galley to the sledge with ropes and signaled for more oxen and men to start pulling.

The crew still aboard the ship couldn't help but let out cries of success as soon as the galley slipped into the cradle. Mehmed was watching the operation from atop his horse and, noticing Al-Khamsa's mane flutter in the breeze, he looked up and felt the wind on his face.

"Unfurl the sails," he called out to the crew.

Zaganos Pashas quickly realized what Mehmed was thinking as he looked over at the sultan and repeated the order, "Quickly, quickly—the sails!"

The crew watched astonished as the wind took to the sails. The winds blowing toward the Golden Horn lessened the burden on the men pulling the ropes to a degree and the ships inched more quickly up the hill. The crewmen were exuberant as ship after ship slid behind the walls of Galata, and many of them for the first time after weeks began to believe this young sultan would be able to take Constantinople—the center of Rome for over a thousand years.

"It's all going much faster than we expected, my Sultan," Zaganos Pasha said. "But then again, at the most we'll be able to land twenty, maybe thirty, ships before dawn.

"No, Zaganos," Mehmed said. "Wait a little longer and you'll see the true bearing of my plan."

The first ships reached the crest of the hill and began to lurch down the opposite slope. As Mehmed had ordered, ropes attached to them ran to the ships coming up the hill, which started rising without nearly any manpower.

"You see now, Zaganos?" Mehmed said. "Didn't I say smaller ships would make our work easier?"

Zaganos was amazed, as were the crewmen, seeing the ships cresting the hill suddenly double the speed of the ascending galleys, pulling them up as they made their way down.

In only two hours, all the ships had completed the nearly one-mile journey.

Mehmed thought about the tales from the *Shahnameh* he had heard from his tutor when he was a boy. What Mullah Gürani had said had been playing in his mind since he first began to plan—*exceptional people at exceptional times must find solutions no one else would think of or even imagine.*

The people of Constantinople woke up to a nightmare with the coming of dawn as they flocked to the city walls. There in the middle of the Golden Horn was the Ottoman fleet of seventy ships, the crescents on their green flags fluttering in the breeze and soldiers in turbans and shalvar standing on deck.

Trevisano, Diedo and Coco were just as horrified and dumbfounded. Even Loukas Notaras, never one to underestimate the Ottomans, was speechless.

This was the first day Constantine reckoned Mehmed was different than the sultans who had come before him.

The Ottoman soldiers were for the first time able to shake their feelings of inferiority and some would say the siege had started anew.

For Constantine, the time to spill blood had come.

101

A soldier from Constantinople in a domed helmet, his mouth and eyes bloody, squeezed a rope tightly knotted around an Ottoman soldier's neck. The prisoner's hands were bound behind him and a chain was strung from ankle to ankle. He had no chance to resist.

More than two hundred fifty of Constantine's solders pushed similarly bound prisoners in front of them from the ramparts above the Fifth Military Gate, the ropes around their necks tied around the battlements along the top of the walls.

Thousands of Ottoman soldiers across the moat watched anxious and afraid of what was happening along the walls. Mehmed ordered all cannons and archers to halt. The attack came to a standstill when it became clear from their turbans and helmets that the prisoners atop the walls were Ottoman.

"They must have been captured in the water pipes," Hasan said in horror to Iskender.

"And the ones Theophilos captured on the Marmara coast."

The gunners dropped their stone cannonballs, the men sitting on the ground sharpening their swords stood up and the cavalrymen dismounted. They approached the moat and looked up the walls curiously at their fellow soldiers as mournful thoughts welled up inside them. Everybody left what they were doing and stared up at the dozens of soldiers on the ramparts.

Constantine smiled as he looked out on the Ottoman soldiers all standing up and the silenced cannons. Giustiniani was to one side of him and Theophilos to the other.

"It seems we've managed to get the Turk's attention," Theophilos said.

"They devilishly drag their ships down the hill to water and we have our walls," Constantine said. "Let them see that. Now let them see true ferocity."

He looked to the commanders behind the prisoners. Kantakouzenos, Lecanella and the other commanders nodded to their soldiers.

Mehmed stepped forward as if he were going to enter the moat, his left hand on the hilt of his sword. "This is barbarity," he muttered to himself.

One of the soldiers lifted his foot and shoved one of the captured Ottomans from the rampart. The rope strained and the prisoner's feet were left swinging ten feet above the ground, his neck broken. Another soldier stepped up and tried to kick another prisoner off the wall, but didn't kick him hard enough. A second soldier joined, picking up the prisoner and throwing him over the precipice. The janissaries, cavalry and foot soldiers facing the wall from across the moat stared, mouths agape, as he fell kicking until the rope suddenly tensed.

"Are we just going to stand here and watch?" Hasan cried, squeezing his fists until his knuckles turned white. "Where is such savagery written in any book of war?"

The men were losing themselves in grief as they thought about their fellow soldiers and commanders on the walls who they had only a few days earlier shared a meal with and fought side by side. Some had shared rooms with them for years.

Iskender and Hasan felt all their blood drain away and their power dry up when they saw Master Ali, the archery instructor, among the prisoners on the ramparts.

Mehmed clenched the grip of his sword and his eyes flashed red. His army's misery grew with every soldier swinging from the end of a rope, wiping away its resilience like the desolation left by a rockfall down a mountain slope. Mehmed felt he wouldn't be able to regroup his army if he didn't take revenge. A hand pressed on his shoulder and he turned around to see Akshamsaddin.

He found the approval he seemed to be seeking.

102

"We must attack now with all our ships at harbor and send them to the bottom of the sea where their cowering," Gabriel Trevisano said. "The Turks' hope has been totally destroyed after the demonstration this morning."

A dozen commanders had gathered urgently at the Church of Saint Mary of the Mongols in the Venetian quarter to discuss how to approach the seventy Ottoman ships anchored in the middle of the Golden Horn. The church itself was one of the most sheltered and serenest places in the city. The city's best naval commanders were lined up in front of the altar along with Constantine and the Venetian and Genoese captains, all going back and forth between each other while mulling what they could do. Everyone was frantic.

"That is exactly what Zaganos wants us to do from where he is with his cannons behind Galata," Aluvixe Diedo said. "We'll fall into a trap if we attack now. We'll lose our entire fleet if we go within a hundred yards of the Turk's ships."

"Then let's first take out the Turks and their cannons there," said Antonio da Corfu, another Venetian. "The cannons there tie our hands in the Golden Horn."

Constantine stood up and walked to the alter with a large golden cross above it. "Those soldiers need to defend the city walls," he said, his voice betraying his loss of hope. "Mehmed will send even more soldiers even if we clear them from behind Galata."

"We must do something," a Venetian captain shouted angrily. "We can't just sit here and watch the Turk make fools of us!"

"I know of something that can be done," a commander said as he rose to his feet.

Those around looked up and recognized the man as Giacomo Coco, who had sailed his fusta from the Empire of Trebizond to aid in the city's defense.

"We will attack suddenly under the pitch black of night. It will not put the entire fleet at risk since we can do it with a few galleys and a couple fustas. All I need is plenty of bundles of cotton, bales of wool and black powder." He turned to Constantine. "You know the mixture for the infamous Greek fire that burns even on water, so little known outside of Greek lands."

"The Turks will form a blockade the moment they see us," Genoese Admiral Zorzi Doria said. "How do you reckon you'll succeed with so few ships?"

"Our capacity to move will be hindered at night, as will theirs," Coco said. "The Turks are still new to their ships. Leave the dark of night beside—they don't even know how to handle their ships in the light of day. It's within our grasp to defeat them at this game of theirs and turn it to our advantage."

"I agree with Zorzi," Aluvixe Diedo said. "This is a very hazardous move."

"I'd forgotten you're as lily livered as the Genoese," Coco spat back, sending the Genoese and Venetian captains into bouts of shouting, accusing each other of cowardice and treachery.

"I see an advantage in Coco's idea," Constantine said, interrupting the quarrels and silencing the room. "Can anybody offer a better one?"

No one answered and it was agreed that Coco would command the attack. The Genoese captains refused to be under the orders of a Venetian commander. Eventually, an agreement was reached for an equal number of Venetian and Genoese ships and captains to participate in the attack.

Zaccaria Grioni, one of the Genoese captains, had been listening intently throughout. He had a deep scar on his neck from a stab wound decades ago.

103

Two hours before morning the next day, at the darkest hour of night, two large galleys weighed anchor, each with a hundred tons of cotton and wool, and rowed out of Neorion Harbor, under Genoese command. Following directly behind were two smaller fustas captained by Venetians—Trevisano on one and Coco on the other. In between and behind the four larger ships were three small fustas loaded with black powder, earthenware grenades, bitumen, brush and the mixture for Greek fire.

The two large galleys in the lead served as a defensive screen, both hiding the fully loaded ships behind and ready to fire their cannons on notice. Having seen it many time throughout his years at sea, Coco knew stone cannon shot would not harm ships covered with bundles of cotton and wool. Coco and Trevisano were to open fire as they approached the Ottoman ships. The small boats would then enter the fray and set light to the Ottoman fleet. Even if they only engulfed one of the ships, they were all next to each other and the flames would spread.

It was quiet and the water was still. The ships were proceeding slower than Coco had thought, as they were weighed down by the bundles of cotton and wool.

Coco went to his chief mate Antonio da Corfu after inspecting the forty oarsmen seated in two rows of two below deck.

"We're going very slow," he said. "I fear the Genoese in the lead will pull ahead and pay for victory with their souls."

"What else can we do but follow?" Antonio said.

"Do you hear how quiet it is, Antonio? The Turks must be exhausted and sleeping like babies. This will be easier than I'd guessed. We should seize this opportunity."

Antonio didn't grasp what his captain was getting at and looked curiously at him.

"We must act now," said Coco, pounding a fist into his hand.

He ran his hand along the gunwale as he walked from the forecastle to the bow, where he leaned over the bulwark. He looked again from the inky waters to the pitch-black sky. There wasn't a single light burning in the Ottoman fleet, its ships broadside to broadside. Coco reckoned he shouldn't let this opportunity go to waste. Destroying the Ottoman galleys meant an end to the war. The plan was his, and so, too, would be the victory. His mind was firm.

He returned to Antonio, took the wheel in hand and turned hard port. "Tell the oarsmen to stroke full force. We're taking up battle positions."

Antonio and the rest of the crew quickly went to their stations. The rowers churned their oars as the barrels of the cannons were each pushed through the gun ports. The bow of Coco's fusta broke from the fleet to Trevisiano and Doria's astonishment and started to speed ahead. The gunners readied cannonballs by the batteries while archers at the bow dipped their arrows with tips wound in sackcloth into buckets of bitumen the crewmen hauled to them, set them alight and took aim at the Ottoman ships. Coco's spirits were high, having overtaken the Genoese galleys—which had been meant to act as a screen—but his face fell as he heard the sound of a cannon as he pulled to two hundred yards from the Ottomans. The smoke over the water in the distance hadn't come from his ship, but from the Ottomans.

"We're taking fire!" the watchman shouted.

The stone shot flew over the ship and glanced off the stern bulwark. A second shot then followed soon after and hurtled directly into the main deck. The hull cracked open and it began to quickly take on water. Its topmast soon disappeared underwater. Coco hadn't even had the chance to fire a single cannon. Much of the crew had started swimming desperately as the ship sank, but none-could see which way they should swim.

The Ottoman captains ordered their gunners to reload and fire continuously. The shots did little harm to the Genoese galleys draped in cotton and wool, but the relentless cannon fire sent up so much smoke that neither Trevisano nor Doria could see what was happening. Under the dark of night, they hadn't even seen Coco's ship go down. Before their bows were ever billowing clouds of smoke. They reckoned either Coco was sending up the smoke from his cannons or the Ottoman ships had caught fire. Looking for his share of victory, Trevisano increased his speed with the fustas loaded with combustibles in tow. He realized what was happening as soon as his ship drove forward and was struck by an Ottoman cannon. The old Venetian sea hand quickly had the holes and cracks plugged with wedges and sackcloth and tried to swing the bow around.

The Ottoman ships then set into motion, rowing for the small fleet. They were superior in number, but they couldn't get alongside the large Genoese galleys. They tried climbing up the boarding ladders and ropes dangling from grappling hooks, but the Genoese seamen beat them back with arrows and stones. The Genoese noticed Ottoman ships were amassing and coming from behind. They turned their bows to the city and managed to evade them.

The Ottoman sailors surrounded one of the galleys with their small ships and finally managed to board. Like ants swarming their prey, they one after another rowed for the galley and the Genoese captain announced his surrender.

A Venetian on one of Constantine's small vessels still unseen reached out a long pole, its tip alight, and set one of the Ottoman ships ablaze. Realizing they wouldn't be able to smother the flames, the other Ottoman ships pulled away from it while its men jumped for dear life.

Trevisano and the other galleys managed to slip away through the larger ships. The Ottoman sailors stopped pursuing them so as not to put themselves in undue danger and turned back for Galata's walls.

Coco swam in the icy water through the darkness and smoke. He was relieved when he came to the rocky shore and a hand reached down to pull him up by the arm. He realized once he was out of the water, though, that this man was no Greek, but an Ottoman soldier—obvious from the man's upturned mustache. Like Coco, many of the sailors defending the city had swum to the wrong shore.

With the coming of day, about forty Greek, Venetian and Genoese prisoners were lined up a yard apart from each other in front of the city's Gate of Saint Romanus. The Ottoman executioners bound their hands behind them and threw them to their knees. The soldiers, all in a miserable state, then laid their heads on the tree stumps before them.

The clashes had stopped for a while. There was no cannon fire or other attack from Constantinople or the Ottomans. The city's people and soldiers on the ramparts watched the grizzly scene unfolding below.

Malik the Executioner stepped to the first prisoner and with the curved blade of his scimitar severed the man's head in one strike. He slowly moved on to the next prisoner and again lopped off the man's head. Heads fell to the ground one by one, some rolling through the dirt to the moat.

Finally, Giacomo Coco's head toppled to the ground.

Mehmed had taken his vengeance for his two hundred soldiers executed on the walls. Those on the city walls were now silent as the Ottoman soldiers cheered their victory.

Next to Mehmed was one of the Genoese seamen—one with a deep scar across his neck.

104

My mood lifted, even if but a little, when they came today and told me Sultan Mehmed had asked for my presence. Meeting with him could bring some light to these dark days. I should say that, in a way, speaking with him puts one at ease and is enlivening.

I frankly wasn't surprised he called for me since whenever he's not with his gunners or soldiers he's with his learned men. They say he talks to them about newfound inventions and social issues. Mullah Lütfi is one of his constant guests.

Mehmed's tent is no different than his chambers in the palace. There are large maps on the walls and drawings of large projects, various contraptions and calculations for the cannons.

I found him busy writing when I entered. When he saw my confused look, he said he was writing a poem, or rather was trying to. I told him I had never heard of a commander who writes poetry in the middle of a war.

He smiled and said he had remembered a story Mullah Gürani had told him when he was a boy—a long tale about what happened between a leader and his philosopher. It's of the value the ruler, whose heart had grown dark from war and bloodshed, placed on his philosopher. He said his relationship with poetry should be the same and it rests his spirit.

He then looked me in the eye and asked who would say thinking of love while at war wasn't a lovely thing.

I was taken aback. It was like he asked as if I was the only one who knew the answer to his question. I felt he knew something about me, but that would be impossible. Then he read a bit of his poem. I'll reproduce it here as best I can recall.

I saw a sun-faced angle, the moon of creation
His black hyacinth curls, lovers' sighs
Clad in black, his beguiling cypress body like the night moon
And yet whose beauty rules the Frankish land

I personally couldn't tell whether he was writing this poem to a lover or the city at whose walls his siege had come to nothing for weeks. I liked it, though, and so tried to remember it and wrote it down as soon as I left. He dislikes what he writes and says it's not as beautiful as what he reads, but still it puts him at ease.

I agreed and told him that writing always does me well, that I couldn't live if I couldn't write.

With the sounds of cannon fire outside, he asked me to recount the battles I have witnessed. I mentioned the battles at sea, our conflicts with Genoa and the few sieges I have seen. He listened carefully. I added that no series of battles I ever encountered had lasted even one-fifth as long as this one.

Then he asked if I missed Venice. Of course, I do. Much in Ottoman lands reminds me of my own city. I told him of the difference between Venice and Edirne as well as the similarities I hadn't known before. I explained that many of the buildings in my city resemble the architecture in Constantinople and Mohametan lands, since, after all, Venetian merchants are influenced by the cities they go to like Jerusalem and Cairo. I mentioned how our two lands and cultures, which we surmise to be so different, are actually quite similar. Of course, in my mind I was thinking of the similarities between Cristina and Nilüfer, but the comparison was true enough for the cities, as well.

After listening to what I had to say, he said he wasn't surprised in the least. He said some try to separate the peoples of the Occident and Orient with borders, but that these are unnatural and that Christians, Mohametans and Jews have lived among each other for centuries, and they have all influenced the other. He believes turmoil holds sway over the world now and that the sundry peoples will put each other to ruin if not ruled over by a single man. He spoke of the necessity for all of them to be ruled over by one hand, an emperor who provides peace and vindicates the right.

If I reckon a guess, this is why he cares so much about this siege. He said Constantinople should now take the place of Jerusalem and Cairo.

He then grew quiet and walked to a map on the wall. He said his forefather Osman had had a dream two hundred years ago. In his dream a great tree grew from his belly and the entire world was spread over its branches. He said they mention this dream when explaining the foundation of their empire. He has had a similar dream, too, he said. In it, the archers ring on his finger grows bigger and wider, and becomes as though it will encircle the world. Then a sparkling gem appears in the center of the ring. The gem becomes the sea and the ring land. He said the first picture in his mind when he awakes is the map he was looking at.

I looked at the map and saw the lands of Europe and Asia truly resemble opposite sides of a ring, cut through by the Bosporus.

He looked back at me and said one empire, one emperor and one center—an emperor to rule to the east and west, over all the People of the Book, in peace and who will serve all man as Alexander the Great, Julius Caesar and Harun al-Rashid once did.

The fire in his eyes was frightening as he spoke. I knew then there was no way this young man would lift his siege, no matter what, and he would never pull his cannons from before Constantinople's walls so long as he lived.

He then said that if one, supreme ruler weren't to come to pass, utter confusion and discord would rule over every land.

Then he pointed on the map to Baghdad and sorrowfully spoke of how the barbarous Mongols had destroyed a centuries-old civilization, set fire to books and burned down libraries. In Spain, he added, other savagery has begun to do the same, putting an end to the peace among the peoples there. I suppose he didn't say those doing so were Christian so as not to offend me.

He believes that without the establishment of an empire as powerful as Rome, as learned as the Abbasids and as all-encompassing as that of Alexander the Great, people will not be delivered from their pain and misery and the small kingdoms and duchies will tear each other apart to ruin due to their fragmentary faiths.

What is important about what their prophet Mohamet said—what they call a *hadith,* or their prophet's sayings—concerning Constantinople, and which has remained on the Turks' lips, lies here. It says that when peace and serenity begin to disappear from the world, the capture of the city will again open the road to centuries of prosperity.

Mehmed believes this with such conviction that he asked me where I want to live once the city is taken. He asked if I would be able to bring artists, sculptors and painters from Venice. Apparently, I'm cut from the cloth to be his civil envoy of sorts between his empire and the republic.

Far from settling the city, I don't believe Mehmed will be able to take it. Many sultan's have attempted it before and none have succeeded. They were all more experienced than Mehmed and instilled more fear in their enemies. Neither Bayezid, who routed the crusader army at Nicopolis, nor Murad, who emerged in victory form the smoke and dust of Varna, had been able to lay a successful siege.

There is a fire in this young man, but it doesn't seem the Ottomans' so-loved God is by his side now. He is, like me, alone, lonely and expended. He doesn't even have his prized Hungarian cannon maker any more, either. His body was torn asunder in front of his gunners yesterday when a cannon exploded after it was loaded with too much powder.

The future, as ever, is entirely uncertain.

105

"This is madness," Jacopo whispered under the dark of night, trying to make his displeasure known to his companion who had convinced him to come with. Over the course of weeks, he had further realized the foolishness of what they had set out to do.

The two men continued along the base of the walls, looking around as they went.

They had gotten quite close to the madrasah. Jacopo had reckoned the compound would be smaller, but now, maybe from his annoyance, it seemed they weren't covering any ground as they walked.

"Don't worry," Manuel said as he walked ahead confidently. "I have everything planned out. There's nothing to be afraid of."

"What do you mean there's nothing to be afraid about?" Jacopo whispered.

His anger was stuck in his throat, he wouldn't yell, but the moonlight on his face betrayed his outrage. He struggled to understand how Manuel could be so calm. He knew janissaries were in charge of keeping order in the city and reckoned they wouldn't be able to return to Florence if they were caught. He had been trying to explain to Manuel from the onset that their undertaking was madness, this being such a well-guarded and safe city with less crime than their own, and on top of that, javelin-throwing janissaries. Manuel had argued that was precisely why they would be able to go about it so easily—two thieves entering the madrasah at night would be the last thing expected in the city. Manuel had finally convinced Jacopo of his plan after many days, but now Jacopo had been trying to dissuade his companion ever since they were seriously set to carry it out.

"Can't you see there're still lamps burning in some of the rooms? What if they see us?"

"Don't worry, they must be students or instructors working into the night. I know about it all—very few go out at this hour. And—"

"And what?"

"And the call to prayer will come in half an hour. That's when they start to stir around for their morning prayer."

"Why didn't we come earlier, then?

"Now is the best time. There are many here who don't sleep until the late hours of night. It's the stillest in the hour before their morning prayer."

Having worked on the ship of Don Pietro—one of Florence's most renowned and shrewdest merchants—gaunt and thin under his ample beard, Manuel Chrysoloras had begun formulating this plan since the moment he first stepped foot into the city to sell finished silk. And if luck was with him, he would be able to crown his profitable expedition with a small fortune.

They continued along the side of a rectangular field and heard a sound when they got to the corner of the wall they had backed up against.

"We're done for," Jacopo said, starting to shake.

Manuel glowered at him. It was always wiser to have a partner in such risky business. It was just one of the many golden rules he had learned, like all merchants up and down the Italian peninsula, but he was annoyed now, seeing Jacopo ready to turn himself over.

A grey cat turned the corner toward them and, pricking up its ears and looking up at the two men for a moment, sprang off into the darkness. They both breathed a sigh of relief and turned the corner to a stone building.

"There, we're here," Manuel said.

"What if the door's locked?" Jacopo said.

Manuel looked at him and smiled. "You think they'd lock the door to the madrasah library?" He lifted the latch on the wooden door. It opened with a click and the two men slunk inside.

"I can't see a thing," Jacopo said in the pitch-black room.

"Just wait a bit. You'll get used to it soon." Manuel opened a satchel.

They were slowly able to start making out the books filling the floor to ceiling shelves as their eyes adjusted to the dark.

"Good Lord, look at these books," Jacopo said as he looked wide-eyed from side to side at the multi-colored shelves. "Which of them will fetch a good price?"

"It'll be worth our pains if we can find these," Manuel said as he took a piece of paper from his pocket.

Jacopo looked at it. "It's all in Arabic. You can't even read Arabic?"

"But you can."

Jacopo finally realized why Manuel hadn't come alone.

"This changes the whole plan," Jacopo said. "Forget about thirty percent."

"What do you want, then?"

"Fifty. Half and half."

"No chance."

"Then I'm going. Find what you're looking for yourself."

With no option, Manuel reluctantly agreed.

"What's your plan to find these books among so many?" Jacopo said.

"There should be a book of records somewhere around. It should have a complete list of all of them."

"What are you talking about, Manuel? All the students and instructors are going to be rising in fifteen minutes. I say we take what we can and get out of here."

Manuel unwillingly conceded that Jacopo was right. The sky had already begun to lighten. They'd have to hurry.

They filled their satchels with the books that had the most beautiful covers. Every once in a while, Manuel asked Jacopo what was written on them.

"It says, ibn Sina, *Al-Qanun*," Jacopo said, looking at a book with a red velvet cover.

"You think it's valuable?"

"How would I know? I can read it, but I don't know what all of it says."

He looked at a book with a brown leather cover. "It's ibn Rushd, but I can't make much sense of the title. It has incoherence written twice—it must be a mistake. Something like *The Incoherence of Incoherence.*"

"Let's not take that one, then. It might be written wrong." Manuel put the book back and removed one with a crimson cover. "What about this one?"

"That one's ibn al-Haytham, *Book of Optics*, and the other is al-Jazari, *The Book of Knowledge of Ingenious Mechanical Devices.*"

Manuel noticed while rifling through the pages of the books stuffed into his satchel that there was some writing in Latin and Greek.

The two men sped out of the madrasah, clutching five sacks of books. Manuel had found the treasure he was seeking. He might not have known its worth, but Niccolò de' Niccoli, the priest in Florence who he would sell them to for cheap, certainly would. A painter in the city would know their true value.

106

Muslihiddin again ignited the cannon, only able to fire three times a day. He had been firing at three points as the sultan had instructed, having said it would be more effective than pounding the same spot. The nearby janissary gunners in groups of five to both sides went running with their ears covered as the gigantic stone ball went flying with a terrific explosion. It arched as if following a rainbow, flew over the moat nearly filled with rubble and careened into the outer wall, which by now was barely standing.

A nine-foot breach crumbled open between the Fourth Military Gate and the Gate of Rhegium. Constantine's soldiers quickly ran out over the rubble.

Mehmed sat on his horse and looked over to Ishak Pasha, who was overseeing this area of operation, after he saw the result he was waiting for.

Ishak Pasha knew this look well. He drew his sword, raised it to the air and shouted, "Attack!"

Thousands of horsemen lunged forward and galloped toward the wall as the soldiers behind them moved forward to take their place.

Commanding this section of wall, Filippo Contarini yelled to the archers lined along the inner wall, "Aim—shoot!"

The cavalry was so large and tightly packed that many in the dark cloud of arrows streaming toward them hit their marks. Some where able to deflect the arrows with their shields, but many fell, clutching their chests, faces and shoulders. Some arrows struck the horses and sent them tumbling with their riders to the ground. They were then trampled beneath the hooves of the charging horsemen.

Contarini ordered his archers to keep shooting. Nearly a tenth of the cavalry fell with each volley. Even though the Ottoman archers were sending arrows up the walls, the defenders sheltered behind the battlements, with almost no one hit, and continued their volleys.

Adding to the defense, Constantine's gunners had predicted this section of wall would fall and had managed to haul a cannon just behind the breach. They fired and sent a shot through the cavalrymen galloping toward them, wrenching more than a hundred of them and their mounts to pieces.

As if knowing what would happen and enraged that it had, Ishak Pasha stepped before his other soldiers and called them to attack in a second wave. Contarini couldn't decide which group his archers should target. Despite having lost more than half their men, the cavalry was now nearly at the moat.

Word had come that the sultan had launched a massive assault and Giovanni Giustiniani Longo appeared at the breach with hundreds of his men. Hundreds of soldiers piled through the wall to meet the oncoming cavalry at the moat as the horses plunged in. The archers lined along the moat could easily strike the soldiers now only yards away. Back on top of the inner walls, Contarini's archers continued to rain arrows down on the Ottoman army. The mangonels behind the walls had also been pulled into place and were ready to hurl stones onto the battlefield.

Some of the horses in the moat struggled to swim with their riders on top of them while others sped over the rubble, having found shallower crossings, and maintained the charge. Many of the cavalrymen hadn't been hit and they dismounted to use their horses to shield themselves from the flying arrows and trudge forward, themselves weighed down by their armor.

Reinforcements had arrived to aid Contarini's archers atop the ramparts, which only added to the showers of arrows. The Greek knight Rhangabes of Constantinople and his men readied themselves to meet the cavalry at the edge of the moat. Many of the soldiers on the walls over the Golden Horn descended and sped on their horses to aid the defense of the land walls.

The soldiers at the edge of the moat didn't give the Ottomans the chance to leave the water. They swung their swords from the breastwork above, each time catching an attacker across the face, neck or chest. Rhangabes was clad in armor from the helmet on his head down his legs—a war machine unto himself—rending all who came before him. Another group of soldiers were plunging their pikes into the Ottomans' chests.

The moat was nearly overflowing with the corpses of Ottoman soldiers, becoming more a mass grave than a body of water.

The second wave of cavalry reached the moat and tried to cross, passing by and through those who went before them. The counter offensive from the city managed to disperse and thin them out. Disregarding the deaths of their fellow soldiers, the Ottomans pushed forward with more joining to replace the dead. The defenders held a more advantageous position and were picking off attackers here and there. Among the cavalry, Ömer Bey furiously entered the water, knowing the armored knight on the other side was commanding the defending soldiers. He pointed wildly at the knight, trying to signal to the mass push of cavalrymen around him that the man was leading the defense. He swung his sword up and through a soldier at the edge of the moat and managed to get his horse up the bank. Dozens of horsemen came flying to the base of the walls with him, trampling stone and corpses under hoof.

More soldiers followed the first Ottomans up and over the breastwork. Ömer Bey cut down Greek soldiers as he fended off blows with his shield, slowly making his way to Rhangabes amid the mob. The renowned Greek knight's face was completely obscured by his helmet, save for his eyes. He deftly wielded his longsword and cut down the Ottomans one by one. His armor was so sturdy that every blow from a sword glanced off with almost no effect.

Ömer Bey lunged for Rhangabes with his sword swinging. Water dripped from the cavalryman's long, dark hair. Rhangabes spotted Ömer Bey coming for him and recognized him as the cavalry's standard bearer. He smiled beneath his helmet and waited. A space opened in the confusion of battle as if readying the stage for their bout. For both Rhangabes and Ömer Bey's soldiers, it was of great importance their leader came out alive.

Ömer slashed his scimitar across Rhangabes' chest, but saw it glance off the knight's armor, which was much stouter than he had thought. With the futile attack against him, Rhangabes lifted his longsword—three times bigger than Ömer's own—and heaved it down at Ömer's neck. Ömer reached up with his left arm and parried off the blow with his armor as he staggered to the side. He found his footing and went for Rhangabes' belly. The knight brought down his sword and cut the blow, then landed an armored fist on Ömer's face. His vision went dark for a moment, but he gathered his senses and swung with full strength down on Rhangabes' shoulder and split the knight's armor. He wrenched out his blade now dripping with blood.

Rhangabes looked at his shoulder, no more wounded than if it had been a scratch. Rage boiled up inside him when he saw his cleaved armor. He swung fiercely at Ömer, who each time deflected the strikes with his shield. Exhausted, Ömer quickly stabbed forward and pierced the knight's armor within inches of his belly. Rhangabes shuffled back onto a stone that had fallen from the wall where the breach had opened. He saw his advantage, took his sword in both hands and lifted it above his helmet.

Ömer gathered his strength to attack the knight's exposed chest, but felt his power drain away with a sizzling burn in his back. Rhangabes swung down and cleaved the cavalry's standard bearer through from neck to waist. Giusitniani caught sight of him and his bloody sword as Ömer's lifeless body fell in pieces to the ground. He couldn't afford to lose one of his best men.

Some of the cavalry tried to recover the body of their standard bearer while others continued to attempted to infiltrate the breach. But with Ömer Bey's death depleting their morale, the defending soldiers repelled them with greater ease amid flashing blades, flying arrow and spears.

Ishak Pasha prepared to send the third wave. He looked to the sultan in wait for the signal, but Mehmed lifted his hand to halt. The cavalry split to the left and right, and through them came a regiment of janissaries.

Mehmed signalled the janissary agha, who had been posted next to him since the outbreak of the assault, and who then turned to his company. Behind him, and waiting for his slightest movement, were dozens of regiment sergeants and hundreds of janissaries waiting for the call. Over a thousand janissaries marched forward in step with cries of *Ya Allah* before they broke into a run.

Contarini was alarmed when he looked down from the walls at the red wave of janissaries quickly descending on the wall in unison stride. His archers took their aim off the cavalry and rained arrows down on the red wave licking at the walls like a raging fire. Many janissaries had fallen by the time they reached the moat, but those behind them marched on as arrows sunk into their shoulders, arms and legs.

The janissaries in the lead laid down hundred-foot-long plank bridges over the moat and tried to quickly stream across. Others were trudging across the moat in places that had filled with rubble and over the piles of corpses, both man and horse.

With word having spread, hundreds of soldiers from the walls over the Golden Horn and elsewhere emerged from the breach to aid in the defense of the janissary and cavalry assault. The Genoese and Greek knights under the command of Manuel da Genoa and Demetrios Kantakouzenos formed a line against the janissaries with a wall of armored men.

One janissary severed a Greek soldier's arm, took off a Genoese knight's fingers and a third plunged his blade into another's belly. Another Genoese knight hefted his longsword and brought it down into a janissary's shoulder as four of Constantine's soldiers cut another down. An eagle-eyed archer on the ramparts struck five janissaries in the neck and face in quick succession.

Hundreds of janissaries and cavalrymen were falling to the defenders with more coming to replace them from behind. Dozens of defending soldiers were also killed and reinforcements came to the battle from behind the walls.

As the battle raged, others prepared timbers and wood blocks, hides, bales of wool and stones behind the wall to close the breach.

The janissary Murad hacked and sliced his way to Rhangabes. The Greek knight was first to attack, but Murad deflected the blow. In full fury, he swung his thin blade up and with the might of his thick arms came down across and plunged his scimitar through Rhangabes' armor and into his body to the horrified looks of his soldiers. Vengeance was done for Ömer Bey's death.

Giustiniani appeared at the mouth of the breach and slayed a janissary as Rhangabes fell lifeless to the field of battle. Murad reckoned Guistiniani was the man holding the defenses together and without him, they would fall apart. He moved quickly for the Genoese knight and leveled his sword at Guistiniani's back. With years of experience in battle, Giustiniani bent forward, sliding the sword over his armor, and swung around from his knees with his sword trained on Murad's middle. He had no doubt this would do the janissary in as it had to so many other warriors hundreds of times before. Murad deftly parried down, however, and knocked the blow from its path. The two men then swung fiercely at each other amid clashing metal in showers of sparks from steel on steel.

Manuel da Genoa and Kantakouzenos were trying to repel the janissaries from the breach with their best soldiers. Now and again, a janissary split from the line and overcame the breach only to be left at a loss as to what to do once at the imposing inner wall across the terrace. Finding themselves trapped, the Constantinopolitan soldiers waiting at the wall quickly set upon them. Many janissaries and cavalrymen were captured alive after having had their hands or arms severed.

Giustiniani had tired under his armor and felt as though couldn't wield his sword. Murad readied a death blow. The Ottoman soldiers would be emboldened the moment Giustiniani hit the ground and would make a final push through the breach. Murad had years before mastered slicing through the rolls of wet felt wound in steel wire, which were thicker than an armored man. He was about to strike Giustiniani a final blow when a hulking Greek soldier on the wall threw his ax end over end at the janissary. Catching sight of it at the last moment, Murad threw himself to the side. The ax cleaved his leg off as he tried to jump out of its path. Giustiniani saw his chance and plunged the tip of his longsword into the back of Murad's neck as he laid sprawled on the ground—no different that the forest boar.

Murad didn't relent, shaking with rage, his sword still up. He collapsed with blood bubbling from his mouth.

The assault lasted three hours, but in the end, Mehmed ordered his army to retreat. The attack had failed. The people of the city and its soldiers were again convinced of their ability to resist and believed the city would now never be captured.

The breach was repaired and as sturdy as ever.

Mehmed had suffered a great defeat. He lost thirty thousand soldiers in one day. The army was devastated

Halil Pasha had been right all along.

107

Something unexpected happened today.

I woke again this morning to the sound of cannon fire. No one knows any more when the sultan will order a bombardment or when he'll silence the guns. Sometimes he has the cannons pound the walls throughout the day and at others, he leaves the Greeks no comfort from night until morning.

They say his strategy is to be unpredictable, to fire the cannons when the city's soldiers are unprepared and to constantly keep them weary. I don't know if they're as tired as Mehmed intends to make them, as they put up terrific resistance to every assault and manage to repel thousands of soldiers every time.

What I do know is this erratic cannon fire is turning me to ruin. Sometimes I get more sleep in the light of day than at night. My sleep is topsy-turvy. I shut myself off in my tent as soon as there is a short respite from the clamor. I pull up one of the embroidered quilts I've acquired since coming and try to doze off.

Then, however, my pounding heart leaves me sleepless. In these moments of quiet, my mind is riddled with thought, I get terribly hot and my brow starts to sweat. Maybe one could grow accustomed to the confusion and uproar outside, but I, for one, cannot bring myself to do it.

Be that as it may, a janissary came to my tent in the late afternoon and changed my whole mood. He came with a package. I thought at first the sultan had sent me something. I had an inkling I knew the janissary's face from somewhere, but figured he must be one of the many soldiers I've seen around. But when he said he had come from Ragip Pasha's villa and the package was from Nilüfer, my heart nearly burst. Then I remembered—he was the janissary who had brought me to Nilüfer's house so many months ago. Ragip Pasha's dutiful guard was one of the few soldiers still at the palace. Apparently Nilüfer had asked him to deliver the package and had been riding for days.

I asked him whether I should open it or not, but he said his charge was only to deliver it and that he didn't know what it contained. His duty was to fulfil Ragip Pasha's request, or more precisely, that of his granddaughter.

I took the package full of curiosity. I waited for him to leave and then breathlessly opened it. Inside was that wonderful case adorned with gold containing her adornment for the eye—what the Arabs call *kohl*. I had asked her many times for it, but she always rebuffed my requests. I asked her for it again as I was leaving the city for it to be a remembrance of her, so I could look on it and think of her, but it was for naught.

She said her grandmother had brought it back as a gift from Mecca. I tried to get my hands on it so many times, but never could. I looked on it for hours and took in her scent wafting from it. I looked at the tarnish and where the enamel had worn away and thought of her graceful hands as she unhooked the clasp, envisioning her almond eyes. That's what the Turks say for women with big, beautiful eyes—that they're like almonds—and I reckon it makes quite a bit of sense.

This fragrance reminds me of her and is like an oasis amid the sharp, acrid smell of burning black powder and stifling, choking, poisonous smoke that now envelopes my life. The rumbling of the cannons has become the rush of waterfalls, the arrows whirring through the air the wings of birds in flight and the clashing of swords the babbling of streams.

How interesting that this little case and its contents used to darken the eye has for weeks brought light to my darkening mood.

There was also a letter in the package. She wrote of an interesting dream she had. She said a Greek man was angrily probing my eye with a small stick. The Mohametans' holy book describes quite extensively how all sinners and who they take as infidels will end up in hell. There I was, wailing amid the fires of hell when all of a sudden, the Greek man turned into Nilüfer and the stick became a *kohl* stylus. My screams stopped and my face became happy.

She had a janissary from the palace called for as soon as she awoke that morning and sent me the case. She said she didn't know why she did it, but that she would always feel awful if she hadn't. I wish she hadn't said that, otherwise I could have taken hope and thought she had changed her mind about me.

But what about now? Still, I am forever grateful she sent it to me.

108

A soldier stopped before the apse behind the altar of the Church of Hagios Ioannes Podromos. He was panting for breath. He had been told the man would be here, but he somehow couldn't find the courage to enter upon hearing voices coming from within.

With the creaking of a table and a woman's cries of pleasure, the soldier couldn't bring himself to interrupt the renowned German at work. The soldier knew the emperor had men searching for him and so, gathering his courage, pounded on the door. The sounds inside didn't stop and the reply was firm.

"Piss off!"

"Sir, the emperor has called for you. You must come at once."

"Go to the emperor and tell him I'm busy, then!"

The man then joined in with the woman's rising, staccato moans.

The soldier knew the emperor would have him killed on the spot if he returned emptyhanded.

"But, Sir—"

"You're still there? Tell him I'll come when I'm done!"

The church's timbers shook with the sound of a tremendous explosion and the rafters creaked. Only a few hundred yards from the city walls, the soldier realized it must have been one of the Ottoman's large cannons as the door in front of him cracked open from the tremor.

Johannes Grandi stood there with a woman bent over the table, his back to the door and half naked. The soldier cracked a smile as he looked on while the middle-aged Grandi pulled up his breeches.

The famous engineer and master of siegecraft approached the solder and said, "Alright, then. Let's see what's bedeviling the emperor already."

On the other side of the walls, Karaja Pasha's Serb master miner Borislav emerged from a shaft and emptied a bucked of earth. He wiped away the sweat from his brow with his sleeve, removing some of the grime on his face and revealing his skin.

They had been digging since night. Mehmed had ordered the digging of tunnels in an attempt to find success underground after it had evaded him on land and at sea. The Serbs—famous for digging mines and tunnels—led a group of foot soldiers Karaja Pasha had gathered and put to work.

Some dug without rest while others erected timbers to prevent the tunnel from collapsing.

"The supports under the walls are making the going quite difficult," Borislav said to Karaja Pasha, who was standing overhead. "I didn't expect them to go down so deep. We're nearly twenty-six feet down already."

Karaja Pasha listened attentively, his eyes bloodshot from exhaustion. He had breathed a sigh of relief when the tunnel had passed under to the other side of the moat in the small hours of morning, but now the foundations of the inner-most wall were causing them trouble.

Borislav climbed back down the shaft to the tunnel, wide enough for five men to come and go at the same time, and went to his men. "Fortunately, I plan to be on the other side of the wall shortly."

The pile of earth coming from the tunneling next to Karaja Pasha was growing into a small mountain.

Johannes Grandi set straight to work once Constantine told him the Ottomans were trying to tunnel beneath the walls.

"I don't know if we're doing right to trust this rascal, Your Highness," Giorgios Sphrantzes said to Constantine, at his side as always.

"He may be a rascal," Constantine said self-assuredly, "but there's no one better in all of Christendom. I'm not paying him heaps of treasure for nothing."

As skilled in poliorcetics as he was in engineering and tunneling, Grandi started to fill the buckets he had prepared with water and ordered the soldiers allotted him to do the same. He then lined the buckets up along the base of the walls at intervals of nine and fifteen feet to the north of the Lykos River where the soil was soft and thick with clay.

He ordered everyone to keep their position as the hundreds of buckets were being placed. A few hundred soldiers also stood at the ready with picks and shovels.

The thousands of soldiers on the ramparts, behind the loopholes and near the walls were complicating Grandi's work. He carefully watched the water in the buckets as he walked up and down the base of the wall, trying to check each one.

"Come on, come on," he grumbled as he ran his fingers through his tangle of blond hair. He bent down nearly to the ground and looked at a couple buckets. Then he ran along the wall and did the same to the others as he went.

"There we go!" he shouted.

The muddy water in the bucket at his feet was trembling with concentric rings emanating out to the rim.

The soldiers set to digging where Grandi indicated and within only a few hours, had reached the walls' foundations. Thanks to the drawings of the foundations Grandi had gotten from Constantine as soon as he arrived in the city, unlike the Ottomans, they were able to move as easily underground as above.

A Serb was trying to get to the end of the Ottoman tunnel. Having spent his life in mineshafts, he could see in the blackness underground as if it were the light of day. With the men around him, he leveled his pick into the waterlogged wall, an unusually large chunk fell to the ground. He was suspicious. The foot soldiers by him thought it would make their work easier to dig the tunnel, but he was thinking about whether to run away or not.

He realized their tunnel had been found and the earth had been weakened from the other side.

The two groups of tunnelers stood there face to face directly under the foundations of the inner wall. Soldiers had come from the city ready for a sudden attack and were well-armed with pickaxes and short blades. Grandi had given them these as there was no space to wield a sword in the tunnels. They stabbed and swung at whoever they came against in the subterranean darkness with daggers, knives and axes. One Greek soldier headbutted a foot soldier in a red turban while the soldier next to him sunk a knife into a Serb tunnelers face. A foot soldier took advantage of the momentary shock of assault and cleaved a Greek soldier's head with an ax. Those at the front of the two groups hacked away at each other while the others trampled over one another as they tried to get the upper hand. A foot soldier pulled a knife from his waist and quickly stabbed three Greek soldiers in the belly, one after the other, but couldn't stop the dagger that plunged into his throat. Although men were falling on both sides, fewer Greeks had been killed and they continued to advance, if slowly, down the tunnel.

Some of the Serbs streamed through the foot soldiers and began to flee, climbing over each other to get out and up the shaft. Waiting at the opening, Karaja Pasha clenched his fists when he realized what was happening. He squeezed his eyes shut and then looked to the sky. He pulled himself together and ordered more foot soldiers into the tunnel, angrily pushing and shoving them down the shaft. They couldn't get through, though, as their fellow soldiers in front of them were being driven back.

At the shaft on the other side, Grandi reckoned the soldiers were making good progress and handed a sack to one of his men. The man descended and went as far as the Greek soldiers. He left the sack at the base of a supporting timber the tunnelers had just erected and unrolled a fifteen-foot fuse. He lit it and quickly made his way back to Grandi, who had planned before to sacrifice his men.

It was too late by the time the soldiers freed themselves from the brawl ahead and looked back.

A rumble came from underground and Karaja Pasha's tunnel caved in. The Ottoman and Greek soldiers were buried along with the Serb tunnelers, many dead and many still alive.

"The Turk isn't the only one who knows how to use black powder," Grandi said with a smile as Constantine approached him.

Mehmed's tunneling attempt was no more successful that his previous assaults.

109

My head has been pounding for days. I've been in my tent day and night, laid out and thinking of my life. I recline on an embroidered sofa as blood is spills beyond my tent and I watch the scenes unfolding before my eyes. I go to another world as I turn within myself and drift into dreams.

Mullah Lütfi saw me a few times in this state. He said I didn't look well and should see a physician. I objected and asked where I would find a physician in all this turmoil. He smiled at this. Sometimes I forget with whom I'm camped. They have physicians everywhere. They treat the injured, use ointments and pastes I've never seen before, and immediately ease their soldier's suffering.

I, however, had no visible injury. Mullah Lütfi said so be it, there are remedies for a troubled spirit and that he would take me to the right man.

There's a sheikh the sultan always exchanges ideas with. They call him Akshamsaddin, sometimes the White Sheikh. They say Mehmed has never left his counsel. He is loved by all and a man of respect. It was he to whom Mullah Lütfi took me. I had no illness for him to detect or offer help.

The sheikh's tent wasn't that big, but then again, twice as large as my own. There were many books strewn around and many different plants stored in glass jars. I was looking over them when the sheikh said he collects them, that there are types here he'd never seen in Edirne and so is taking samples.

I was amazed he would go around to collect plants in the encampment and further afield while hundreds of soldiers are falling in battle. Then, as if he knew what I was thinking, he said war will end but science will remain—empires fall but science builds on itself and persists.

He told me about the herbs in his glass jars for a while and then turned to me and asked if I had ever had a serious illness before. I said I was once nearly stricken with plague, but priests prayed and I was delivered.

He laughed and said the money did nothing, and that I simply hadn't been stricken by a pestilent affliction. Akshamsaddin has strange ideas about sickness. He believes they are all caused by small creatures or mites, and if one avoids these, then so will he illness.

He then told me about the plants that protect one from or treat these creatures. I suppose he had reckoned my ailment wasn't without, but within, and he was trying to warm the chilliness between us. He rattled off the names of many plants and which illnesses they ease. He showed me in his book where he had detailed notes on all of them. I didn't understand many of the names of the plants in the book or the ones he said. I did know the occasional Greek and Latin words in his book. These were the names Hippocrates and Galen, the Greek physicians of old, used. There were also some names from the languages of Hindustan and Cathay that I know.

I told him this was all very confusing and I didn't understand much of it. He said everything has a simple foundation and the Creator gives his servants countless signs. Akshamsaddin known their holy book like all Mohametan scholars. An Ottoman scholars' power of mind is outstanding—nearly all I've met have memorized word for word the hundreds of pages of their holy book. He picked up a walnut, cracked it in his palm and showed it to me, asking if I didn't think it resembled a brain. Its fissures and creases really did look like a diminutive brain. He gave me a piece to eat. He himself was fasting in the mode of the Mohametans, not eating or drinking during the daylight hours to try and nourish the spirit. Many of the soldiers are also fasting.

He said this nut that looks like a brain also strengthens the mind and drives away distress. According to him, plants growing above ground cure the upper body and those that grow underground and roots the lower body. He said that according to a plants shape and color, they benefit certain parts of the body. Cherry, for example, resembles a blood clot and so is good for sanguine illnesses.

Of course, this has all come from the results of long trials and experiments, he said. These general rules direct a man at first, but only scholars knowledgeable in the field can reach any final result.

It seemed he had been carefully studying my reactions and expressions as we talked. I also mentioned that I hadn't been able to sleep, that I've been afflicted with frequent headaches and that I am always lost in dreams and fantasy.

He took my wrist to take the rhythm of my heartbeat and asked me to speak of my days in Venice and Edirne and some other short questions.

I wasn't expecting it when he said my trouble was love. I was speechless. He said I needed to listen to music in a heavy mode and speak with the people I know intimately. He waited a moment and then said or I should marry the woman I couldn't drive from my mind.

I asked how he knew it was love and told him my wife had passed years ago. Enough of that, though. From where did he know I had become smitten with a woman in Edirne? I haven't told a soul.

He said he knew from my heartbeat, since it changed the moment I mentioned Edirne.

I tried to look as though I believed him, but I don't much reckon I convinced him. I was about to ask him not to mention it to anyone when he told me not to worry and that what passes between physician and patient is not meant for anyone else's ears.

Then he told me not to forget that real love is not of the one within whom it wells, but from the Creator. Love is only love if it draws one closer to the one who creates it. He said that brooding for days with one's head in their hands and drowning, laid out lost in fantasy, might make one a deeper person, but that if I don't want to drown in those depths, I must see the light, face the Love of God and pray. He said every day is a new day, the sun rises for the servants of God, the rain falls for me, trees come into leaf for man and flowers emit their fragrance for us all—the world is under the command of man.

He gave me some nigella seeds, told me to boil them and drink the water, and I'd feel better. Then he sent me on my way. He had much more work for the day.

I was still thinking of what he said when I got back to my tent. How lucky—or providential, as the Turks say—for Mehmed to have this man who seemingly read my entire spirit after only fifteen minutes, perpetually at his side.

I've now decided that in terms of wise men, Akshamsaddin is for Mehmed what Aristotle was for Alexander the Great.

110

Ten Ottoman foot soldiers struggled with the tree trunk the were carrying before they dropped it to the ground.

It sent sawdust and wood shavings scattering among the many timbers of all sizes already there. Dozens of sawyers were working in twos with crosscut saws to cut the trees where they had been marked with ink. The lines, some thirty-three, some sixteen, some ten and most three feet apart, weren't easy to see in the dark of night, but the men's eyes had adjusted over the past three hours.

One of the sawyers took off his red turban wrapped in white muslin and scratched his head. He wondered what they were going to do with all this wood. The cannon carriages were all in place and the entrenchments were complete, so he couldn't make sense of what these gigantic logs would be used for.

A man went around with a red jug to quench the parched laborers' thirst. The sawyers guzzled down the water, spit into their hands and picked back up their saws.

The water carrier made is way along and got to a man sewing together sheets of camel hide. The leatherworker eased a large needle through the hide and back up. Fastened together, the hides spread out nearly ten square yards with just as many seamsters as leatherworkers. Regardless of the darkness, they squinted with their heads lowered as they worked their needles through the stiff hide.

Five foot soldiers came, rolled up the finished hides and brought them over to the janissaries a little farther away. They left the hides tied up with thick chord in a small square and then went off to fetch the small timbers.

In order for the construction be done perfectly, Mehmed had ordered Jafer Agha to have his men do the work according to the plans, as he didn't want there to be any mishap in its assembly. Jafer Agha had handed the work to Vahdeddin, who had set to work with fifty men from his regiment.

Iskender hefted a long timber the foot soldiers had just brought and laid it between two posts on a hundred-square-foot carriage propped on wooden wheels. Another janissary took hold of the other end of the timber. Iskender looked up as he wrapped a long rope around the timber and poles to hold it upright.

The length of the timber made him hopeful about the shape this war machine would take. He leaned his head farther back and looked to the sky.

The weather was clear and the stars were twinkling. He wondered if Mariam was looking up at the same stars—maybe she saw the sparkling star he was looking at right now. Was she safe? Was she being used for the defense of the city? At worst, wouldn't the women of the city be undertaking tasks far from the walls? What if a soldier had taken a liking to her?

The scenarios running through his head made him angry, heated and annoyed, as if he were wrapping the rope around his neck instead of the timbers.

"You look pensive again, my boy," Mullah Fenari said.

Iskender relaxed when he heard the man's voice next to him. He had poured out his heart to Mullah Fenari countless times, but had never been able to mention Mariam. Fenari, though, always listened as if to understand why he said what he had and would respond with words of comfort.

"I'm afraid," Iskender said.

"He who believes in fate is protected from sorrow," Mullah Fenari said.

And so it was again. The man's velvety voice quenched his burning heart like a spring rain.

Iskender was about to look back and express his gratitude, but Fenari had long disappeared. Iskender knew he was going around to pray with the soldiers and strengthen their morale.

"What do you say? You think this will work?" Hayrullah said, holding the other end of the timber.

"It has to," Iskender said. "Maybe not only one, but if three are used together they'll be much more formidable."

"They say the sultan will order more be made according to how this works out."

"I hope there won't be any need for more."

The thought of spending another night outside the city walls was torturous. The siege had been ongoing and intense for weeks, and being this close to Mariam yet unable to see her was wearing.

They lifted another timber and started fastening it slightly above the first. Hayrullah noticed Iskender lost in thought.

"You still thinking of her?" he said, breaking the silence. Other than Hasan, he was the only other person to know of Iskender and Mariam.

Iskender nodded and looked up at Hayrullah. "What about you? Aren't you afraid?"

He smiled. "I'm from a village in Mostar." He reckoned that this night, he could tell Iskender his story. He had never told anyone before.

"Vlad of Wallachia has always tried to take our kingdom into his own. He attacks our land and his savage armies take all the Bosniacs they find in the villages and burn them alive. Every time, he brings a group of prisoners back with him for his own amusement. They say he gleefully has them impaled on stakes at dinner in a courtyard of his castle. He attacked many of the villages around my own many times. My parents dressed me in my best, clean clothing when the men from the Devshirme came to take the tribute boys and sent me out to them." His eyes began to well up, his face was flushed and his voice started to crack. "Like everyone in the village, my parents knew they took boys who were well-groomed and sturdy. The Devshirme official liked me and took me. That's how I came. I remember my father's excitement as if it were yesterday. The next day, Vlad's men raided our village and put everyone to the sword. I only learned of it weeks later in Edirne."

He was silent for a moment before he continued. "Now it's eight years later. I heard Vlad's soldiers are aiding Constantine in defending the walls. Being part of this holy war doesn't frighten me one bit, Iskender. Rather, it fills me with joy. What I'm afraid of is if we are forced to flee, then those men will laugh at us. That's something I would never be able to get over."

Iskender couldn't think of anything to say and looked at Hayrullah's bloodshot eyes. Then the two young men went to the pile of timbers to go get another fifteen-foot log.

An engineer walked among the dozens of janissaries working with the timbers, holding his drawings and checking on each group. "This needs to go three hands deeper," he said to one. "This plank needs to be three fingers thicker," to another. "This needs to be tied better," he said, overlooking the construction that was slowly turning into a gigantic contraption.

Farther down from the timbers and hides were hundreds of laborers in a line, swinging their pickaxes. A trench began beside the piles of timber and earth in the encampment and extended out, growing deeper as it went and wide enough for a few men to run along it side by side. The diggers worked under cover of night toward the base of the city walls hundreds of yards away.

A group of foot soldiers left water buffalo and ox hides behind the diggers, readying them as the trench progressed.

There was a foot soldier holding a torch as he searched for

something along the furrow. The sudden cuffing he got to the face made him feel he'd been trampled by a horse.

"Didn't we say absolutely no light?" a janissary overseeing the digging growled.

"My dagger fell from my belt," the man said from where he sat on the ground. "I'm looking for it."

"Oh, is your dagger more precious than these hundreds of men you see, you miscreant?" the janissary seethed as he pointed at the diggers at work.

The man quietly got to his feet and looked off in the distance to the cannons relentlessly firing on the walls rising from the Marmara coast. It was an impenetrable night, lit up only momentarily by the constant streaks of cannon fire.

The crashes of cannonballs into the walls made known the incredible bombardment that night. The man, however, had thought that was the sturdiest section of wall and couldn't make sense of why the sultan was targeting that particular spot.

Come morning, not only this foot soldier with a welted face, but the people of the city, too, would wake in astonishment as they learned the reason behind it.

111

Georgios Sphrantzes, hurriedly tried to rouse Constantine in the old Great Palace at the Acropolis Point at the edge of the city. He had reckoned it would be much safer for Constantine to stay there for the night rather than at Blachernae Palace on the city walls.

"Your Excellency, wake up, wake up—something terrible has happened!"

"What is it, Georgios?" Constantine grumbled as he turned over, half asleep.

"It's the Turk. It's terrible. He's built an unbelievable tower!"

Constantine's eyes still weren't fully open as he quickly rode to the walls of the Fifth Military Gate under the first light of dawn. With the word from his close confidant, he had torn out of the palace without taking time to close his shirt. He ran through his soldiers and up the steep stairs to the ramparts of the inner wall. The din raised by the soldiers and people looking out from between the battlements made him all the more disconcerted.

He looked out from the rampart and saw why the people were raising such a commotion. He couldn't remember ever hearing of a tower of such size in the stories he had heard of the dozens of sieges the city had experienced over a millennium.

Standing twenty yards away from the outer walls on the far edge of the moat was a gigantic, wooden siege tower, thirty-feet tall and looking down on the ramparts. It was so large that it had maybe a hundred men over its many levels. Constantine reckoned the timbers looked so well fastened with rope that it wouldn't be any sturdier even if it were made of stone.

Worse still, a trench starting from underneath the tower extended back to the Ottoman encampment, covered over with water buffalo and ox hides to fend off any arrows. The Ottoman army could now ensure a constant flow of men and supplies to the tower.

Janissary archers had already begun to shoot on the battlements before Constantine had been able to overcome his initial astonishment. As if taking revenge for their ineffectiveness over the previous weeks, each archer loosed sixty arrows every minute. Posted on the top level of the siege tower, they looked down on the soldiers along the wall and skewered them easily.

It took Constantine's soldiers time to pull themselves together after the assault began. Hundreds of them lay dying, screaming in pain with arrows lodged in their throats, heads, eyes and chests. Coming from such a close range, some of the arrows had pierced through and through. The soldiers still standing had arrows raining down on them before they could find the opportunity to escape.

The defense of the walls around the Fifth Military Gate was overseen by Theophilos. He shouted, enraged, at his dazed soldiers, unwaveringly brought them back to the fight and had his archers return the assault with flights of arrows.

The Constantinopolitan soldiers were afraid to stick their heads out from behind the battlements and crouched down as they moved along the rampart. One peaked over and took an arrow to the eye, sending him writhing to the ground. He screamed in agony as another archer, like most of the rest, raised his bow above his head to shoot. With a sting, he lowered his arms and screamed in horror when he saw an arrow through his arm. He jumped to his feet only to be sent back down with ten arrows to the back. The soldiers on the wall were falling left and right along the ramparts. Those still standing were struggling to strike any of the Ottoman archers looming over them.

"How could you have let this happen?" Constantine shouted as he watched the scene, exasperated, from the inner wall. "Such a thing takes days to build and you saw nothing! Nothing!"

"Your Excellency, you know we were busy defending the city in the south throughout the night," Sphrantzes said, his hands trembling. "There was constant bombardment. All our attention was focused there."

Constantine got a second jolt.

"It looks like this young sultan is more cunning than we'd suspected. He must have completed it throughout the night with the countless men he has at his command. He built a tower and dug a trench right under our noses while we trifled away at the southern walls like fools."

A group of soldiers on the second level of the tower began to throw earth, stones, wood and whatever else they had into the moat from behind the camel hides stretched across its frame. Already half filled by the soldiers in the tower and the rubble falling from the walls, the moat could easily be crossed on foot in no more than a few hours. Men were running from the encampment and through the trench with handcarts of more stone and earth to replenish the supplies as they ran out. More also came with more arrows for the janissaries.

"We must bring reinforcements from the other walls," Constantine told Megaduke Loukas Notaras amid the unceasing shower of arrows.

Notaras looked along the miles of walls and saw there was no letup in the bombardment anywhere and foot soldiers maintained their attacks at points along the fortification.

"They're pressing on our entire line of defense. It will be difficult to find unencumbered reinforcements to bring," he said before leaving the rampart.

Having demoralized the city's defenders, Karaja Pasha ordered a regiment of a hundred foot soldiers into the trench to prepare for an assault. Two foot soldiers hefted axes and hacked away the ropes from the timbers at the front of the tower, letting drop a wooden bridge. It fell over the moat like a drawbridge and settled level to the ground. The ropes holding it in place tensed under the weight. With the width of the moat and its considerable distance from the inner wall, it fell a few yards short of the battlements.

Karaja Pasha gave the cry for attack and foot soldiers climbed up the ladder to the bridge, dashing over it and throwing themselves onto the ramparts. The janissaries continued their arrow assault as the foot soldiers tried to take out whatever defense they could.

They came in waves of ten and twenty, carrying maces, axes and daggers as they jumped from the bridge to the walls with cries of *ya bismillah—in the name of God.* Most of them made it over while others fell short or cracked their heads against the stone and tumbled bloodied to the ground. Those not maimed from the fall pulled themselves to their feet and tried to scale the wall with grappling hooks, leaving behind those with shattered limbs where they fell.

The foot soldiers who made it to the rampart were splitting heads with their axes, cracking bodies with maces, and severing arms and hands with their swords. Battle-hardened Greek soldiers who were sheltered from the flying arrows stood ready and cut them down as soon as they made it further along the wall.

Notaras had now been able to set up reinforcements of Serb archers in the bastions to both sides of the siege tower. Now, with their arrival, the battle fell in the Constantinopolitans' favor. Mehmed knew the dangers these bastions posed, but there was no escape from the regularly spaced towers protruding from the walls. With their rounded façades built out from the walls, the hundred archers in each tower took aim from above and behind the battlements at the flow of foot soldiers over the siege tower's bridge. Caught between arrows flying at them from both sides, the foot soldiers began falling to the base of the wall and into the moat like over-ripe mulberries in summer. Very few could cross, and those who did were killed as soon as they made it over the wall.

Hayrullah took notice of the Wallachian archers and turned away from the screen of two layers of camel hide. These were Vlad's archers—clear from their hats and bows. He reached to his quiver and within a split second fitted an arrow to his bow, drew the string with his thumb and let go. The arrow whistled through the air and found an eye peeking out from the battlements. He let loose dozens of arrows in succession, emptying his quiver each time it was refilled. Almost none of his arrows missed their mark, the Serbs slumping down, riddled with arrows. The other janissaries were turning from side to side and started to take aim at the bastions. The Serbs were being picked off, but Notaras had more to take their place.

Some Greek soldiers saw their chance as the arrows flying from both sides thinned the Ottoman assault and threw torches onto the siege tower's bridge, catching the Ottomans off-guard as it went up in flames and engulfing the foot soldiers on it. Some managed to escape the inferno by tossing themselves into the moat below.

Karaja Pasha saw the flames and quickly ascended the tower. He grabbed an ax from a soldier's hands and hacked at the ropes holding the bridge to the tower.

The flames were growing and leaping toward the tower.

Utter confusion broke out in the siege tower. The foot soldiers started streaming back, but the janissaries kept their arrows trained on the bastions and walls. Karaja Pasha swung the ax at the ropes and timbers with all his strength again and again. The flames had spread so close that he had to turn his head away and could still feel the heat on his face.

He didn't have much further to go before he chopped all the way through the timbers. He threw the ax to the floor, held on to a timber overhead and stomped down with full force. Again, he stomped on the timber.

Then, just as the fire was climbing to the tower, the bridge fell away to the base of the wall with flames trailing behind. The tower was safe.

The bridge continued to burn and Karaja Pasha ordered the siege tower to be rolled back two yards.

Constantine heaved a deep sigh of relief, smiled and looked knowingly to Sphrantzes.

With no sign of relenting, Karaja Pasha ordered the foot soldiers back and the janissaries to prepare for another attack.

The tower got reinforcements of men and arrows and then was again rolled toward the wall as Constantine looked on.

Karaja Pasha again ordered the assault and arrows started taking flight anew from both sides. A group of janissaries pulled up the assault bridges from the back of the tower, laid them across to the ramparts and set out in groups of fives and tens. The Greek soldiers took hold of the ends of some of the bridges and toppled them to the ground. The janissaries threw down more bridges in their place one after another. The first thing the janissaries who managed to cross had to take care of was the soldiers dispatching the bridges, and they laid into them with their blades. Hayrullah dropped his bow, leapt onto one of the bridges and managed to bound his way across. He drew his scimitar from its scabbard and hacked off the arms of a soldier as the man reached out to dislodge one of the bridges. Another came up behind him, but he sent the man over the wall with a kick, then broke another's jaw with a quick elbow as he opened a path for himself, slicing through those who stepped before him. Known for his mastery with a sword, Theophilos lifted his head with a disdainful sneer, turned to both sides with a flourish of his blade and then made for one of the janissaries' heads. The janissary blocked the blow and the two men started at each other in the middle of the commotion.

The Bocchiardo brothers, responsible for the defenses of the northern walls, then appeared with their men at the battlements and set into a savage battle with the janissaries.

Paulo knew he had to stem the flow of janissaries from the tower. He took a load of torches, set them alight and threw them at the siege tower. They flew through the air, but struck the hides and tumbled to the ground. The soldiers inside managed to extinguish and toss out the torches that had found a way in.

Troilo stood with a sword in each hand, slicing through the janissaries challenging him, sometimes also cutting down an errant Greek soldier without mercy.

Then came the man to put an end to the battle.

The Greek powder boss came to Paulo with a bucket, flashing a sly smile as he pointed to its contents. He was a beastly man, his smile betraying his blackened teeth. Karaja Pasha saw that something had turned and new he had to do something to stop Paulo, who had been raining fire onto the siege tower since he appeared on the wall.

Paulo took a torch and dipped it in the incendiary mixture, half liquid and half grit. He set it alight and flung it at the siege tower without trying to hit the archers. Flames spread over the surface as soon as it struck the hides. The blaze crept over the entire structure before the soldiers inside understood what happened and many began to burn.

Hayrullah noticed the flow of soldiers over the walls had stopped when he looked back and saw the siege tower now engulfed in flames. Theophilos in that moment swung his sword across his body and took off his head.

In a final throe of hopelessness, Karaja Pasha took his sword and hurled it at Paulo. Antonio and Troilo painfully looked on as their brother dropped to his knees with the sword stuck in his chest. Antonio's eyes burned as he looked at Karaja Pasha. He thought to jump over the wall onto his brother's butcher, but Troilo held him back when he tried.

The flames worked their way down the siege tower, engulfed the barrels of black powder and sent a terrific explosion ripping through the structure. Karaja Pasha managed to jump as the tower hurtled into the air in pieces. Uninjured, he returned with his men to the trench and back to the encampment.

"Why!?" Mehmed cried with resentment as he watched from afar in the encampment when the tower was blown to pieces, squeezing his fists until they looked they would crack.

112

"Now's the perfect time to attack and sweep them out," Theophilos said with his fist raised to his chest. Dried blood was caked over almost his entire arm. "The Turk has failed in almost all of his assaults. We must attack while this defeat is still fresh."

All the commanders had gathered in one of the audience halls of Blachernae Palace along the walls.

Theophilos pointed to the northern walls on a map. "We should attack with two prongs, one from here and another from the Golden Gate in the south, and slaughter everyone before us."

After Theophilos' fiery speech and gesticulations, Giovanni Giustiniani Longo thoughtfully turned to Constantine. "What news is there of the Turk? Is he still not thinking of retreating?"

"It's true, Mehmed's army is spent and wretched," Constantine said. "The soldiers' belief in their sultan is also waning more and more. Leaving the walls and meeting them face to face would be suicide, though. We have no need for that anyway. We believe Mehmed will give up shortly."

"I agree, Your Excellency," Giustiniani said. "The Turk is close to relenting."

"The provisions in the city are nearly gone," Notaras said. "There's enough for a week, at most. Then there won't be any potable water or even a sack of wheat. As you know, Mehmed blocked off the aqueducts. I think it would do good to consider any peace offer, gentlemen."

"What are you saying?" Cardinal Isidore snapped angrily. "Did you not hear what the emperor just said? Have you not witnessed with us the defeats the Turk has suffered these past weeks? What peace are you talking about? The sultan is going to pot right before our eyes."

"The cardinal is right," Giustiniani said. "The megaduke's concerns are baseless and embarrassing. It's difficult sometimes to reckon which side he's on."

"I won't be lectured about loyalty by some Latin," Notaras growled. "I heard the stories my whole childhood about how you Latins sacked and invaded our city. Your murderous forefathers made rivers of blood flow through the streets for days and slaughtered all, even women and children. You stole our precious statues, Egyptian obelisks and all our wealth."

Isidore and Giustiniani both started shouting at Notaras. The hall was filled with fevered passion. Giustiniani grasped his sword and walked to Notaras. If the man entering the hall at that moment hadn't put an end to the quarrel, the knight would have taken off the megaduke's head.

"You argue for nothing," Orhan Chelebi said as he entered, a grandiose turban atop his head and clothed in a caftan with yellow embroidery over a long, black shirt. He looked to be around forty and had a birthmark above his neck. "The young sultan's enterprise will soon end."

He walked to the center of the hall. He was confident, spoke slowly and was the only man in such attire those around him would listen to. He knew very well he held the greatest advantage.

"The soldiers will start to grumble and grutch once Mehmed is defeated. It will also grow with influence from the pashas at the palace and in the army. They'll remind the soldiers of their glories from years past."

He passed a shining, red apple from hand to hand as he spoke, sometimes lifting it up and holding it before his face.

"Revolts will break out in Edirne, and the city will sink into flames and confusion. In only a few weeks' time, Mehmed will either lose his head or be driven from the throne." He stopped and turned to the men around the table. "Then I will be the only heir to the House of Osman and I will assume the throne, not to trouble you in Constantinople again."

The commanders looked as though they thought him right.

"Now, though, I have to go and check the harbor," Orhan said as he approached the door. "They're uneasy with me and send a few ships every day to look over it. We must keep our eyes open."

With this, he walked through the door and left.

"I'm curious, Your Excellency," Cardinal Isidore said. "What will change—delivered from one Turk only to bring another to power?"

"Don't believe everything you see or hear," Constantine said with a smile. "We will be delivered from the Turk, but who said we would install another? And Orhan is beholden to us and our word."

After debating for a few hours, Constantine and his commanders decided there was no need for an attack and it would be best to maintain the line of the city's defenses with the arms and men they had at hand. They all believed they would be celebrating victory in only a few days' time—all, save Notaras.

Megaduke Loukas Notaras was deeper in thought than ever.

113

A delegation of Hungarians came to the encampment today. They were Hunyadi Janos' men. He whom they call the White Knight. They say they will bring a mighty war against Mehmed if he doesn't lift the siege at once.

He reminded them of the peace treaty they had agreed to only a couple years earlier in Edirne. The simpleton Hungarians were quite pleased to sign the agreement back then, as well. Now it seems this White Knight has doubled back and hatched a plan to be able to defend Constantinople against the Turks.

The men in the delegation said Hunyadi has renounced his regency and thus any agreement signed while he held the position was now void. Ladislaus V is apparently finally king. They handed their copy of the agreement over to Mehmed and asked for his. It was a very open show of the broken contract between the two realms. I saw in Mehmed's own lavish tent, and with my own eyes, how calm he acted.

He said he would return his copy of the agreement, but that it would take some time to arrive from the palace. Then he invited them to rest in the camp.

He ordered a pasha to take the Hungarians through the encampment and have them see the war machines, the cannons in particular. The Hungarians at first misunderstood him calmness, but realized the reason later when they saw the towers and cannons large enough to rival their own. I can't get the horrified looks on their faces when they saw these tools of war out of my mind. One of them spoke in Latin so no one else would understand and said that this was an official challenge laden with intimidation.

I'm sure the thousands of disciplined soldiers in the hundreds of tents in the encampment was something they'd never seen before. I don't know if what these fiends saw in the camp will have any effect on changing their leader's mind, as they showed no fealty and hobbled an agreement not yet passed its first year. What is certain, though, is that Mehmed is truly vexed. They say Halil Pasha has taken the Hungarians' threat seriously and is trying to convince Mehmed to lift the siege. Those who trust Halil Pasha's discretion are many, indeed. It isn't only the Hungarians, either. Word has spread that the voivode of Wallachia is also preparing to move against the Ottomans.

If what they say is true, a large Hungarian fleet will come by sea, the Wallachians by land to attack the encampment from behind, and the Ottomans will take an onslaught on three sides. They would thus be easily defeated. The pope has again realized the seriousness of the situation now as the siege has prolonged and there's word his men have ridden off in all directions for reinforcements.

I now see better how Constantine's city has been able to withstand dozens of sieges over a millennium and how the city's soldiers dismay their attackers no matter what they try. No sane man could sustain this siege much longer. And they haven't. But therein lies the rub, as this young sultan's wisdom is either nonexistent or outshines all of ours. Mehmed would have long ago returned to Edirne if he weren't so young and full of fire.

114

The executioner of Myrelaion glared at the two prisoners sat in a small dungeon soiled with human filth and reeking.

The screams emanating from the dungeon, far underground, seemed as if they could be heard over the rumble of cannon fire and confusion outside.

The Myrelaion cistern in the heart of the city was below an old monastery. Sheltered from the outside and with massive walls, it had for years been used to torture prisoners, those declared heathens and heretics, and no less than heirs with a possible claim to the throne.

Since the Constantinopolitans considered their emperor to be the regent of Christ on earth, they would not abide any deformity or impairment. An emperor who came to the throne, if he hadn't already had his rivals killed, would have them blinded or their ears sliced off.

With such experience, the executioner of Myrelaion was well-handed at torture. He was at ease when two more prisoners from the Ottoman ranks were delivered in the evening hours. One had been captured in a tunnel and the other during another assault. He had to find out where the other tunnels were and hoped the men might talk. In no hurry, he sauntered over to his table and picked up a knife he knew quite intimately.

He shot a look to his jailors behind the prisoners. He no longer spoke much and a look was all his men needed to understand.

He walked to the two soldiers who had been sat in chairs. The prisoner closest to the iron door, a Serb, stirred as if he were trying to stand up, but his hands were bound behind him to the chair. The soldiers' legs were also tightly bound to the chairs with thick tethers. The Serb jumped, taking the chair and himself just off the floor and back down.

"It's not your turn yet," the executioner said.

He motioned to his jailer, who then went behind Vahdeddin—his face growing more unrecognizable with each strike from the cane—and took hold of his hair with both hands.

Vahdeddin could still hold his face up despite the beating he'd taken. He'd received dozens of kicks to the face already since the moment the city's soldiers had captured him and his janissaries in a tunnel.

The executioner wiped the knife on his leather butcher's apron out of habit. It was the only thing covering the top half of his corpulence, spattered with dried blood, vomit, excrement and other filth.

He grabbed Vahdeddin's ear with his left hand and then with his right, slowly drew the knife through.

Vahdeddin let out a deep groan. He was in no state to scream. He tried to pull his head away, but the jailer behind him held it firmly in place.

The Serb next to him was terrified. "Aren't you going to ask a question before you go in with the knife? Maybe he'll give an answer!"

Sphrantzes appeared from the darkness at the back of the cell and, since the executioner didn't understand Serbian, was happy to answer. "First we show that our intentions are serious. First agony, then questions."

The terror on the Serb's face turned to dismal dread.

Sphrantzes then turned to Vahdeddin and switched to Turkish. "Tell me, then, which gates are you tunneling under?"

Having slumped over in pain, Vahdeddin lifted his head. Sphrantzes was pleased, thinking he'd answer. Vahdeddin only cracked a smile, though. He lifted his brown eyes from under his swollen brow caked with blood and looked up at Sphrantzes.

"He's having fun with us. Continue," Sphrantzes said, switching back to Greek.

The executioner looked back to his jailer, who let go of Vahdeddin's head, walked to the table and picked up a leather strap. He walked back and tightly fastened it around Vahdeddin's forehead from behind. He took the end of the strap and squeezed it in his fist. He knew he'd have to do more this time to restrain the prisoner. He lifted a leg and planted his foot against Vahdeddin's back. There was no way he could move, if but a little.

Seeing all was ready, the executioner wiped the blood from his knife on his apron again and brought it to Vahdeddin's nose. He shook violently, and not expecting it, both the executioner and jailer lost their balance and fell down.

"Hold the bastard tighter!" the executioner barked.

They started again, but somehow couldn't keep Vahdeddin still.

"I don't get it. How can he still move?" the jailer said.

The executioner was well angered and punched Vahdeddin in the face with the force of a maul. He then went back to the table, dropped his knife and picked up a large, iron hammer.

"He's very fidgety. Let's take care of that first," he said before laying the hammer into Vahdeddin's knee. He then shattered his other knee while Vahdeddin was still groaning.

The Serb looked on in horror.

The executioner went back for his knife, wiped it off again and started to slice off Vahdeddin's nose.

Vahdeddin was unrecognizable when the executioner stepped away.

Sphrantzes stepped in front of him again. Vahdeddin's head had slumped down, so Sphrantzes leaned over and looked in what was left of his face. "Where are the tunnels? Where are you trying to enter the city?"

Vahdeddin slowly pulled his head up. He gave no answer, and instead spat blood in Sphrantzes' face.

Sphrantzes, with years of experience, was unsurprised. He wiped his face with his sleeve, looked to the executioner and then at the Serb.

The executioner took hold of the Serb's ear.

"I'll talk, I'll talk! Just kill him already! I'll tell you everything I know!" he pleaded just as the executioner brought the blade to his ear.

Vahdeddin craned his head to the Serb and cried, "No!" His eyes streamed, a mix of blood or tears.

Sphrantzes hadn't been mistaken in his estimation. The Serb would talk. By evening, action would be taken on all the tunnels, each one would be destroyed and they would take hundreds of more prisoners.

115

"It's been fifty-six days," Mehmed said. "A full fifty-six days. I can't understand somehow, hodja, how have we still not been able to attain victory? Why? Have I not done everything correctly and fully? If it's faith, I have faith. If it's power, I have power. If it's the army, I have an army. I don't understand."

Mehmed was pacing back and forth inside a green tent. The intricately patterned carpet and his caftan were of the same blushing red. He was troubled.

In a corner of the tent, sitting behind a book on a stand was Akshamsaddin.

"The measure of every slave of God's test of faith is difficult, Mehmed. It will be as arduous as the strength of one's faith. Patience, however, is the key to unlock all problems. Patience must not only be shown upon the first difficulty—patience must be shown as calamities come one after another. The first bite is as bitter as a poisonous weed, but the result is sweeter than all the world's fruits."

Mehmed stopped pacing at the corner opposite Akshamsaddin. He lifted the skirts of his caftan and his scabbard and knelt down. He left his right knee up and rested his elbow on it in despair.

He started rubbing his face and beard. "My soldiers are being done away with, my people are dying, they're tortured and carved to pieces. My heart can't accept it and my spirit is shriveling. When one of them suffers, it's as if I feel the pain of them all. They die once, but I die over and over again for each one."

"Being sultan is no feather pillow, Mehmed. It is pain, distress and understanding." Akshamsaddin looked up at Mehmed. "Suffering for a just cause is a trait of prophets. Did Pharaoh not inflict all tortures on the Israelites when Moses supplicated to God? Did Pharaoh not torture Asiye to death on the stake for her welcoming the spirit of the Angels? And did God not give to her a palace of pearls in paradise? Or Jesus and his Apostles? Were they not victims of Rome's most brutal torture? The life of our prophet was shrouded in constant tears. The *i'lâ-yi kelimetullah*—the profession to spread the word and glory of God and wage jihad for it—is the legacy of prophethood."

They both fell silent for a while.

"The soldiers' belief is dwindling and there's unrest."

Akshamsaddin responded in Arabic. "*You will see those within whose hearts is a sickness and who hasten among the people, saying we fear lest misfortune befall us. But perhaps God will bring victory or a command of His will and they will become regretful for what they had concealed within themselves.*" He stood up, lifted the curtain and looked out the window. "Your war is not only beyond those walls. The difference between believers and unbelievers is revealed in war. This is how it was at the Battle of Uhud and those before it, as well. *As Jesus son of Mary said to his disciple, Who will stand with me for the cause of God? His disciples said, We will stand for God. Then a group of the Children of Israel believed and a group disbelieved. So, We thereupon strengthened the believers against their enemies and they became victorious.*"

Mehmed listened in silence with his head hung down. Akshamsaddin walked to him, took hold of his shoulder and pulled him to his feet.

"Patience, Mehmed. Once you believe, you will not be defeated again even if all your viziers break out in revolt. Angles become soldiers, and soldiers, angels."

Mehmed was taken aback, as he hadn't mentioned his grand vizier, other viziers or anyone else concerning unrest.

Akshamsaddin smiled. "Don't be surprised, Mehmed. They don't call me the White Sheikh for nothing."

116

Mullah Lütfi visited my tent today for a meal. He has a student who never leaves his side these days. They call him Sinan the Student. It's part of the hierarchy of the madrasah—first, one is a student, or *softa*; then a manservant, or *lala*; and finally, a mullah. A student constantly watches his teacher and never makes him repeat himself. Mullah Lütfi says Sinan is a very bright boy with great aptitude for painting and mathematics. When I said I didn't get how the two were compatible, Sinan opened his eyes wide and said they're the same thing in actuality, and that we have both eyes and a mind. He really is an interesting boy, like his teacher.

Mullah Lütfi asked if I missed eating at a table as I was knelt on the floor spooning out the meat pilaf.

I won't lie. My legs have never gotten used to kneeling like this and I always stand up with a little pain.

Then he asked if I miss my own food, and specifically asked about pork.

Like all Mohametans, his face turned sour and full of revulsion when he said the word. Mohametans, like Jews, run from pork as if it were a Cerberus himself.

I told him he should try it and that it's just as tasty as the beef and mutton they eat.

He chewed very slowly and didn't speak until he swallowed. What I said had slightly disturbed him.

I asked if he would fast tomorrow and he nodded. I told him I heard it wasn't necessary to fast if one is traveling. I heard right, he said, but we've been here for weeks with no end to the siege in sight, and that if one stays in the same place for more than fifteen days, then he is obligated to fast.

He stopped and then said one mustn't forget the true jihad when waging war for the smaller jihad.

I asked him if he knew that Christians fast, as well. I told him we fast for the forty days of Lent during Eastertide, during which we eat nothing at all two of the days, and for the rest, we have a small meal of bread and vegetables at noon and then a small supper, but never meat, eggs or dairy.

He said he's heard of it, but had difficulty understanding its meaning. Their fast, he said, is to discipline the body's desires.

I told him that we do the same thing, though, and eat little, suppressing our appetites for repentence.

Mullah Lütfi said the Mohametan fast is quite the opposite. He claimed Christians increase their desires while fasting. He said when we look at the writings of Galen, Hippocrates or Avicenna—who the Mohametans call ibn Sina—they say the body's desires cannot be suppressed by eating a little, and that this rather further stirs up those desires.

I told him we also don't eat any kind of meat. No beef, chicken or anything else—only fish—but they eat red meat when they break their fast. I think ours is more sensible.

He agreed that fish is healthier than red meat and even a small amount can fill one's belly. He insisted, though, and said to fast is to not have anything pass one's lips from dawn until dusk, no matter what, but that for them, they can eat what they are permitted—what the Mohametans call halal—as much as they please within moderation.

Then I asked him why Mohametans abstain from pork. He apologized and said he didn't want to spoil my appetite. Then he said that pigs are filthy animals and only eat filth. He also said there are verses in the Bible itself that say pigs are filthy.

He said it should be in Matthew of the New Testament, if he wasn't mistaken. He then spoke of the verses from Matthew I remember from Sunday services. It was the story of Jesus passing through Gadara, where he came across two men possessed by demons. There was a herd of thousands of pigs feeding in the hills. The demons told Jesus that if he were to cast them out, then to send them to the swine. Jesus told them to go, which they did and went to the pig herd. Then the pigs all rushed down the hills and drowned themselves in the sea.

I told him that I know the verse, but asked what connection he made between exorcising demons and pigs.

Like the rest of the prophets, he said, Jesus was sent for the happiness and peace of mankind, so in his interpretation, why would he create obstacles to a man's earnings and livelihood. He said, as he reads it, it is very clear in the symbolic language of the verses that evil creatures are in league with each other.

I told him I thought he was creating his own unnecessary meanings from the verses, and if pork were forbidden, it would be written more clearly. He fell silent for a while and then said something in Arabic that means, more or less, *my religion for me and your religion for you.*

Then I asked him about wine and why they refuse to drink it. For example, I've searched relentlessly for a lovely wine to go with the pilaf we were having, as it would be delightful. He mentioned the senses, said that God is man's greatest blessing and wine makes one lose one's senses and do what one otherwise would not normally do. I countered his protestation by saying it does no such thing if one drinks in moderation.

He said that whereas I may be well-educated and well-cultured, a wine drinker can lose his moderation from time to time and drink too much. This made me smile and I told him that in such a case, the sin does not lie with the wine, but with he who knows not how to drink it.

This reminded me of what a Hungarian emissary once told me—that the Turks have much sense, as they should, since their punishment will be greater for not believing in our Lord and Savior Jesus Christ.

He said one can find the forbidding of wine in Luke, about which I, of course, asked him to say the verse.

He asked how Zechariah and Elizabeth praised God when they had their son John. This I remembered and easily recite—*For he shall be great in the sight of the Lord and shall drink neither wine nor strong drink.*

He asked if this verse is not proof, then, that abstaining from drink is not greatness in the eyes of God, or in other words, a virtue.

I agreed that it signifies the greatness of John the Baptist, but added the we, ourselves, are not prophets.

He then asked if the prophets weren't men and if they came to show goodness to mankind, then they came to show us how to live by example of their own lives.

I told him that whereas he and the Mohametans may consider the prophets to have been men, for us Christians, Jesus Christ is the Lord God.

He claimed we do not glorify God by humanizing Him, but rather diminish Him, and then went on to say our understanding of the Trinity of the Father, the Son and the Holy Spirit was the work of Constantine the Great's council that was held within these city walls that have given them such trouble. He seems to think that after Christianity spread through the empire, Constantine accepted the faith so that the pagans could find something familiar in Christianity.

I told him I knew Constantine the Great was the first emperor ever to accept Christianity.

Then he got to his argument. If it stopped there, then fine, he said, but Constantine synthesized two religions together to stop conflict. For example, the ancient Greeks had tripartite gods, as in Zeus as the god of the heavens, Poseidon as the god of the sea and Hades as the god of the underworld. They are, of course, gods and not mortal. He said that the bishops needed to compete with the old, deep-rooted religion, so they omitted that Jesus was merely mortal and presented him as God. According to him, the Trinity was their response to the pagans' tripartite deities.

I objected and asked about what's written in the Bible.

He asked which Bible I was talking about, because, as he said, there are so many versions. He said there were no less than three hundred versions in Constantine's time and it was the bishops of Christendom who compiled what we now call the Bible at the Council of Nicaea.

I had nothing to respond with and there's no way to know if the version of history he knows is correct or not.

He went on, saying that wasn't all. He said Constantine only thought about maintaining peace in his empire and so made the Christian holidays match the pagan festivals. As an example, he said that as we know, the celebration of Jesus' birth is on the twenty-fifth of December, but that is the day the Babylonians celebrated the birth of the goddess Ishtar, wife of Tammuz. He said the Christian Lord's Day also comes from pagans, and that the first Christian's observed it like the Jewish Sabbath on Saturday.

I asked him where he knew this from. I had nothing other to say in response. He laughed and said I must have forgotten that he is the head of one of the greatest libraries of the ages.

It's true, although I think it was unfair, as he was giving examples of things that I didn't know the accuracy of in the moment.

Then he moved on to the similarities because, as he said, discussing differences does no one any good. He said no matter how much the Bible changes, it maintains the essence of Christianity.

It is a principal in both Christianity and Mohametanism, he said, to clean with water. I agreed and added that we also baptize our babies. He mentioned that we also touch the holy water when we walk into a church and said that both faiths use water for purification for worship.

I told him that their worship could be much longer and intricate that ours. He agreed, but told me not to comment too hastily and told me he knows of many priests who cannot pray without prostrating to God.

I once saw a cardinal like this in Rome. Not only do they prostrate, they lay flat with their face to the ground in praise of God.

He said there's also a similarity in theme among the holy days—Christians have Sunday, Jews have Saturday and Mohametans have Friday. That is to say that each religion has the principle of gathering in congregation at least one day a week. I obviously agreed, because the unity of the congregation is the unity of society.

He finished eating and went out to wash his hands and face. These Turks are always splashing in water. Drums of water and pitchers are ever-present even in the army encampment.

When he came back, he asked if I knew what truly piques his curiosity. Apparently, it's the Hagia Sophia, well behind the walls in the city.

He said it has a dome and that domes are Mohametan architecture as a representation of the sky. He surprisingly said he'd never seen any domes on churches or cathedrals in Italy or the east of Europe.

When I think about it, many have spires and sharp projections.

He asked why, then, the Church of Hagia Sophia is so different than Christian churches in Europe. I reckoned it's because it was built so much earlier than the rest.

He said that was precisely it—before Mohamet and his religion.

I asked him why that mattered. It's important, he said, because before Mohametanism, the true prophet was Jesus, and His original message had not yet been spoiled. He claimed this shows that those who built it were Mohametans.

I was incredulous and asked how he could be so sure they were Mohametans.

He said he knows from the time his prophet was sent, since at that time, the true faith had been corrupted and so there was need for a new prophet. He also mentioned the Biblical prophets. What he said this means is that in the centuries before Mohamet, there were people who still believed in Jesus' true message.

I asked what this had to do with domes. He said it should be clear enough that those who built the dome were Mohametans, or at least not like the Christians of today.

When I asked him what he had to say about the mosaics of Jesus Christ and the Virgin Mary, and the crosses on the walls, he alleged they were added centuries later, but what he was getting at was the shape of the dome and the direction the building faces.

Now we were talking about direction. He said Hagia Sophia faces thirty-three degrees south of east.

He claimed it deviates very little from facing the Kabba in Mecca. He said this deviation can be explained by how land moves over great time. I'm not very convinced of this theory of his. I'll have to do a lot of research.

I asked him if he had mentioned his theory to the sultan. He said he had briefly, but Mehmed didn't find it very important and said every religion predicts the next and that he thought the ground was prepared for him. Mullah Lütfi was certain, though, that when Mehmed turns the church into a mosque and opens it to Mohametans, he will believe it's returning to its true essence.

He gave me enough to think about tonight, as if I need any more.

117

"The Christian alliance in the city is very effective," Karaja Pasha said. "The knights gathered around Giovanni Giustiniani and the Bocchiardo brothers along with Theophilos' soldiers are putting up incredible resistance and cutting down everyone who attempts to breach the walls. They have everything to their benefit—the massive walls, high towers and cover among the battlements. No matter what great warriors the janissaries are or how determinedly the cavalry attacks, we're still slaughtered. In every assault, we've lost ten soldiers to their one. If we lose a thousand, they lose a hundred—or not even that."

The Divan was meeting in the sultan's spacious tent with all of the commanders of the siege and viziers present. The red tent was outfitted the same as a room back at the palace, lined with couches and sofas, and with a carpet with a dragon motif spread over the entire interior.

"Karaja's right," Ishak Pasha said. "Jacopo Contarini and Demetrios Kantakouzenos repair any breach in the southern walls with earth, bales of wool and hides as soon as we open them. And although the cannon balls damage the walls, they do next to nothing to these soft reinforcements."

All eyes were on Muslihiddin in expectance for an explanation from the army's chief engineer.

"That's correct," he said. "The walls are more durable than before when they repair the breaches with timbers from behind, so the cannons should be directed elsewhere."

"Now is the right time to make them accept a heavy annual tribute and pull back," Halil Pasha said standing beside the sultan, as he reckoned this was the best opportunity for his proposition. "It would be best to evaluate all of it when we have a proud withdrawal in hand. We should prepare a treaty with very severe conditions and make Constantine accept."

Karaja Pasha and Ishak Pasha hadn't expected such a proposition. The two commanders hadn't deceived themselves or anyone else and were only thinking of informing the sultan, not of withdrawal. Hamza Bey had earlier reported the miserable situation on the sea and was trying not to bring the defeat to mind.

Zaganos Pasha was the most irked by Halil Pasha's overture. "If it had been left to the grand vizier," he said angrily pointing to him, "then we would've never come and engaged in any of this. Talk of withdrawal after all of this is unacceptable. It's true, we have amassed many casualties and the skilled and battle-hardened Christian armies have been quite successful in their defense of the city, but we've known of Constantine's cunning as we have of the emperors before him. It's also true the Greeks have defended their city from behind these walls for a thousand years and it can't be denied they have the best defenses ever seen. We knew all of this already. It's what we were expecting. But we've started to demoralize them at the same time. Their arms are running thin and all the entrances to the city are under our control."

"And what happens when a second fleet arrives from Rome?" Halil Pasha said. "What happens when reinforcements come from Venice, Genoa and Naples, with arms, sacks of wheat and barrels of water? How can we counter the pope's vast fleets when we haven't even enough power to face three ships?"

"What you say is just your works of fancy," Zaganos Pasha spat back.

Halil Pasha and the others at the Divan were surprised Zaganos Pasha had come out this strongly against the grand vizier. No one had ever been able to do so out in the open or as grandiosely.

"The Christian kingdoms have sent all the assistance they will. The rest is Rome's mind-war against us. Their intention is to frighten us with the existence of aid, demoralize the soldiers and ensure we retreat." He made little effort to mask his insinuation. "It's unfortunate there are those among us who give credence to these rumors and then spread them among the men."

"I suspect Zaganos Pasha is tired," Saruja Pasha said in support of Grand Vizier Halil Pasha. "He's expended much effort throughout the assaults and must not hear what's coming out of his mouth. Isn't the best plan that which considers all possibilities?"

"There's a difference between possibilities and delusion," Ishak Pasha said unexpectedly. "Delusion creates unrest, divides the men and demoralizes them. Once unrest spreads in the army, even if most oppose it, they'd be most ineffective."

Mehmed had been listening to them all, but didn't show what he was thinking. He made no expression of approval or anger—in fact, his face had no expression at all.

"Can the cavalry pull together one more assault?" he finally asked Karaja Pasha once everyone's opinions had been made clear.

"The cavalry is weary, but hasn't lost heart. They await your orders, my Sultan."

Mehmed then turned to the janissary agha after receiving similar responses from Ishak Pasha and Hamza Bey.

Jafer Agha was steadfast. "The janissaries have only now stretched their legs. They think day and night of their brothers-in-arms who died before their eyes. They're itching to enter the fray and await your orders, my Sultan."

Mehmed said he would announce the hour of the final assault later and the soldiers should be ready at all times.

"I can't tell if there are those among us fighting for us or for Constantine, Sultan," Zaganos Pasha said once everyone had left the tent. "I can't help but wonder why you didn't give it to them."

"I know, Zaganos. I know them well. But trouble among us now does us no good. The men you speak of have value and importance for the soldiers. It would stir up discord and create disorder. There's a time for everything."

Before Zaganos Pasha left the tent, Mehmed instructed him to send an envoy to Constantine for the third and last time, and said for it to be the lord of Kastamonu, Jandaroghlu Isfandiyar Bey.

Mehmed handed Zaganos Pasha a paper from his pocket with the specifications for everything. Zaganos Pasha realized then that he had planned the assault much before anyone spoke at the Divan.

"You understand, Zaganos, don't you?" he said. "Either I'll take Constantinople, or it will take me."

Zaganos Pasha knew failure to take the city spelled his end as much as it did for the sultan.

118

Jandaroghlu Isfendyar Bey and two men, one on each side, proceeded, all blindfolded, on their horses. Constantinopolitan soldiers led their horses, all surrounded by palace guards.

Their blindfolds were finally removed when the horses stopped after they had passed by the scenes of the city and anything that would reveal the arms caches or plans for the defense. Isfendyar Bey dismounted and looked at the inscription carved in stone above the gates of the palace. He smiled as he read the Greek inscription of the emperor who built it and the history of his time, but he shuddered inside.

"Heraklios, 610 to 641."

"What is it, Sir?" one of his men asked when he saw the look on his face.

"I thought of Abu Sufyan, who told Heraklios of the prophet, and of his companion Dihyah al-Kalbi, who extended a letter to the emperor from the prophet."

"They sent their first call to the emperor eight hundred years ago, and now we have a similar assignment," his other man said.

Isfendiyar Bey looked at his men. "Let's hope ours is the last."

The figures in the shining mosaic floors transfixed Isfendyar Bey as he walked with his men, palace guards before and behind them, through courtyards and long, columned corridors to the audience hall.

Mythological beasts in the mosaics looked as though they would spring to life—a wolfman baring fangs and ready to pounce; a seahorse half equine and half fish; a Pegasus with wings spread; a winged and beastly dragon; a chimera with a goat head on its back, a snake for a tail and the head of a lion; and many others. Isfendyar Bey had read many stories of these and seen them in paintings in Anatolia and Europe, but this was the first time he'd seen this many.

The emperor's throne was raised up three steps at the far end of the audience hall. Around Constantine were his senior commanders and advisors, including Giovanni Giustiniani Longo, Theophios, Demetrios Kantakouzenos and Loukas Notaras. Along the walls to the right and left were dozens of the city's leading patricians and members of the royal family.

The high ceilings of the hall lent it a spacious ambiance despite the press of people.

Everyone was waiting in anticipation for the message from Mehmed. Constantine and Giustiniani's relaxed air attracted the attention of everyone in the hall. The rabble shouted insults at the three Ottoman envoys as they took their place before Constantine who, like most everyone else, was expecting to hear a demand for a steep tribute in exchange for the lifting of the siege.

Unperturbed, Isfendyar Bey stood haughtily and delivered Mehmed's message in fluent Greek. "Sultan Mehmed, son of Murad Khan, demands all Ottoman prisoners in the city be released, the keys to all the city's gates be handed over to him, the city's soldiers to drop their arms and that the emperor surrender the city."

The message fell on the hall like one of Mehmed's massive cannonballs and a roar erupted as Constantine and his men's faces dropped.

Isfendyar Bey paid no concern to the tumult. "If these conditions are met, Sultan Mehmed will permit the emperor, his family, the leading families of the city and all others who so wish to leave unharmed. Other than the emperor and his family, all others may stay in the city. Their lives and property will not be touched and their dignity will not be sullied." The shouts from the hall raised in pitch. "If they are not met, however, the sultan can guarantee neither life nor property. As you know, if the city is taken by force, the emperor, his people and all their property will be the possession of the sultan. *O People of the Book, come to a word equitable between us and you—that we worship none but God.*"

Constantine said nothing as he waited for the hum of the crowd to fall—his eyes angrily trained on Isfendyar Bey.

Theophilos drew his sword from his scabbard. "Permit me, Your Highness, and I will straighten out this man's arrogance forthright!"

Constantine raised his hand as Theophilos stepped forward. He stopped and sheathed his blade.

"I'm curious," said Constantine. "In what does the sultan trust to send such a message? He has many soldiers, they are well-armed, his cannons are mighty, but so far, he has yet to attain any worthwhile success. Does he not see our coming victory?"

"Victory belongs to God," said Isfendyar Bey. "And so it is His will that will be."

Laughter trickled from the crowd.

"Your God hasn't wanted you to take the city for two months, then," Constantine said. "Why do you defy Him?"

"Great victories are painful. Jesus experienced hardship for a great while as he spread his word." Isfendyar Bey looked straight at the Latin knights behind Constantine as he spoke. "When the Apostle Peter told Emperor Nero of the true faith, Rome brought torture and persecution that lasted hundreds of years."

The commotion in the hall fell slightly more hushed.

"Do you not see our armies fight heroically?" Constantine said. "Do you not know that the pope's fleets will arrive at our harbors at any moment with thousands of men?"

"As God has written, so shall it be. These are the sultan's commands."

Constantine rose from his throne and slowly descended the steps to the emissary.

"The sultan gives you one day to decide your actions," Isfendyar Bey said. "This is all we have come to say."

Constantine walked around the three emissaries as he replied. "Does Sultan Mehmed truly believe the great city of Constantinople will fall? Does he believe that I, Constantine XI, will be remembered as the emperor who handed the city to the Turk sultan. Does he believe the House of Palaiologos will hand him on a silver platter the legacy of Julius Caesar and Constantine the Great? Does he not know that Constantinople is the crown of all Christendom and its kings, that they will forever support us against you Mohametans and we will remain an indestructible fortress against you? Neither Attila the Hun, Caliph Muawiyah, Sultan Kaykhusraw nor Caliph Harun al-Rashid ever succeeded in overcoming us. Thousands of hopes lie dead and buried outside our walls. It was there we slaughtered your prophet's men. As I live and afterward, Constantinople will stand."

"*Hüvelbaki,*" said Isfenyer Bey when Constantine finished.

"What does that mean, Constantine said as he turned back to face him.

"Only God is eternal," one of Isfendyer Bey's men said.

Constantine pulled a knife from his belt and plunged into the man's neck from behind. "I didn't ask you," he said as the man fell to the floor with blood spurting from his neck.

If his weapons hadn't been held, Isfendyar Bey could have taken Constantine's life on the spot. He furiously stepped to Constantine, only to be met by the palace guards, their swords leveled at him and his remaining man.

"There's no need to wait a day," Constantine said, raising his head in defiance. "You've received your answer. Now, you may go and tell your sultan."

119

A cook took his yard-long spoon and stirred the pilaf in a cauldron that stood to his waist. The rice, glistening in the darkness, had already been cooked and the glowing embers left under the cauldron were keeping it warm.

He spooned out two heaps onto the plate a janissary held out to him. The janissary then went to the next cauldron and ladled some roasted meat next to his pilaf. Unlike the other janissaries, Iskender never cared to mix his rice and meat. First rice, then meat. He made his way to a third cauldron and got a glass of grape compote from the cook, then made way for the men in the line behind him.

Hundreds of janissaries filed passed the dozens of cauldrons set up side by side, then returned to their regiments to fill their bellies around the fires they'd built. More brimming cauldrons came as they emptied and those still hungry came back for a second helping.

"Look, I found someone with the same name as you," said Hasan as he came up behind Iskender with another janissary with him and two plates of pilaf in one hand.

"Looks like you're starving again," Iskender said with a smile.

"Twice as much as you. You'd eat this much, too, if you were as big as me. And I'm haggard from fasting all day."

"The less I eat the smaller my appetite is," said Iskender. "I took this only to keep me from wasting away."

"You'll be our patron saint if you keep up like this," Hasan said cheerfully. "You eat little, drink little and sleep little. No, no, let me fix that. You eat nearly nothing, you don't drink anything and you never sleep."

"There'll be time for us to rest, eat and drink."

"Look, now you're talking like a mullah," Hasan said, giving them both a chuckle. "His name's also Iskender," he said to the janissary with him. "He's from the archery regiment. I haven't seen him for ages."

Iskender bowed his head and greeted the young man. The other Iskender responded in kind.

"He has a nickname, though," Hasan said. "Iskender the Woodsman."

Iskender wondered how he'd gotten this epithet, but didn't ask since they had just met.

"He's the best archer in the regiment."

"It's nothing that grand," the other Iskender said. "I'm as good as any janissary."

Iskender looked at his arms and reckoned he could string any bow he pleased.

"Don't pay attention to him," Hasan said. "He didn't used to be so modest. The master archers found bows we'd never seen and challenged anybody who thought they could to string them up. He muscled a bow together that even champion wrestlers couldn't get it to budge."

The three young men walked amid torches toward their tent. Iskender the Woodsman parted to return to his own regiment.

"He's not much of a talker," Iskender said.

"He's quiet. Now more than usual, but he still talks more than you," Hasan said, laughing.

"Why do they call him the woodsman?"

"It's an interesting story. I'll tell you."

They got to the field with their regiment's tents and sat down among the others around a fire. They took their spoons from the holder in their hats and started eating.

"There aren't many know who his people are or which village he's from. He also won't tell anyone."

"It's certainly in the Devshirme registry," Iskender said indifferently. He was lost in his own thoughts and wasn't much for listening to a story at the moment. Hasan knew this, but went on to get Iskender out of it.

"Certainly someone's looked. What everyone says, though, is that the Devshirme official was a real crank and didn't take a liking to anyone easily. He said they needed real men for the palace. The aghas told him there were few boys to take conscripts from and he snapped that they had nothing to do where they were since most of the boys were no good. They went to another village, but he didn't like any of the boys there, either. Some were too short and others were too scrawny. For every boy he looked over he said they had no luster in their eyes and their destinies were unclear."

Hasan chewed a spoonful of pilaf and went on. "Then he saw a boy carrying wood in the village square. He caught his eye on first glance since he weas very well-built. The boy was still very young, but his arms were as big as the logs he was carrying. He asked who the boy was and they told him he had no mother or father and carried wood to the villagers for money. The Devshirme official snatched him up and brought him to the hearth. Ever since then they've called him Iskender the Woodsman."

"Now it makes sense how he could string those bows," Iskender said. He took a sip of his compote. Again, he'd only picked at his food—a couple spoonfuls of rice and a few pieces of meat.

"You're in a mood again, Iskender," Hasan said.

Iskender said nothing. Hasan didn't insist and instead turned to the other soldiers around the fire.

Iskender looked off sorrowfully. He strained to see the city walls half a mile away beyond the dozens of tents. All of the walls were shrouded in darkness and fog. *One more day,* he thought, *just one more day.*

Feverish work was going on behind the walls.

A farmer in tatters tipped out a wheelbarrow of stones at the base of a wall. Having delivered a dozen carts of stone, the farmers at the top of the walls began to pull them up. Ropes stretched from the four sides of a wooden apparatus through pulleys and to the workers' hands. One of the men stopped often to oil the ropes to keep them slick.

"Why are you standing around? Get back to work!" Theophilos shouted before he slapped the old farmer across the face when he saw the man stop to take a breath. With a bloody lip, the old man grabbed hold of his cart and took off for where they were loading the stone. Hundreds of peasants were stacking stones along the base of the walls as commanders watched over them. They had set up a variety of ways to haul the stone up the walls.

Giustiniani was having timbers and brushwood piled at the walls around the Fifth Military Gate. As many women and children as men had been put to work stacking wood up at the base of the walls to be used to boil the cauldrons large and small nearby in preparation for the imminent assault.

Johannes Grandi went to Giustiani with two boys carrying casks. "Be careful, you brats, you'll blow yourselves to kingdom come," he shouted when the children, hidden behind filth, set the casks down too hard.

"The kegs are ready, as you asked," he said, turning back to Giustiani.

"How many?"

"With these, it's all fifty."

Giustiniani smiled happily. He reckoned fifty casks of black powder would do to ignite the Greek fire, which would burn on the surface of the sea and under rainfall. He could see himself as ruler of Corfu, as Constantine had promised.

Two other children who had managed to slip out from the hard work hid on the ramparts and looked out from above the Gate of Saint Romanos. Unable to see over the battlements, one climbed on the other and stood up on his shoulders. They wavered as they tried to keep their balance.

"What do you see?" the one on the bottom said as he struggled.

"A whole bunch of stars," the other said, blinking in wonderment.

"You moron, not up there, look down at the ground."

"That's what I'm doing."

"Those are torches."

"Torches are orange, these are white."

"They're not torches?"

"There are—a bunch of them. There're a bunch of tents, too. But behind them farther away there're a bunch of white lights. It looks like they're moving."

"Get down, you idiot," the boy said as he sent the other boy tumbling off. "Get up, it's my turn now."

He climbed up on the boy's shoulders and looked at the field below. The sprawling sight of burning torches and red, white, yellow and green tents through the cloud of fog drifting by dazzled him. Like the other boy, he also saw white lights in the distance that looked to be coming closer.

The boys noticed a soldier coming toward them. And took off down the stairs to disappear into the night.

Mehmed closed the flap over the window of the green tent and turned around.

He had left his tent without his guards, as he did when he went to inspect his army, and made his way to Akshamsaddin's tent. He didn't want to disturb the sheikh, having found him in prayer with his forehead to the ground.

Someone bumped into his shoulder as he walked between the

tents with his head down in thought. He looked up and saw a janissary, like himself, lost with his head down walking among the tents.

"Forgive me," Iskender stammered as soon as he recognized the sultan and went to bow. Mehmed took hold of his shoulders and held him up.

"You look to be far off in thought," he said as he looked at Iskender. "Like me, you must be thinking of something you so greatly desire."

Iskender nodded silently, not knowing what to do. Mehmed liked the depth of the expression on Iskender's face and his eyes were drawn to the coral necklace around the janissary's neck. He had a feeling there was something different about this soldier—a different fire burnt inside him.

"Coral doesn't look like much at the bottom of the sea," Mehmed said. "It only reveals its true splendor once out of the water. This is exactly what is necessary at times to be victorious. Every victory has its price. Go and rest now. Tomorrow will be a grand day."

It never crossed Iskender's mind as he walked back to his tent that he was the first soul Mehmed had told the time of the final assault.

BOOK FİVE

Pespective

120

A painter excitedly pulled books out of his bag, having memorized their lines and taken notes on them for days, and placed them on the ground. If it were another time, he would have arranged them with more care, never having let anyone else leaf through them. Now, though, he was at the final stage of his weeks of experimentation and was darting back and forth to the looks from his friends Bartolommeo and Costanzo.

The few people passing through Venice's grand Saint Mark's Square couldn't quite make out what the few men a hundred yards from the basilica were busy with.

The painter excitedly walked to the basilica and counted his paces back to where he came from. Bartolommeo and Costanzo looked curiously at each other as they tried to make sense of what their friend was up to.

The painter took three steps past his two friends and said, "Bring the easel here. We should have the canvas right here."

The painter stood in the middle of the square and counted the surrounding arched columns from left to right as he took care to set up his easel in the exact spot he had determined the day before. He took note of the Oriental carpet hanging from the balcony in between the twenty-seventh column from the left and the thirty-second from the right. Although many of the balconies had small carpets hanging from them as ornamentation, the only one in that spot between a few columns was this one. He made sure his easel was where he wanted between two points. He then unwrapped a canvas and placed it on the easel.

He took out a mirror as big as the canvas from his bag of paints and brushes.

"Where did you find such a big mirror?" Bartolommeo asked. "It must have been expensive."

"It cost me a painting," the artist said. "Another painting of the Madonna with child to a church. That's all."

His friends knew he constantly made paintings with religious themes for the churches, but also that he was fed up with painting the same things on end. Like every painter in need of money, however, he was fully aware he had no other choice but to paint these scenes if he wanted to support himself with his art.

He dipped a brush into a thick, black paint he used to mark the stones and looked at the notes in his book in his other hand. He marked the two points on the ground about a yard apart as he kept one eye on the basilica.

"Now we're getting started," he said, straightening up. "Costanzo, you hold the mirror." He took the man by the shoulders and placed him in the first spot he'd marked, turned his back and handed him the mirror.

"Bartolommeo, you stand right here and hold the canvas like this over your face." He went opposite Costanzo with his face turned from him.

"But Gentile, you've put the backside of the canvas to my face," Bartolommeo said. "How am I going to see?"

"Just do as I said. There's a hole in the canvas, down at the bottom, right in the middle. It's small." He'd placed it almost directly in front of Bartolommeo's right eye. "Now close your other eye and look through it."

"I can't see anything. Lift up the sheet."

Gentile adjusted the mirror in Costanzo's hands and brought it perfectly opposite the canvas. "There, hold still," he said. "Bend down when I say and then straighten back up."

"You ready?" Gentile said. Costanzo and Bartolommeo were now growing quite impatient. They were also very curious about what Gentile was working on, as he had been constantly disappearing day and night.

Bartolommeo couldn't believe what he saw through the hole when Gentile removed the sheet from Costanzo and was struck dumb for a moment. Costanzo nearly dropped the mirror from amazement upon seeing the canvas appear before his eyes.

Gentile waited a moment and then turned to Costanzo. "Now bend forward with the mirror."

Bartolommeo was just as surprised when the mirror in front of him came down. The same sight as the painting he had just seen reflected in the mirror still stood before him.

"This is unbelievable," Bartolommeo marveled. "It's the same—the scene of your painting itself. There's no difference between it and your painting. Fantastic. Simply magnificent."

Then Bartolommeo and Costanzo traded places and admiringly looked on at the basilica and its depiction on the canvas. The only thing different was the few people walking in front of the actual basilica who, naturally, weren't in the painting. They laughed as they watched the people seem to magically disappear as they looked back and forth from the painting to the basilica.

Gentile had just recreated an experiment, but on a grander scale, by renowned painter and architect from Florence, Filippo Brunelleschi, who had earlier done so with the small Florentine Baptistry. The Florentine painter's life had changed months ago with the acquisition of a book. He had no idea that Niccolò de' Niccoli, the book merchant he frequented, had gotten his books from two thieves who had made off with them in Constantinople. Niccolò this time sold him ibn al-Haytham's *Book of Optics*, having earlier sold him al-Kindi's work on optics. Works supported by al-Kindi's research, having critiqued and surpassed those by Euclid, Ptolemy and Galen from more ancient times, were a treasure to a painter, showing how to depict true to life on canvas using mathematical principles. From Venice, Gentile had been on the lookout for translations of al-Kindi and ibn al-Haytham as soon as he heard of them. With the help of ibn Sina's *The Canon of Medicine* in his own library, he also planned to figure out how to transfer what he saw true to form onto canvas. In line with ibn al-Haytham's suggestions of investigative experimentation, he had chosen Venice's grand basilica.

City folk came and lined up to marvel at the true to life depiction of the basilica as Gentile, Bartolommeo and Costanzo embraced each other excitedly.

"It's exactly the same. The same as in real life!" one said as he walked away.

As the crowd dispersed, three horsemen, one slightly in front of the others, rode toward the painters. It was clear from their dress they were Ottomans. Their caftans signified wealth and fame in Venice in the 1470s. One of the horsemen was also obviously a janissary. The people in the square couldn't help but gawk at the Ottomans' richly adorned clothing and marvelous swords hanging from their belts.

"Which of you is Bellini?" Isa Bey, leading the other two, said in perfect Venetian as he looked down from his horse.

Gentile looked disconcertedly at his friends upon hearing his name. "I am," he said, curious.

"The famous Venetian painter Gentile Bellini, son of Jacopo, brother to Giovanni?" Isa Bey said, this time addressing Gentile directly to be sure. He'd known that for ages, one of every two painters in this city was named Bellini.

"I am he," Gentile said.

Isa Bey and the janissary looked to each other, pleased they'd found the man they had been searching for over the past two days in all of the studios and every other nook and cranny in Venice.

"They call me Isa Bey. I am an emissary from Sultan Mehmed II, Khan of the Sublime House of Osman, son of Murad Khan, Sultan of the Lands and Emperor of the Seas, the Shadow of God over Men and Spirits, Deputy of God in the East and the West, Champion of Water and Land, Caesar of Rome, the Conqueror of Constantinople." He paused for a moment and cracked a slight, unexpected smile at the lucky man before him. "Fortune smiles on you. The sultan is calling you to the capital, to Constantinople. We held all the meetings with the doge and we've been looking for you for two days."

It took a moment for Bellini to shake off his bewilderment. "Why me?"

Isa Bey carefully looked at Bellini. "Because you're the best. Sultan Mehmed chooses the best."

Gentile Bellini had met many painters who had gone to Ottoman lands. Word of the Grand Turk's fondness for painters and art and had spread to Venice, as it earlier had to Florence and Naples. He had never hoped for such an invitation for himself as he had so suddenly right now. The idea to escape religious paintings for the Church and be able to see different places and people sounded enchanting to him from the first instant. He wondered if he'd already also grown bored of painting portraits of Venice's shrewd politicians and priests. He'd also heard that the Ottoman sultan paid good money to the artists he was pleased with. He had already made up his mind since the first moment.

"When do we depart?"

Isa Bey smiled. "You're a wise man, Signore Bellini. The sultan will be pleased. He doesn't care for hesitation at all. There's one more thing, though. The sultan also has want for a master medallion maker of your choice."

Bellini looked over at Costanzo. "Well, then he's found his man."

Costanzo da Ferrara felt fortunate he had come from Naples to spend these past couple of months at his friend's studio in Venice.

Bellini spoke up just as Isa Bey turned his horses head away. "You speak Venetian like it's you mother tongue. I can't tell if you're Venetians or Turks."

Isa Bey smiled again and turned back to the painter. "There is no Turk or Venetian in the Sublime State. We are all Ottoman." Then he looked out over Saint Mark's Square, on which he hadn't set foot for thirty years, and thought of his wife back in Constantinople whom he missed so.

Cristoforo Moro from the Great Council of Venice looked on from among the crowds, but not at Isa Bey or the janissary. He had been following every step of the third man in the delegation—Yakup, the sultan's vizier, a Jewish convert to Islam. He was certain now.

121

Yakup Pasha's mind was racing as he waited in the darkness. He had met with Cristoforo Moro from the nearly untouchably powerful Council of Ten the day earlier and was told he would meet him where he was now.

Three people appeared from out of the black. From his right, his left and directly in front of him came the senior members of the Council of Ten, Giovanni Mocenigo and Stefano Malipiero, along with the man you had arranged this secret meeting in Saint Mark's Square, Cristoforo Moro.

Yakup Pasha looked around anxiously to see if there was anyone watching.

"Don't be afraid, dear Vizier," Mocenigo said. "Everything is under control."

"We've arranged everything," Malipiero said.

"What you ask of me is madness," Yakup Pasha hissed through his teeth. "That you even proposed such a thing is testament to your stupidity."

"Don't rush to a decision," Moro said.

"The Senate is even willing to pay one hundred thousand gold *zecchini* in the event you succeed," Mocenigo said from the side.

"Not only for you, this is enough for your children, their children and their children after to all live like kings," Malipiero said.

Yakup Pasha flashed a mocking smile. "My family and I already live like that at the pleasure of the sultan. What could you even give me that the Ottoman sultan couldn't?"

The three conspirators from the Council of Ten looked at each other as if this was the response they had expected.

"Freedom," Moro said.

"We know you're a Jew converted."

"That's no secret," Yakup Pasha said.

"You live a life of freedom, but what about those hundreds of Jews in Venice confined to their quarter?"

"Or those in the dungeons of Rome?"

"What would I be able to do for them?" Yakup Pasha said, now starting to feel disconcerted. He wondered what these men's proposal actually was.

"If you accept our offer, you will receive one hundred thousand gold *zecchini* and hundreds of Jews will be released upon order from the pope. There are records that show that dozens of them are your relatives."

Yakup Pasha swallowed the lump in his throat.

"If you reject our offer, they all die."

Yakup Pasha's brow started sweating. He took out a handkerchief from his caftan and wiped his forehead. "This is rubbish! You ask something of me I could never do. Even if I accept your offer, how would I manage to do it? And then, would I come out alive? The janissaries would butcher me straight away!"

We thought of that, as well," Mocenigo said.

"You are both his vizier and his physician," Moro said.

Malipiero took a small bottle from his pocket. "You tell him this will be good for him and add one drop of it to his food every day. You needn't hide anything—it's all out in the open. No letters, no secret messages, no messengers at risk of being caught. You add one drop to his food every day for weeks. Nothing will happen to the sultan after only a short while, so no one will suspect you of anything. But then, day by day, his condition will worsen and after six months, his body will lose all vigor."

Yakup Pasha was hesitant about whether he should take the bottle or not. "Why are you getting up to such a thing? I don't understand," he said hopelessly. "You have every privilege in the straits and you can engage in all types of trade in his realm."

The three men looked back and forth at each other again. "There's nothing to understand, dear Vizier," Moro said. "The sultan's fleet is growing stronger and our domination of the sea is decreasing steadily."

"Above all, though, we've gotten word the sultan will soon attack Otranto in the south," Malipiero said.

"How could you know that?" Yakup Pasha asked. "He doesn't even tell his closest men where he will go on campaign. I don't even know."

"He continues to build his fleet," Mocenigo said. "It's only a matter of time before he tries to set foot in Italy and take Rome."

"If Rome falls into the hands of the Turk, then he would make all of Europe Mohametan," Malipiero said. "We will not allow that to happen."

"If you won't do it, we'll find someone else who will. Don't doubt that," Mocenigo said.

"Remember, hundreds of Jews will be saved thanks to you," Moro said.

Yakup Pasha looked at the bottle Malipiero was holding out, racked with indecision. This was undoubtedly the worst day of his life.

BOOK SİX
Perspective

122

A janissary quickly entered when he came to the Numerical Sciences building of the Sahn-i Seman Madrasah in Constantinople. His brow was covered in sweat from running. He took out a silk handkerchief to wipe it away and continued walking quickly as he tried to catch one of the teachers before he went into class. He quickened his pace when he saw a young teacher in a green caftan among the students. The *fiqh* classes on Islamic jurisprudence he had taken came to mind as he thought about how this young teacher's hair, which stuck out from the sides of his turban, was going grey. He was thankful for having become a janissary, as he reckoned scholarship was much more difficult and intricate than soldiering.

Sinan Bey had already entered the classroom and closed the door without noticing the janissary trying to reach him. Now the janissary was forced to wait until class let out. Sultan Mehmed's orders had been clear—no teacher should be disturbed in lessons. The janissary folded his arms and set to waiting by the door.

"The eye is the master of all," Sinan Bey said to his students, who were hanging on his every word. "Thanks to the eye, we see the world and we create maps of the stars. Eyes make maps and eyes plan buildings. It is the eye that makes algebra possible from the beginning. There is an understanding of everything on earth, no matter what it is, and it was the eye that first discovered it. That is why we say, we have eyes, therefore we understand."

He looked over his students. "Now, do as I say in the order I say it. First, take your rulers and measure your arm from the elbow to the wrist and write down the measurement in your books."

The twenty boys who filled the classroom curiously set to doing what they were told. They were sat in a circle and each of them behind a low, wooden desk. Some sat cross-legged and others were on their knees, all of them hunched over as they worked. Their straw yellow paper was in complete contrast to the ornamented, red carpets spread over the floor.

Sinan Bey walked around his students and looked over their shoulders from time to time to check if they were doing their work correctly.

"Now measure the length of your hand from your wrist to your fingertips. Then find the proportion of these two measurements."

"809 over 500," one student said immediately.

"204 over 125," said another.

"908 over 500," a third said.

"Well done. Those who found 809 over 500, or 1.618, are correct. This will be your result if you measure carefully and don't slip up."

He walked back to the center of the classroom. "Now, lets do the same thing for the three knuckles of the pointer finger. Try to find the proportion between the space from the first knuckle to the second and the length of the whole finger."

"It's the same, teacher—809 over 500," the first student said, again first to answer.

Sinan Bey walked past his students, looking at what they were writing and checking if they'd found the same result. Then we went back to the middle of the class and picked up a large sheet of paper, big enough for all the students to see.

He dipped his pen in the inkpot and said, "Now, try to find the order in the sequence of numbers I write down." 0, *1, 1, 2, 3, 5, 8, 13, 21, 34, 55, 89, 144, 233.* "This sequence can go on forever."

"Each number is the sum of itself plus the number before it," one of the students said after a while.

"That's correct," Sinan Bey said. "Now for the real question. What is the relationship of 809 over 500, or 1.618, to this sequence of numbers?

Some of the students did various calculations in their heads while other worked with pen and paper to find the answer.

"It's the ratio the numbers have to each other, teacher," one said before too long.

"Very good. You will always get 1.618 from 233 over 144, 144 over 89 and 89 over 55. What this shows us is the mathematical order many things have."

Sinan Bey took the pine cones from his table that the students had been curious about since the lesson began and distributed them to the boys.

He kept one for himself. "For example, look closely at these wonderous pine cone's seeds. You will see spirals emanating out from the bottom. Now, every two boys count the lines swirling out to the left and right and then tell the rest of the class."

"Fifty-five and thirty-four," one said.

"Eighty-nine and fifty-five," said another.

"Now divide," Sinan Bey said.

"It's 1.618,"

"Well done, boys. Flowers, pinecones, how tree branches grow, sea shells and many other things have this golden ratio of 1.618. Al-Khwarizmi wrote about it and the power of numbers in detail in *The Compendious Book on Calculation by Completion and Balancing.*"

One of the students stood up. "Teacher, my father went to Pisa last summer and brought back a bunch of European manuscripts. One of the books had numbers in it, so I looked through it all right away. I remember now there was something like this written in Latin. Do you know about that?"

"You must be thinking of the mathematician Leonardo of Pisa. I've seen his book, as well. He lived a couple hundred years ago and its clear to me he got his findings concerning this golden ratio with knowledge of al-Khwarizmi's work. He always mentions al-Khwarizmi in the many versions of his manuscripts. And as we all know, al-Khwarizmi lived over six hundred years ago and is one of the founders of our mathematics. To think otherwise makes no sense. There are many translations of al-Khwarizmi in Latin and Greek throughout Europe, especially in Spain and Andalusia. I've told you already about the crusaders I saw in Jerusalem who were used to Roman numerals and how they thought our numbers were sorcery when they saw the Arabs doing arithmetic with them."

The students smiled with their teacher again as they remembered the story they'd found so amusing when they first heard it.

"But, teacher," another said, "what is the result we get from these numbers? Why is it?"

"I was going to ask you all the same question. What do you say?"

"It signifies the order of creation."

"What does it signify about that order?"

"The order points to an arranger and that everything is created within an arrangement."

"Let's look at the Holy Quran, shall we?" Sinan Bey said. "Do any key verses come to mind?"

He waited for a moment.

One student moved his lips silently as he went through the hundreds of pages and thousands of verses in his head. He came to the one he was searching for and recited it in Arabic. "*Verily, God has appointed a due proportion for all things.* Surah *At-Talaq,* verse three."

"*And He created the seven heavens, one above the other. You will see not any imperfection in the Most Compassionate's creation. So look again—do you see any flaw?*" another student recited. "*Then look twice again—your sight will return to you frustrated and weary.* Surah *al-Mulk,* verses three and four."

"Well done, boys," Sinan Bey said cheerfully as he left the room.

"You have a prize waiting for you—weave prepared a feast of roasted pine nuts for you. Tomorrow, you'll see how this golden ratio is used in complex equations. And don't forget to look at the third volume of al-Khwarizmi in the library."

Sinan Bey saw the janissary waiting by the door as soon as he stepped out and knew straight away the sultan was calling him to the palace.

"What's the reason?"

"A painter has come from Venice and the sultan wants you to meet him."

In a strange coincidence, both the janissary and Sinan Bey mounted their identical, sable Bulgarian horses and rode off for Topkapi Palace.

123

Sinan Bey, who was also a miniature painter, had been chatting with Gentile Bellini for two hours in one of the spacious rooms in the palace.

Bellini walked to him at the window as he spoke in Venetian. "That's it," he said. "Perspective produces exactly what you see from this window. There's no difference between what you paint from here and the scene outside. It's true life itself."

Sinan Bey stood at the window with his hands clasped behind him. He looked outside and then turned back to Bellini with a smile. "The truth isn't something that fits in a window. You merely reflect the depth of the world on canvas as an illusion using mathematics and geometry."

"But it doesn't matter if it's an illusion or not, Sinan Bey." Bellini was still struggling to pronounce the man's name even though he had now been in the city for days. Sinan Bey was speaking fluent Venetian, whereas the pronunciation of the man's name annoyed him and made him slightly embarrassed. "The important thing is to capture the truth in all its detail."

"Signore Bellini, I reckon I agree that details are the best reflection. I'm not saying there's no place for detail in painting. Miniatures have much detail and they're very important, after all, and much attention is paid to the depiction of the subjects, people, objects and nature. There is much detail in miniatures—as much as on the patterns of our caftans and rugs."

"Then what you're saying is the same as what I'm saying. Is not detail and perspective the same in a sense?"

"Not at all," Sinan Bey persisted. "It's rather that perspective harms the truth of the detail. What you see from this window is limited to one line of sight—your viewpoint. If you capture ten details, then you miss a hundred since they aren't in your field of view and you don't notice them."

"I understand what you're saying, but would I not be capturing the reality from this point?"

"You're partly right, but I don't agree with what you say. You still see reality as the whole of the objects you can observe and you accept your painting as a reflection of reality. What you see on the other side of this window, however, is no more than an illusion. This Justice Pavilion you see, the chimneys of the caravanserais in the center of the city and the specks of people in the distance are all a reflection in themselves. In your prison of perspective, the minaret of that mosque is no bigger than my finger and the people no more than the tip of your brush. The majestic mountains on the horizon are as big as chickpeas. Isn't that right?"

"That is how they look from here, though, isn't it?"

"As you say, you're right. That's how they look. But reality isn't so. We believe in Plato's allegory of the cave. All we see is but a pale reflection of true reality. What you do is nothing but depict the shadow of a shadow, glorifying a false reality in your painting while thinking you reflect truth. And as you do, you're twice removed from the reality you think you've caught."

"But, do you not depict the world in miniatures?"

"We do, but we don't emphasize the reality you hold so highly. It's quite the other way around for us. We try to go beyond the thing and capture its meaning instead. A thing has no value in our eyes—the true value is its meaning. We love cypresses because they remind us of death and the Creator. We love flowers and paint them in many colors because they evoke God the Shaper of Beauty. Our sultan is always at the center because his duty and responsibilities are greater than the rest of ours. Our reality is boundless and cannot be imprisoned in a small window. Let me say it like this—you say you capture reality, but you actually draw away from it whereas we go beyond illusion and capture true reality, or try to. My teacher Mullah Lütfi always said what a painter does is not depict what is seen, but what is felt, known and believed. You remind me of a very old friend of his."

"Why don't you give objects depth, then?" Bellini said.

"Who said we don't? You imprison depth in space. In miniatures, there are leaps in space and time. They explain both how events were and as they will be. They show the passage to events in the future and in different places. A singular view and path of time are limited, but a multiplicity of views and leaps in time better reflect reality. You look out from one place, but we watch the world from the ninth heaven. Let me say one thing more. If this perspective you so praise were really that precious, then it would have been used for the past thousand years. Perspective is based on geometry and optics, and as far as I know, these topics you know by heart have been investigated for centuries. Euclid, Galen, ibn Sina, Ptolemy, al-Kindi and ibn al-Haytham all did these calculations over the past thousand years, but nobody, or none of the people who have read them, have abandoned themselves to this perspective you speak of. Don't get me wrong, though—I'm not saying perspective is something bad. Not at all. What I'm saying is it's a style to follow and continue, but it can't be said to be better or worse than miniatures. And you do it admirably so, as well."

"But miniatures look—how should I say this—a little childish."

"I've heard that from another Europeans before—that they're childish." Sinan Bey smiled. "Now let me ask you a question, Signore Bellini. When a child looks to the sky, he sees blue heavens, and when he looks down, he sees the brown of the earth. Isn't that so?"

"It is."

"Pray tell, which of our miniatures have a blue sky?"

"Sometimes it's purple and sometimes its golden," Bellini said. "I've been curious about that, actually. We always use the shades of blue and other colors like that."

"So, wouldn't that make it so you have the childish view you assert we have? You said it yourself."

"I don't understand."

"Let me explain, then. Let's say we take a boy, close his eyes, take him to the base of a tower and then open his eyes. He will look up and think it is the tallest tower ever built, wouldn't he? Then, let's say we take him to a house a ways off and have him look out from the window. Then he would think that large tower was no bigger than a reed pen. This is what childishness is, isn't it? You're right on that point. We do try to capture the naivety of a child in our painting. You reflect mathematics in your painting—we try to see the purity of a child's mind."

"So children see gold and yellow everywhere?"

"Going beyond the importance given to an object's detail requires just as much sensitivity. Embellishments to the sky or some other part of nature—a cloud, the sea, mountains—the different colors all have symbolic and abstract meanings."

"I admire the importance you give to time, since perspective also employs the angle of the light and thus, the mastery of shadow."

"Yes, however, light and shadow can only capture a specific time and place and then fix it there. Just as you imprison the painting in your one view, so too do you imprison it in a single point in time and space. We try to destroy time and capture eternity."

"Although by saying you capture eternity, you miss the moment."

"There, now you've started speaking a little of our language," Sinan Bey said. "If the Creator so wanted a moment to be captured, then He would always hold it fixed and wouldn't exhaust his servants so much, would he? This moment you speak of is nothing. Can you capture something always on the move?"

"It's interesting that your theology directs your painting."

"You are the last person I would expect to say that, Signore Bellini. All the European paintings I've seen have been of churches, the Madonna with child, Jesus, and Saint Peter and the other Apostles. The portraits you paint are of bishops or dukes involved in works of faith. Jesus on the cross you believe He was nailed to takes precedent in many Christian paintings."

Bellini knew Sinan Bey was at least partly right on this and had nothing to respond with.

"Do you see a single crescent in our miniatures, though? A shining moon would be nice in the place of honor in our miniatures, wouldn't it? Do you think we're unable to do it? Haven't you looked at most of them yourself? Didn't you see the flowers, gardens, battles and libraries we paint—the scenes in history books, the paintings of medicines and treatments in medical books? Leave that be. What about the paintings of beautiful Layla in her sumptuous clothing or Majnun engulfed in madness? It is you who so unceremoniously puts your religion at the center of life and your paintings. This is why so many of your artists grow tired and want to escape it. The rupture of religion from art and science starts there. Our paintings, however, show every side of life and the beauty of everything in the world."

124

"According to legend," Mehmed said, "there was a Persian padishah long ago. The city's astrologers said he wouldn't live to see the age of forty. No matter which astrologer looked at the stars, they saw that same short life. What would you do if you knew you would die before forty, Gentile?"

Bellini stood behind a canvas a few yards from Mehmed, painting his portrait as the sultan sat still and looked out over the city from a large balcony. Bellini had been waiting for this for weeks—after having made the drawings earlier, now he was finally adding color. As a master at his craft, he had painted portraits of many Venetian doges and European kings, but now in Mehmed's presence, he felt himself a novice or apprentice of sorts. He hadn't even been this excited when he painted Holy Roman Emperor Frederick III or renowned leaders and knights on return from crusade.

"I suppose I would travel so I could see the whole world, Sultan," he said, adding the single title as fluently as Mehmed spoke Venetian.

"Well, do you know what this king did? What would the ruler of a large empire with far-off boarders, countless soldiers and an overflowing treasury be able to do?"

Mehmed's face was paler today than usual and looked weary, but Bellini was overly pleased with the cordiality the sultan showed him.

"I suppose he would have traveled those boarders and had a bit of fun as he so pleased," Bellini said.

"Not at all, Gentile. He closed himself off in his palace and gathered all the poets, artists, painters, calligraphers and wise men there were to be had around him and worked to learn all of the arts. He painted for months and wrote for years—books with hundreds upon hundreds of pages. He competed in the palace gardens with the best archers the world had seen." Mehmed looked out to the mountains over the horizon. "Then one day, at thirty-eight, he fell from his horse and died."

Bellini swept his brush through the red he'd mixed to capture the tone of Mehmed's caftan and brought it to the canvas.

"Sometimes I feel like that man," Mehmed said. "I'm cursed by unease and can't go anywhere. My only consolation are these paintings and books. Art and science are the only hope for man to achieve immortality. Without the roads he built, who would remember Julius Caesar, and who would remember Alexander the Great without the writings of historians?" Mehmed looked to Bellini, which he rarely did. "And here you are making a record of it. Just as Khosrow and Shirin first fell in love with the paintings of each other, so too will people believe in your painting."

Mehmed turned his gaze to the Bosporus. "What the historians write will be truer than history," he said as the calm breeze carried the fragrance of the water and gardens under the sun to him. "People will remember me as you paint me."

Emboldened by Mehmed sharing his thoughts, Bellini reckoned he could ask the question that had been on his mind for some time. "Many of the miniaturists at your command turn their noses up at the Venetian style and belittle perspective. Why do you want your portrait painted this way?"

Mehmed smiled. "Baba Nakkash used to tell me all the time when I was a child in Manisa, but I never understood then. He would ask me what truth is—is it what we see? I thought about what it would be if it weren't what we see. But then imprisoning reality in the material is barbarism itself. My miniaturists are in pursuit of abstraction. Perspective limits the material. Those who see your portrait of me will think they see me and those who read about me will think they understand me. Very few of them, though, will be able to see the hidden truth behind the vantagepoint of the portrayal. Truth, however, can be captured through the use of different vantagepoints. None of them do so by themselves, though, since reality is them as a whole or none at all. My miniaturists understand all of this, but I wouldn't reckon they totally discount perspective."

"You're right. I suppose they are as affected by perspective as I am by miniatures."

"As much as I am their sultan and regard their rights, so too am I for my subjects who aren't Muslim and must take care to regard their thoughts similarly. That is empire. When one becomes sultan, his body goes in service to his realm. Every moment not in service to the people is a sin for a spirit and body devoted to service of the true God. My realm stretches to east and west. You also have a warrant over me, Gentile, and you're exercising it now."

"And you see no sin in that?"

Mehmed stood up. "Come here, Gentile. Let me show you something."

Bellini set his brush down beside his paints. They left through a back door in the room accompanied by Yakup Pasha and walked down a long corridor that grew darker as they went. They turned a corner and Mehmed stopped in front of a door. Bellini looked down curiously at the light streaming from the gap above the floor. Mehmed looked to Yakup Pasha, who them produced a key from his belt, unlocked the door and stood aside.

Bellini was astonished by what he saw as he entered the small room—a gigantic painting of the Virgin Mary with candles in front of it.

"I—I thought you were a Mohametan," he stammered.

"Of course, praise be to God, I am Muslim." He placed his hand on the engraved hilt of his sword, his face set and sure. "And this is the sword of Islam."

Bellini didn't know what to make of it as Mehmed continued. "But it is the duty of every Muslim to tolerate all the People of the Book. There is even a verse about Mary in our book. This painting is hundreds of years old. If my Christian subjects venerate it, then I, too, want to understand them."

Bellini looked in admiration at the room, itself a small display room. There was a magnificent sword engraved with the double eagle that he reckoned once belonged to a Roman emperor in the city, along with weapons that had been given to the sultan when he assumed the throne.

"The Orient and the Occident belong to God," Mehmed said. "Perspective is also so, Gentile. My miniaturists believe painting only by mathematics is too mechanical. If not, then it is also one of God's arts, as man's pleasure and the many interpretations of art are the manifestation of His name, the Shaper of Beauty, in His worldly servants."

Bellini found himself more comfortable as Mehmed spoke. Only when he returned to Venice, would he realize this was one of the most delightful moments he'd experienced.

"I don't want to disturb you, You're Excellency," one of the viziers said as he walked up, "but they say Ali Bey has entered the city."

after having his men keep an eye on the man for months, Mehmed was delighted to hear word the renowned astronomer Ali Qushji had come. The scholar had set off from Samarkand upon invitation from Mehmed, leaving his own land to live in the queen of cities.

"I'll come a little later," Mehmed said before he turned back to Bellini. "But tell me now, Gentile. Do you understand why the Persian padishah gave himself over to art and science?" Bellini looked curiously back at Mehmed. "Because he realized the only hope to attain immortality lay in these two practices. It's precisely because of this that true power and rule lies not with the sultan, but with the scholars and artists. We pass through this world, but art remains, as does science. I, too, will one day return to the earth, but your painting will remain." He smiled. "Paint well so the people remember me well."

125

A watchman in a tower nudged his fellow guard awake when he heard the pattering of feet growing nearer an hour past midnight. Everything was shrouded in a thick fog.

They couldn't tell at first whether it was an assault and couldn't make anything out no matter how much they squinted through the darkness. One of the watchmen looked up, but there were no stars and the moon was the slightest sliver. The sound of footsteps would be faster if it were an attack, he thought, and these were very slow.

The other watchman then noticed something and peered down from the battlements to check. He hadn't been mistaken. There were thousands of white turbans wrapped around the red caps of the *bashibozuk* irregulars who were slowly advancing. From one end of sight to the other, countless white, muslin rings slowly marched toward the moat.

He jumped for the bell and began ringing it wildly and shouting, "They're coming! We're under attack! They're here!"

Thousands of soldiers took their positions in front of the wall as the sound of the bell broke the silence.

Mehmed looked to Jafer Agha. The janissary agha ignited the signal arrow ready in his hand, aimed and launched it into the sky.

It split through the dark, flew over the thousands of foot soldiers and fell like a shooting star in front of the city walls. With the signal, the foot soldiers broke into a run, sending up clouds of dust into the fog and blocking all sight.

"Archers, to your positions!" Theophilos bellowed.

They immediately took to launching arrows from between the battlements, but couldn't much see who they were aiming at and bewilderedly shot out at the wide field stretching out from the walls.

The foot soldiers couldn't see anything above them either as they ran over the field, but heard a buzzing draw nearer. An arrow pierced one's chest. Another plunged into a Hungarian soldier's cheek and other struck a soldier's hand clutching an ax. Hundreds of soldiers fell in the darkness. Another buzz came and an arrow lodged into an adventurer who had come from a village near far-off Malatya. He was pleased when he saw the arrow sticking out from his shoulder—he thought he narrowly escaped a quick death and let out a deep breath to push forward when another arrow lodged into his heart, leaving him lifeless on the ground. Hundreds of slaughtered irregular soldiers remained were trampled under the feet of those following behind.

Constantine stood in a tower with his aides as he looked out on the unfolding scene and tried to figure out which gate the attack was targeting. As soon as he could tell, he would send reinforcements to the area, but then Loukas Notaras spoke up, only adding his dismay.

"They're not attacking one point", he said. "They're along the entirety of the land walls."

"Why would they take such a broad line when soldiers are falling in the Lykos Valley where the walls have been so weakened?" Sphrantzes said.

"To keep our soldiers spread out along the walls, that's why!" Notaras said. "I suppose this is his final trick."

Foot soldiers were still running toward the entire length of the more than four miles of land walls. The watchmen in the high towers realized when they got closer that the assault was coming in three main branches, flowing straight to the city like roiling rivers.

One was descending in between the northern-most Gate of Blachernae and the Gate of Charisios, the second in between the Lykos River and the Fifth Military Gate, and the third from there to the Third Military Gate.

The foot soldiers began to flee from the shower of arrows, running over the areas of the moat full of debris and bodies. Those who lost their footing while crossing started to thrash about as they tried to swim in the ice-cold water. A Macedonian who, like many of the soldier, didn't know how to swim, sunk like a stone through the water to the bottom.

A third of the foot soldiers who were now on the moat were now easily visible and the archers on the battlements skewered them effortlessly. They were so crowded together that the Greek, Venetian, Genoese, Wallachian and Hungarian archers didn't even have to aim. It was enough to simply loose arrows down the walls.

"It will be very easy to defeat these inexperienced soldiers," Constantine said.

"It seems to me the sultan is distracting us," Notaras said. "Our soldiers are getting tired."

"You worry for nothing, Loukas," Constantine said. "Just watch and see."

The foot soldiers who made it to the outer walls put up the tall ladders they had brought and tried to make it up. Ladders went up along all of the four miles of walls. The foot soldiers scurried up the ladders, one behind another, ten and twenty to each, but the city's defenders quickly reached over the battlements and tipped them over. The soldiers on the walls had something more lethal waiting for those who had reached close to the battlements or for those whose weight made the ladders too heavy to throw off.

"The cauldrons!" Theophilos yelled.

His soldiers brought the steaming cauldrons and buckets prepared the night before up to the top of the walls. Four soldiers, two in front and two behind, toted a cauldron belching steam slung from a poll to the edge of the battlements. They labored the cauldron up and tipped it over, spilling boiling oil over the heads of the soldiers trying to scale the walls. Everyone on the ladders fell to the ground with bloodcurdling screams. The oil scalded everywhere it touched, melting flesh as it streamed over them and sometimes sizzling to the bone. It fell on the foot soldiers on the ground, flowing over their heads, shoulders, arms and chests, crackling and burning as it went, leaving behind severe burns. The defenders on the wall emptied the cauldrons and bucket of all sizes over the ladders, frightening those who managed to evade it so much that they fled.

The heavy stones the defenders dropped drove off the foot soldiers still trying to make their way up.

A fierce-eyed soldier from Moldavia decided to turn back to the assault, but his decision soon crumbled, as he found himself under a shower of burning oil that scalded him tortuously in his tracks. He had thought the assault with this many soldiers would be much swifter work. He turned face and retreated back through the oncoming assault along with some units of irregulars who had been of the same mind, making his way back across the moat. Once there, however, he saw something that made it abundantly clear there was no other choice but to fight.

The assault commanders in the field across from the moat were spinning their scimitars like a whirlwind, making it known they would cut down anyone who fled. The soldier, like the others, caught the commander's eye, realized this was no ruse and turned on his heels back to the walls. He took hold of a ladder to help reposition it. A second group of soldiers came with more cauldrons of boiling oil and stones and took their place atop the battements, giving no respite. Foot soldiers had made it to the top of the ladders and become targets for the swords of the Latin and Greek defenders they met. Those who set foot on the ramparts managed to cleave some heads with their axes.

One soldier wielding a spiked mace attacked a Greek defender with such speed that he had trouble pulling his mace back out of the man's skull and was run through by another defender from behind. A Hungarian with a mace flung it over his head and took down defenders in twos and threes. The foot soldiers managed to slice their way forward a few yards, but with the ladders behind them tipped over and the shower of boiling oil and stones, the city's soldiers made short work of them in a slaughter.

"I told you," Constantine said with a chuckle. "These marauders can't harm us in the least."

The assault went on for two hours before the foot soldiers were called back.

Just as the city's soldiers were celebrating the defense, the resounding cries from Karaja Pasha and Ishak Pasha resounded for attack. The cavalry then spurred their horses forward along the three main prongs of attack.

Mehmed had been able to get his cannons in place close to the walls throughout the night as the foot soldiers wore down the defenses. With the sign from Mehmed, the gunners ignited the touchholes and turned with their ears covered. The explosions out of the muzzles illuminated the night like flashes of lightning bolts, the night falling back to darkness in between. The defenders on the ramparts couldn't tell if the mass of soldiers appearing before the walls that they saw in the flashes of light were real or only an illusion. The city's bells were tolling, calling all the city's soldiers and people to the walls.

Cannon balls started to careen into the land walls with more force than ever, inflicting mighty impacts from north to south.

"They're attacking again," Sphrantzes said as he grew more trepidatious.

"They've sent in the cavalry," said Notaras. "They're like incessant waves pounding the shore."

Constantine was silent.

Having gotten his signal from the sound of cannon fire, Zaganos Pasha prepared his men on a sliver of coast after crossing the Golden Horn from the opposite shore and ordered them to attack. Cannon fire pounded the sea walls from across the narrowest part of the Golden Horn as the soldiers climbed up.

The sea commander Hamza Bey, having taken Baltaoghlu Süleyman's place, had been waiting in the darkness at the mouth of the Bosporus as Mehmed has ordered. With the attack on the Golden Horn, he hauled anchor and brought his ships around the Acropolis Point and toward the sea walls along the Marmara coast. The snarling, stone lions in front of the walls were there to meet Hamza Bey's men, as they had all the uninvited for centuries.

The ships in the Golden Horn lifted anchor to beset the walls rising from the water. Trevisiano and Diedo noticed their movements and brought their large galleys into battle position.

The cavalry jumped off their horses at the base of the walls and quickly started ascending the ladders. Boiling oil again came pouring down, but unlike the foot soldiers, their helmets and shields lent them some protection. Like a line of hundreds of tortoise shells one after another, the cavalry climbed the ladders as the boiling oil flowed off their shields.

"The stones!" Giustiniano yelled out.

The defenders began dropping stones where the oil was being poured. The Greek, Venetian and Genoese soldiers rained them down on the coming cavalrymen and drove them to the ground. The stones thudded against their shields, with some striking the ladders and splintering them to pieces. The cavalrymen who had made it to the ramparts had inflicted more casualties than the foot soldiers before them, but with the broken flow of reinforcements, the course of the battle was little changed.

Then the constant cannon fire in between the Fifth Military Gate and the Gate of Charisios opened two breaches.

The cavalrymen called out to each other to head for the cracks in the walls.

They threw themselves through the breaches while the defenders where still stunned. They collided with the soldiers coming out to meet them in close quarter combat. The cavalrymen hurtled through and over the outer wall, striking down all who came before them in front of the inner walls. There were nearly three hundred of them in the terrace.

Giustiniani, Theophilos, and Antonio and Troilo Bocchiardo quickly amassed their men in front of the breaches. The knights formed a wall of steel as archers in the towers above launched showers of arrows on the heaving mass of cavalrymen.

The defenders still on the wall on both sides of the breach continued to pour boiling oil on the cavalrymen below as it dawned on them that the city had yet another unexpected weapon.

In addition to oil, the defenders also poured a mixture of black powder and pitch onto the Ottomans and then immediately shot flaming arrows as soon as it stuck to them. The field beyond the breach erupted in a roiling inferno amid their screams and wails. Giustiniani ordered his men and the other knights back from the flames.

"Now maybe the smell of his roasting soldiers will demoralize the sultan," Constantine said with a grin.

The Greek and Latin soldiers quickly surrounded the three hundred Ottomans who had made it through the breaches and who were now caught with no route for escape. The city's defenders tightened around them and slaughtered them, running them through with swords and spears, and breaking their bodies with maces.

Contarini and Kantakouzenos at the southern walls, Giustiniani and Theophilos at the Lykos Valley, and Antonio and Troili Bocchiardo to the north used the same tactic against the coming cavalry, repelling them with boiling oil, stones and inextinguishable Greek fire. The corpses of Ottoman foot soldiers and cavalrymen lay piled up outside the walls like pyramids.

The defenders along the walls broke out in cheers of victory as the cavalry began to retreat.

126

"We've done it, we've done it!" a soldier cried out as the cavalry fell back.

"It's finally over!" Contarini yelled.

"They're running away!" another shouted as he and his fellow soldiers held their fists in the air and congratulated each other.

Notaras, however, had a feeling Mehmed wouldn't have given up so many men for nothing.

Al-Khamsa stamped his hooves back and forth and side to side as if he were standing on glowing coals due to the excitement of the sultan on his back.

"My pashas, aghas and brothers," Mehmed shouted out to the janissary regiments lined up in front of him, "no one before us has surmounted these towering walls. This grand city has never opened to anybody!" He steered Al-Khamsa back and forth in front of the janissaries as he spoke. "The great Osman sent his best ships here, but it was for naught! Caliph Muawiyah sent his son Yazid here, who then returned with empty hands! Harun al-Rashid—the greatest of the Abbasid caliphs—even agreed to tribute!" All the janissaries stood silent as they looked upon Mehmed. "Not the Huns, not the Slavs and not the Avars—no one has passed over these walls!"

He halted his horse in front of the middle of the lines of janissaries. "How will we be victorious, then? How will we take this pearl of a city?"

The janissaries looked at each other and then back at Mehmed. A smirk spread over Halil Pasha's face as he started to reckon this was the beginning of the retreat.

"We will take it because we do not go to pass over the walls, but to die at the foot of them! We run not to victory, but to death, to dirt! My brothers—man is buried in the earth he was created from. Today, our absence from home ends. We are going home!"

The janissaries raised a sky-splitting cry of *Ya Allah.* Al-Khamsa reared back as the sultan drew his sword and turned to the walls of Constantinople. He broke into a gallop with a shout, "Attack!"

The city's soldiers along the ramparts heard the deafening beat of davul drums. Their faces dropped as they looked out over the ramparts and realized they had celebrated too soon. As dawn began to break, Mehmed charged forward, the janissary aghas to his sides and the red wave of his army spreading out from him. Hundreds of standards rose above their heads and forked, tasseled flags rippled in the wind from the Marmara coast to the north extreme of the walls.

The bells of the city's hundreds of churches started to toll frantically.

The din of the *mehter* davuls resounded with ear-splitting power rhythm in a signal that the actual assault was now beginning.

Mehmed reached the moat and stopped with a regiment of a thousand archers. Marco Barbari de Piero of the Knights Hospitaller and his best warriors emerged from behind the breach and marched toward the sultan.

Iskender the Woodsman pulled his bow from his quiver. His muscled strained as he strung up his bow in one quick motion and looked out to catch sight of the Genoese commander as the sultan had instructed.

Three thousand janissaries continued to march toward the walls.

The rain started to fall harder and the field was turning to a mire as they struggled through the mud. Iskender strained his way across the moat, stepping on corpses, earth, rubble and anything else that came underfoot. Hasan took hold of a loophole in the breastwork and pulled himself out of the moat. Abdullah of Bosnia heard the whisper of coming arrows and ducked, crossing back and forth as he ran to the breach.

There was now a line of crimson stretching along the four miles of walls. Oxen and men slowly hauled the wheeled, wooden siege towers toward the moat. The tunnelers were also working to get above ground in many places.

Hamza Bey brought his gunships broadside the walls above the Marmara coast and ordered to open fire. Cannon muzzles emerged from the gun ports one by one and fired in succession. Another group of galleys with dozens of siege ladders tried to get as close to the walls as possible.

On the other side of the sea chain, a fleet of sixty smaller ships surrounded Trevisiano and Diedo's large galleys and tried to hinder their movement.

"We're under attack on all sides," Notaras said. "They're coming from land and sea, north and south. There are nearly no soldiers left in their encampment. This is their final stand."

"You Excellency," Sphrantzes said, "it's time you went to a more secure place inside the city."

The resounding booms of cannon shot against the walls shook the tower where the stood.

Constantine looked hopelessly from Sphrantzes to Notaras and back.

Waiting at the north of the Golden Horn, Zaganos Pasha called for the remaining soldiers under his command to attack and charged forward with them.

Iskender and the other janissaries flung the ladders back against the walls and flew up and onto the battlements before the defenders had a chance to get the cauldrons of boiling oil. A soldier leading two others swung his sword at Iskender's head, but he dropped down and deflected the blow. He ran through the men to the right and left before he raised back up, and as he did, he planted a foot against the front soldier and pushed him over the battlements to the mud below.

A mass of janissaries had made it to the ramparts by then. Iskender went left as another group went right and set to battle with the Greek defenders of the city. Then arrows bore down on the janissaries—from where was uncertain—and they were cut in their speed. There was a unit of archers hidden in a round tower twenty yards to the south. Their arrows gave no respite. They drew their bows with such fury they sometimes hit their own men on the ramparts teeming with soldiers of all kinds, and the speed of the janissaries made them hard to mark. Iskender saw the man commanding the archers and knew it was his destiny to be here this day. There stood Theophilos atop a tower only twenty yards away.

Hasan and the rest of his regiment attacked the breach at the Fifth Military Gate. He reaped through the Greek soldiers as they trod over the bodies who had come before him. No matter how many souls he parted from their bodies, though, more units came from behind them. There was no way to enter the narrow breach due to the showers of arrows, stones and boiling oil from overhead. Superior moral was still with the Constantinopolitan soldiers as the Ottomans fell left and right. Hasan lifted his head for a moment amid the confusion of battle and looked up at a tall tower with a flag emblazoned with the double-headed eagle and a many-pointed star fluttering above its main door. Mullah Fenari flashed in his mind and he knew what he had to do.

Mehmed, Jafer Agha and a janissary regiment were in a clash of swords with the knights surrounding them.

Karaja Pasha and more janissaries had hurriedly run to the breach by the Gate of Charisios and were breast to breast with the defenders flowing out against them. Overseeing the defense of the gate, Antonio and Troilo Bocchiardo acted as soon as they saw Karaja Pasha.

"That's the Turk who killed our brother, isn't it?" Troilo said.

"The very one!" Antonio snarled.

The defense of the city had fallen by the wayside for them and their sole mission was now to kill the Ottoman commander at all costs. Antonio gripped his ever-present mace. Its spiked head gave no quarter to those it met. A knight for decades, Antonio, clad in thick armor and carrying a massive shield, trusted he could easily rout any mostly unarmored army. He swung his mace furiously above his head and pounded it into the mud before he set off for Karaja Pasha. He swung wildly, knocking everyone out of his way, friend and foe alike, sending them bloody and battered into the muck.

Abdullah of Bosnia was in a heated battle with a knight who wore a white tunic with a red cross over his full armor outside the Fifth Military Gate. The knight's sword was twice as long as Abdullah's and nearly as broad as a man's hand. Despite its size, the armored knight wielded it with a deftness Abdullah had never seen before. He swung it again at Abdullah's face.

One of Hamza Bey's ships had run close to the walls on the Marmara coast.

"The ladders, the ladders!" he shouted.

The crew landed five siege ladders against the walls and the soldiers started to hastily make their way up. Then fourteen more galleys drew alongside the walls and threw up another hundred ladders. Some of the ships couldn't get close to the rocky shore, so the soldiers jumped onto the boulders jutting out and threw themselves into the sea to get to the base of the walls onshore.

Iskender was felling Constantinopolitan soldiers one by one with his sword, fists and elbows. Some he stomped down before they could attack. He ducked down as he proceeded, weaving back and forth to evade the arrows. He grabbed a Greek soldier as he neared his mark and used him as a shield as he made his way to the tower with fellow janissaries from his regiment behind him. He rushed through the door of the tower and found Theophilos standing there before him.

Theophilos looked at the young janissary and paused for a moment with surprise washing over his face. He stiffened as he recognized the young man by his eyes. Iskender was the last person he expected, or hoped, to see.

He gathered himself and flashed a wry smile. "I know you," he said. "I even remember your name—Alexandros. Let's see if your blood is as sweet as your sister's."

They started to circle each other in the round interior of the tower, like two wildcats weighing the other up for a fight.

"I've waited many long years for this moment," Iskender said. He lifted his sword above his head and charged.

Theophilos jumped to the side and neatly tumbled back to his feet. He swung at Iskender, who was finding his feet after falling forward from the force of his attack. He leapt to the side, but Theophilos' blade caught his left arm and sunk in nearly to the bone. He again found his footing and took guard. Theophilos took his broadsword in both hands, stepped forward and swung across at Iskender's belly.

"You're still a wretched peasant boy, Alexandros," Theophilos said.

Antonio reached Karaja Pasha and twirled his long-handled mace as he made his way, crushing the heads of everyone nearby, both attackers and fellow defenders. Troilo and the other knights were busy fending off the janissaries from Antonio. He heaved his mace down at Karaja Pasha's head. Karaja Pasha raised his shield, but with the force of the blow, found himself in the mud. He jumped back to his feet and prepared himself for battle with the two brothers standing opposite him. Troilo's eyes burned with vengeance, blinded by rage. He spun his sword as we walked toward Karaja Pasha. He flashed his blade out at Karaja Pasha, but received just as quick an answer. Karaja Pasha rolled to the ground and swung at Troilo's legs, splitting his armor and hitting bone. He shuffled back and saw the flash of Antonio's mace as he righted himself. He lifted his shield, but it was too late and he fell to the field at Troilo's feet. Despite the deep gash in his leg, Troilo lifted his sword, its tip pointing down, and swiftly stabbed down to the ground.

Iskender the Woodsman recognized Giustiniani the Genoese knight, whose name he had heard before, from the boar on the man's crest. His group of janissaries was surrounded by defenders, butchering the soldiers the found themselves up against. Iskender, however, skirted along the moat on the trace of the commander of the defenses, as the sultan had ordered. He saw nothing else among the thousands of soldiers on the battlefield. He spied the Genoese knight from a hundred yards away, and despite the distance, the man appeared terrifically monstrous. He disappeared from view and the field again was empty in his eyes. Just as Yildirimli Baba had said—even if there is a tremendous horde around the target, it is as desolate and empty as a desert to an archer. It's enough to only spy the target. He climbed up a mound where he was to be able to see over the battle. A Greek soldier hurling spears noticed the janissary intently peering out the other way and, without waiting to breath, launched a shaft at him. It plunged just behind Iskender the Woodsman's liver and lodged next to his spine.

Orhan and the Catalan defenders under his command were pouring boiling oil over the soldiers on the ladders extending up from Hamza Bey's galleys. Already unstable as they bounced along with the ships, the soldiers struggled to keep hold and fell screaming onto the boulders below. The tumbling janissaries' heads cracked open and their backs splintered as they hit the rocks the stone lions in front of the walls oversaw.

The archers next to Orhan ignited the mixture of pitch and

black powder that had been prepared earlier in the city and tossed it over the towering cliff of the walls onto the ships, immediately sending two up in flames.

The galleys under Trevisiano and Diedo's command had already sunk ten Ottoman ships with their cannons. The fleet of small ships around the hulking galleys couldn't harm the Venetian and Genoese commanders in the least.

Messengers continuously ran from the sea walls to report the state of battle to Constantine.

"You see, Loukas? We leave their bedeviling siege towers and their men in ashes. Our knights are besting Mehmed's janissaries. Not a single one has gotten over the walls—not along the Marmara coast or the Holden Horn. They're done for. There's no difference between this assault and the others."

Notaras was silent. It seemed Constantine was right—the red line of janissaries was falling apart and becoming more ineffective as the battle raged on. He had even seen units attacking the sultan's regiment surround the enemy.

Barbari de Piero fought his way to Jafer Agha, who was cutting down knights to all sides. He leveled his sword and plunged it through the janissary agha's chest. Mehmed's top soldier fell from his mount to the mud to the horrified looks of dismay from his soldiers nearby. They lowered their weapons in the disarray only for some to soon drop dead from the defenders' relentless counterattacks.

Hasan picked up the banner as a standard bearer who'd held it fell beside him. He ran for the breach, trodding over stones and bodies and started to climb the wall.

After a laborious mile of pushing and pulling through the mud, five wooden siege towers finally came to the edge of the moat. Janissaries launched arrows at the defenders along the walls as the soldiers on the lower levels tried to fill the moat with earth, stones and rubble. The city's defenders had learned earlier the towers' vulnerability, however, and set their bridges alight with Greek fire, engulfing the towers from top to bottom in flames.

Iskender the Woodsman was unaware of everything around him and was focused on his target. He picked up his bow from the pools of blood at his feet. He caught sight of Giustiniani behind the breach, fitted an arrow to the string and drew it back. He held his breath, took aim, remembered what Yildirimli Baba had whispered in his ear the day he received his *ijazah* certificate, and let go. He collapsed to the blood-stained mud as the arrow sped through the air.

You don't shoot—God does.

127

"Lord Christ, save us!"

"Mother Mary, drive off these heathens!"

Cardinal Isidore and Gregorios Mammas led a procession of the people carrying an icon of the Virgin Mary through the city's streets. They were now passing the *Milion* in the heart of the city. All the city folk had been praying day and night as the sound of cannon fire against the walls and battle resounded over them. The days of pouring rain was making the going difficult as they carried the icon on their shoulders. The streets were slogged with mud and nearly unwalkable.

The people had always believed the Virgin Mary, in whose glory they carried the icon, would be their salvation when earthquakes struck the city, in times of famine and of war, and throughout any other catastrophe.

One of the elderly men holding up the icon slipped in the mud as the procession passed by the Forum of Constantine, and the fifteen-foot icon fell to the ground to the thunderstruck looks of the people.

"Lord in heaven!" Gregorios said. "Nothing like this has ever happened before!" The men stooped down and lifted the icon back onto their shoulders. "Forgive us, Mother Mary!" Gregorios cried. "Drive off these heathens!"

"Amen!" the procession responded in unison as they continued in prayer down the road.

They approached the Forum of Theodosius—built by the same emperor who built the city walls centuries ago—and again, the icon fell with the men holding it into the mud. The procession erupted in cries of horror.

"Have mercy, Lord Christ!"

"What does it mean?"

"Will the Virgin no longer deliver us?"

"I say we place it back to Hagia Sophia at once," a woman at the back of the procession said. "The streets aren't safe for us!"

"Yes, yes," said the woman at her side. "The angels will protect us there. We have to go now."

The men again lifted the icon out of the mud as part of the procession fled for the Church of Hagia Sophia. The whole icon, particularly the Virgin Mary's face, was now thickly caked with mud.

After only a couple dozen more steps, and despite their extreme care, the towering icon again fell to the street.

"Mother Mary has abandoned us!" a man cried.

"This can't be!"

Cardinal Isidore and Patriarch Gregorios looked worriedly at each other.

A strange blush fell over the sky.

One of the children pointed up. "Look, look! It's the crescent of the Turks!"

The people looked up aghast as they saw the crescent moon in the sharp curve of a scimitar in the strangely rubicund sky.

"The Lord God no longer resides in this city," Gregorios said, having lost all hope.

The people abandoned the icon in the mud and fled to Hagia Sophia and the other grand churches nearby.

128

Giovanni Giustiniani fell to the ground as an arrow struck him out of nowhere. It pierced his chest armor, its tip jutting out from the steel plates over his back. The knights around him didn't know what to do. They were soon joined by other soldiers flocking to the commander sprawled out on the ground. Having received the same blow just a little earlier and now with the enemy commander dead, the janissaries set upon the soldiers again.

As word spread of Giustiniani's death, Hasan ran along the ramparts to the tower where the imperial flag of Constantinople was flying. He cut off the arm of a Constantinopolitan soldier who stood to counter him and sent another one's head tumbling, but had lost his sword as he grappled with two knights. He set off the rest of the way unarmed as he swung out his fists and elbows as he ran. No one could stop his massive bulk.

He finally came to the city's flag. He beat down the two soldiers there, snatched the flag by its wooden pole, snapped it in half and threw it over the wall. He took the standard and wedged it in between two stones of the thousand-year-old tower. He spotted Mehmed atop Al-Khamsa in the distance and raised a fist as if asking the sultan to bear witness.

Hasan fell to the ground as the green flag emblazoned with a white crescent whipped in the wind. There were no less than forty arrows in his back.

Mehmed took off the last of the knights' heads with his sword, its hilt inlaid mother of pearl, where Jafer Agha—whom he had always been with since childhood—had been killed. He looked up and saw the flapping crescent atop the ramparts.

"Come now, my lions!" he shouted to the nearby soldiers. "Gird your fervor—surrender is near!"

His soldiers pulled together and began to force the defenders back.

Karaja Pasha saw the fluttering crescent on the walls just as Troilo's sword was about to fall and extinguish his life. With great fire, he whipped his shield up and deflected the blow. He stood up as Troilo saw the flag and his attention wavered. Karaja Pasha's sword was already in his belly once he snapped his head back. Antonio circled around Karaja Pasha with his mace in one hand and a shield in the other. He then spun the mace over his head and at Karaja Pasha, who met the blow with his shield and swung his sword up at Antonio's belly. Antonio fended it off with his shield, stepped forward and headbutted Karaja Pasha in the face. The sharp protrusions of his helmet opened a gash over Karaja Pasha's brow. Antonio hefted his mace as Karaja Pasha's eyes darkened. The Ottoman commander managed to recover, but had dropped his shield. Emboldened, Antonio came flying at him even faster. Karaja Pasha barely managed to evade the blows, then brought up his blade and caught the mace by one of its spikes. He pulled with all the strength he could gather and pulled Antonio forward as the knight held on firmly. Karaja Pasha leveled his sword and plunged it through the mail in between Antonio's helmet and armor into his throat. His men then sped forward emboldened.

The helmet of the knight opposite Abdullah looked to him to be an overturned bucket. The only difference were the narrow slits for the eyes and nose in the shape of Saint Anthony's cross and the breathing holes. With deep gashes to his arms and legs, Abdullah knew, though, that he shouldn't make light of the knight.

The knight's movements were hindered by his fifty pounds of armor. He wasn't agile, but he wielded his sword, thick and heavy like his armor, on the mark. Abdullah was quick and nimble, but his blade did no more than glance off the knight's armor. He also struggled to keep hold of his blade as he fended off the knight's strikes. He remembered what Vahdeddin had said—*this grip will drop no sword or bow. This grip will flash before a knight's face.*

He reckoned the rest would be easy if he could just pierce through the knight's armor once and sink his blade into his flesh, but the knight parried each his attacks. The knight made a swing for him, but Abdullah then brought his calloused hand—trained against marble—down and slapped the top of the knight's helmet. It caved in and spun around, the eye slit off to the side, leaving the knight confused and feeling as though he'd been struck by a maul. Abdullah swung across his body and slipped in the mud as his blade met the knight's armor and lost his balance. The knight trained his sword where the blow had come from and ran Abdullah through. Barbari de Piero removed his helmet as Abdullah collapsed to the muddy field. He burned where he'd last been struck. He fell back behind the wall and removed his loosened breastplate. There was a deep, fatal gash in his belly and he felt the ground slip from under his feet.

Orhan's men disappeared one by one when word reached the ramparts over the Marmara coast that Giovanni Giustiniani had died. The soldiers below aboard Hamza Bey's ships also began to again scale the ladders one after another.

Sparks flew as Iskender and Theophilos' swords clashed. Iskender charged. Theophilos fended off the blading flashing before him and then jumped in between the tower's battlements. Iskender followed and sprung at him, swinging down as Theophilos planted his feet back on the ground just in time to evade the attack. Their swords met, pressed against each other, one leveled at the wall and the other at the ceiling. Theophilos had his sword in both hands as he forced Iskender down. Iskender was pushed back farther the more Theophilos strained against him.

Just a few more steps back and Iskender would be at the edge of the tower over the drop. He grabbed the blade of his sword and pushed back with both hands. Theophilos leaned into him as Iskender resisted. Just when he was about to go over the edge, he reared his head and cracked it into Theophilos' face. Theophilos' vision fell dark for a moment and he stumbled back. His nose was broken. Iskender came at him, brandished his scimitar in a challenge. This time it was Iskender striking again and again as Theophilos reflexively fended off the blows. They came to the edge of the rampart over the drop, both of them teetering back and forth to keep their balance.

Iskender saw an arrow flying for him from a nearby tower. Theophilos saw his opportunity and kicked him to the ground. Iskender dropped his sword over the precipice as he fell. Theophilos jumped on him and set the flat of his blade against Iskender's throat. He pressed down as Iskender tried to push it off his neck. The veins on Theophilos' brow were bulging and his lips strained into a smile as the sword edge slid on Iskender's throat and drew blood.

"You're still just a peasant boy, Alexandros!" he snarled.

He was about to take off Iskender's head when the janissary reached into his belt and stabbed Theophilos in the neck with a dagger.

"I am not Alexandros—I am Iskender!" he shouted as he sent Theophilos falling over the battlements to the muddy field below.

The Constantinopolitan soldiers faltered with Theophilos' death and hundreds of janissaries started to ascend the ladders.

Constantine rushed down when he saw the death of one of his closest and most trusted men.

Orhan looked around desperately from a tower on the walls over the Marmara coast. He took a final look at the crescents of the Ottoman flag unfurl one after another along the city's outer walls, like wildflowers coming to bloom on a hillside. He took a deep breath as he made his way along the ramparts and then jumped to the sea.

Aluvixe Diedo realized something had changed in the city when the ships surrounding his galleys dropped oars and made for shore. Every Ottoman ship was heading for the coast. He went to the stern to see what was happening. Then, an Ottoman sailor who had managed to get aboard came at him with an ax. Diedo jumped to the side as the ax caught his leg.

129

"One, two, three—heave!" Fifty janissaries chanted as they hefted a gigantic battering ram into the wooden gates. They were trying to break through the three main gates in the Lykos Valley while others had set fire to another and were waiting for it to burn through.

The soldiers atop the inner walls didn't know what to do, as many of their commanders had been killed, and those who hadn't had begun to flee. They drew their bows indecisively and were reluctant to continue the fight. Many were ready to drop their arms and surrender. Ottoman flags were fluttering from the towers along the outer walls.

Mehmed ordered a full assault on the inner city once the gates had been opened and sections of wall were torn down. He had gotten word the city's defenders had taken cover in the alleys and side streets and so didn't want to leave anything to chance. All the soldiers in the camp—foot soldiers, cavalry, Muslim and Christian, from Rumelia and Anatolia, and the remaining janissaries flooded into the city.

Less than half a mile from the invasion, Constantine ran in fear down the Mese road with Georgios Sphrantzes, Don Francisco de Toledo and Demetrios Kantakouzenos, flanked by knights, toward the ships in the Golden Horn.

"Your Excellency, you must get rid of your clothes," Sphrantzes said in a panic. "They won't come after you if they think you're an ordinary man."

" That would sully my honor, Georgios. How could I? The city has fallen, but I am still standing. Leave me to fight," Constantine said, his voice trembling, although he didn't much believe what he was saying.

"This is no time for that, Your Excellency. First, we'll spirit you away to Crete, then we'll send word to the Christian realms and knights for relief. After that we'll take back the city from the Turks with a glorious Christian army."

Constantine removed his cloak, his breastplate embossed with the two-headed eagle and his engraved armbands as he ran and threw them to the street. He was left in only his undergarments and boots.

"Your crown, as well, Your Majesty," Sphrantzes said.

Constantine dolefully took the crown from his head, looked at it a final time and tossed it to the ground.

"They've come—there, to the right!" Don Francisco said.

"You keep going. We'll stall them," Kantakouzenos said.

Constantine and Sphrantzes entered a narrow street and kept running.

Ishak Pasha quickly rode over when he saw two knights from atop his horse.

A dozen of his men surrounded the knights.

"Throw down your weapons," Ishak Pasha said. "There is nothing you can do any more."

Don Francisco and Kantakouzenos were hesitant, but they saw they had no other choice. They slowly knelt down and placed their swords on the street.

Constantine lost Sphrantzes in the confusion and panic as they ran through the side streets. The city folk were running in every direction in search of places to hide, believing the Ottomans would slaughter them.

He reached the Column of Constantine—erected by the city's founder—and hastened his pace, knowing the Golden Horn wasn't far off. He felt a cold sting in his back as a spear sunk into his body.

Twenty yards behind him, an Arab lifted his fist with a cry of *Allahu Akbar—God is Great.* "I bring you greetings from Abu Ayyub al-Ansari!"

He had recognized Constantine as the emperor from the eagles on his boots.

Constantine collapsed to the ground next to the towering Column of Constantine with the spear still rising from his back.

130

Among the first units to enter the city, Iskender stopped when he passed through the gate. The rain was pouring. He closed his eyes and took in the city's air with deep breaths for minutes under the falling rain. Then he opened his eyes as if he'd been reborn. He slowly turned his head and looked around. He beheld the trees of his city, the columns, churches, aqueducts, the houses of all sizes and the palaces as if reuniting with his beloved after years of separation.

He was now only a short run away from his true beloved, though—his childhood sweetheart. Mariam was the only memory he held dearly from his past and his only reason to live. He had waited for years, night and day, to see her again.

He set off running with his sword in hand. He sped up the Mese road and veered off into the side streets. He knew them as if he had only left the day before. He passed through the neighborhoods where had been up to all kinds of mischief as a peasant boy with a soiled face and hands, bare feet and a hungry belly.

The people fled in terror when they saw him, a formidable janissary, knowing the city had been seized, and didn't dare cross before him.

He waded through the fields he had tilled so many years ago and remembered the moments he and Mariam had run through them hand in hand, each one passing before his eyes. The day they met in the palace garden, when he gave her the coral necklace, their furtive climb of the Maiden's Tower and when they met at the *Milion* were all vivid in his mind.

He finally reached the neighborhood where Mariam's family lived when he had fled. He stepped to the door, stopped, and without any further thinking, thrust his shoulder into it.

The door cracked open and he saw her—Mariam, standing there.

He looked into her eyes—she was terrified. Her eyes the color of the sea and her golden hair were just as he remembered. Looking on Mariam was like setting eyes on the rising sun.

Mariam looked at the Ottoman soldier standing in her doorway and saw the boy from long ago behind his mustache. She saw the red coral necklace around his neck. She wanted to say his name but her mouth wouldn't move. She stood staring at his white felt hat, the scimitar in his hand and the red sash around his waist. Thoughts raced through her head—was this not her childhood love she'd waited nights, weeks, months and years for, her first and only love, now there across from her?

Iskender looked down to the baby whose mother was holding tight with dread. The baby was sleeping peacefully despite the tremendous clamor on the streets. Then he felt someone appear at his side. He slowly turned his head and saw the boy he had saved on the walls so many years ago, now grown. Ioannes also recognized his old friend who had rescued him from death so many times.

Iskender felt the thousand years of Constantinople's history crash down on top of him. He felt in his spirit the pain of the hundreds of thousands of Constantinopolitans in that moment and could barely keep his knees from buckling.

He looked on Mariam again before he stepped back. She saw the string of coral still around his neck. He shut the door and turned from the house.

"Alexis!" Marian cried out behind him. She left the baby with Ioannes and ran after him. Iskender turned around. They ran for each other and met in an embrace.

The tears streaming down their cheeks mixed with rain drops.

"I thought you were dead," Mariam said. She cried as she spoke, struggling to tell him of all the stories over the many years as fast as possible. "They killed your entire family after you left. I waited for weeks, and then months and years. I had to get married, I had no choice. I married Ioannes to always be reminded of you."

"I understand," Iskender said as he looked into her eyes. "You don't have to explain anything. I've also thought of you for years. I dreamt of this moment, of seeing you, every night."

Ioannes appeared at the door with the baby.

Iskender put his hand on Mariam's shoulder. "The Turks call this destiny. It can't be any other way. Go now, your baby and husband are waiting for you. Go and shut the door tight. It will take time for calm to return."

He took off running under the rain. His knees went out as he turned the corner and he broke out in sobs. He wailed to the heavens and then fell to his hands in the mud.

The people of the neighborhood couldn't make sense of who this janissary was or why he was heaving wretched tears in the street.

131

"Mehmed the Conqueror!" the soldiers amassed between the walls chanted amid cheers for the young sultan walking through them.

Mehmed entered the procession at the Gate of Charisios where the city's main Mese thoroughfare began. To his left and right were Zaganos Pasha and Yakup Pasha with his other viziers, the janissary aghas, Karaca Pasha and Ishak Pasha. Following behind were his teachers—Akshamsaddin, Mullah Gürani and Mullah Hüsrev.

Standard bearers hoisting banners of all colors flying the crescent led the procession behind the sultan, with archers beside them, followed by palace officials and soldiers. His imperial guards flanked the length of the procession. Mehmed looked out and saw the city's buildings behind the waving crescent flags of green and crimson. Beyond, he saw the imperial star and decided this would be the symbol of his empire—the crescent of Islam and the star of Rome together, the center of east and west.

Whether from the hardships the commanders put them under over the past two months or not knowing what else to do or what the sultan would want, some of the people of the city came to the procession to bow before the young conqueror. One man thought an old man in the middle of the procession in a white turban and white robe was the sultan. He reckoned none other than this wise-looking man could attain such a success.

Akshamsaddin smiled at the people who came to his horse and pointed in front of him. "No, no, not me—he is the sultan," he said motioning to Mehmed.

The people looked surprised at the young sultan and ran to his side. Akshamsaddin looked to Mullah Gürani and Mullah Hüsrev at his sides. None of them couldn't stifle their laughter.

"I am the sultan," Mehmed said to them in Greek with a smile, "but still, you went to the right man first."

The procession stopped as it passed the Blachernae Palace. Mehmed dismounted Al-Khamsa. He bent down, took a pinch of earth and sprinkled it on the muslin of his turban.

"Victory!" he cried.

When the victory of God has come and the conquest—then exalt your Lord with praise and ask forgiveness of Him.

"Why did he do that?" one of the foot soldiers asked another, although he was just as bewildered.

"So as not to succumb to the grandiosity of the self," Mullah Lütfi said from behind them. "We came from earth and so too shall we to it return. Victory belongs to God alone."

Then a knight who had shed his armor and mixed in with the crowd of city folk thought he found the chance he'd been waiting for and charged the procession with a dagger in hand. He broke through the imperial guards caught unaware and ran for Mehmed with his dagger trained on his neck.

Mehmed reached out and grabbed the knight's arm with the dagger only a hair's breadth from his neck. He twisted it around, elbowed the man in the face and snatched the dagger as the would-be assassin fell to the street. Blood flowed from the man's mouth from where his teeth were smashed out. Mehmed threw the dagger to the ground as the imperial guards carried the man off.

They press of people taking refuge in the Church of Hagia Sophia were trembling with fear. As during services, the upper galleries were full of women and the men filled the floor below.

"Don't fear. The enemy will come as far as this grand church and then an angel of God will descend and drive them from the city," one of the priests said again, as he had been for hours. He was speaking to an elderly man, although it seemed he was most afraid.

"Yes, it's true," another said. "This is a prophesy foretold for centuries. This city cannot fall to a heathen invasion."

"The angels will save us!"

Every priest was trying to calm the crowd, but the people's fear and confused cries continued unabated. It was as if Armageddon had arrived. Men had forgotten their wives and the women their children as they thought of the tortures the sultan would inflict on them. The Latins had imprisoned women and children in the city two hundred years earlier, and the stories of them bound together one behind the other in a train of spoils as they were boarded onto ships flashed through their minds, among many other tales of horror. If Christians had left no stone standing, they thought, who knew what Muslims would do.

A dozen priests were huddled in the recesses of the church only they knew—chambers in the dome and roof, and the cisterns below ground—praying the catastrophe would pass them by.

Mehmed looked up at the Church of the Holy Apostles, the Valens Aqueduct, the Forum of Theodosius and the Column of Constantine of the city's founder as the procession continued along the Mese road. He ordered a janissary agha to place his men around them to stave off any looting by the irregulars.

He dismounted in front of Hagia Sophia and stood for a moment as he looked up at its magnificent dome before he entered accompanied by his imperial guards. He walked through the front courtyard and stopped before the large bronze door the janissaries had been trying to open for hours.

"What are you doing?" he yelled at a foot soldier trying to pry off a gem-encrusted cross from the wall just as it fell.

"I'm taking what's mine by the right of God," the soldier said assuredly.

Mehmed drew his sword and smashed the man's face in with the hilt. "God does not command you to despoil!"

He knelt down and picked up the cross.

The fearful crowd in the church at first thought an angel had come when the large doors to the church slowly opened and sunlight streamed in. As they got closer, though, they saw the shadow of the sultan in the doorway emerge into the light.

Mehmed craned his head back and looked up at the dome. He gazed at the mosaic of Jesus at the top, as if suspended in air, surrounded by golden tiles. Its splendor and brilliance reminded him of a single verse—*God is the light of the heavens and earth.*

Four priests then ran and fell to their knees before him.

"Forgive us!"

"Have mercy on us!"

"Stand up," Mehmed said.

He saw an older man waiting and watching him carefully and in silence from behind them. He reckoned the man was different from the others and approached him. He handed the cross to Gennadios Scholarios and turned to the people.

"No harm will come to you or your property. Now go to your homes and see to your work."

The men, women, elderly and children stared in bewilderment at each other. Everyone embraced and held who they found next to them in relief.

A young man raised his fist in the air and cried out, "Long live the Turk, the emperor!" Some others then followed in kind.

Mehmed turned back to Scholarios and the priests around him. "I will choose from a among you a new leader of your faith. The patriarch will have all the rights he had before and the Christians of the city will continue to be able to worship freely. You will celebrate Easter and the other Christian holy days as you always have.

"This glorious church, however, is now mine and I shall leave another one of your large churches to you as your center.

"Now go and tell your people to get back to work and return to their homes. Tell them their lives and property are safe. My commanders will meet with you in a few days and then tell me of your troubles."

The priests were speechless. They bowed and tried to kiss Mehmed's hand and robes, but he stopped them. "Theologians do not bow before an emperor or anyone else."

Scholarios looked at Mehmed with a smile and a slight bow of his head.

Mehmed turned to Zaganos Pasha and pointed to the paintings and mosaics on the walls. "Have these idolatrous images painted over, but don't harm them. Have the position of the qibla determined and have a mihrab made to match the space without damaging the walls or floors."

As he would for the city's Christians, Mehmed would he choose the chief rabbi for the city's Jews and allow them to continue worship in their synagogues.

Mehmed sat on the throne of Constantinople in the Blachernae Palace. Zaganos Pasha was at his side. The Genoese *podestà* of Galata handed him the key to the quarter. Mehmed had ordered all the walls around Galata to be torn down at once and all weapons be handed over. In exchange, the Genoese residents there could continue to live as they had had before. Mehmed was surprised, though, when the *podestà* told him some of the people had fled on ships.

"Did they run from me?" he asked.

He ordered Zaganos Pasha to have the town criers announce as soon as possible that no arm would come to the residents of the city.

"Send letters to those who have already left the city. Their houses and land will be under my care until they return. I will return their properties if they return and, if not, I will give them to my soldiers for their service in taking the city."

Two janissaries hauled a prisoner before the sultan as the *podestà* was leaving the palace. He fell to his knees with his hands and feet bound in chains when he came to the sultan.

"Megaduke Loukas Notaras," one of the janissaries said.

"Look at the state of this palace," Mehmed said to Constantine's chief minister.

Abutting the city walls, the palace had been hit by cannons throughout the weeks of the siege. The magnificence of the imperial palace had been reduced to cracked walls, collapsed columns and piles of debris and marble—in ruins, like much of the city.

"Both we and you lost many men," he said. "I have always heard you are a smart man—a man of the palace not quick to anger or who falls prey to incitement, who rejects tyranny and knows the path of good sense over prejudice. Please tell me. Why did you put up so much resistance to the siege? The lives of many men were in your hands to save."

Notaras looked up in a wretched state from his knees. "We believed throughout that you would turn back."

"Did you not see the great number of my soldiers from the walls and towers? You can see for miles from there. And did you not see my massive cannons, my war machines and my fleet?"

"We thought you would turn back because there were constant messages from your camp to the emperor. They said each time that we should bear out a little longer and that you would give up soon."

Zaganos Pasha and Yakup Pasha looked to each other. Ishak Pasha and Karaja Pasha wondered if what they had just heard was really true.

Mehmed was unsurprised, as if he had expected it. "Who did you get these messages from? Who was your informant among us?"

Without a word, Notaras turned his head to Halil Pasha at the sultan's side. "He was to provoke the soldiers when you retreated, overthrow you and replace you with Orhan."

"Is the sultan going to believe a Greek man's ramblings as he tries to save his own life, or the words of his grand vizier?" Halil Pasha growled. "This man doesn't know what he's saying for fear of death."

He then stepped forward and drew his dagger from his waist. He had to get Notaras to stop talking and began to walk to him. Mehmed signaled his imperial guards just as Halil Pasha was about to stab Notaras. In an instant, he had a dozen swords trained at his throat.

He looked first to the guards and then to Mehmed, his eyes full of dread. "I am a Chandarli. Three of my forbearers have been grand viziers for the House of Osman. Nobody could have established this realm without the Chandarli family. We manage the realm and these soldiers are my soldiers!"

The imperial guards looked at Halil Pasha unperturbed. If it had been no more than one day earlier, this man could have turned the palace over with one word.

Mehmed rose to his feet and walked to Halil Pasha.

"Order comes not by sedition, but by the hand of a strong ruler. The realm is ruled by monolithic power, not secret plans." He pulled a piece of paper from his pocket and showed to Halil Pasha. "I knew of your scheme since the day I took the throne. My spy Burhan among the Greeks didn't sacrifice his life for nothing." He felt a pang of grief when he mentioned his childhood friend. "I am Sultan Mehmed the Conqueror, son of Murad. I am sultan of the House of Osman, padishah of the east and caesar of the west." He raised his finger to Halil Pasha. "This is a traitor. Cut off his head and distribute his wealth and property among the soldiers. Carry out his punishment without delay!"

As Halil Pasha, Loukas Notaras, and the patricians and leaders of the city and Galata were being beheaded in the towers of the Golden Gate, six priests filled in the grave they had secretly dug in the grounds of the Church of Hagia Sophia. Mehmed had ordered his men to find Constantine's body and the priests were fulfilling his command to secretly bury him. The new patriarch, Gennadios Scholarios, had told Mehmed it behooves an emperor to be buried with his predecessors, but for Constantine, in a place no one would know or find.

Mehmed thought of Constantine the Great as he stood among the ruins of the palace. He thought of the Roman Empire of Julius Caesar, the Macedonia of Alexander the Great and the Baghdad of the Abbasids. How temporary are kingdoms and transient are empires, he thought, and recited lines he had memorized as a child.

The owl keeps watch on Afrasiab's trellis,
The spider draws the curtain at the Caesar's palace.

132

That divine light, the angels the people of the city were waiting for in Hagia Sophia, has entered my spirit. My heart is as large today as its grand dome, and I feel as unencumbered as the horizon over the Marmara Sea.

I reckon I'll find myself on my way back to Venice the next time I return to these notes. The assault that began that night has changed everything. Just as Mehmed tore down the thousand-year-old walls of Constantinople, so did I the walls I made within myself.

I entered this magnificent city with the sultan's procession as soon as the city was under their control. Much of the city is in order, but still, much of it is in tumult. The people who still do not know Mehmed look for places to run from his soldiers while others have already declared him their new emperor.

When Hamza Bey's soldiers were flowing into the city from the shores of the Marmara Sea and Golden Horn, the Venetian and Genoese sailors tried to make a quick escape from the Golden Horn, thinking Mehmed wouldn't forgive them for their part in the defense. While the sultan hasn't touched them as of yet, the Venetians are fleeing the city, as these Turks can change their mind in an instant. Constantine's man Georgios Sphrantzes is among them.

Aluvixe Diedo was one of the captains of the fleeing ships and, amid the commotion at the harbor on the Golden Horn, he didn't recognize me at first. Me in my Ottoman caftan, he must have thought me a Turk. As soon as he did, though, he implored me to come with him and said we must flee at once. He said he was sailing straight for Rome, where he would inform the pope of the situation.

His leg was wounded and I can't get the forlorn look on this great commander's face out of my mind. He and his crew say the Turks will decimate the city and tear it apart. A physician named Niccolò Barbaro on his ship told me Mehmed was the antichrist himself, that the world had ended and civilization had fallen into the hands of barbarians.

These men speak so of Mehmed because they don't know him. The sultan has already commissioned his sergeants to safeguard the city folk's life and property. The town criers are everywhere announcing in Greek and Latin for everyone to return to home and work. Far from killing the city's inhabitants, Mehmed has sent his men far and wide to call for scholars, artists, craftsmen, architects, engineers, masons and carpenters from Europe and the Orient to come and make this city the center of his realm.

Barbaro is beset with delusions.

No, the world did not end today—it has begun. Today the Occident and the Orient have come together, the sultan has become emperor and the myriad peoples will mingle. The sun rises in the east today more alive than ever and with more splendor.

The Turks have sheathed their swords and are readying their pens. Calligraphers, scribes, painters and sculptors will meet in Constantinople. My love will also sprout in Mehmed's garden, in this city.

I've kept these notes for a long time. I will now deliver them to Aluvixe Diedo so those in Venice and elsewhere who don't know the Ottomans or misunderstand them can know better. With these notes, I bid farewell, or good riddance, to my dark memories.

I have Nilüfer's swan in hand and it looks back at me. In this new city, this queen of cities, as I wait for my queen, with a contented heart, I can finally read what she wrote.

There is no god but God and Muhammad is His messenger.

133

A janissary put on a sandy robe as dawn broke. Below his knee-length shalvar was red cloth wound down to his ankles.

He looked out the window of his tent as he fastened the many fine buttons from his waist up. The fiery sun was slowly rising over the sparkling waters of the Bosporus and the soft russet land to both sides. Days of rain had given way to clear skies.

His robe was tight around his muscled chest and hung down to his ankles. He fastened the final button of his collar and wrapped his sash of sea blue around his waist. He also fitted golden bands around his arms for the ceremony that would be held at the Friday prayers.

He hung the engraved sword in its scabbard the sultan had given him as a gift for his success to his left. He lifted his white felt hat with golden bands with both hands and placed it on his head. He placed a white plume in the front, hung his quiver to his right and slung his bow over his left shoulder.

He stepped out of his tent, pulled on his yellow, gazelle-hide boots and straightened up under the fully lit sky.

He looked out at the Bosporus and brought his hand to the string of coral around his neck. After a while, he slipped the necklace under his collar and set off for the ceremony at Hagia Sophia. Today was the first day he was to take Jafer Agha's place.

The newly risen sun burned the same hue as the coral around his neck.

134

"Excuse me, sir. The museum is closing in fifteen minutes," a guide said just as Beyazit finished reading the last of the notes.

The day had turned to evening. He put the notes back into the envelope and walked left the Art Institute of Chicago as the lights in the galleries were shut off.

The sanguine rays of the setting sun shined on the lion statues at the base of the wide staircase as Beyazit walked to the street.

Sultan Mehmed II remained on the throne for thirty years following his conquest of Constantinople.

He conquered the Empire of Trebizond and the Morea in 1461, taking the last remaining territories of the Eastern Roman Empire.

He removed Vlad Dracula as voivode of Wallachia in 1462.

He conquered the Crimea in 1475, putting an end to Venetian rule and ensuring Ottoman domination of the Black Sea.

He captured the lands of Serbia, Wallachia, Bosnia and Albania.

His army attacked Otranto in southern Italy in 1480, but it retreated when he died of a suspected poisoning.

In the following centuries, Sultan Bayezid II reinforced the realm's European territories, Sultan Selim I conquered Mecca and Medina and Sultan Süleyman the Magnificent took Belgrade and reached as far as the gates of Vienna.

All of these lands were lost over time, but Constantinople, first taken by Mehmed, remained under Ottoman rule for centuries, and is now the city of Istanbul in Turkey.

Many historians agree with the claim that if Mehmed hadn't died at forty-nine and had lived another decade, the history of the world would be different and the present concepts of East and West, Occident and Orient, would not have their present meanings.

SOURCES AND ACKNOWLEDGEMENTS

It was not possible to keep a list of all the sources I used over the five years I wrote this novel. When I think of it, it is impossible to count all the books, articles and texts in both English and Turkish, paintings, maps and manuscripts, or track the memories of Alexander the Great, Alberti Balbi and Sultan Mehmed II. In other words, it's only as possible to track the sources for this book as it is for the sources of a person's map of ideas and power of imagination. What I can say, though, is that as of the beginning of 2009, I had looked at almost anything written in English and Turkish on the conquest of Constantinople, Sultan Mehmed the Conqueror, and Ottoman history, culture, social life and the janissary corps. The European and American sources were on the brink of becoming small towers of their own in my small room. In addition, I should mention the dozens of books and articles I read during my doctoral studies, which while not directly related to the novel, undoubtedly nurtured its creation.

What I truly must mention, though, are the books that markedly affected the novel and the other sources and works that came to the forefront. The most important of these are the *Shahnameh* of Ferdowsi and the accounts of Alexander the Great found in this epic poem and in the many versions of *Iskandarnameh.* The influence of the tales of Dede Korkut that surrounded Sultan Murad's young prince were unavoidable. The character of Alberti Balbi, of course, was influenced by the dozens of travelers, emissaries and envoys who later wrote about the Ottomans. The fairest among them were British orientalist Edward Lane, Flemish writer and diplomat for Austria Ogier Ghiselin de Busbecq, Lady Mary Wortley Montagu—the wife of an eighteenth-century British diplomat in Constantinople—Patrick and Alexander Russell of the Royal Society, whose sympathy for the Ottomans is clear in their writing, and of course, the themes in Alberti Balbi's notes. The main tracks of the religious dialogues between Mullah Lütfi and Balbi were inspired by many works, including Ahmed bin Qasim's memoirs. Works by Steven Runciman, Roger Crowley and Reşad Ekrem Koçu were the primary influences for the historical details of the conquest and Julian Raby's dissertation was the source material from which I learned of Sultan Mehmed's interest in medallions. I used works by historians who have studied Mehmed the Conqueror, such as Franz Babinger and Süheyl Ünver, along with many others. For the history of the Roman Empire, I heavily relied on the works of Edward Gibbon and John Romer.

If only a few colors can be used to paint a picture of Mehmed's garden, then this bibliography of sorts represents this novel. But further to the point, it is not enough. Not only a page, but a book, or at the least a thorough essay, should be written on the sources presented in this novel. The Ottomans of old spoke of *the relaters of news and the conveyors of works.* Perhaps this is more accurate than the title of author. In short, the above people and many others played a role in the success of this novel. All flaws are mine and mine alone.

B.A.